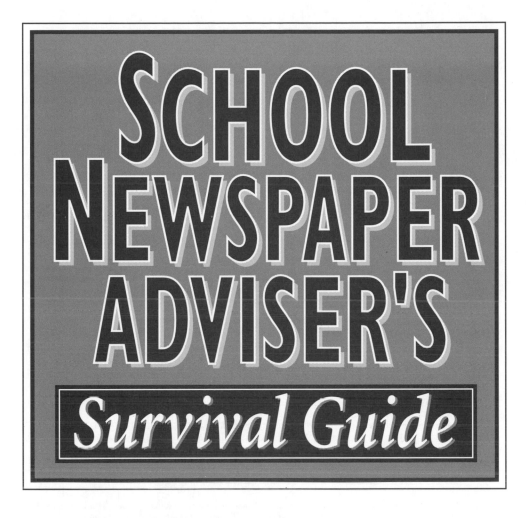

SCHOOL NEWSPAPER ADVISER'S Survival Guide

PATRICIA OSBORN

JOSSEY-BASS
A Wiley Imprint
www.josseybass.com

Published by Jossey-Bass
A Wiley Imprint
989 Market Street, San Francisco, CA 94103-1741   www.josseybass.com

Jossey-Bass books and products are available through most bookstores. To contact Jossey-Bass directly call our Customer Care Department within the U.S. at 800-956-7739, outside the U.S. at 317-572-3986 or fax 317-572-4002.

Jossey-Bass also publishes its books in a variety of electronic formats. Some content that appears in print may not be available in electronic books.

Library of Congress Cataloging-in-Publication Data

Osborn, Patricia.
    School newspaper adviser's survival guide / Patricia Osborn.
      p. cm.
    ISBN 0-87628-891-3
    ISBN 0-7879-6624-X (layflat)
    1. Student newspapers and periodicals—United States—Handbooks,
  manuals, etc. I. Title.
  LB3621.073 1997
  371.8'974—dc21   97-23288

FIRST EDITION
HB Printing 10 9 8 7 6 5 4 3 2 1

ACKNOWLEDGMENTS

Special thanks to:

Carolyn Barnes, adviser, *The Rebellion*, Bowsher High School, Toledo, Ohio

Jim McGonnell, adviser, *The Blue and Gold*, Findlay High School, Findlay, Ohio

Linda Glomski, coordinator, Great Lakes Interscholastic Press Association (GLIPA)

Tony Garver, computer technician, U.S. Air Force reserve

Mike Hiestand, attorney, Student Press Law Center

Connie Kallback, editor, and Win Huppuch, publisher, Prentice Hall Direct

...the approximately 150 journalism advisers throughout the country whose papers and surveys contributed to the breadth of this book

... and especially the students and advisers whose excellent work is sampled here

ABOUT THE AUTHOR

Patricia Osborn is a graduate of Bowling Green State University in Ohio where she received a B.A. in journalism and earned her teaching credentials. She has also attended the University of Toledo and Instituto Mexicano-Norte Americano in Mexico.

Ms. Osborn has taught English in grades 9-12 at all levels, basic to honors, in Toledo, Ohio. As well as required English courses, she has also taught electives in journalism composition, Russian Literature, and drama; advised high school newspapers; and served as English department chairperson. Before becoming a teacher, Ms. Osborn was a general news reporter on the *Marion Star* and an advertising copywriter for a Toledo department store. A writer of fiction and poetry as well as books and articles, her work has appeared in magazines ranging from *Educational Digest* to *TV Guide*.

Ms. Osborn is the author of *Reading Smarter*, published by The Center in 1995. She has also written a number of other books and articles concerned with language arts and education. These include *How Grammar Works, A Self-Teaching Guide* (1989, John Wiley & Sons, Inc.) for both personal and classroom use; *Poetry by Doing* (1992, National Textbook Company); and *Finding America* (1995, AMSCO School Publications, Inc.), a multicultural anthology of literature.

ABOUT THIS RESOURCE

School Newspaper Adviser's Survival Guide is designed to help you, the school newspaper adviser, make the most of your time, your staff and your resources. Newspapers don't run themselves, and—unlike professionally published papers—in most schools editorial and business staffs combine under the leadership of one person. That makes the job of school newspaper adviser even more involved and that's why this resource was created.

The survival guide format offers useful and practical solutions to the concerns and problems that you as an adviser confront every day. Brimming with time-saving tips for organizing your staff, your workspace and the myriad details involved in producing an effective paper, the *Guide* also includes reproducible workshop activities that introduce and reinforce the major tenets of good newswriting style and the journalistic approach.

School Newspaper Adviser's Survival Guide is divided into four easily accessible units:

1—GAINING PERSPECTIVE, GAINING CONTROL

Unit 1 applies to your role as an adviser, taking up such matters as defining your goals and a school paper's purpose, clarifying your position as buffer between newspaper staff and school administration or faculty, selecting a staff that really works, and facing the challenge of protecting journalistic rights and instilling a sense of ethics.

2—NEWSWRITING WORKSHOP

Unit 2 takes up the lifeblood of a good newspaper well-written, well-chosen and well-researched stories. By an author experienced in both professional journalism and high school newspaper advising, this book includes, but goes beyond the basics of summary lead-inverted pyramid newswriting to develop a journalistic sense of weighing, choosing and valuing words. In this unit you'll find interesting, up-to-date suggestions and exercises on everything from editorials to sports, as well as guidelines for getting the most out of interviews and suggestions for stories you can use or adapt to your school's needs.

3—NEWSPAPER LAYOUT: THE SENSE BEHIND THE STYLE

In producing a newspaper, first impressions count a lot. Unit 3 will advise you how to show your stories to the best advantage and make the most efficient use of your students' computer skills. You'll also discover the most effective ways to use advertising, photographs and sidebars to make your paper attractive and powerful, without becoming gimmicky.

4—MANAGING TO FIND TIME, FINDING TIME TO MANAGE

Unit 4 will help you cope—by managing your time more effectively, getting the school newsroom organized more efficiently and making technology work for you!

School Newspaper Adviser's Survival Guide is packed with the ready-to-use forms and exercises you need—for advertising, beat coverage, reporter's guidelines, newswriting exercises, and more. You'll also find innumerable ideas for making a good paper even better—ways to brighten your pages, lists of potential advertising prospects, a wealth of story ideas, and guidelines for self-critiquing.

In short, this guide helps you make the most of your time and organizational skills so that not only will you survive, but your school paper will thrive.

Patricia Osborn

CONTENTS

Unit 1

GAINING PERSPECTIVE, GAINING CONTROL

Unit 2

NEWSWRITING WORKSHOP

NEWSWRITING WORKSHOPS

Unit 3

NEWSPAPER LAYOUT: THE SENSE BEHIND THE STYLE

Unit 4

MANAGING TO FIND TIME, FINDING TIME TO MANAGE

APPENDICES

GAINING PERSPECTIVE, GAINING CONTROL

FOCUS: Your role as adviser

No one said it was going to be easy, yet the role of school newspaper adviser can be the most stimulating, rewarding and satisfying part of your school day. It's one of the original hands-on classes, where you find yourself working shoulder to shoulder with student staff members as co-players aiming for the same goals—with a definite product to show for the time and effort you expend. . . . That's the plus side.

So much to do, so little time

There are times when an adviser inevitably feels pulled from all directions. *Who* next? *What* next? *Where* is . . .? *Why* did I ever agree to take this job? The 5 W's and an H crowd around you in the guise of all the claims on your time and attention. It seems impossible, and no wonder.

Professional papers are run by experts in the four major areas of endeavor required to produce and publish a newspaper:

1. Editorial
2. Business/Finance
3. Advertising
4. Production/Circulation

School newspaper advisers are usually given responsibility for all four—even when they have no special knowledge or training of any kind in journalism, and that's not all. Expectations include advisers' being knowledgeable in:

1. Desktop publishing
2. Design and layout
3. Staff management
4. Photography
5. Newspaper law and ethics
6. Being a full-time teacher, of course, fits in somewhere!

Once the range of responsibilities is realized, the job seems overwhelming. Yet most advisers simply buckle down and do it—only stopping for breath once in a while to lift up their heads and wonder "How?" and "Why?"

There is little chance of changing the job description, but there are definite ways to ease the pressure *and* produce a more successful paper.

A key to success: FOCUS

| F | lexibility | O | rganization | C | oping skills | U | tilization of strengths | S | upport |

Having FOCUS means you've zeroed in on your goal: that you don't let yourself be derailed by those nagging little distractions tugging at you from all sides; and that you take up problems in their order of importance, let minor ones solve themselves and avoid getting bogged down in a mire of minutiae. To be in focus, work on developing qualities that enable you to operate more effectively.

FLEXIBILITY—A newspaper without a crisis is like peanuts without salt. Because of deadlines, crisis is a built-in element of every school paper—and for some, it's a major part of the excitement and stimulation. In your role as adviser, it's essential not to let yourself be overwhelmed by crises—and one way is by being prepared.

The sports picture didn't turn out? Keep an updated file of feature photos on hand to plug into the space, with clever captions and cutlines.

You can't prepare for every possibility, but encourage your staff to start looking for solutions instead of fanning the first flames of crisis when problems arise. A flexible, problem-solving attitude and approach helps you take challenges in stride.

ORGANIZATION—The idea of "a place for everything and everything in its place" seems ludicrous in regard to a typical school paper office.

Yet a place for "things" is just one small part of the organization needed by a newspaper adviser. You also must organize the staff and assign tasks so each staff member knows what is expected and when.

Don't think of organization as a constraint on creativity and initiative. It's actually a way to clear up the mundane details that cause constant problems and to free you and your staff for true creativity and innovation.

COPING SKILLS—Students like to look to their adviser as the reasonably calm and assured center in the midst of the storm. Although this is sometimes difficult, the manner and attitude of the adviser is generally contagious.

It's deadline time! It's panic time! Don't let it be frantic time. A little excitement and tension can help your staff do their jobs better; a newspaper by definition is a last-minute project. Yet everyone will work better holding the belief that no problems are too big to cope with and solve.

UTILIZATION OF STRENGTHS—It's all too easy to dwell upon your needs—more money for computers and programs, more support from the school administration, a better pool of candidates for the staff. It's more productive to build upon your strengths. If you do, even an inexpensive-to-produce, Xeroxed paper can be lively, readable and attractive while a multipage tabloid with color may not be—even though produced from the latest programs and equipment.

It's essential to make the most of what you have—so the rest can follow.

SUPPORT—One of the joys of working with and on a school newspaper is the opportunity for staff and adviser to work together as a team. Not everyone is equal in responsibility, but everyone can share equally in the same goal. The sense of team spirit arises from adviser, editors and staff developing a positive, "can do" attitude. This comes from the adviser's being supportive of editors and editors' being supportive of staffers. By giving support to one another, everyone shows awareness that the inevitable foul-ups are not deliberate acts of sabotage and that the rewrites and corrections are not a form of punishment but a means of helping the individual, the staff and the paper grow together.

The paper hasn't enough support from the administration and community? Creating a sense of cohesion and mutual support within the staff itself can sometimes activate the rest!

FOCUS—**F**lexibility, **O**rganization, **C**oping skills, **U**tilization of strengths and **S**upport—is the theme of this book, providing you with ways for you and your staff to develop the qualities needed to produce a better paper with less wasted time and effort.

Priorities and expectations

What grade would you give yourself as an adviser?

Being teachers and possibly perfectionists, most advisers would be hard put to decide what grade to assign themselves—just as they find it difficult to grade the students on their staffs. If grades were given for effort, long hours and pursuit of high standards, most advisers would not quibble about deserving an A. But, if judged by their self-determined goal of excellence, the grade becomes another matter.

An adviser of an award-winning paper, a person prominent in state and national journalism circles, blamed herself for her increasing inability to maintain the school paper's traditional number of yearly issues. Yet she alone set the demanding production schedule. The principal didn't care whether a few papers more or less were published yearly. His main concerns were a trouble-free paper and good public relations. Although he was satisfied, she wasn't.

Standards self-assigned by a perfectionist are, by definition, impossible to reach. It may be necessary to step back, assess your standards and decide which are realistic, which need to be changed and which deserve priority.

A SCHOOL-FULL OF CRITICS—In addition to measuring themselves against self-set standards, newspaper advisers, unlike most teachers, are in charge of classes that create a product—concrete results for everyone to read and freely criticize. It often seems the most avid critics are not students, but administrators, teachers, parents and special interest groups, eager to pounce on every flaw and poised to challenge the paper's introduction of any controversial or sensitive issue.

To ease the pressure of perfectionist standards and outside criticism, begin by assessing your strengths—and then building on them. Start by deciding where you are and what you and your staff need to work on first. Use the "Priority and progress assessment" sheet or let it serve as a guide for devising a list of your own (Figure 1-1 on page 5). Of course, just because an area is under control doesn't mean you don't want to aim even higher. Yet the assessment will give you and your staff an idea of the areas to tackle first.

Once you've identified the areas needing concentrated effort, it's a good idea to sit down with the paper's editorial board and plan a definite campaign to accomplish your goals. Avoid tackling more than your staff can complete successfully, especially if this is your staff's first project. Throughout this book, you'll find ideas, strategies and materials to help you formulate and carry out your plans. Remember that success breeds success—and the first successful steps, though small, will lead to larger ones.

You may want your editorial board or even, perhaps, your school principal to participate in making this assessment.

SETTING PERSONAL PRIORITIES—As well as setting major goals for the paper and staff, it's also important that advisers set personal priorities for the hundreds of details that crowd upon them from every side.

"What do you think of … ?"
"I really need you to help me …"
"This will only take a minute …"
"This is really, really important!"

A newsroom by nature is a busy, sometimes hectic, place—but there are times an adviser must decide where to draw the line. Each time one student interrupts another, having decided his or her problem is more pressing than someone else's, it results in a waste of time and often causes the first problem to need reviewing or reworking when taken up again. Besides, it's just plain rude—a symptom of an era when too many kids and adults think "me first" is an acceptable attitude. As a valuable lesson in office procedures, as well as a way to save time and avoid constant interruptions, it's helpful to establish ground rules such as the following:

Staff ground rules for successful teamwork

1. Avoid interrupting an editor or adviser when he or she is consulting or helping another staff member, unless asked to do so.

2. Before seeking help, first try to solve problems on your own. An asset for journalists is resourcefulness.

3. Remember, other people probably think their problems are as important as yours. Interruptions are not only rude, but unfair.

4. Tolerating rudeness breeds discord and resentment.

CREATE A TIME LINE—The flurry of final deadlines . . . printing and distribution . . . editorial board meeting . . . posting assignments. After assignments are up and news gathering begins, there is often a fallow period in the news room when it becomes hard to tell whether reporters are productively planning their interviews and assignments or merely making time befor rushing their work through at the last minute.

One way to ease the pressure from all sides at final deadline time is to create a staggered time line. For example, if your paper comes out every four weeks, the deadline for having all advertising sold, ads drawn up and pages laid out for ad space might be two weeks before the deadline for newswriting assignments.

If the editorial board has planned a special investigative reporting spread assigned to a team of reporters, this too needs a distinct deadline. If started an issue in advance, it can be finished—complete with graphics, photos and layout—well before other stories scheduled for simultaneous publication.

Priority and progress assessment

PART 1. Rank the items listed by the following scale:

| + | Under control or accomplished | **o** | Not a goal at this time |

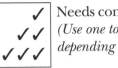 Needs concentrated effort *(Use one to three checks, depending upon need.)*

_____ 1. Issuing a paper on time on a regular schedule

_____ 2. Having sufficient funds to publish scheduled number of papers

_____ 3. Adhering to the fundamentals of journalistic style

_____ 4. Improving computer skills of staff members

_____ 5. Seeking funds to buy equipment, expand paper, add elements such as color

_____ 6. Increasing number of issues published each term

_____ 7. Reaching an acceptable level of grammar: spelling, usage and punctuation

_____ 8. Increasing readership and interest of student body

_____ 9. Becoming an award-winning paper

_____10. Brightening the paper with up-to-date design elements and graphics

_____11. Gaining more support from administration and/or community

_____12. Getting staff members to maintain deadlines

_____13. Going beyond basic news to in-depth coverage of issues, profiles and features

_____14. Having every staff member pull his or her assigned weight

_____15. Developing a more mature, professional environment

_____16. Providing the tools students need for more effective communication

_____17. Training students in the principles of good journalism

_____18. Increasing advertising revenues

_____19. Achieving more coverage of in-school activities and events

_____20. Becoming more open to ideas, debates on issue, society as a whole

PART 2. Assigning priorities

When you have finished Part 1, rank those checked as needing concentrated effort in the order of importance to the success of your school paper. List them in descending order in the blank spaces below, with the one you hope to accomplish first as number one.

1. _____

2. _____

3. _____

4. _____

5. _____

FOCUS ON YOUR GOALS—Avoid letting editors or other staff members get side-tracked and waste their time—and yours—on details that may be interesting in themselves but only hinder you and the paper from attaining its primary goal. The main goal of a newspaper is to publish interesting, well-written and informative stories. The rest is actually window dressing.

A simple 8-1/2″ × 11″ mimeographed paper with lively, properly handled stories can be much more appealing than a flashy, graphics-laden tabloid with dull, awkwardly written prose. As an adviser, then, encourage staff members not to waste time worrying about attracting attention with art and graphics if the reporting itself lacks substance and vitality. Such elements as infographs can add a valuable dimension to a story, but the gathering and writing of the news in that story must come first.

Whose paper?

To make the most and best of your time, avoid letting staff members cast you in a parental role—as someone who "cleans up" or "takes over" for students who do their assignments halfheartedly, then come begging for help. Students must think of the paper as theirs, which of course it rightfully is. Make a point of giving the editor, editorial board and staff members as much responsibility as they can handle. This means relying on them to check with administrators or make phone calls that you could just as easily take care of yourself. Kids who know they are trusted to take responsibility tend to feel a deeper commitment to the paper than those who don't, yet, you, as the newspaper adviser, are always placed in an ambiguous position. Even while emphasizing the students' role, you symbolize the newspaper's continuity—the one who remains after each year's crop of students graduates and goes on. As an adult, you should expect to take the ultimate responsibility for every decision made and every item published in the paper.

As an adviser, you often tread a fine line—trying to maintain the position of truly advising, not commanding, while at the same time alerting students to possible problems, helping them see the ramifications of their actions and guiding them to make the right choices—and, sometimes, letting them take steps that you may think unwise, just so they can discover the consequences of their decisions.

Because you can do a task more easily, faster and better, it is sometimes tempting to do it yourself, but you are something more important than a fence mender. You are an adviser, whose job is to develop in students the skills, the self-confidence and self-discipline to do the job themselves.

WANTED: A staff that works

What works . . . works

According to our survey of schools large and small from coast to coast that publish school papers, the following data emerge. The majority of responses came from four-year high schools, although junior highs and six-year secondary schools also participated. Enrollments range from 220 to 3000 students.

Survey results:
journalism offerings

➤ Nearly 75% of the schools surveyed report having one adviser supervising both editorial and business operations.

➤ Staff sizes range from as few as 6 to as many as 70.

➤ In close to 63% of the schools, the newspaper meets as a regularly scheduled credit class.

➤ An additional 7-1/2% of schools have a combination of regularly scheduled class and extracurricular participation.

➤ Almost 30% of the schools offer journalism classes in addition to the newspaper. Of these, nearly half have 16-30 students enrolled.

➤ Of the rest of the schools, approximately 36% report having more than 30 students in journalism classes—with the largest boasting 120—and the rest 15 or fewer.

The makeup of a school newspaper staff depends in large part upon the size of a school, the makeup of its student body, and the support and backing you receive or can cajole from the school administration, school board, parent groups and the community at large.

BEGINNING THE SELECTION PROCESS—According to nearly 60% of newspaper advisers responding to the survey, acceptance to their staffs requires the approval of the adviser alone or a combination of the adviser and the editorial board. To gain acceptance, candidates must also meet certain prerequisites according to policies set by nearly 50% of the schools.

According to the six prerequisites most often listed, candidates must

1. Have taken journalism, basic photography or mass media class.
2. Meet specific grade requirements.
   In some schools, C or better; in others A's or B's or better; in one, enrollment in a college prep course.
3. Have a teacher or teachers' recommendation; generally at least one is required to be an English teacher.
4. Take part in an interview with adviser/editorial board.
5. Have attained junior or senior status.

Other prerequisites include the ability to work on the paper outside of class hours, being computer literate and having the recommendation of a school counselor.

While the selection process and prerequisites vary from school to school, approximately 40% of the advisers surveyed reported staff membership was based on open enrollment: elective, not selective. Potluck.

THE PROS AND CONS OF OPEN ENROLLMENT—Open enrollment sounds dangerous—tempting to do-nothings looking for a place to waste their time and yours. Yet if a staff is open to any students wishing to enroll, much depends upon what they find after they get there. There can be certain advantages to a class that comes by choice, not recruitment. In one case, a D student in English with a genuine interest in journalism joined the newspaper staff as a sophomore and showed such dedication, determination and initiative that he became editor in chief his senior year. Although spelling never became his forte, he was a thoughtful leader who inspired his staff to do an outstanding job of investigative reporting.

Another reporter, who barely scraped C's in English, experienced a rise in her verbal scores on college aptitude tests, which her mother attributed to participation on the school paper. Indeed, according to the authors of *Journalism Kids Do Better: What Research Tells Us About High School Journalism in the 1990's,*[1] journalism students do better on grades, ACT tests and Advanced Placement exams than those without a journalism background.

HOW TO STAFF YOUR PAPER—How you proceed depends upon your major goals—which themselves may change as the paper progresses. Word gets around and even without formal recruitment, a kind of informal recruiting inevitably goes on, with friends encouraging or warning friends just what to expect.

With regard to staffing, the biggest problems facing advisers surveyed are related.

1. How to attract a top-notch staff when the newspaper competes with other classes needed in students' majors and with after-school jobs and home obligations that eat into available time.

2. How to motivate students to produce a quality paper, meet deadlines, come up with creative story ideas, follow through and stick with a tough story.

3. How to recruit the kind of staff you need to produce the kind of paper the staff, the student body, the school and you as the adviser can be proud of.

The problem facing the school paper adviser is similar to the football coach's: A winning team attracts a bigger and better field of candidates, a losing team discourages students from trying out. The obvious question: How do you pick a winning team from a limited selection of talent?

Although the greatest number of advisers reported having staffs of 16 to 20 members, approximately 10% were produced by staffs with only six to ten members. And, another adviser with a staff of 30 considered it too large.

What's the minimum number needed to produce a good paper? Some might say as few as one. A biography of Robert Frost describes his frustrations as editor of his school paper when he was unable to get his fellow students to turn in their stories on time. Disgusted, he went home one night and wrote the entire edition by himself. Frost didn't have much success as a schoolteacher either—obviously a better writer than a leader—yet his frustration in trying to get stories written can be shared by almost any adviser.

GAUGING YOUR NEEDS—What does it take to publish a good paper? According to the survey, there are also papers with as many as 70 staff members, with some accepting freelancers working on an extracurricular basis. Most publications fit into one of two

---

[1] *Journalism Kis Do Better,* Jack Dvorak, Larry Lain and Tom Dickson, ERIC/EDINFO Press, 1994.

categories: 8-1/2″ × 11″ papers and news magazines of 4 to 16 pages or 11″ × 17″ tabloids with 4 to 28 pages.

The size of the staff and school determines the size of the paper and its frequency of publication—and the type of paper you plan to publish dictates the size of staff you need, if you are free to choose. The key to success is having a staff that works.

One way to begin tailoring a staff to fit your paper's profile is through a staff application ("Staff application," Figure 1-2 on pages 12 and 13), which serves two purposes.

1. It gives you an idea of an applicant's potential. It also gives would-be staff members a sense of what will be expected of them if accepted.

2. Once distributed and returned, applications allow the adviser, with or without input from the editorial board, to select new enrollees who fit the categories and exhibit the qualities the staff seeks.

You may also ask current staffers to refile an application ("Application for editor and staff positions," Figure 1-3 on pages 14 and 15) for their chosen positions each year. This can reveal the surprise departure of someone you counted on to return, since students sometimes hesitate to announce their intentions to leave, fearful of being pressured, of hurting their adviser's feelings or even of its having an effect on their grade.

If your school permits, you can do active recruiting on school television and over the PA system, as well as in English classes. Even if there hasn't been a rush of applicants in the past, good promotion can help enhance the impression that being on the school newspaper staff is an honor.

THE CONSTANT: CHANGE—One of the constants of a school newspaper staff is that it changes every year. It's a fact that offers frustration, challenge and promise. Like the coach of a winning team, you may find yourself faced with the loss of a cadre of experienced, talented seniors and a year of rebuilding to do. One year, a would-be crusading journalist may join the staff and prod other staffers to share his activist stance and fervor. In another, the staff may have a core of sincere, dependable workers but lack a natural sparkplug to lighten up and brighten up the paper's pages.

WANTED: THE IDEAL STAFFER

Inquisitive	Motivated	Knowledgeable
Full of ideas	Responsible	Imaginative
Industrious	Independent thinking	Cooperative
Self-disciplined	Resourceful	Active

Of course, this paragon doesn't exist—and schools today no longer stress many of these qualities as traits desirable for students to develop. Yet all are valuable not only for the professional journalist but for any young person.

Although you cannot pick any staff whose individual members exhibit all of your ideal qualities, you should also not limit your search to those who possess a narrow range of attributes. A staff made up of industrious and cooperative students may lack a free spirit with the flash of imagination to bring dull pages to life, yet a plethora of self-proclaimed young geniuses may not be able to bring themselves to conform to deadlines or the demands of newspaper production.

THE NEWSPAPER STAFF AS A MIRROR—The ideal staff should represent a cross section of the student body. One danger of a staff that is too narrowly selected is its tendency to become inbred—believing everyone thinks the way they do, likes what they do, and—if others don't, ought to. Such a staff, sometimes unconsciously, reflects the idea that they are producing a paper strictly for those who count—those like themselves.

By representing a cross section of the student body, a newspaper opens itself to a whole new realm of story possibilities, mirroring the real world. Yet some members of minorities—social or ethnic—may hesitate to apply, rightly or wrongly feeling themselves unwelcome. In some cases, advisers may also feel uneasy about seeking "token" representation when minority students have shown no desire to join. One way to begin making the paper truly reflective of the student body is to introduce broader coverage of student concerns through profiles, interviews or in-depth reports. This alerts potential candidates of the newspaper's genuine devotion to the entire spectrum of the student body, not just an elite few.

If a school offers journalism, it is usual for high school newspapers to limit acceptance to juniors and seniors. If not, staffs are regularly opened to sophomores as well as the two upper classes. This enables a better balance between staffers in training, those who are seasoned, and soon-to-graduate seniors.

CHANGING YOUR EXPECTATIONS—A concern of many advisers is that top students with excellent writing skills are often not able to work on the paper because of schedule conflicts or other obligations. Yet it's well to remember that journalism itself is a cradle of good writing. The journalistic style has nurtured many of America's best authors, from Mark Twain and Walt Whitman to Ernest Hemingway and John Steinbeck. Students with a true desire to write, to learn and to work on the paper often become better staff members than straight A students who may think of the paper as "down" time in their rigorous schedules and of themselves as granting favors by agreeing to participate. You may get better results by enrolling students who care than those cajoled into joining the staff—better results from those who know they don't know than from those convinced they already know and who find the strictures and structures of journalistic style hard to accept.

As you choose and balance your staff, also consider the job descriptions of positions you need to fill. Those attaining editorial positions will develop as they work on the staff, but incoming staffers need certain skills or you must make accommodation for their lack.

THE COMPUTER RULES!—The power of the computer has become an overwhelming element in school newspaper production. In some newsrooms, the computer threatens to reign so completely that news itself is viewed as a tiresome necessity, useful only as a source for type blocks of varying sizes needed to create ingenious page designs. From this viewpoint, the real joy and purpose of working on the paper are to manipulate type, invent striking graphics and create an eye-popping impact on every page.

Computer whizzes on the staff can cause an adviser who's not equally confident and competent to temporarily lose focus—and control. Graphics can be spectacular, but too many typographical and visual tricks distract readers and warp body copy into unreadable twists and shapes. If there are enough computers available, it is good to have as many staffers as possible computer literate. It is not good to have an overabundance of staffers who are so obsessed with the computer that they rank it above all else.

The business of a newspaper is to print the news. All else is cosmetic—sometimes enhancing the presentation of the news, but never successfully masking an absence of meaningful, well-written stories. For those on a school paper staff, learning to write well comes first and deserves the adviser's main concern.

If there is a shortage of computers, you may want to staff the paper with several students whose primary task will be to word process stories on disks to a standard format, to be later fed into the paper's desktop publishing program—or you may want to coordinate your efforts with a business computer class.

CREATING ESPRIT DE CORPS—By its nature, the school paper is an organization that requires its adviser to spend much time giving individualized attention to staff members and coping with innumerable details. In some cases, it creates the illusion of free time on the hands of some staffers, and that can lead to a multitude of problems.

- Students slipping out of class on made-up errands to hobnob with friends.

- Staffers marking time while waiting to go for an interview or simply procrastinating about beginning their stories, sometimes as if the "free time" were rightful perks for their joining the staff.

- Staffers who are industriously engaged in their duties becoming resentful of the slackers and tempted to slough off themselves.

- The wide variation in responsibilities, duties and experience of novice and seasoned staffers causing advisers' nightmares, especially at the end of each grading period.

- Hardly least, finding that the need to give individualized attention saps the adviser's time and energy, making it impossible to devote needed attention to the planning and organization.

Creating a sense of teamwork and responsibility

The problems must be addressed from three directions:

    A. Development of team spirit

    B. Staff and editorial board organization

    C. Clear-cut system of grading

DEVELOPMENT OF TEAM SPIRIT—Your role and relationship as adviser is inherently tricky. Even though it would be nice to say, "This is truly a student newspaper. It's all theirs. I only advise them when they come to me with questions," the practice is necessarily somewhat different. If the adviser also holds the grade book, students are aware of the power of the pen and the wages of defiance.

The school newsroom is still a classroom, and the adviser is also a teacher. And, unless the school has an especially strong journalism program, the student staffers presumably still have much to learn—including professionalism and ethics.

In addition, school newspaper staffs change completely every two to four years. The adviser is the constant—as long as he or she persists. Being an adult, almost always a member of the school faculty and presumably the best versed on journalism practices, the adviser must ethically bear the responsibility for everything done by members of the staff with regard to producing and issuing the paper, both with or without his or her knowledge.

As a result, as an adviser you are in an ambiguous position. Knowing that you must accept responsibility for all that appears in the school paper, you must also instill the idea that the school paper is not your paper. It is theirs. You are "merely" its adviser.

YOUR PAPER'S
LOGO

Staff application

for the school year _____ to _____

1. Name _____   Next year's class ranking _____

2. Current English teacher _____   Current grade _____

3. Cumulative GPA _____   Are you computer literate?   Yes _____   No _____

4. Check the areas that most interest you. (*You may choose more than one.*)

_____Newswriting and reporting   _____Photography

_____Sports   _____Cartooning, artwork

_____Feature writing   _____Computer design, Infographs

_____Humor   _____Ad design, layout

_____Proofreading   _____Advertising sales

_____Business   Other _____

Note: Editorial positions usually require previous staff experience and are made on a separate application.

5. List your proposed academic schedule for next year	6. List the extracurricular activities in which you plan to participate
1. _____	1. _____
2. _____	2. _____
3. _____	3. _____
4. _____	4. _____
5. _____	5. _____
6. _____	6. _____

7. Do you expect to work after school next year?   Yes _____   No _____

    If so, in what job? _____? About how many hours weekly? _____

8. As a member of the newspaper staff, you will be expected to research and complete assignments outside of as well as during class time, just as with homework for other classes. Will anything hinder your doing so?   Yes _____   No _____

    If yes, please explain.

    _____

9. If extra work is needed for paper production, when would you be available?

____Before school   ____After school   ____Free period   ____Lunch   ____Study hall

10. List three positive qualities that would make you an asset to the staff.

_____

_____

_____

11. Rank your ability on the computer:

Word processing: ____Whiz   ____Plugged in   ____I'm trying
____Where's "On"?

Design/Graphics: ____Whiz   ____Plugged in   ____I'm trying
____Where's "On"?

12. What other special abilities and/or interests do you have that you want to have considered?

_____

_____

_____

_____

_____

_____

_____

_____

_____

_____

_____

_____

13. List two additional members of the faculty or administration who can give you a recommendation.

Name	Department or Office
_____	_____
_____	_____

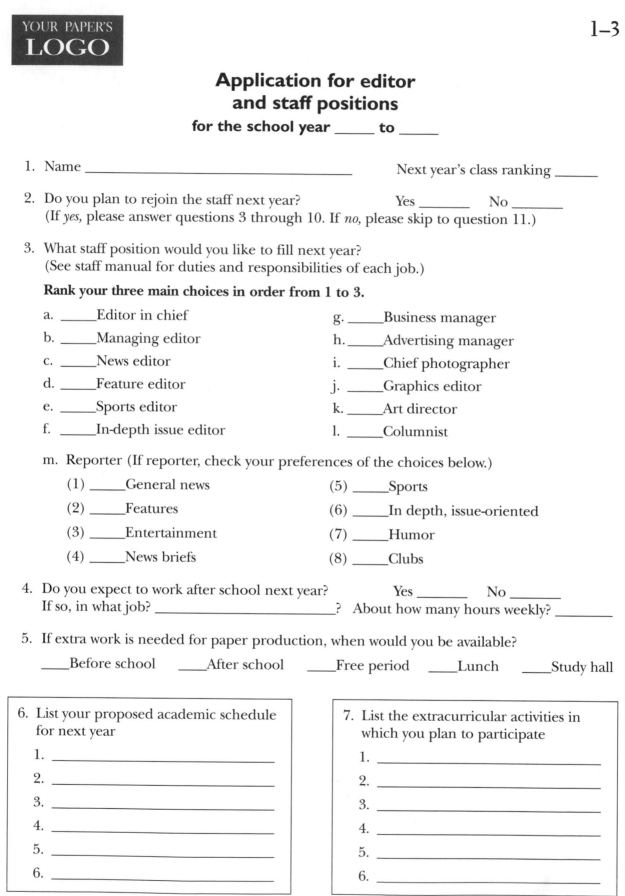

YOUR PAPER'S LOGO

Application for editor
and staff positions
for the school year _____ to _____

1. Name _____   Next year's class ranking _____

2. Do you plan to rejoin the staff next year?   Yes _____   No _____
   (If *yes*, please answer questions 3 through 10. If *no*, please skip to question 11.)

3. What staff position would you like to fill next year?
   (See staff manual for duties and responsibilities of each job.)

   Rank your three main choices in order from 1 to 3.

   a. _____ Editor in chief   g. _____ Business manager
   b. _____ Managing editor   h. _____ Advertising manager
   c. _____ News editor   i. _____ Chief photographer
   d. _____ Feature editor   j. _____ Graphics editor
   e. _____ Sports editor   k. _____ Art director
   f. _____ In-depth issue editor   l. _____ Columnist

   m. Reporter (If reporter, check your preferences of the choices below.)

   (1) _____ General news   (5) _____ Sports
   (2) _____ Features   (6) _____ In depth, issue-oriented
   (3) _____ Entertainment   (7) _____ Humor
   (4) _____ News briefs   (8) _____ Clubs

4. Do you expect to work after school next year?   Yes _____   No _____
   If so, in what job? _____?   About how many hours weekly? _____

5. If extra work is needed for paper production, when would you be available?

   ____ Before school   ____ After school   ____ Free period   ____ Lunch   ____ Study hall

6. List your proposed academic schedule
   for next year
   1. _____
   2. _____
   3. _____
   4. _____
   5. _____
   6. _____

7. List the extracurricular activities in
   which you plan to participate
   1. _____
   2. _____
   3. _____
   4. _____
   5. _____
   6. _____

8. If named to the position of your choice, what changes and improvements would you like to see?

   _____

   _____

   _____

   _____

   _____

   _____

   _____

   _____

9. After having been on the staff, what do you think are the paper's greatest strengths?

   _____

   _____

   _____

   _____

   _____

   _____

   _____

   _____

10. Would you be able to attend a journalism workshop in the summer? _____Yes _____ No

    (*Note:* Participation in a workshop will be both a valuable experience and helpful to you as an editor or department head.)

11. If you do not plan to return, please explain your reasons.

    _____

    _____

    _____

    _____

    _____

    _____

    _____

    _____

Steps for instilling team spirit

1. **Emphasize a common goal.**

    The purpose of the staff is to produce a paper that both its members and the student body can take pride in. Having both staff members and their parents or guardians subscribe to a staff contract and code of conduct ("Code and contract for staff members," Figure 1-4) can also help verify the impression that newspaper staff members are part of a specially focused group.

2. **Show awareness of staff hierarchy.**

    Encourage novice staffers to take their questions to student editors first—then come to you, if necessary. Avoid publicly contradicting an editor or allowing one staffer to play off you to win an argument with another.

3. **In questions of ethics, explain alternatives thoroughly.**

    Assume that students, being inexperienced, are not fully aware of the consequences of some of their "bright ideas." A thoughtful explanation works far better than a flat-out "no" and can help students learn the skills of effective decision making.

4. **Take a positive approach.**

    As a result of TV "one liners," negativism has become fashionable, especially among kids. Show appreciation of good work, try to make students see that criticism is meant to help not hurt and discourage cruel banter among students as unprofessional.

5. **Avoid the impression of having favorites.**

    Because it is often necessary to spend time with editors, younger staffers can feel left out, unnecessary and unimportant. Try to sit down with inexperienced staffers and give suggestions on assignments in progress as often as you can.

6. **Make sure everyone has a special duty assignment.**

    One way to avoid suspicions that everyone isn't doing his or her fair share is to give a definite, additional job assignment to anyone not having an editor's or manager's position.

7. **Create a staff manual.**

    With examples from this book—plus additions and alterations, if necessary, tailored to your situation—you can give students the satisfaction of knowing there is a definite framework within which the paper operates. Including a style book, job descriptions and other information, the staff manual can also save you time by being the answer book for students' questions.

8. **Show interest in work in progress.**

    Some students, who seem to be malingering, claim they can't work amid the hustle and bustle of newsroom activity and prefer to work at home. Explain the importance of learning to concentrate in spite of distraction and the inefficiency of wasting time. Suggest they do make the effort or help out on other staff projects.

9. **Be supportive.**

    Show support of individual students, the students' ideas and your mutual desire to create an outstanding paper. When differences arise, urge students to withhold judgment until all the facts are known—then accept the majority's will.

Code and contract
for staff members

for the school year _____ to_____

To students and parents of students accepted as members of the school paper staff:

Participation on the school newspaper affords students with more freedom than most other classes. It also requires them to take responsibility and exhibit a high degree of maturity and good judgment.

As members of a group that produces a concrete product that will be distributed to and read by both students and adults, those named to the staff can expect to be held to accepted journalistic standards and ethical practices.

As individuals, they are recognized by many as representatives of the paper, whether actually on assignment or not.

To show that you fully understand the responsibilities of staff membership, please have the following contract read and signed by both you and a parent or guardian.

I, _____ *(Your name)*, as a member of the school newspaper staff, agree to abide by the following code of conduct.

1. I will not take advantage of the freedom given staff members to leave class to cover assignments and do other work for the paper. I will not use journalistic duties as an excuse for playing around outside of class, leaving the building or disturbing other classes.

2. I will meet deadlines for assignments, rewrites and other newspaper projects. If I find that it may be difficult or impossible to meet a deadline, I will inform the editor and/or adviser at the earliest possible moment.

3. I understand that I am expected to devote time to completing assignments and other production work for the paper, just as I expect to do homework for any other class. This means for a class that meets an hour a day, I am willing to devote the equivalent of up to five hours weekly, although this may not be required on a regular basis.

4. I agree to produce at least 10 inches of publishable material each issue. This includes stories and headlines, graphics, and/or advertising—or its equivalent in adviser-approved effort.

   Due to limitations of space, the work produced may not necessarily be published in the issue for which it receives credit. Such work not published cannot again be used for credit if published in a following issue.

5. As a representative of the newspaper staff, I agree to abide by standards of good behavior, avoiding rudeness and disrespect to both students and faculty. I realize that the ability of a student press to cover sensitive issues may be questioned if individual staff members are observed acting in a childish or irresponsible manner.

I understand that failure to abide by the terms
of this contract can lead to my dismissal from the staff.

Signed _____
Student

Date _____   _____
Parent or guardian

10. Schedule private meetings with key staffers.

Try to meet privately at least once a week with the editor in chief and advertising/business managers, and with other key staffers as needed, so that you can discuss mutual problems and strategies without interruptions.

Staff organization and editorial board

A staff that works is one that knows what is expected of its members. An important adjunct to example is to have the duties of each position spelled out as clearly and realistically as possible in the paper's staff manual. How ably and how creatively any job is done will naturally depend upon the individual holding the position, but it is vital that the manual not be a "pie-in-the-sky" wish book. It should provide definite guidelines for students to follow and the adviser to use as a reference during student progress reviews.

Some papers choose to assign editorships by pages, with editors being in charge of one or two pages, depending upon the size of the staff and number of pages published. In this case, the job descriptions match the content of the assigned page.

The advantage of assigning editorships—except for that of editor in chief and managing editor—by content is that it permits an editor to see that reporters follow through and to help with every phase of a story, from inception to final editing. Once approved for publication, some stories may be pooled to use wherever most needed or effective.

With small staffs, certain positions such as business manager and advertising manager may be combined. With larger staffs and bigger papers, there may be a need for a managing editor in addition to editor in chief, and such positions as feature editor may be divided into several categories, for example, feature and entertainment.

You may reproduce the outline of editorial duties in the "Staff manual: job descriptions" (Figure 1-5) or use it as a guideline for developing one of your own.

ACHIEVING BALANCE: SPECIAL DUTY ASSIGNMENTS—As every adviser knows—or soon learns—the last-minute crisis is standard for the school paper nearing its final production stages. Last-minute news . . . botched photographs . . . the crash of a computer. . . . And that means extra work—sometimes after school, in the evening, before school, over lunch hours, during free periods—any time the adviser and key personnel can snatch some free minutes.

It's often wonderful how this "in" group of editors and staffers can show such pride and determination. They freely dedicate themselves to the last-minute pressures and extra hours of deadline time and feel a great sense of victory and accomplishment each time they've won.

Of necessity, the pressures of deadline weigh upon experienced staffers versed in desktop publishing, layout and paste-up. If the entire staff tried to take part, many would be dead weight and justifiably feel they were wasting their time. Yet it can seem patently unfair, when the paper is a school class or activity—that hard-driving editors may receive no higher recompense in credit or grades than classmates with less demanding responsibilities. The sight of some of their classmates, apparently at ease, can prove irksome to editors consumed with the need to meet and beat that deadline.

Staff manual: Job descriptions

Editor in chief

1. Serves as spokesperson for the staff, sets its tone and represents the paper in dealings with school administration and community.

2. Checks with principal, school offices, activity schedule and beat reporters for story leads before each issue, or delegates authority for one or more of these tasks.

3. Conducts editorial board and staff meetings, then posts assignment sheet.

4. Oversees staff assignments and checks with other editors to resolve problems and verify that work is progressing and deadlines are being met.

5. Writes the lead editorial, which represents the agreed-upon policy of the paper.

6. Consults with the adviser at least once a week outside of class.

7. Copy-edits assignments after they have undergone first revision, and then submits same to adviser. If time, the two sit down together to co-edit.

8. Responsible for overseeing layouts, progress and production of entire paper.

9. May also write stories and headlines, give staff members guidance and make suggestions for improvement.

10. Encouraged to be a creative leader who determines the direction the paper takes during his or her tenure as editor in chief.

News editor

1. With input from the editorial board and other sources, makes up the list of news assignments for the coming issue.

2. Hands out assignments, discussing possible angles and approaches, tips on news sources, and the types of photos, graphics and sidebar material to gather. Checks on progress of reporters daily.

3. May sit down with reporter after preliminary research to discuss what elements to stress, additional sources to seek and additional questions to ask and answer.

4. Responsible for copy-editing first through final drafts.

5. After first revision or revisions, submits edited drafts to editor in chief.

6. Assigns self and writes news stories and headlines.

7. Approves or rewrites headlines, photo captions and cutlines for news stories. Checks to see that everyone in photos is identified correctly.

8. Does news page layouts on computer or on paper for reproduction by computer desktop publishing program.

Feature editor

1. In charge of originating, selecting and assigning feature stories, which may include profiles, human interest, entertainment and news features.

2. Encourages feature writers to generate own ideas, then presents assignments under consideration at editorial board meeting for discussion and additional suggestions.

3. Works closely with feature writers to discuss progress and make recommendations for covering and strengthening them.

4. Responsible for copy-editing first through final drafts.

5. After first revision or revisions, submits drafts to editor in chief.

6. Assigns self and writes feature stories and headlines.

7. Approves or rewrites headlines, photo captions and cutlines for feature stories. Checks to see that everyone in photos is identified correctly.

8. Does feature page layouts on computer or on paper for reproduction by computer desktop publishing program.

Op-ed editor

1. Responsible for overseeing opinion pieces and editorials, including editorial cartoons, masthead, statements of policy, letters to editor and columns.

2. After consulting with editor in chief about lead editorial, presents projected pieces to editorial board.

3. Makes and keeps track of assignments, discussing progress and making suggestions for strengthening.

4. As well as editor in chief, may author unsigned editorials or write bylined opinion columns.

5. Responsible for copy-editing first through final drafts.

6. After first revision or revisions, submits drafts to editor in chief.

7. Approves or rewrites headlines, cartoons and other graphics.

8. Does op-ed page layouts on computer or on paper for reproduction by computer desktop publishing program.

Sports editor

1. Keeps track of all sports events, schedules, coaches, team rosters, records; assigns stories on basis of greatest interest to fans and fairness to participants.

2. Because of seasonal nature of most sports, may have reporters work on assigned beats to increase familiarity with coaches, players and records.

3. Presents story ideas to editorial board for discussion, putting special emphasis on features, advances, profiles and other pieces with broad student interest.

4. Works closely with photographers to see that sports pages have effective action shots; also seeks human interest sports photos that tell the story and need only caption and/or cutline to be complete.

5. Makes assignments and checks on progress. Also writes sports stories, edits first through final drafts of sports stories. After first revisions, submits edited drafts to editor in chief.

6. Approves or rewrites headlines, photo captions and cutlines for sports stories. Checks to see everyone in photos is identified correctly.

7. Does sports page layouts on computer or on paper for reproduction by computer desktop publishing program.

Team/In-depth report editor

1. Coordinates coverage of stories requiring investigative research and team reporting, concentrating on school and community involvement in an issue of far-reaching interest and effect.

2. Works with a team of reporters to obtain in-depth coverage of subjects that may require extended deadlines.

3. Presents editorial board with topics of choice for advance issues, after brainstorming to explore possible resources, angles, sidebars, potential for infographs, photos and opinion polls.

4. Meets with reporting team to assign stories to members and self, making sure each understands the overall issue and his or her special segment.

5. Works closely with team to discuss progress and make suggestions. After editing first draft, edits then submits subsequent drafts to editor in chief.

6. Envisions an overall design and theme for the spread, makes graphics assignments and layouts accordingly.

7. Approves or rewrites headlines, graphics, photo captions and cutlines for in-depth reports. Checks to see that everyone in photos is identified correctly.

8. Does in-depth report layouts on computer or on paper for reproduction by computer desktop publishing program.

Chief photographer

1. Works closely with editors and seeks suggestions on elements desirable in photo illustrations assigned to accompany stories.

2. Originates ideas for photo stories or single shots that can hold their own as human interest items, spreads or features with the addition of cutlines or captions.

3. Makes sure proper identification is obtained for all photos.

4. Oversees the taking and finishing of all photos taken for the paper.

5. Responsible for making sure of dates and times for special events, such as sports, so no one-time photo opportunities are missed.

6. Shows proofs of photos to assignment editor for choice of most effective shot and cutline/caption writing; crops and/or prints photos to size needed.

7. With the approval of adviser and need of paper, works with other student photographers, on staff or freelance, and oversees their work.

Reporter

1. Fulfills assignments by doing necessary research and interviews, submitting stories correctly spelled and written in proper journalistic style, complete with suggested headlines, on or before assigned deadlines.

2. When first draft of assigned story is copy-edited and returned, has one full day to make suggested revision and resubmit. (With approval of editor, extension may be granted if further research is needed.)

3. Successive drafts will be reedited, then either approved or returned to reporter for further revision until written correctly in acceptable style.

4. Reporter also provides data for infographs and factoids for sidebars; suggests brief, punchy excerpts to use as pull quotes; and writes needed cutlines and captions to accompany photos.

5. Should notify editor as soon as problem arises concerning deadline so a solution may be found or another story assigned.

6. Is expected to complete at least 10 inches of approved and publishable copy for each issue. Full credit will be given whether or not space allows publication.

7. If assignment will not pan out by deadline, the reporter, at the editor's discretion, can be given another assignment, choose a feature or news feature from idea file, or have an editor okay an idea of writer's own.

8. Each reporter will check his or her beats before each editorial board meeting, giving promising ideas for news stories or features to the editor in chief. Writes up those suitable for news briefs and submits drafts to appropriate editor.

9. In addition to reporting, each staff member not having an editorial or managerial position will be responsible for an extra duty assignment.

All staff members

1. As the basis for grading, each staff member is required to keep a reporter's portfolio, complete and ready to hand in by an assigned date before the end of each grading period.

2. Should keep up-to-date on professional coverage of national and world concerns, and, for each upcoming issue, should clip at least three professional newspaper or magazine stories, pertaining to people their age, which should be handed to the appropriate editor as possible story leads.

Art director

1. Works closely with editors to provide artwork needed to enhance pages, including cartoons, sketches, graphics and choice of clip art. May also provide art for advertisements.

2. If familiar with computer draw programs, may also create computer-based illustrations and infographs.

3. As art director, has responsibility for seeing that all types of artwork are complete, acceptable and ready on deadline, whether done by freelancers, another staff artist, or self.

Note: If there is no staff artist in a given year, the editor in chief or adviser should contact the art department chairperson at the beginning of the year about candidates interested in various types of art. Those selected should be contacted by editors as soon as assignments are made, and be given details on their projects and deadlines.

Advertising/business manager

The advertising/business responsibilities may be managed by one person or divided between two. The duties break down as following:

Business:

1. Accurately keeps the newspaper's financial records.

2. Prepares a business report for every issue, including amounts spent for printing, photography, supplies, etc., and the income from advertising and any other sources. Draws a comparison between actual figures and the projected budget.

3. Keeps an accurate inventory of supplies and purchases, informing adviser when supplies need to be purchased.

4. Sends out statements with tearsheet or complete paper to each advertiser immediately after publication of each issue, following up each delinquent account, if any, both by phone and by letter.

5. Prepares needed payout slips and works closely with school treasurer, according to official procedure.

Advertising:

6. Prepares and maintains a list of current and prospective advertisers; takes charge of selling campaigns as well as doing actual selling.

7. Makes sure all ads are designed to proper size and complete before deadline.

8. Designs and writes copy to advertisers' specifications or works closely with advertising artist/designer given this assignment.

9. Decides ad placement on pages, working with editors to adjust spaces to allow for editorial matter, if necessary.

10. Conducts periodic surveys of student body and advertisers to assess effectiveness of ads and potential for growth.

Duties of the editorial board

1. The editorial board meets before assignments are made for the upcoming issue, with editor in chief conducting the meeting and adviser as observer/consultant.

2. In addition to editor in chief, board members include other staff editors, chief photographer, art director and business/advertising manager(s).

3. Other members of staff or guests may be invited from time to time to present their ideas or special issues but shall not have a vote in board decisions.

4. Editor in chief will present a list of story ideas gathered from school administrators, school's activities calendar, future book and items gathered by beat reporters.

5. Each editor will present and be given ideas for his or her area, open for discussion.

6. The board will also hear the planned subject or subjects of editorials for the upcoming issue, discuss and approve views that represent the paper's official editorial policy and stance.

7. Passage of those topics representing official staff policy requires a two-third majority; passage of other votes needs only a simple majority.

8. Special meetings of the editorial board may be called when needed by the editor in chief and/or the adviser.

THE ADVANTAGES OF AN EXTRA DUTY ROSTER—One way to solve the problem of staffers without editorial positions having too much time on their hands is the staff duty roster. By assigning special duties, you provide each staffer with a meaningful task to perform when not actively working on a story assignment. You can also achieve a higher level of organization, preparedness and accuracy that can cut down the time spent working outside of class. In preparing an extra duty roster, try to devise areas of responsibility that require approximately the same amount of time and effort per issue.

You, as the adviser, should have concrete proof of a job well or poorly done, as well as be able to tell by observation whether a student is performing his or her job. You may wish to assign two staffers to some of the areas and allow those assigned a given task to ask other staffers for help if the work loads fall at different times.

Depending upon your staff size and organization, you may want to include assistant photographer and artist positions among the special assignments on the duty roster. With this type of assignment, students can see that they are not just being given "busy work" but are making a definite contribution by helping the paper be better organized and run more smoothly. The goal is a job well done.

You can include a job description of each assignment in the paper's staff manual ("Reporters' special duties," Figure 1-6), and use or adapt the "Special duty assignment sheet" (Figure 1-7) to post on the staff bulletin board.

TIP

During or before editorial board meetings, have less-experienced staffers proofread the just-published issue and mark errors in:

Spelling	Punctuation	Usage
Headlines	Cutlines	Clarity
Hard-to-read type	Mechanical errors	Other mistakes

See who can find the most errors; you may give a "prize" such as a candy bar or soft drink. Discuss how this kind of mistake can be avoided in the future.

You may wish to make a list, a la Ben Franklin in his *Autobiography*, and have the staff strive to make the next issue totally free of one targeted error. By concentrating on one error at a time, the need to avoid it entirely can become firmly planted and improvement come more easily than if all problems are tackled at once.

Grading: the need for creative solutions

One of the biggest headaches for any adviser comes from the need to assign grades to newspaper classes offered as credit courses. With everyone on the staff having differing levels of responsibility—some staffers more experienced than others, editors devoting extra time to production and editing—there is really no firm basis for making the comparisons needed to establish a grading scale. It's like comparing apricots to zebras.

The problems become compounded if you add other requirements, such as selling a given amount of advertising or spending a stated number of hours working for the paper outside of class. There's often no way to determine whether a staffer's claims and/or excuses are valid or invalid unless the adviser turns detective—not only time consuming but also ruinous to morale.

Reporters' special duties

1. **Exchange editor**—compiles and keeps a record of names and addresses of schools and other organizations to which each issue is sent. Carefully looks through each exchange paper received for usable ideas. Calls attention of appropriate editors or adviser to stories inspiring similar coverage, striking graphics and layouts. Upon request, puts a copy in the idea file under proper heading: features, sports, etc.

2. **Proofreading**—Because of the unreliability of computer spell-checks in catching words spelled correctly but lacking the intended meaning when read in context, goes over computer-processed copy to read for words passed over—such as "tat" for "that." Also checks for punctuation errors, other mistakes.

3. **Mail clerk**—Picks up newspaper/journalism mail from school distribution point and delivers it to appropriate editor or adviser. Hands notices of activities, posters and circulars of interest to adviser, editor or bulletin board clerk. Also follows proper mailing procedure for letters and other mail sent from newspaper office.

4. **Compiler of future book**—Makes sure the future book is up-to-date, adding and deleting items as necessary. Filed by upcoming issues, the future book contains a list of scheduled activities that need coverage for that issue; copies of advance stories printed in previous issues that require follow-up; timely press releases that can be rewritten as news briefs or researched further for stories; copies of beat coverage forms; and other possibilities for future issues.

5. **Assistant to business/advertising manager**—Helps as needed with ad layouts, design, art, sales, recordkeeping, mailings, etc. Helpful to have computer experience, interest in art and/or business.

6. **Gofer for editors**—Is on call to run errands for editors, checks on details and facts, does paste-up jobs and other necessary tasks. Duties include keeping track of supplies—pencils, rulers, scissors, etc., at end of each hour and reporting needs to business manager.

7. **Pollster**—Responsible for preparing and conducting opinion polls of students and/or faculty on a variety of subjects, including polls used as part of in-depth reports, readership surveys and infographs running solo. Needs system for fair coverage, avoidance of repeaters.

8. **Bulletin board clerk**—Sees that bulletin boards are eye-catching, informative and up-to-date. Checks daily to remove old notes and put up new ones. Changes boards dramatically at least once per issue—installing pages and items from exchange papers, stories and ideas from professional media, posters, bulletins and notices as well as keeping up a special section for assignment sheets, duty rosters and messages to staff.

9. **Names-in-news monitor**—Before each story is set in final form, goes through printout of student body and faculty directory to make sure all names are spelled correctly. Checks other sources for names outside of school. Also has the responsibility of placing a hatch mark after a student or faculty member's name each time it appears in the paper so certain students and teachers are not favored.

10. **Clipping clerk for staff portfolios**—Goes through two copies of each issue and clips out each story, photograph, piece of artwork and advertisement. These should be kept in folders and handed out to each staff member for use in his or her portfolio. Also responsible for checking in filing clippings from national and professional press brought in by staffers, later added to portfolios.

11. **Distribution crew**—Takes charge of counting out papers after publication of each issue, taking them to distribution points, and seeing that they are properly distributed. Also needs to count out papers for advertisers and exchanging.

Special duty assignment sheet

Effective dates _____ to _____

Duty	**Staffer or staffers in charge**	
1. Exchange editor	_____	_____
2. Proofreader	_____	_____
3. Mail, supply clerk	_____	_____
4. Assistant to business ad manager	_____	_____
5. Gofer for editors	_____	_____
6. Librarian for future book	_____	_____
7. Pollster		
8. Bulletin board clerk	_____	_____
9. "Names in news" monitor	_____	_____
10. Clipping clerk for portfolios	_____	_____
11. Distribution crew	_____	_____

Other assignments

12. _____	_____	_____
13. _____	_____	_____
14. _____	_____	_____
15. _____	_____	_____
16. _____	_____	_____
17. _____	_____	_____
18. _____	_____	_____

Not only do grades cause headaches. They also create controversy among staff members and even bitterness toward the adviser. "Why did Kim get an A, when I spent twice as much time working for the paper and got only a B?"

The frequent differences in age and experience make it frustratingly complex to grade each draft and revision of a reporter's story. Is it fair to hold a sophomore, new to the staff, to the same standards as a senior editor? The questions have no definitive answers.

AN ALTERNATIVE TO RECORDKEEPING—There are a number of ways to wriggle out of the necessity of spending hours mulling over grades for the newspaper staff. Before adopting a method that is highly creative, it is best to discuss your plans with your principal.

Pass or fail says that a staffer did the work expected of someone in that position, or that he or she didn't. On a newspaper staff there is, in a sense, no middle ground. Either a staffer contributes to the newspaper's production or becomes a detriment—wasting editors' and adviser's time by missing deadlines, submitting shoddily written stories, fooling around and being ready only with excuses. If the absence of grades is not acceptable in a newspaper class offered for English credit, you can still create a version of pass/fail by issuing either A's or F's.

Presumably the newspaper staff is a hand-picked group, whose members joined because they want to have a part in producing the school paper, not for competition in getting good grades. The only competition involved should be to better the paper each issue. If it is an elective course, you might also discuss the advisability of dropping a staff member who receives a failing mark or F for two consecutive grading periods or two successive issues of the paper.

After adopting either of these systems, you can explain to the staff at the beginning of the year that, as far as the newspaper goes, grades aren't important to you and needn't be to them either. What really matters is each staff member's effort, enthusiasm, spirit of cooperation and determination to make the best school newspaper possible.

GRADING: THE REPORTER'S PORTFOLIO—Another alternative to time-consuming, meticulous grading on a daily or weekly basis is to have each staffer compile and prepare a reporter's portfolio. Introduced as a tool for composition classes, the portfolio is a natural for the newspaper. It provides the objective criteria you need for an honest evaluation, especially of students who don't hold an editor's position and whose contributions aren't always apparent. The portfolio also provides a concrete basis for comparison, because the staffer who is lazy, slipshod and late with other assignments is likely to be just as sloppy and undependable with his or her portfolio.

In establishing grades, you may want to weigh the extra time spent working by editors as points equivalent to some elements of the portfolio, which they may lack time to prepare, or encourage (or assign) other staffers to help in compiling editors' portfolios.

To prepare their portfolios, you may provide students with the following forms: a list of expected contents ("Portfolio content," Figure 1-8), progress report ("Progress report: special duty assignments," Figure 1-9), and calendar for recording their daily staff diary ("Daily staff diary," Figure 1-10).

YOUR PAPER'S LOGO

Portfolio contents

Grading Period _____

Dates _____ **to** _____

Include the following in your portfolio.
Make sure that all are neatly mounted and labeled.

1. Clippings of all articles, photography, advertising or graphics that you wrote or created. Indicate issue number, date of issue, page number and a statement of your contribution, if not bylined.

2. Final, approved versions of articles or other material that you did during this grading period, which was not published but okayed.

3. Daily diary/schedule of work done for paper during and outside of class this grading period.

4. Progress report on special duty assignments, if given.

5. List of work you did for the paper this grading period, in addition to that represented by clippings.

6. Copy of forms used for beat coverage, kept in portfolio as reference.

7. Other material, requested by adviser or illustrative of work you have done this grading period.

Progress report:
Special duty assignments

Grading Period _____

Dates _____ **to** _____

Name _____ Assigned Duty _____

Week No. _____: **Assessment of progress**

(Check one)   Outstanding ☐   Satisfactory ☐   Needs ☐   Unsatisfactory ☐
Improvement

Comments: _____

Signed: _____

Name _____ Assigned Duty _____

Week No. _____: **Assessment of progress**

(Check one)   Outstanding ☐   Satisfactory ☐   Needs ☐   Unsatisfactory ☐
Improvement

Comments: _____

Signed: _____

Name _____ Assigned Duty _____

Week No. _____: **Assessment of progress**

(Check one)   Outstanding ☐   Satisfactory ☐   Needs ☐   Unsatisfactory ☐
Improvement

Comments: _____

Signed: _____

Name _____ Assigned Duty _____

Week No. _____: **Assessment of progress**

(Check one)   Outstanding ☐   Satisfactory ☐   Needs ☐   Unsatisfactory ☐
Improvement

Comments: _____

Signed: _____

Work done for this issue in addition to clippings and assigned duties:

1. _____

_____

2. _____

_____

3. _____

_____

4. _____

_____

5. _____

_____

6. _____

_____

7. _____

_____

8. _____

_____

9. _____

_____

10. _____

_____

Daily staff diary

For each day, list your activities during period as briefly as possible.

Name _____   **Dates:** _____ **to** _____

	MONDAY	TUESDAY	WEDNESDAY	THURSDAY	FRIDAY
Week 1: During class hour					
Outside hours: *state time*					
Week 2: During class hour					
Outside hours: *state time*					
Week 3: During class hour					
Outside hours: *state time*					
Week 4: During class hour					
Outside hours: *state time*					
Week 5: During class hour					
Outside hours: *state time*					

Defining your publication's purpose and personality

Questioning your role

A list of twenty-one questions up for discussion at a symposium of journalism advisers touched on the following concerns:

> Have you literally lost sleep over the school paper?
> Has your involvement with the paper caused you to fear losing your grip on everything else in your life?
> Do any of your colleagues understand and sympathize with your efforts and goals as an adviser?

Such questions are clearly intended to reflect the feelings of a substantial number of advisers.

In every specialized area of education—from athletic coach to band director to dramatics adviser—there are women and men who think of their positions as genuine callings. They seem to glory in their roles, and, though they grouse from time to time along with the rest, consider their sacrifices worth making. Their zest and confidence as leaders often prove contagious, and their enthusiasm attracts students who reflect their sense of purpose. Yet such dedication is rare. While losing sleep because of a crisis can happen to anyone—the fear of losing your grip on everything else in life and alienation from colleagues are signs of more serious problems.

Assess your position

As a class, the school paper occupies only a fraction of the school day. Unless journalism is a fully scheduled department, it may be only a fraction of your day as a teacher. It can be—it deserves to be—a highlight of your school day and that of each staff member. But it shouldn't so consume your time and your life to seem the be-all and end-all of your existence.

What is the major concern of the school newspaper?

If someone asked, "What is the purpose of a French class?" the answer would appear self-evident: "To teach students French."

Asking "What is the purpose of a newspaper class?" would likely produce a different answer: "To publish the school paper."

For the school newspaper, the product often obscures the genuine education taking place. Even for students trained in beginning journalism, the experience of actually producing a paper is different and far more demanding. To student editors or reporters, the main goal is to produce a paper, but their adviser must focus on this goal and the equally valid one of making students' participation in the newspaper a significant learning experience.

The masthead of a school paper often includes a policy statement expressing the paper's goals. Yet remember—and remind the school administration from time to time—that the newspaper is a class or activity created as an adjunct to a student's education.

If it begins to seem like a destructive force, pushing the adviser to the edge of martyrdom and facing alienation, it is time to step back and assess the purpose and benefits of the school paper, both for the students on the staff and the school at large ("Purpose and advantages of publishing a school paper," Figure 1-11).

Purpose and advantages of publishing a school paper

Benefits for students on staff

By becoming staff members, students:

1. Gain awareness of the power of written communication by publishing their work and receiving valuable feedback from readers.

2. Develop the skill of maturely handling interviews and staff business on a one-to-one basis with the adults whom they contact as student reporters/editors.

3. Face the need to weigh and make decisions about ethics and values, and to resolve conflicts between rights and responsibilities.

4. Acquire writing skills that in the future will prove assets in professional, technical and vocational fields, as well as those allied to journalism.

5. Accept the requirements of meeting deadlines and fulfilling assigned duties in order to succeed as part of a production team with clearly outlined goals.

6. Take over meaningful leadership roles as student editors, designers and managers.

7. Receive grounding in practical and professional applications of modern technology.

8. Have an outlet for expressing their creativity and communicating their ideas.

9. Make a positive contribution to their school and feel an integral part of the school community.

10. Become aware of the necessity of accepting responsibility for, and the consequences of, submitting their work to public judgment.

Purpose and advantage to school and community

For the student body and faculty as a whole, the school paper:

1. Provides the only news periodical specifically addressed to the school and its unique community.

2. Serves to unify the student body by appealing to its members' common interests and concerns.

3. Provides a forum for student expression and ideas.

4. Offers a medium for written communication of information that can be conveniently disseminated in no other way.

5. Attempts to provide fair, well-rounded, unbiased coverage of the school as a whole.

6. Promotes high standards in journalistic writing and shared ethics for writers and readers alike.

7. Helps students see the importance of print journalism to citizens of school, community and country.

8. Deepens students' understanding of troubling issues by exploring them from the viewpoint of students and their schoolmates on the student press.

9. Underscores the importance of being literate, via the school's sponsorship and support of the newspaper as a valuable source of information.

10. Forges links that help make students feel more like knowledgeable participants in the educational process.

In a fundamental sense, the process of publishing a school paper is as important as the product. For you as the adviser, its goal is not only turning out a superior paper, but the growth and education taking place as students learn to function as editors and writers, managers and technicians. Yet, as a staff gains experience, you must always face the frustrating truth that you can never take even your most talented staffs as far as you'd like. School is actually a rite of passage. Graduation is always coming some tomorrow.

REMEMBER THE PROCESS AS WELL AS THE PRODUCT—Frustration is natural and probably inevitable. Though each new crop of kids may seem less prepared than the one before, much of the inadequacy is built into the system. It's not the kids' fault. It's not your fault as their adviser.

Compare it to any other kind of class. First-year math, for example. Or, even a class of first graders. Just as these have much to learn, so do the incoming members of a school newspaper staff. It's vital to remember that you are a teacher, even though you bear the title of adviser, and kids are but kids.

THE WORTH OF AN OPINION—It's convenient to define *adviser* simply as someone who gives advice—an opinion or suggestion. For those who assume that one opinion is as good as another, this puts the school paper adviser in an ill-defined position. To what degree should you attempt to steer or control the direction that the newspaper takes?

It is preferable to stay as much in the background as possible, allowing students to exercise their leadership and decision-making skills and to accept responsibility for their own choices and actions—yet the title *adviser* implies someone whose opinions weigh more than uneducated guesses. According to the dictionary, *advice* involves "the making of a recommendation as to a course of action by someone with actual or supposed knowledge, experience, etc."

By accepting the title *adviser* instead of *director, coach* or *teacher,* you choose to guide students in subtle ways through reason, not command. By making a distinction between choices that are truly optional and those that are crucial, you can give students both the freedom and support they need. When dire consequences loom, make special efforts to validate your opinion with both facts and examples, while leaving room for students to question, participate and learn.

Accept the fact that you don't have all the answers. Don't apologize for what you don't know; some of the best educational experiences take place when you are learning along with your staff. For successful learning, follow-through is as essential as generating ideas. Martyrdom results when students are eager to formulate plans, but the adviser is forced to carry them out.

Whether you're starting out fresh as an adviser or want to update an established paper's image, the possibilities before you present an infinite chain of choices. What size paper? How often to publish? What directions to take with contents? As a basis for making educated choices, acquaint yourself and your staff with what other schools are doing, and compare your situation with theirs.

A MATTER OF TIME—The advent of desktop publishing has multiplied both the tasks and the time it takes to produce a school paper. Both a boon and a burden, computers work fast—but much of the work once done outside of school now falls on students and advisers. Administrators find this hard to understand. In fact, advisers don't always appreciate how much they're expected to know and do—and blame themselves for not being able to publish as many papers as in the "good old days" of weeklies and biweeklies.

In the era of desktop publishing, managing to come out monthly is *good*. In fact, more than 80% of school papers surveyed publish at intervals of a month or longer. This factor alone has a major effect on the expectations and demands advisers and staffs can place upon themselves, as well as affecting the contents and personalities of school papers.

Settling on size

A PAPER OF COMMON DIMENSIONS—The majority of papers surveyed fit the category of tabloid size, while 30% measure 8-1/2″ × 11″, the size of a sheet of typing paper or *Time* magazine. This smaller size, such as *Devils' Advocate* (Example 1-1), may be easier and more economical to produce. The 8-1/2″ × 11″ size encompasses news magazines that feature striking, page-size photographs or artwork (Example 1-2), and concentrate on magazine-type articles, features, and in-depth reports on issues of special interest to students.

With creative design and editorial planning, the 8-1/2″ × 11″ paper or news magazine can choose, adapt and incorporate the most promising new ideas in layout and coverage to fit its space and page size.

THE TABLOID, STILL THE LEADER—Why do 70% of the schools surveyed publish tabloid-size papers (Example 1-3) on newsprint stock? One reason is that tabloids look more like professional newspapers. And, they may be traditional at schools where sizing down seems like retreat. With pages approximately twice the size of typing paper, tabloid pages allow scope for greater variety of stories and versatility in makeup, but they are also less forgiving. Overly long stories, weak headlines, fuzzy photos and too little white space lead to a vast, gray uniformity that is more deadening to large pages than smaller ones. Tabloid-size pages also run a greater risk of looking jumbled.

Producing a tabloid page may also present a greater challenge, especially considering the constraints of desktop publishing. If your school lacks sufficiently large computer monitors or other needed equipment, it becomes both difficult and time-consuming to change focus from actual size to fractional when working on different phases of design and production. The need to run proofs on undersize sheets that require overlapping and pasting further compounds the problem.

Yes, producing a tabloid page presents a challenge—and that may be just what you and your staff will thrive on. Weigh the pluses and minuses of each size page before settling on the one that's best for you, your staff and your school.

A DEFINITION OF JOURNALISM—There's something about being on a newspaper, about being a journalist, that generates excitement. A pocket dictionary defines journalism as "the work of gathering news for, or producing, a newspaper, etc." Although that "etc." might be a magazine, the *jour* in journalism means *day*, so journalists' sense of seeking news of the day and being up to date comes naturally.

Ironically, because of desktop publishing, the school newspaper is often pressed to keep to a monthly schedule, let alone offer news of the day. In fact, one long-time adviser estimates that computer technology doubles the time it takes him and his staff to produce their school paper.

As one result, school papers are devoting more space to pages of opinion, features and entertainment, while relying less on what traditionally passed for news but was often stale accounts of past events.

Example 1-1. *Devils' Advocate*, 8-1/2" x 11" offset, Hinsdale Central H.S., Hinsdale, IL.

Example 1-2. *Compass*, 8-1/2″ × 11″ glossy, Reynoldsburg H.S., Reynoldsburg, OH.

Example 1-3. *Cougar Chronicle*, 11″ × 17″ newsprint, Palmyra Area H.S., Palmyra, PA.

PLANNING TO PLAN—As preliminary steps to fine-tuning your paper's image, plan to sit down with the editorial board or the entire staff, if feasible, and brainstorm ideas about the paper's editorial concept and direction in makeup. Since ideas are hard to snatch from thin air, gather other papers, especially those you judge worthy models, as well as professional newspapers and magazines that may provide inspiration for stories or design. Allow more than one session to develop your plan of action. Ideas need a chance to percolate, and staffers need the opportunity to seek examples of their own.

What works—what doesn't

As a preliminary to your planning session, ask students to analyze the differences between print and electronic journalism: what are the advantages of each and what types of coverage does each handle more effectively as a result ("How medium affects message," Figure 1-12).

You may wish to extend your discussion to include the Internet. Clay Felker, director of the Felker Magazine Center at the Graduate School of Journalism at Berkeley, comments about on-line publications, "Nobody wants to read very much . . . . Our eyes get tired quicker on a computer screen. Plus it isn't very practical. People look at a screen as work, not pleasure. It doesn't have the portability of print. As a result, you have to write differently in order to keep people interested." (Quoted in the *New Yorker,* May 13, 1996)

In your discussion, avoid commenting on the benefits or purposes; concentrate, as Felker does, on the strengths and limitations of other media.

ADDING SCHOOL PAPERS TO THE EQUATION—As a result of their comparison, students can validly decide that both television and newspaper have a vital place among American media and that print journalism has assets all its own. They should also notice how advantages come with disadvantages and vice versa. For example, television's fleeting image upon the screen provides immediacy but inhibits reflective thinking and thoroughness of coverage. The "sound bite" leaves viewers no time to pause, chew or digest an item before another topic—or even a commercial—comes their way.

From this springboard, discuss what a school newspaper can and can't do well, especially considering the problem of timeliness. First, try to elicit a list from staff members, or note the items below and ask them to discuss why each presents a coverage problem.

School newspapers have difficulty covering

Spot news: By the time such stories appear, further developments have likely outdated them. With news of wider interest, professional media get there first and leave little or nothing new to say.

School sports: In each sport, teams may play up to four or more games between issues, with the most recent happening too late for deadline. The earlier ones have disappeared into the record book.

World and national news: A school newspaper can give only secondhand coverage to subjects taking place in other parts of the country and world. Approached as hard news, such stories seem redundant in student papers.

Follow-up stories on school events: Here timing and angle are everything. If it happened soon after the previous issue came out, it's probably too old to cover effectively as straight news. It might make a good feature if well-conceived and executed.

How medium affects message

1. Comparing television and print journalism, list three main elements that television uses to deliver its message and three used by newspapers.

    Television: _____   _____

    _____

    Newspaper: _____   _____

    _____

2. What are three advantages of each type of news coverage?

    Television

    1. _____

    2. _____

    3. _____

    Newspaper

    1. _____

    2. _____

    3. _____

3. What kind of coverage can each medium do best?

    Television

    1. _____

    2. _____

    3. _____

    Newspaper

    1. _____

    2. _____

    3. _____

4. Comparing a traditionally oriented paper, such as *Wall Street Journal*, to *USA Today*, what influences of television's impact can you note? _____

_____

_____

_____

5. In what ways, if any, does TV journalism lack important qualities of good news coverage?

_____

_____

_____

_____

6. What is the advantage of a newspaper's existing in tangible form, on paper, rather than as an image on screen? _____

_____

_____

_____

7. Which medium, TV or newspaper, appeals more to the emotions and which to logical thought? State reasons for your choices. _____

_____

_____

_____

8. What advantages does the Internet have over broadcast and print journalism?

_____

_____

_____

_____

What disadvantages? _____

_____

_____

_____

Reviews: This is a touchy subject. From across the country, school papers seem to revel in reviews of CDs, movies, concerts, restaurants. Album and record reviews can tempt some to hard-to-detect plagiarism or cause young writers to attempt professional jargon but not quite get it. Concerts, like school events, quickly turn into old news, unless the reporter can grab an interview or take the reader behind the scenes.

How many reviews are too many? It's a good area to leave up to student choice—with warnings against overdoing.

Scholarly articles: Topics such as "Medical advances in the late 20th century," which sound like research papers written for other classes, sometimes substitute as in-depth reports. These are not news or features—they don't belong.

THE SPECIAL PROVINCE OF SCHOOL PAPERS—What's left? Plenty! In fact, your staff should find more than enough ideas to fill every issue. Assign stories on the basis of what students in your school need and want to know. Aim to inform, help them keep track of what's going on, give them insight into school concerns and policies, provide local aspects of national and world issues, provide a forum for student opinion . . . and don't forget to include entertainment, sports, academics. Then be sure to package it all appealingly on readable, well-designed pages with crisply written stories on every page.

WHAT SCHOOL PAPERS DO WELL—The best and brightest papers develop techniques for making their papers lively, informative and appealing. Is it next to impossible to cover spot news? Then make news easy to spot. The number-one targets for sprucing up pages are those two- or three-paragraph stories that, scattered throughout the paper, look limp and lost. Group them together in a single column down the side of a page or otherwise packaged together under a standing headline. The simplest choice: news briefs (Example 1-4).

Each news brief deserves its own headline, and make sure there is enough white space between items so they don't run together and make the column go gray. Also, warn reporters against falling into the dull habit of starting every tidbit the same way: "The French Club plans . . . ," "The National Honor Society elected . . . ," "The Booster Club will sponsor . . ." Such beginnings are sure to have a deadening effect on page-organizing columns that students will scan with interest.

BRANCHING OUT—With beat coverage, reporters' discovery of more such short news items can provide opportunities for creative packaging. All news briefs? Yes . . . but to liven your pages, try grouping them under special categories, possibly with catchy titles, as in Examples 1-5, 1-6 and 1-7. Other possibilities:

Club news = *The meeting place*
Honors and awards = *Making the grade*
Activities = *Happenings*—or—*Coming Events*
Sports = *Shorts in sports*

Some school papers, inspired by columns in professional publications, such as *Time* magazine's "Winners & Losers," have created their own columns of positives and negatives, such as "Pluses & Minuses" or "Problems & Solutions." In a school paper, however, be careful about being too blunt in your choice of column heads. Such headers as "Cheers & Jeers" can lead to a type of personal attack that is hurtful at best, gossip or even libel at worst.

Example 1-4. "News Brief," *The Epitaph*, 11″ × 17″ newsprint, Homestead H.S., Cupertino, CA.

Example 1-5. "When & Where," *The Colonel*, 8-1/2″ × 11″ offset, Theodore Roosevelt H.S., Kent, OH.

Example 1-6. "Gym Shorts," *Falcon's Cry*, 11″ × 14″ newsprint, Jordan H.S., Durham, NC.

Example 1-7. "Quick Takes," *TJ Today*, 11″ × 17″ newsprint, Thomas Jefferson High School for Science & Technology, Alexandria, VA.

GRAPHIC SOLUTIONS—Ideal elements in a school paper combine information worth noting with eye appeal. In your planning sessions, encourage your staff or editorial board to discuss these and their own ideas.

Calendar of school events: In graphic form, list the events scheduled during the weeks between one issue and the next. If attractively packaged, it becomes a standing graphic element that encourages readers to save each edition for reference. (Example 1-8)

Game Highlights: Design a graphic way of presenting scores and perhaps capsule accounts of games played since the previous issue. Start with the most recent and go backward in chronological time. Older games may deserve only scores. Sports are tricky. Avid fans attend games and get the rest from the local paper, TV and game post-mortems with friends and student athletes. Those who don't care won't bother reading.

It's a question of good reporting. Write previews of upcoming games, and encourage sport writers to dig for information worth printing. Try to exchange papers with key rivals. Their papers' sports pages hold promise of offering background about your opposition that will add dimension to your coverage.

Another approach is to feature a "Player of the game" in each sport covered. Along with the charted score and play stats, include a mug shot of the chosen player, plus one or two paragraphs, reporting his or her contribution to the game and season, along with a quote by the coach, the featured player, or a teammate. (Example 1-9)

Firsthand stories: Much that is old to some people is news to others. ("Do you mean women weren't allowed to vote till over 130 years after this country was founded?") That it is news to some doesn't mean it belongs in the paper. Too much of too many school papers relies on stories that were better covered elsewhere. Some are rehashes of material from other sources—little better than space fillers, chosen because they appeal to kids' interests—music, fun and entertainment—and seem deceptively easy to write.

Local coverage/primary sources: As far as possible, these two factors should be of first consideration in choosing story assignments: local coverage, primary sources. They may not be the exclusive criteria, but such stories should predominate. The basis may be a news event, an advance story, a profile, an analysis of an in-school problem or in-depth coverage of the local aspects of a broader issue. Columns and opinion pieces make some of the most interesting and readable additions of all—as long as they are backed up with sufficient examples and cogent observations, not just top-of-the-head ramblings.

How much space should a paper devote to primary coverage? As much as possible. There are certain gray areas where opinion affects the decision. Is it a sincerely written column or merely a writer's feverish emptying of random thoughts into the word-processing program—anything to meet a deadline? Well-written, well-researched, "honest" stories hold up and are interesting, even for someone not associated with the local scene. The others show their weaknesses. Judge on local angle, sources and readability.

On this basis, one outstanding school paper included in the survey had seven-eighths of its editorial matter devoted to local coverage and primary sources, with the rest devoted to seemingly frivolous columns and opinion pieces—some of them "throwaway" topics.

Example 1-8. (Top to bottom:) *The Chronicle*, 11″ × 17″ newsprint, Harvard-Westlake School, North Hollywood, CA; *Devils' Advocate*, 8-1/2″ × 11″ offset, Hinsdale, IL; *The Prospector*, 11″ × 17″ newsprint, Cupertino H.S., Cupertino, CA.

Example 1-9. (Top examples:) *The Chronicle,* 11″ × 17″ newsprint, Harvard-Westlake School, North Hollywood, CA; (Bottom example:) "Spring sports watch," *Academy Times,* 11″ × 17″ newsprint, Charles Wright Academy, Tacoma, WA.

Nowhere, ever, should a writer begin a column or opinion piece like this:

> Well, since I'm expected to have a column in the paper, and I've got to get this in tomorrow morning or my name will be Blah, I'll try to pick a topic that will interest as many of you as possible.

> Let's see—sex, skipping school, sleeping in. Maybe I should just forget about the column, and try to work all three into my day tomorrow . . .

Ask staff members how much of the "column" consists of empty words. They should come up with 100%—the whole thing. This kind of writing is dishonest—an attempt to fool the reader into believing it says something when it doesn't. Such stories do not qualify as local, primary or source-related, but are indulgent and self-serving.

Members of a newspaper staff should not capitalize on their positions by putting one another, their adviser or themselves in the spotlight unless involved in a genuine news story. Features and profiles about staffers should be taboo as well.

FINDING PRIMARY SOURCES—When a story involves a school activity, the news source is often obvious—the principal, student leader, athletic coach or award winner clearly designated. Sometimes the source may be too obvious. In the case of an unpopular policy or controversial issue, especially well-rounded coverage demands that reporters contact all sides. News stories are not places to play favorites nor alienate those of opposing views. Editorializing should be left to the editorial page.

"The school is tightening its athletic code, and players are grumbling." Talk to the principal, the coaches—yes. Players, too. Don't just use students' quotes as an inquiring reporter exercise. Share specific concerns with those responsible for the new rules, and ask them to explain their reasons in the light of student objections. Cut to the story's core and report its true significance.

Finding primary sources is more difficult—but the result is rewarding—in coverage of problems in the national spotlight: pregnancy, drugs, underage drinking, one-parent families, inability to meet the demands of the workplace, censorship . . . . Topics that once could shock have become standard fare, but that fact does not make such topics valueless.

Yet a school newspaper should never merely rewarm a story because it seems daring or fashionable. Unless a story has a definite focus and provides students with a special dimension and understanding of how the subject affects and concerns them and their classmates, the "shock" headline may gain attention, but the rest will prove a letdown. Along with the ho-hum reaction comes the question: Why was this story in the paper—to fill up space or just to cause a sensation?

WHERE TO BEGIN?—Tackling an in-depth report of a national issue such as teen smoking requires extensive preplanning. It should go far beyond patching together a research story from magazine articles and previously published reports. It means sitting down with a chosen few: editor or editors, reporter or reporting team and adviser, and brainstorming to see what direction to take, what leads to follow.

Here's how you might approach such a story as teen smoking:

1. Discuss ideas about whom to consult first: The head of the local Cancer Society? A hospital administrator? The school counselor? You don't need to know all the answers in the beginning, nor even all the questions. Do some preliminary digging. Your first contacts might not yield interviews but names of people to see.

2.   Take a representative poll of students that can be broken down in classes and by male or female. Be sure to seek a large enough sample. Ask: Do you smoke? How much? When did you begin? Do you wish you could stop? Do you think you could stop if you wanted to?

3.   Interview individual students who smoke, asking how and why they started and why they don't quit. One school got a group of five or six smokers together for a private discussion of their feelings about smoking. The exchange was taped and published as dialogue, with the reporter choosing representative answers, using such aliases as Marlboro Man and Virginia Slim to conceal the participants' identities.

4.   As a separate story, a reporter could contact the local police and try to elicit their cooperation in letting staffers attempt to buy cigarettes from various local establishments, However, even after seeking police cooperation in their investigation of cigarette sales to minors, a high school in Missouri ran into censorship, according to an article in *Student Press Law Center Report* (Spring 1996). Two of eight local businesses illegally sold cigarettes to the student investigators. The story, which named the stores, was censored after the school principal allegedly received calls, expressing fear of the story's effect on business.

5.   Another angle: How do nonsmoking students feel about smokers' rights? Are they too strictly limited?

6.   Omitting names if so requested, interview teachers regarding their attitudes toward smoking.

7.   Check old issues of your paper to learn the attitudes of the administration, editorials and student groups toward smoking in the past.

8.   Use infographs and sidebars for statistics and related factoids.

One reason the shock topics of the day can create such great interest is that they strike close to home and stir personal feelings. It is not wrong to include several quotes garnered from professional media; this ties the local story to the broader issue. *Proximity* and *magnitude* are two factors that make news news—and firmly tying a local issue to a national one makes use of both.

GET THE INSIDE STORY

"It should be a great show."

Why?

"The *Broncos* are without a doubt our toughest opponents so far."

What makes them that way?

"Since coming here as dean of girls, I've found everyone most helpful and friendly."

Can you give some examples that show this is so?

It's natural for school reporters to feel nervous and uneasy when doing an interview. They want to get it over as quickly as possible, so they settle for the first answers, the easy ones. Settling for the superficial results in dull, lifeless stories that tell nothing new. "Ask the questions that readers would like to ask if given the chance" should be every reporter's motto.

The best answers take thought—so the good reporter is a good listener, too. At times, showing willingness to listen to the silence of someone searching for the right words or example is the best way of expressing genuine interest and earns the best quotes.

GOOD NEWS GATHERING: CENTRAL TO THE EQUATION—The choice of topic and the actual writing are only part of the story. The job done in gathering the story makes or breaks it. To tune up your paper's pages, concentrate on news gathering as well as coverage and writing. Here are four approaches that will enable students to analyze and sharpen their interviewing skills:

1. **Conduct an in-class press conference.** Invite a news source, such as the principal, dramatics department chairman or another prominent newsmaker, to participate. Let the entire staff or beginning staffers plus an editor or editors serve as press corps. Have them prepare questions in advance, but encourage staffers to be on the alert for answers that need follow-ups.

   Discuss the session's effectiveness afterward, and ask novice reporters—or everyone—to write an interview story for comparison, further discussion and grading—with the best chosen for publication.

2. **Stage a "live" interview for staffers.** Let an editor or seasoned reporter do an interview, with other staffers present as audience. It may be done for an actual assignment or based on a preplanned, fictional topic—such as an interview with Daisy after the death of Gatsby.

   Allow the class to ask questions and discuss the techniques of interviewing after it's completed.

3. **Team a novice reporter with a seasoned one.** At the beginning of the year, pair reporters going out on interviews. Although the novice participates solely as an observer, an introduction to the news source allows the reporter to become known before going out alone.

4. **Professional stories don't just happen.** Have students analyze stories in professional papers and try to discern what questions were probably asked, what facts were elicited and how they were researched.

SPOTLIGHT ON THE INDIVIDUAL—In general, it's not just what you do, it's how you do it that makes the difference between a weak paper and a strong, lively one. The same is true of stories about individual students or teachers. In school papers these fall into two main categories.

1. **The true profile:** Chosen not because of popularity but because of accomplishment, the subject of a profile promises rewarding interviews of students and teachers. The true profile starts with a special focus. It may spotlight someone with a special hobby, such as rock climbing; a special mission, such as belonging to a group that rescues greyhound dogs; or even with a special handicap, such as being bound to a wheelchair.

   The profile can also have a news angle, such as a student skater chosen to appear in an ice extravaganza or entered in a major contest. The goal is to increase readers' awareness of other facets of students' characters and get them personally involved in their lives. When they result in good interviews and writing, profiles are both read and talked about.

2. **Senior Standouts:** Without special handling, this type of feature can further the impression that the school paper is a cliquish organization that caters to the "right" people—the social set, athletes and those with good grades. The stories too often follow a formula, a listing of extracurricular activities, a recital of courses taken and plans for the future, plus a few quotes giving expected answers to uninspired questions. A real, rounded person rarely shows through. Too often the spotlighted seniors seem like a who's who of students whom everyone (who's anyone) knows.

    The cure? The first possibility is to turn this stale feature into a true profile, with a newsworthy reason for every choice. You need not limit your choices to seniors. You can also build your senior spotlight around a series of unexpected and thought-provoking questions, for a dialogue-box feature that combines imaginative answers and a special insight into the subject's personality and lifestyle.

    THE DIALOGUE-BOX FEATURE—With a standing head such as *Speaking out* or *Getting the last word*, the personal close-up becomes less a writing assignment than an eye-catching feature, similar to that in professional newspapers and magazines. Your paper's chosen dialogue box can ask about favorite foods, heroes, sources of inspiration; the possibilities are endless. The only warning: Avoid questions that unduly embarrass the featured student, family and friends, or that provoke suggestive answers.

    Before settling on a list, test the questions on other staffers—not for publication, but to see if they provoke both thoughtful and amusing answers.

    You may use the sample dialogue box ("Dialogue box: Your chance to speak out," Figure 1-13) as given or as a springboard for creating your own. Once chosen, repeat the questions through successive issues. Much of the fun comes from readers' making up their own answers and comparing their responses with those in print.

    Allow time for the chosen students to complete their answers. For most newspaper assignments, allowing written responses to reporters' questions is a no-no that prevents asking follow-ups, but this deserves additional time and thought.

    Seek to include students who represent a cross section of the student society. Don't concentrate on the social, athletic and academic elite, but include various fields of study—business and vocational as well as college prep—and the school's range of diversity.

School newspapers as a laboratory for learning

In many ways, working with the school paper, either as an adviser or staff member, consists of conducting experiments to discover what works and what doesn't—constantly seeking better ways of doing things, and being willing to strike out in new directions when a promising approach appears. It also means profiting from errors—not bemoaning or blaming—for out of experiments comes growth.

In planning to fine-tune your paper's coverage, you may use the following checklist ("Checklist for fine-tuning your paper's coverage," Figure 1-14) as a basis for your discussion.

Dialogue box:
Your chance to speak out

Please write out your answers to each of the following questions. You and they will be featured in a dialogue-box format in a forthcoming issue of the paper. When you have finished, please return them to the newspaper staff office or to _____, staff reporter.

Your name _____

Class or year in school _____ Nickname _____

Complete the following:

1. The accomplishment I'm most proud of:

    _____

    _____

    _____

2. Most of my teachers would be surprised to know:

    _____

    _____

    _____

3. The fictional character I'd like to meet in real life: *(Also explain why.)*

    _____

    _____

    _____

4. My favorite excuse for not turning in homework on time:

    _____

    _____

    _____

5. I like to spend my free time:

    _____

    _____

    _____

6. My biggest regret about high school:

    _____

    _____

    _____

7. What most adults don't seem to understand about kids:

    _____

    _____

    _____

8. Three words or phrases that describe me best:

    _____

    _____

    _____

9. When I was younger, I used to imagine myself as:

    _____

    _____

    _____

10. The biggest change I'd like to make in myself:

    _____

    _____

    _____

Checklist for fine-tuning your paper's coverage

DIRECTIONS:

Every paper—school or professional—can be fine-tuned in news coverage, design, headline writing. Don't be too hard on yourself, but try to give honest answers. Score 5 points for each "yes."

Do not expect to achieve 100%, as even outstanding papers can always be fine-tuned and certain items may not relate directly to your kind of coverage.

If you rate at 70 to 75%, congratulate yourselves—then keep going!

	YES	NO
1. Over half of our paper's coverage concerns school-related news, activities and primary sources.	_____	_____
2. News pages emphasize advance stories or newsworthy insights into past ones.	_____	_____
3. News briefs are grouped together as readable design elements.	_____	_____
4. The page one lead story qualifies as news, not opinion or background.	_____	_____
5. The paper strikes a balance between news briefs and longer stories.	_____	_____
6. Coverage of student-related national issues features primary coverage by student reporters.	_____	_____
7. The paper is free of issue-related stories written primarily from research in books, magazines, etc.	_____	_____
8. Reviews of CDs and movies avoid jargon and aren't used as fillers.	_____	_____
9. Inside pages highlight school news, news features, student profiles and close-ups instead of leaning heavily on personal opinions, reviews.	_____	_____
10. The paper includes a calendar of activities.	_____	_____
11. At least one editorial expresses the paper's view on a timely issue.	_____	_____

	YES	NO

12. Each issue includes a masthead, school name, address and the paper's policy statement.

13. Infographs and sidebars present statistical data and related background of stories.

14. All columnists clearly have something to say, instead of just filling up space.

15. Entertainment stories give both those who attended and those who didn't a sense of shared experience, sometimes taking readers behind the scenes.

16. In-depth reports contain meaningful interviews with local authorities and student quotes that contribute to a better understanding.

17. Profiles are newsy and insightful, not simply formula summaries of subjects' backgrounds.

18. Columnists offer a fresh approach to topics their readers can relate to.

19. Sports stories avoid dwelling on past events, either in leads or by their length.

20. Sports pages include a variety of profiles, graphics, briefs, features and columns as well as advances and round-ups.

Students' rights . . . and *Hazelwood*, too

The need for student press freedom

Two Supreme Court decisions, nineteen years apart, stand as signposts for student press rights.

Strangely enough, the *Hazelwood*[1] decision, allowing school officials the ability to censor school papers in order to "set high standards for the student speech that is disseminated under its auspices," came at a time when professional media were relaxing their strictures under the influence of tabloid exposés and cutthroat competition.

In those states or school districts that have not legislated otherwise, administrators have the right of prior review and the power to censor the student paper on the grounds given in the Supreme Court's *Hazelwood* decision of 1988.

DRAWING THE LINE—In writing the *Hazelwood* decision, the United States Supreme Court declared that administrators could censor any forms of expression deemed "ungrammatical, poorly written, inadequately researched, biased or prejudiced, vulgar or profane, or unsuitable for immature audiences," or any expression that advocates "conduct otherwise inconsistent with the shared values of a civilized social order" or any expression that is "inconsistent with its basic educational mission."

The decision provided wide latitude for administrators desiring to censor school papers.

Quoting from the *Tinker*[2] case ruling of 1969, the *Hazelwood* finding cited the premise that students "do not shed their constitutional rights to freedom of speech at the schoolhouse door." Yet the *Hazelwood* decision further declared that "[i]t is only when the decision to censor a school-sponsored publication, theatrical production, or other vehicle of student expression has no valid education purpose that the First Amendment is so 'directly and sharply implicate[d],' as to require judicial intervention to protect students' constitutional rights."

According to the 1969 *Tinker* case, "a prohibition against expression of opinion, without any evidence that the rule is necessary to avoid substantial interference with school discipline or the rights of others, is not permissible under the First and Fourteenth Amendments."

However, citing a 1986 case, *Bethel* vs. *Fraser*[3], "A school need not tolerate student speech that is inconsistent with its basic educational mission," the *Hazelwood* majority opinion stated, "A school must be able to set high standards for the student speech that is disseminated under its auspices—standards that may be higher than those demanded by some newspaper publishers or theatrical producers in the 'real' world—and may refuse to disseminate student speech that does not meet those standards."

Further, "In addition, a school must be able to take into account the emotional maturity of the intended audience in determining whether to disseminate student speech on potentially sensitive topics . . . ."

---

[1] *Hazelwood School District* vs. *Kulhmeier*, 1988

[2] *Tinker et al.* vs. *Des Moines Independent Community School District et al.*, 1969

[3] *Bethel School District No. 403* vs *Fraser*, 1986

THE CASE FOR STUDENT PRESS FREEDOM—Two notable organizations dedicated to helping secure rights for the student press are The Freedom Forum, a foundation established in 1935, and the Student Press Law Center, established in 1974.

The Freedom Forum publishes *Death by Cheeseburger,* the "bible" of student press freedom, and the pamphlet, "Talking About Freedom," a teacher's guide to the First Amendment. Single copies of each are offered free to high school journalism teachers or daily newspaper editors. According to The Freedom Forum, all of its many publications and activities are dedicated to supporting and encouraging an independent, free press worldwide on both the professional and school levels.

Along with its center in Arlington, Virginia, the foundation has established The Freedom Forum Media Studies Center at Columbia University in New York City; The Pacific Coast Center in Oakland, California; The Freedom Forum at Vanderbilt University in Nashville, Tennessee; and The Freedom Forum World Wide Web page.

Address:	The Freedom Forum
	1101 Wilson Blvd.
	Arlington, VA 22209
Phone:	(703) 528-0800 Fax (703) 284-3570
	(800) 830-3733 for ordering material or information
E-mail:	News@freedomforum.org
Home Page:	http://www.freedomforum.org

Student Press Law Center provides cost-free legal services to student journalists, faculty advisers and anyone working with the student press. This includes analysis of cases and legislation, letters offering legal opinions, free telephone consultations and evaluations of existing publication guidelines and help in developing new ones.

In addition to *SPLC Report,* a magazine published three times a year, the center publishes *Law of the Student Press,* a legal handbook, and *The Hazelwood Packet,* which includes model guidelines and policy statement.

Through its education outreach program, Student Press Law Center serves as a clearing house for information on legal issues confronting the student press, provides speakers for journalism seminars and workshops, and sponsors the Scholastic Press Freedom Awards.

Address:	Student Press Law Center
	Suite 1910
	1101 Wilson Blvd.
	Arlington, VA 22209
Phone:	(703) 807-1904
E-mail:	splc@capacess.org
Home Page:	http://www.splc.org

POLES APART—Few advisers and administrators would disagree about the need for high standards for the student press, but the question is how those standards can best be reached.

Realistically, in some schools, the question of students' rights as school journalists never comes up. Although to some journalism advisers, this may seem like the impossible dream, this position may fall at one of two extremes. The blessed work with an administration that genuinely believes in student press freedom and trusts the adviser to counsel students about legal and ethical problems that lie in their path. At the other extreme is the controlling principal or administrator who wants to direct and supervise every facet of school business. The school newspaper, being open to public view, earns particular attention; however, even this type of administrator may not be a complete ogre and may yield to tact and diplomacy.

Just as the best classes are self-directed, self-motivated and self-disciplined, so are the best school papers. Achieving high standards and self-determination is best accomplished through cooperation and communication, instead of through challenge and censorship.

In an age of confrontation, communication can occur only when someone acknowledges a certain validity to the other's viewpoint. In a journalism adviser-administrator situation, the reasonable attitude should come first from the adviser—because objectivity is one of the press's guiding principles.

WHEN CENSORSHIP IS A THREAT OR A PROBLEM—Begin by preparing a list of reasons the school paper should not fear censorship. Avoid claiming that school officials don't deserve that right; under *Hazelwood,* they do. Yet, by granting the rights of a free school press, an administrator creates a relationship that allows a publication to be more thoughtfully edited, mature and responsible editorially than those produced by students who are censored.

The word *censor* has, for many, a totally negative connotation, yet everyone censors his or her speech to a certain degree—whether from the desire for "political correctness" or consideration of the effect of one's words on someone else. The real evils of censorship occur when the choice of topics and words is dictated and imposed by someone else. In the case of a censored publication, the press becomes merely someone else's mouthpiece, and writers write, not as they think or believe, but according to a set of other-directed standards, out of fear of reprisal or punishment.

Because kids are kids and advisers are hired staff, the censored student press sometimes faces the need to "please the principal" without being sure what, exactly, might arouse displeasure. Can they report a teacher accused of sexual harassment? Can they review a bestselling record with questionable lyrics? The key word becomes not "should" but "can" or "will." Can we get away with it? Will it be cut? Will we get in trouble with the principal? Will the noose of censorship get tighter?

With a censored press, there's no use in asking: How will our story on the accused teacher contribute to our readers' understanding? Is it our responsibility, not our right, to cover it? Nor is there any point in asking: Why is this album the best choice for this issue? Because the concern is whether it can get by the censor.

EXPLORING *HAZELWOOD*—As you and your staff explore the ramifications of *Hazelwood,* it will be helpful to discuss some of the circumstances that led the Supreme Court to make their decision. The following exercise ("It's the law!" Figure 1-15) will serve as a basis for discussion and forming knowledgeable, objective opinions about its values and the problems it creates for the student press.

THE SCHOOL PAPER AS A PUBLIC FORUM—The *Hazelwood* decision cited the *Tinker* case concerning the status of the school paper as a public forum that "precluded school officials from censoring its contents except when 'necessary to avoid material and substantial interference with school work or discipline . . . or the rights of others.'"

Hazelwood further defined *public forum* by stating, "School facilities may be deemed to be public forums only if school authorities have 'by policy or by practice' opened those facilities 'for indiscriminate use by the general public' . . . or by some segment of the public, such as student organizations."

Name _____   Date _____

It's the law!
Hazelwood School District vs. *Kuhlmeier*
January 13, 1988

PART I

Supreme Court Decision: In 1988, the majority of the Supreme Court concluded that administrators of Hazelwood East High School in suburban St. Louis, Missouri, had the right to censor a story concerning teen pregnancy and another on the effects of divorce on students from an issue of a school-sponsored student paper, *The Spectrum,* published in May, 1983.

According to the principal, the three pregnant Hazelwood East girls used as examples could be identified, even though given assumed names, and the subject of teen pregnancy, with references to sexual activity and birth control, was inappropriate for some of the younger students. He also felt the divorce story violated the principle of fairness because a student sharply criticized her father, who was given no opportunity to defend himself or reply.

With the paper already subject to prior review, the principal deleted two pages. When the paper came out with two pages missing, *The Spectrum* staff filed a lawsuit complaining their First Amendment right had been violated.

Upholding the administration, the U.S. District Court for Eastern District of Missouri held that no First Amendment violation occurred. Although the U.S. Court of Appeals of the 8th Circuit in St. Louis later reversed this opinion, upholding the rights of the students, the Supreme Court then found in favor of the Hazelwood School District, creating the limitations currently in place.

DISCUSSION:

1. Did the Hazelwood East principal have valid objections to the article on teen pregnancy:
   a. concerning the problem of the pregnant girls being identifiable among a small student body, assuming this is true?
   b. concerning the subjects of teen pregnancy, sexual activity and birth control being inappropriate for younger students?

2. Did the principal have valid objections to a one-sided story in which a student's parent was made to look bad, but was given no chance to defend himself?

3. Should the stories have been published "as is"? Why or why not? Was the principal right to delete them? (Note that the paper came out in May. How might that have affected the situation?)

4. What is your opinion of the Supreme Court decision? Why?

PART II

In granting school officials the right of censorship, the Supreme Court also set out a number of specific examples by which a school newspaper might justifiably be censored.

All were based on the opinion that schools need not tolerate forms of student expression that were "inconsistent with its basic educational mission." In other words, censorship is valid in instances where a school paper does not uphold the same principles, standards and goals that the educational system seeks to accomplish.

DISCUSSION:

A. With this in mind, discuss why the Supreme Court felt each of the following areas was important enough to consider specifically, by stating that the failure of a school paper to adhere to any one of these standards made that condition censurable.

To avoid being censored, a school publication should

1. be grammatical
2. be well written
3. be adequately researched
4. not be vulgar or profane
5. not be biased or prejudiced
6. be suitable for immature audiences
7. be an advocate of conduct consistent with shared values of a civilized social order and the basic educational mission
8. set high standards, conceivably higher than those set by some newspaper publishers in the "real" world

B. Explain your attitude toward the above standards. Which do you consider justified or unjustified grounds for censorship? Why?

PART III

The following are also areas in which school newspapers and professional publications are open to legal action:

1. Obscenity: articles or language considered filthy and offensive as judged by community standards regarding sexual conduct.
2. Libel: any false statement, published or broadcast, that results in a person's being hated, shunned, or avoided, or suffering financial loss.
3. Articles causing "material and substantial disruption of school activities": specifically defined as rioting, unlawful seizures or destruction of property; student boycott, sit-in, walkout or other related form of behavior.
4. Invasion of privacy: Publications may not intrude on a person's private life nor expose it to the public for comment, criticism or ridicule.

DISCUSSION:

1. How are these areas essentially different from those in Part II?
2. Do you feel that the rights of free speech should protect writers from being sued for one or more of the above? (Explain fully.)

Note: You may obtain more extensive information and guidelines from such sources as The Freedom Forum, Student Press Law Center, and school journalism organizations. Since a number of state legislatures have passed bills to provide protection for student publications and because laws concerning libel and obscenity may vary from state to state, you may wish to do further research locally.

Therefore, if a student press is school sponsored, having been lent the school's name and resources, and can be described as part of the school curriculum, it can be subjected to censorship as a result of the *Hazelwood* decision unless it is considered a public forum or there is a state law to the contrary.

Even under *Hazelwood,* school officials must show a valid educational purpose for censorship, nor can their action be an attempt to silence a particular viewpoint with which they disagree or which is unpopular.

There are two ways to publish a school paper as a public forum if not already protected from censorship by state law.

BECOMING A PUBLIC FORUM BY POLICY—If you are unsure whether your school has adopted an official policy regarding the curricular status of school newspapers, check with your principal, superintendent or school board. You may not find an official policy concerning censorship and prior review and, in certain states, laws may make them unnecessary.

If a policy concerning censorship does not exist or does parallel *Hazelwood,* you can explain the advantages of establishing the student press as a public forum (Figure 1-16). Further model policy guidelines are available from Student Press Law Center.

BECOMING A PUBLIC FORUM BY PRACTICE—If you do not wish to work through official channels, you may try to establish that, by practice, your publication is a "public forum for student expression."

The newspaper's policy ("Sample policy statement," Figure 1-17) should be briefly but precisely stated in the masthead or boxed on the editorial page, where it appears each issue. Staff records should include a fuller version of the same policy, dated and signed by the adviser and editor.

The establishment of the paper as a public forum will date from that time and the acceptance of this policy, by becoming published and practiced, becomes a de facto matter.

You may obtain a fuller statement of policy suggested by the Student Press Law Center in its *Hazelwood Packet.*

The masthead should also include school name, full address of the paper, including room number, phone number and, if applicable, subscription or per-issue price, along with data about advertising rates and specifics, plus submission deadlines.

Where you fit in as adviser

With the newspaper as public forum, it may seem that a safety valve is taken away from the adviser. If acting as official censor, the principal bears the final responsibility, with or without sufficient knowledge of the legal concepts governing all publications. If the principal assumes the role of censor, in lieu of the statement of public forum policy, your staff may wish to add, "This paper is subject to prior review," to alert its readers that censorship takes place.

In case of a public forum, Student Press Law Center suggests a statement of policy concerning adviser job security:

> The adviser is not a censor. No teacher who advises a student publisher will be fired, transferred or removed from the advisership by reason of his or her refusal to exercise editorial control over the student publication or to otherwise suppress the protected free expression of student journalists.

The student press as public forum:
Right for schools and students

1. The public forum teaches democracy in action by allowing students the rights granted American citizens in the First and Fourteenth amendments.

2. The integrity of the school is protected by Supreme Court decisions that permit censorship of material that can be reasonably forecast to cause "substantial disruption" of schoolwork or discipline, or as an invasion of the rights of others.

3. By making the school press a public forum, the school thereby encourages students to develop mature judgment and exert meaningful responsibility.

4. The public forum allows student journalists necessary freedom to test and weigh their opinions while gaining awareness of laws regarding libel, obscenity and invasion of privacy.

5. If a school adopts a written policy not to exercise prior review and/or prior restraint, court decisions indicate that a school will likely be protected from liability.

Sample policy statement

Published _____ times a year, the student newspaper of _____
school is a public forum, with its student editorial board making all decisions
concerning its contents.

Unsigned editorials express the views of the majority of the editorial board.

Letters to the editor are welcomed and will be published as space allows.
Letters must be signed, although the staff may withhold the name on request.
The paper reserves the right to edit letters for grammar and clarity, and all letters
are subject to laws governing obscenity, libel, privacy and disruption of the school
process, as are all contents of the paper.

Opinions in letters are not necessarily those of the staff, nor should any
opinion expressed in a public forum be construed as the opinion or policy of the
administration, unless so attributed.

The adviser advising

Advice: practical recommendations as to action or conduct, an opinion on what to do and how to handle a situation

In practice, there is a fine line between the words *advise* and *guide,* although one dictionary uses the example "to guide a mule" as part of the latter's definition.

Truly adopting the role of adviser is one of the trickiest acts in the repertory. Students, who generally do not have all the confidence they exude, are both unworldly and sometimes unwise. They need someone whose opinion and judgment they can trust, yet they dislike being treated like mules.

Successful approaches for advising without begging or threats

1. Whenever possible, provide students with choices so that you are not merely giving them the option to agree or not, but encouraging them to make decisions and accept responsibility.

2. Explain the ramifications of publishing questionable articles that seem subjects for legal action or likely to arouse contention.

3. Encourage students to think of the probable effect of their articles on their readers. Ask them to consider the purpose of their words and the likelihood of their achieving the desired outcome.

    If an editorial is intended to persuade, will it achieve its purpose if it outrages those who oppose its viewpoints, or will if be more effective if it makes them think?

    If a sports column targets a specific group of athletes, is the writer willing to take the verbal and possible physical abuse that might be—and has been in some cases—the result? After a story is published, an adviser is hard-pressed to protect a student from the results, but he or she should outline the possibilities beforehand.

4. Stress that accepting rights demands maturity. When granted responsibility, students should be willing to accept the consequences of their choices and not blame someone else nor excuse themselves from responsibility as one student leader did, by crying, "Hey! What do you expect of me? I'm just a kid."

5. Make students aware of the implications of what they say. As in *Alice in Wonderland,* students may genuinely mean what they say, but don't always say what they mean. Student attempts at satire can be notoriously heavy-handed, causing them to seem cruel and insensitive instead of clever.

6. Encourage students to see the importance of details such as grammar, spelling, precision in use of quotations and accuracy in reporting facts. As a teacher, you must monitor writing and grammar.

7. By standing back and advising, you help your staff develop a spirit of professionalism and maturity, along with an appreciation of the power and influential medium they have in their hands as student journalists.

Defining your paper's mission

One of the most potentially serious problems that faces the school newspaper is the danger of developing a siege mentality. Faced with criticism and pressures from inside the school and out, the staff can come to see its position as Us versus Them. Not surprisingly, the adviser, admittedly or not, is often driven to feeling like one of the besieged. The ideal perception for staff and adviser should be "We *for* Them."

Although being on the school newspaper is an experience beneficial to its members, the product also should have the clear purpose of benefiting the entire school community, not just gratifying the wishes of staff members for a vehicle of self-expression.

One way to clarify the position of the paper is to devise and publish a mission statement ("Mission statement," Figure 1-18). It may, but need not, be published in the masthead of every issue, but it should at least appear in the year's first edition. A copy should be posted in the staff newsroom and be readily available for reference and, if need be, a reminder. You may also wish to include it in the staff manual.

Working along with the editorial board, you may use the mission statement given here as a source of inspiration, adopt it as written, or with some alterations.

FACING THE CONSEQUENCES—According to an article in *Student Press Law Center Report* (Spring 1996), a high school newspaper adviser faced possible loss of her teaching credentials as the result of a story on bestiality. Published in a high school located in a farming community, the story cited studies showing a fifth of farm boys engaged in sexual conduct with animals and included quotations from the school counselor.

The adviser reportedly alerted students to the possible consequences but allowed student editors to make their own decision to run it.

QUESTIONS OF RELIABILITY—In writing on controversial subjects, students should be warned against counting on uninformed or prejudiced opinion.

In a story on natural herbs being advertised and sold as mood-altering pills said to provide safe highs, a student commented, "The government okayed them for sale. If you can buy them legally, they must be okay." The article contained no counterbalancing expert opinion, warning of possible side effects and health risks. Professional media later reported that such pills had allegedly contributed to a number of deaths.

Writers should also beware of quoting sensational figures, such as "one out of five farm boys engage in bestiality," as if they were totally valid. Polls may be inaccurate, purposely slanted or inadequately sampled, sometimes to reflect sought-after conclusions. Then these same figures get quoted again as fact, acquiring a force and influence they don't deserve.

According to an Associated Press report, a study on the effect of divorce in California contained gross errors, yet the conclusions were cited as valid in more than 175 newspaper and magazine stories, 348 social science articles, 250 law review articles, 24 appeals and a Supreme Court case. And that's not the first time the results of so-called scientific studies have been discredited.

ANTICIPATING PROBLEMS—Debate or conflict at crunch time can lead to disastrous consequences: censorship and even the threat of the adviser's dismissal. It's better to prepare for potential differences between editorial board and adviser, or more drastic action later, by establishing ground rules for publishing stories that might prove volatile and even censurable ("Ground rules for reporting sensitive and controversial topics," Figure 1-19).

Your goal should not be to avoid the controversial issues but to channel potential controversies so that they lead to true enlightenment and positive results.

Mission statement

The student press of _____ *school has adopted this as its mission:*

1. To publish news, information and opinion articles for and about student, faculty and administration activities, interests and policies.

2. To maintain high ethical standards with regard to fairness, personal and legal rights, responsibilities and accuracy.

3. To provide a forum for free and responsible expression of student opinion and present well-balanced, locally researched coverage of issues of broader student interest.

4. To strive for a high level of competency in the technical aspects of writing, including grammar, spelling, clarity and precision.

5. To welcome diversity and increase the scope and depth of our coverage in order to heighten mutual understanding and awareness throughout our entire school community.

Ground rules for reporting sensitive and controversial issues

1. Articles should have a definite local news peg, need and purpose that may be stated or implied, but are known and can be clearly and concisely expressed and supported by the reporter and/or editorial board members.

2. The subject of the article should apply to or directly concern a significant number of students.

3. Coverage of the story should rely on primary research involving school or local sources who are knowledgeable about the subject.

4. Articles on controversial subjects should be well balanced and evenhanded, giving informed views from each side.

5. Reporters should refrain from unethical or illegal lapses that can be construed as libelous, obscene or invading privacy.

6. The paper should observe restrictions concerning preservation of anonymity and the need for parental permission by minors under conditions having legal ramifications.

SEEKING CONTROVERSY OR TRUTH?—Students should not shun controversial stories having a good purpose, but should avoid the appearance of seeking sensation for its own sake or as a test of their limits. Striving for the shock effect makes the paper seem to be crying "wolf" and saps its power to attack sensitive issues with truth and vigor. Encourage your editorial board to explore all the possibilities and ramifications before going ahead with a story that sounds attention-getting and different.

In an early meeting with your editorial board, you may wish to discuss how your paper would deal with certain controversial and sensitive issues ("Controversial and sensitive issues," Figure 1-20). Because of the variations in school and community, there is no one right way for every newspaper, but such a discussion will lay the groundwork for future decisions. You may find similar situations to use as a basis for discussion in issues of *Student Press Law Center Report*.

Outside and inside pressure groups

Have you ever lost friends because of the school paper? Do you wonder whether you should share inside school information and confidentialities with editors? Do colleagues understand your goals as newspaper adviser?

Tabloid, yellow journalism, newspaper, in-house newsletter—in many ways the school paper is a unique arm of the press. Much of the trouble with the perceptions of the student press held by administrators, other faculty members and members of the community comes from their views of what a school newspaper ought to be and its failure to measure up to their own measures.

In some views, the school paper should be like a corporate tool, dedicated to printing positive news about school management and showing the school's best face to public view. Except for content, the school paper often fits comfortably into the newsletter slot: published for a clearly related circle of readers and generally supported materially if not sponsored by the management. How then can the staff of a high school paper dare to turn upon those who sponsor and support it?

COLLEAGUES OR CRITICS?—Thanks to desktop publishing, it's easier than ever for a school paper to achieve a professional look—and the more professional the look, the higher the standards to which others will hold it. Make no mistake, others will be out looking for errors. Especially if the newspaper has adopted a crusading stance, faculty and administrators can grow uneasy about being next in line as potential victims.

Avoid pitting yourself against both colleagues and administrators on the grounds of students' "rights." It is not only *Hazelwood* that makes this position hard to defend. For it is also true of a school-sponsored publication that the school provides space, possibly supports the paper financially and pays the adviser's salary. Without this official recognition, there can be no paper.

It is best for the faculty, administration and you as adviser to accept the view of the paper as a laboratory for learning. The paper is a place for experimentation, and an outlet that receives positive and negative feedback—both valuable parts of the learning process. Students may even learn lessons of intolerance from outside pressure groups who seek a ban on certain books or protest given subjects as unfit for a student publication. Here, above all, you, as the adviser, must keep in focus to prevent creating the illusion of the paper as an armed camp. Let colleagues know the primary purpose is to aim for free and fair coverage of the truth.

Name _____   Date _____

Controversial and sensitive issues:
What course to take

DIRECTIONS:

Printed below are brief backgrounds of situations that might serve as the basis for possible stories. Acting as a member of your paper's editorial board, read each one and decide which course your paper should take and why.

Remember, there is not necessarily a right or wrong answer, but one may be best for your school and community. After making your decision, discuss the story as a board or class, and seek input from your adviser, before or after a student consensus is reached.

ISSUE I

A well-known student athlete, a senior who is legally an adult, has been arrested and charged with rape. The identity of his alleged victims will not be released, but there are two accusers, reportedly from other area schools, though possibly other victims have yet to come forth. The story has been widely covered in local papers and on TV, including interviews with his coach, teachers and counselor.

Should your paper? (*Check one*)

_____   A. Decide not to cover it as the story has no valid purpose but sensationalism.

_____   B. Briefly recap the story with new quotes and an emphasis on the question of the accused's past in contrast to his possibly ruined future, if found guilty.

_____   C. Do some investigative reporting and see if the school rumor channels can reveal prior knowledge among students and details of symptomatic behavior.

_____   D. Do a story on rape and its consequences, assigning stories not only on the physical and psychological damage to females, but its consequences to males.

_____   E. Link the issues of rape to wider social issues, such as the prevalence of pornography, portrayals of serial rapists on movies and TV, the heightened sexuality of talk shows and acceptable advertising.

Write your reasons for your choice:

_____

_____

_____

_____

_____

ISSUE II

Although there are school rules against gambling, someone calls attention to the different types of gambling taking place on the school campus. This includes athletic pools, both professional and collegiate. Some are run by students, but faculty members are known to run pools of their own. Some teachers also let students play cards before school and during free periods—at times gambling for money.

Now, the paper learns that the Boosters Club is planning to sponsor a Monte Carlo Night, featuring gambling with fake money, to raise funds for school improvements.

Should your paper? *(Check one)*

_____ A. Decide to cover just the Monte Carlo story as news and dismiss the gambling as harmless fun—not to be taken seriously.

_____ B. Do separate stories on the Monte Carlo night and gambling going on in school, then link them in an editorial, concerning adults' setting bad examples for students.

_____ C. Do separate stories, but run the Monte Carlo night first and—as its follow-up—the gambling story, with or without editorial, in a later issue.

_____ D. Write an in-depth report on the proliferation of gambling in the United States and the availability of gambling outlets in your community and school.

_____ E. Use the incidence of gambling as part of a report showing how official school policy is unrealistic in a number of ways, and editorially propose that, instead of just being ignored in practice, much should be abolished or changed.

Write your reasons for your choice:

_____

_____

_____

_____

_____

STEPS FOR COUNTERACTING OUTSIDE CRITICISM AND PRESSURE

1. As an adviser, avoid writing permission slips or signing requests or excuses for students' absences from class to work on the paper, thus implying your work is more important than theirs.

2. Emphasize the importance of details—spelling, grammar, getting names and dates correct—since excessive mistakes in these areas lead others to believe students are unqualified to confront larger issues.

3. Be prompt and willing to publish retractions, when necessary, but impress staffers with the damaging effect of errors and retractions on the paper's reputation.

4. Impress upon staff members that, given the right of a free press, they cannot justifiably hold others to higher standards than those to which they hold themselves. Therefore, they can expect their own conduct, whether directly representing the paper or not, to be under close scrutiny.

5. Try to build a relationship of trust between yourself and your colleagues, recognizing that privileged information is often shared at professional journalistic levels and ethically kept secret. If there is a question, ask whether a colleague wishes you to consider a statement "off the record" if you think it may lead to a story. This is professionalism.

6. Work to establish a relationship of trust between yourself and reporters, as well as an understanding of the relationship between reporters and their news sources.

7. Avoid the appearances of the paper's being either an elite clique with a secret agenda or the source of underground gossip—too hot to publish but okay to whisper.

8. Be open to suggestions and ideas without taking them as personal attacks or being on the defensive, for by advising the paper as a laboratory or public forum, you're allowing students the greatest of opportunities—the opportunity to learn by experimenting, by doing, by experiencing for themselves the problems and promise of journalism.

NEWSWRITING WORKSHOP

GOOD REPORTING: The key to good papers

What makes a story newsworthy

DEFINING NEWS—Among the many definitions of news, one of value for the school press is "reports of timely events or information that people want or need to know about." To deliver the news, a paper must know its readership—toward whom its coverage is directed. At times, newspapers must consider the advisability of serving unfelt needs—by covering stories that its readers weren't aware they needed to know, but that cause them to exclaim, "Wow! I'm glad I learned that!" and "Isn't that something!"

With reference to time, there are two kinds of stories a newspaper can cover:

1. **Advance:** a story written about an upcoming event, detailing plans and expectations, along with facts needed by someone planning to attend, such as day and date, hours, place and price.

2. **Follow-up:** a story written anytime after an event takes place, relating what happened, its effects, and what is likely to be the next step—in this way leading to possible follow-ups of the follow-up.

FACING FACTS ABOUT TIMELINESS—That news, with reference to time, is limited to these two kinds of stories causes special problems for school newspapers. If published at monthly-to-longer intervals, student papers often can't cover either advance or follow-up stories in a timely fashion. Lead time needed to process stories compounds the problem. Limited class time, novice staffs and inadequate facilities make it unfeasible for schools to rival professional newspaper coverage—just as newspapers can't possibly rival TV's on-the-spot reporting.

"Old news" is an oxymoron. If it's old, it's just not news. Yet, in addition to widely separated dates of publication, additional problems dog school papers and harry advisers who try to publish the news "as it happens." Special events like big games and school plays have a way of taking place at awkward times in reference to publication dates. Often, full details aren't decided in time to write good advances, and the following issue comes out so long "after the fact" that the story's grown stale.

How to find "hard" news for a school paper

Just as today's newspapers have adapted because of television, so have school papers adapted because of changes in print journalism. While altering their coverage and design, school papers still seek to offer what can justifiably be called news: "reports of timely events or information that people want or need to know about."

The typical eight-page school paper often breaks its coverage down as follows:

PAGE 1—FRONT-PAGE OR MAIN NEWS

- Changes in school policy
- Special events and activities
- Hard news, such as vandalism
- Schoolwide projects
- Honors and prizes
- Especially newsworthy features
- Column of news briefs
- Teasers highlighting inside stories

PAGE 2—EDITORIALS OR OPINIONS

- Editorials and columns
- Editorial cartoon
- Masthead
- Letters to the editor
- Additional news briefs or updates on club activities, perhaps in calendar form

PAGE 3—NEWS/FEATURES

- Secondary news and timely features
- Usually the first page carrying advertising (The first two carry news and editorials and are traditionally left free of allusions to mercenary motives.)

PAGES 4 & 5—THE CENTER SPREAD

- In an eight-page paper, the only pages that can be laid out as a single unit, being the entire center sheet opened flat. (For example, 8-1/2″ × 11″ papers consist of 11″ × 17″ sheets folded; 11″ × 17″ papers, 17″ × 22″ sheets folded.)
- Often used for in-depth coverage of a single topic, bringing a national concern home via investigative reports of its effect on the local scene.
- Photo stories running either across the top half of both pages or vertically down their outer sides, can also make dramatic use of center spreads.

PAGE 6—ENTERTAINMENT

- Columns
- Television, movie, record and book reviews
- Profiles of visiting entertainers
- Places to go, things to do—written by student reporters who have been there

Pages 7 & 8—Sports and sport features

- Schedules of upcoming games
- Overviews of team seasons
- Profiles of athletes
- Columns
- Sports not in the mainstream
- How many pages are devoted to sports coverage depends upon their importance in individual schools.

Where stories come from

Ideas for stories are everywhere, although not everyone can recognize them. It's traditionally called a "nose for news"—but it's really being curious, asking questions, being interested in people and things, wanting to know why things are as they are, not being satisfied with what's on the surface and being determined to get the inside story.

Can the attitude be taught?—A newsstand tabloid has as its motto, "Inquiring minds want to know." The first steps in satisfying their wishes is taken by the inquiring minds of reporters who research and write news stories and features. Instead of passing over the "same old, same old" scene, top reporters train themselves to look with fresh eyes and keep their ears open. A casual comment can lead to a feature story that gets people talking.

Of course, not every news brief or club update contains more than a paragraph or two of copy.

French Club to view slides of Paris trip

Bonjour! Members of the French Club hold their first meeting of the year Thursday, Sept. 24, after school in room 201.

Miss Elise Baumgartner, French teacher, will show slides of her vacation in Paris last summer. Refreshments will be served.

That's it, in most cases. But, wait! Did someone say Miss Baumgartner got a part as an extra in a Hollywood movie being filmed in Paris? And she appeared in a scene with the star? And he kissed her hand?

Of course, most club stories are routine, and beginning reporters shouldn't expect a big story to be lurking within every small one. Nor, in trying to impress, should novice writers be tempted to pad and embellish their stories with empty words and useless adjectives. In good journalistic writing, often less is more, and the right words in the right places count most.

Yet, student reporters should train themselves to keep their eyes and ears open and their "inquiring minds" at the ready—lest they miss a real gem.

FINDING THE NEWS—The school press has three main sources of news:

A. School

- Clubs
- Activities
- Curriculum
- Codes of conduct
- Sports
- Student Council
- Awards, scholarships
- Policy changes
- Educational standards
- Counseling
- Improvement of facilities
- Noteworthy individuals

B. Community

- Laws, such as curfews, affecting students
- Community concerns, such as gangs or graffiti
- Entertainment
- Local youth programs
- Job opportunities
- Volunteer possibilities

C. National and world issues

- Close-up coverage of wider concerns as they directly relate to students in your school

School Coverage

Getting on the beat

One of the best ways to help insure that your paper doesn't miss important stories is to make each reporter responsible for covering assigned beats. Through beat coverage, faculty and students also become more aware of the paper's active interest in gathering all the news, not just feeding on its own interest and ideas. This awareness encourages potential news sources to think, "This might be something for the paper" and tip off a reporter or the adviser.

AROUND THE SCHOOL—As soon as possible, obtain an updated list of all clubs and activities in your school, along with their advisers. Depending upon their numbers, divide such clubs as chess, speech, African-American, foreign language and so forth among first-year reporters.

Clubs

1. As a first step, each cub reporter should see assigned club advisers to ask for the yearly schedule of meetings, current list of officers and planned or proposed events for the coming year. A copy of every club's beat coverage form goes in the paper's future book as well as in each reporter's portfolio (Figure 2-1).

2. Before each issue, reporters should check portfolio listings, then interview advisers or presidents of clubs on their beats to gather information about meetings and other story possibilities. Interviewers should make a point of being polite and interested. If they appear eager to rush away, the adviser may not take time to make additional comments—and the result is a missed item.

3. Regular meetings should be written as news briefs or included in the paper's club calendar. Reporters should check with an editor about suggestions that seem to deserve fuller news or feature coverage.

4. Every issue, reporters should record each club's coverage and include clippings in their portfolios. These also will serve as a basis for grading.

Student Council

1. An editor or seasoned staffer works best on this major beat.

2. Student Council, which has various names and functions in different schools, can generate a variety of stories throughout the year—including decisions that affect the entire student body and Council-sponsored activities.

3. Reporters can plan to attend council meetings, as well as interview officers, committee chairpersons and adviser, depending upon the story.

School administration

1. The editor in chief or page one editor is the main candidate for checking with the following administrators:

   a. Principal
   b. Activities director
   c. Dean of students
   d. Director of curriculum
   e. Head counselor
   f. School nurse

2. The principal and the activities director are two prime news sources and should be contacted before each issue's editorial board meeting. If possible, the editor should schedule regular interviews with each to explore story ideas. Doing so establishes that the paper operates on a professional level.

3. Editors should try to develop a respectful rapport with top school officials. For the paper to succeed, their doors must be open, yet the administrator-student relationship should not overpower journalistic responsibility to cover stories as objectively as possible.

4. If feasible with regard to time and distance, you may wish to assign reporters to attend Board of Education meetings. Since this allows students to see a governing body at work, the assignment may be passed around. Knowing the agenda in advance will let the editor decide whether a meeting needs coverage by a seasoned reporter.

Beat coverage of clubs

Name of club or organization: _____

Name of adviser _____ Room no. _____

Schedule of meetings

List Day/Month/Date   Time *(if known)*

1. _____   _____

2. _____   _____

3. _____   _____

4. _____   _____

5. _____   _____

6. _____   _____

7. _____   _____

8. _____   _____

9. _____   _____

10. _____   _____

Other planned activities *(Include dates, if known)*

Officers:	Name	Class Rank
President	_____	_____
Vice Pres.	_____	_____
Secretary	_____	_____
Treasurer	_____	_____
Other	_____	_____

Coverage in paper *(State issue number, whether news brief or story, and headline in paper. Include clips in reporter's portfolio.)*

Issue no.	Type of coverage	Headline
_____	_____	_____
_____	_____	_____
_____	_____	_____
_____	_____	_____
_____	_____	_____
_____	_____	_____
_____	_____	_____
_____	_____	_____
_____	_____	_____
_____	_____	_____
_____	_____	_____
_____	_____	_____
_____	_____	_____
_____	_____	_____
_____	_____	_____

Staff Reporter _____

Faculty department chairpersons

1. Beat reporters should contact the building's department chairpersons at the beginning of the school year and before each issue's planning session.

2. Departments may include:

English	Math	Social studies
Business	Art	Industrial arts
Science	Music	Library
Home economics		Foreign language

3. In opening interviews, reporters should try to determine the department's plans and projects for the year, such as concerts scheduled in the music department, state math contests, distributive education conventions, Right to Read week and art shows. Whether or not the plans are fully set, the first interview alerts the chairperson to the type of stories to have in mind when the reporter returns. ("Coverage form: Department chairpersons," Figure 2-2).

4. Other stories that can be generated from tips by department chairpersons include:

   a. Prizes won by students, such as for art and science projects

   b. Unusual class activities, such as a mock wedding in Life Choices class

   c. Faculty accomplishments, such as appointments to a state panel

   d. Profiles of students with unique stories to tell, whom the chairperson may have in class or have heard about from other teachers or students

5. Reporters covering department chairpersons should also fill out beat reports, with copies in their portfolios and the staff future book. You may wish to have interviewees initial each entry for this and other coverage forms.

Sports

1. Sports are usually covered as individual reporter's beats. Because of their seasonal nature, they are usually assigned by time periods and writers' interests.

2. At the beginning of the year, the sports editor should obtain the schedules of all school sports. Games should be listed in the calendar sections of the future book as well as kept in the sports editor's portfolio.

3. At tournament times, the editor should also be on the alert for games and tournaments not previously scheduled.

4. During each team's season, the editor or sports writer should also obtain a roster of players and their positions.

Building on beats

- In all areas of reporting, it is vital to spell people's names correctly. Seeing their names misspelled is like a slap in the face to most people and implants the image of careless reporting.

Coverage form: Department chairpersons

Name of department: _____

Chairperson _____ Room no. _____

Department activities planned for year

	Type of Activity	Date (*if known*)
1.	_____	_____
2.	_____	_____
3.	_____	_____
4.	_____	_____
5.	_____	_____
6.	_____	_____
7.	_____	_____
8.	_____	_____
9.	_____	_____
10.	_____	_____

Awards, contests, conventions, etc., in which students participate under department auspices

	Description	Date (*if known*)
1.	_____	_____
2.	_____	_____
3.	_____	_____
4.	_____	_____
5.	_____	_____

Additional notes

Coverage in paper *(State issue number, whether news brief or story, and headline in paper. Include clips in reporter's portfolio.)*

Issue no.	Type of coverage	Headline
_____	_____	_____
_____	_____	_____
_____	_____	_____
_____	_____	_____
_____	_____	_____
_____	_____	_____
_____	_____	_____
_____	_____	_____
_____	_____	_____
_____	_____	_____
_____	_____	_____
_____	_____	_____

Staff Reporter _____

- For checking, obtain a computer printout of the entire student body from the school office and insist that reporters and editors use it.

- Beat reporters realize many contacts will be fruitless. The goal of beat reporting is to cover the news, not manufacture it, but they should always be aware that a show of genuine interest in a contact may elicit an unexpected lead.

- It is also essential to both broaden and deepen school coverage. Your job as adviser is to encourage staffers to give equal attention to all clubs and activities that appeal to all segments of the school population.

OTHER NEWS SOURCES

Hard news

It may happen infrequently, but there are times when the opportunity comes to report news—either good or bad—of wider interest. It might be vandalism, an accident in the school chemistry lab, a grant to renovate the school library or a revised dress code. Such stories, because professional media cover them first, should not become a rehash of other sources but should involve firsthand reporting and interviews. Avoid letting an inquiring-reporter-type list of random opinions take the place of a thoughtfully researched story that deals with the consequences and effects of a major event that the school paper must cover after the fact.

Once-a-year activities

Every school has a number of traditional events that require advance or follow-up stories, often both. These include:

a. Homecoming week c. Class plays c. Magazine drives
b. Blood donor campaigns d. Proms f. Spirit week

As straight news, these stories often become trite recitals of the same old thing. Encourage editors and reporters to seek a fresh angle to feature along with the mandatory Who, What, When, Where, Why, How.

For an advance story on a school play, the reporter might sit in on tryouts or even read for a part, if willing to take the role. An eyewitness account of the process can bring the story to life, with the announcement of cast members, "teaser" summary of the plot, and production dates included. (In one school, a male reporter participated in "cross dressing" day during his school's Spirit Week. His trying experience became a compelling story—and, without editorializing, was a powerful commentary on insensitive planning of school activities and the cruel side of some students' "fun.")

Human Interest

Human interest stories appeal to the softer side of human nature—people getting in touch with and caring about other people—or show the puzzling and unpredictable side of human behavior. There is sometimes a fine line between human interest and features, but all reporters should be on the lookout for those unique stories that don't fit into any other special category.

"It's not polite to eavesdrop." According to contemporary etiquette, even that old saw's not true. It's okay to eavesdrop, just don't be too obvious. For advisers and reporters, eavesdropping—or simply being alert—can provide leads to some of the most interesting stories in the paper.

Where to begin? Listen to students chatter before and after class. Pay attention to what they are doing, what and whom they talk about. Gossip is definitely taboo for an ethical school paper, but watching and listening can give clues to pastimes and fads that are ripe for coverage.

Here are two examples:

1. A student who normally keeps to himself is seen poring over a magazine on model trains. Questioning him reveals his intense enthusiasm, the extensive layout he has constructed himself and is continually enlarging, and his frequent participation in hobby shows and model train exhibits.

2. A senior girl drives a "classic" car called Miss Molly, which has been in and out of the school parking lot for years. Her uncle owned it first, then her two older brothers, and now she is the last of the family to claim this somewhat battered, faithful old "prize."

Be careful not to concentrate on personal friends of staff members or give too much play to the "in" group of students, which every school has. Make an effort to give fair coverage to all segments of the school population—not only ethnic groups but also those who do not rally to the traditional athletic/social/sports ethos.

Some schools have done remarkable stories about students with disabilities. With sensitive reporting, these students can be especially receptive to questions about the feelings, problems and reactions they have, attending a school where the majority is not physically challenged. The resulting story can have value—not only in enlightening the rest of the student body, but in recognizing those students often regarded as "different" and consequently left feeling shunned.

Casting for ideas

How do you find stories? There are really only two ways: Either you go looking for leads or they come looking for you. For someone not in the profession, it may be surprising to learn how many suggestions for stories come to the newsroom—by mail, by phone, or in person. Some are worth following up—others impossible.

Once students and faculty know the paper is genuinely interested in covering all aspects of school life, you may begin to get tips from a number of sources. You'll want to develop those that conform to the definition of news or human interest, and devise a polite way to explain why you can't use those unsuitable for coverage.

Community coverage

With regard to school papers, the current media immersion deserves thanks for one thing at least—broadening the scope of student awareness and therefore releasing school journalism from the narrow confines of school itself. To broaden your paper's outlook, you can turn to the community for both primary and secondary coverage. As secondary resources, the community provides a wide range of organizations and authorities that reporters can contact to verify and elucidate important aspects of both local stories and national-world issues. On the primary level, community resources fall into four categories.

Local concerns

Local news, such as proposals to build a new city sports complex (Will school teams play there?) or to enact curfew laws (Will this affect school activities?) is natural fodder for school papers. Reporters can attend council sessions and interview local and school officials.

You may want to assign local council sessions as a learning experience, as a regular beat or for specific issues. As with the school board, attendance at every council meeting may prove unprofitable—both from its failure to consistently produce stories of interest to students and the possibility that talky, unproductive-sounding sessions may "turn off" student reporters assigned to this beat.

Community problems and possibilities

Gangs, graffiti, drugs, alcohol, violence . . . although these are also national concerns, they bedevil each community to a lesser or greater extent. School papers trying to confront these problems can combine research on community responses to crime, student perceptions of themselves as both victims and accused, and local efforts to deal with these issues.

With negative news and sensation most appealing to professional media, the school press can afford to concentrate on the positive—and underscore the fact that most students also want to see the problems solved. One approach is to spotlight community youth agencies, volunteer possibilities, and job programs as feature stories or profiles of student participants.

Entertainment and activities

What's to do? Students are often unaware of the number and variety of events scheduled in their community. Instead of picking up old news already announced by professional media, entertainment news will be more timely if the school paper concentrates on direct coverage. Almost every music presenter, local theater group and entertainment venue—as well as community attractions like museums and zoos—publishes and mails publicity releases about upcoming performances and events to local media. If your paper is not already on such mailing lists, the entertainment page editor may write to publicity directors of local groups and request inclusion.

Fledging reporters can gain practice by boiling down pertinent releases for use as entertainment briefs, phoning for further details—such as availability of student discounts—about those of special interest. Although not considered plagiarism, most professionals object to copying word for word all or any part of news releases.

If one or more student performers take part, local theater and music groups also provide the basis for news features. Casting calls or announcements of auditions that accept school-age performers are also news that students may seek.

Keeping up with the local movie and concert scene can be an "iffy" business since school reviews often appear after interest has peaked and is fading. Reviews of popular records and movies also hold out temptations to plagiarize the pros—or to indulge in trite and effusive rambling. Good reviews require writers with a special flair, talent and knowledgeable opinions.

If there is a wide range of activities in your community, you may want to create an entertainment calendar, listing those taking place during the time period between issue dates.

Participatory journalism

One of the most innovative forms of school newspaper story goes into the community, but comes out of the head of an imaginative, sensitive and thoughtful student reporter. It might be called participatory journalism. With professional media being what it is, the world outside the classroom can look daunting to students, though they try to hide their fears of such things as taking driver's tests, giving blood, being interviewed, registering to vote and voting, or giving mouth-to-mouth resuscitation. Remember, in a typical high school, one quarter or more of the paper's readership are the same freshmen who were scared "green" in September by thoughts of starting school in an alien setting.

Participatory journalism can be either serious or light. It is an eyewitness account, allowing readers to experience unfamiliar sights, sounds, smells and feelings along with the reporter. Its success depends upon the ability of the writer to note the telling details and choose apt words to describe them. It also requires the writer to assume that readers will share the writer's perceptions and responses. The story need not be third-person objective, but, as in all cases, reporters should use the first person sparingly.

At one school, a student reporter responded to news of increased AIDS exposure among teens by having herself tested for HIV, just so she could describe the experience for her paper's readers. Another went behind the scenes at one of the nation's few remaining circuses performing under the big top, combining his report with a lively photo story. Other possibilities include visiting the community's juvenile detention center or attending a trial for drunk drivers, going for a limousine ride or participating in an out-of-the-ordinary sport.

National and World Issues

Bringing the world closer

Most school papers no longer ignore the world outside and its direct effect on every student, inside the classroom and out. Teenage parenthood. Life overrun by technology. The constant assault of media alarmism and excesses.

How should the school paper respond to contemporary issues? The chosen approach must be within the framework of each particular school and community. A system that bans *The Catcher in the Rye* from its reading lists will hardly condone including explicit details in an article on birth control methods.

Opening the school paper's field of coverage to include national and world issues allows some of its best stories as well as its longest and dullest. The difference in effectiveness is less a result of the choice of topic than the manner in which the reporter or team of reporters attempt to bring the subject home to their readers. The prominent and sometimes "hot button" issues affecting teens, which have made the transition from the professional media to the high school press, include news and findings regarding the following:

1. Guns, gangs, and violence
2. Education
3. Science and technology
4. The environment
5. Laws relating to teens
6. Drug and alcohol use
7. Sexuality and parenthood
8. Health and fitness
9. Ethnic and gender equity
10. Entertainment

When reporting on a phase of any of these topics, or others currently receiving media attention, it is vital to remember that a school paper cannot break the news. It can only focus closely upon it from the viewpoint and for the benefit of its readership.

To make coverage fresh and enlightening, issue-oriented stories must have a clear local angle. Reporters should first ask themselves such questions as:

1. How will this directly affect me and my fellow students?

2. To what degree does this fit the situation, conditions or profile of students in our school? (You may want to conduct a survey if precise data would add authenticity to the story.)

3. What other sources in the school or community can reveal local aspects of the issue and, if a problem, offer help?

Avoiding pitfalls of issue-oriented reporting

A false promise lurking within major issue stories is their wealth of details and material. This can lure inexperienced reporters to believe they need only pluck facts and quotations from previously written articles. The results sound like it—a dull, uninspiring string of paragraphs pasted together without focus or purpose. The reader probably will and should react, "What's this got to do with me? Are they just trying to fill up space or something?"

Issue reporting can also tempt some writers to turn to the uninspired approach of treating it as an inquiring reporter story. "Do you think the Supreme Court was right in upholding the recent challenge to _____?" The answer is predictably "yes" or "no," with reasons showing that the respondents had little interest in the question or answer, only in getting their names in the paper. The reporter showed insufficient interest as well.

Inform, educate and persuade—but do not alienate—There is no Hippocratic oath taken by members of the press, but in an age of media excesses perhaps one would help. Nor do the general purposes of a newspaper, which traditionally include such goals as "to inform, educate, entertain and persuade" include "to alienate, titillate and shock."

Even as it opens its pages to admit wider issues, the school press exists in a very close circle. This should be remembered in coverage of such sensitive issues as homosexuality, criminality and teen parenthood. Steeped in the "tell all" atmosphere of television talk shows, some students—or even faculty members—might unwittingly reveal information to an interviewing reporter that makes them the objects of cruel gossip or ostracism. In the confines of a school population, there is little room to hide.

If, as an adviser, you believe in freedom of the press, you agree that no subject should be taboo to high school journalists. A commensurate belief should be that stories should be handled with responsibility, maturity and an understanding of the paper's readership.

In a conservative community, a forthright or controversial approach would offend and alienate the very readers the paper seeks to educate and influence. It is well to remember, whether writing an editorial or reporting a controversial subject, that your side always "wins" when you present your views to someone who already agrees with you. Success in influencing someone who differs, however, calls for forethought and good judgment, especially when dealing with an issue that could shock, cause outrage or even provoke censorship.

Even as members of a staff with no true fears of censorship, student editors and reporters should keep in mind the need for a clear, firm purpose for choosing a "hot-button" issue as a lead story or center-page spread. Is it because students need to know how this national concern pertains directly to them? Or because last issue's topic created a sensation, and this will push the limits even farther? These are questions worth asking.

Getting the issues in focus

To prepare for responsible issue-oriented reporting, members of your staff should keep up-to-date on professional coverage of national and world concerns. Assign them to clip at least three newspaper or magazine stories relating to people their age per issue, and post examples on a bulletin board as inspiration for future coverage. (The clippings can later be included in each staffer's portfolio.)

Before each editorial board meeting, the editor in chief may meet with concerned editors to discuss a choice or choices of issues, along with their focus and ramifications, for later presentation to the board as a whole. Editors should also discuss how best to write each story:

1. As an individual news feature, with or without an accompanying survey or sidebars highlighting related aspects, or

2. As a team reporting assignment, with separate stories assigned to several reporters for an issue that calls for rounded coverage.

GETTING TO THE SOURCES—Issue-oriented stories will usually be based on news published earlier in professional newspapers or magazines. Although reporters should consult, as far as possible, knowledgeable school or community sources, stories may include as background facts, figures—and even exact quotes from other publications—as long as they are brief, to the point and properly attributed. Student reporters must also be aware that scientific-sounding facts and figures can sometimes create false impressions. For example, professional newspapers sometimes present misleading impressions by not distinguishing between the number of students who admit to having cheated once—which might be a sign of basic honesty—and those who are habitual cheaters. When a story contains data and conclusions that rely on surveys or results of experiments, its sources must be qualified and identified.

It is relatively easy to lie and mislead with unsubstantiated facts and figures, intentionally or unintentionally. There are repeated instances of one writer quoting a statistic, another picking it up from the secondary source and its being passed along as "fact" although its origin is forgotten. At times, although the "fact" is proved false, it becomes so widely accepted that the truth can't prevail. Novice writers should try to avoid this trap.

THE ISSUE STORY: A TRIAL RUN—How your paper decides to develop an individual story depends upon the issue and its source, its effects on your school's student body, the angle you choose to pursue and the leads student reporters discover in the process of pursuing it.

Truancy: Symptom or Cause of Juvenile Crime?

For example, assume that a story in the local paper states that a nationwide study shows truancy has risen steadily at the majority of schools throughout the country in the past ten years. Authorities blame the rise on two main factors:

1. Funding cuts have eliminated positions for truancy officers in many schools.

2. Juvenile courts are overwhelmed with young lawbreakers accused of major crimes, making them unable to deal with truants.

Furthermore, the study shows a clear link between early truancy and later involvement in serious crime. According to the study, case records of over 90% of the youth detained for major offenses reveal that habitual truancy was present as an early symptom of their future criminal behavior.

"If the schools were committed to prevent truancy, we could begin to reverse this worsening trend," declared study author Dr. Dwayne Gregory of Midhaven University. "However, school spending cuts have eviscerated truancy programs, juvenile crime continues to rise and, in response, less attention is paid to truancy as more money goes to punishment, not prevention."

Those are the "facts." It is a classic example of a national issue that is ideally suited to the school press. How should it be handled?

The first step is to discover how the percentage of students truant daily in your school compares with the percentage, presumably given in the original article. The principal probably has access to statistics like these. Is truancy at your school higher or lower than the national average? The answer will dictate the direction the story takes. If higher, how do your school and system plan to respond? If lower, who or what deserves the credit?

Other sources can include:

1. The superintendent of schools, who can speak for the entire system.

2. The head counselor or dean of students, who may provide a profile of the type of student who becomes a habitual truant, outline the steps your school takes to control truancy and explain the types of punishment called for.

3. Students known for frequent truancy. The reporter may even be able to quote them, as long as their identities are withheld or disguised. This kind of story can cause problems if names of truant students are published; however, if composite portraits or aliases are used, that should be clearly stated in the story or footnotes.

4. Juvenile courts in your community. How overburdened are they? Do local court authorities and the director of the juvenile detention center agree that truancy is a forecaster of more serious crime? Here is another area to pursue.

With approaches such as these, the story promises to go beyond information lifted from other published sources or random inquiries. It can develop into an investigative feature or spread of related stories that are fresh, revealing and original—and may make a valuable contribution by enlightening members of the student body and your community.

The basic requirement for effective issue-based stories is student reporters who have direction, determination and enterprise, along with the encouragement and guidance of their adviser.

More "fit to print ideas" for stories

1. Build on the news report of a study about the extent of computer use in college. What percentage of faculty members in your school use computers at home? In their classes? What about students? For what purposes?

2. Instead of asking the usual questions like, "What do you like best about America?" link stories about foreign exchange students to news items, perhaps one comparing American education with that in other countries. Or, run in-depth interviews about a single facet of life in their homelands—for example, dating customs.

3. Exchange papers with other schools, including those from your area and throughout the country. Ask students for names of friends and relatives who will help you make contacts. Join journalism associations and exchange papers with other advisers. Exchanges are a good source for ideas about layout as well as story ideas you can adapt for your use.

Examples 2-1 to 2-4 illustrate outstanding student stories based on various types of coverage.

Getting good interviews

Newsworthy stories begin with an idea, but they also depend upon reporters' powers of observation and, to a large degree, their interviewing skills.

Yet the very thought of going out on an interview—be it for a job or a news story—intimidates many students.

That's another advantage of assigning incoming staff members to regular club beats. It allows them to hone their interviewing skills on assignments that are generally less involved than major news or features.

In addition to giving cub reporters practice in writing stories of a few paragraphs in basic journalistic style, the club beats help them gain confidence, poise and ease when they start covering stories that require more intensive coverage.

One of the first rules that reporters should learn is, "Don't be afraid to ask." Whether it's a question for the editor, adviser or the person being interviewed, no question is foolish if it's sincere. And, asking questions can save time, avoid awkward gaps and missing facts in stories, help prevent errors, and provide leads to unsuspected angles that will enhance the story.

Sign Prom Promise--Win a Chance to Dunk a Principal

by Kristin Cockerill

Want a chance to dunk your favorite awareness aide or administrator? This is just one event that Students Against Drinking and other Drugs are considering to promote Alcohol Awareness Month in April.

Lauren Coffee, sponsor of SADD, wants to have a dunking booth if 75 percent of the students sign the prom promise pledge. SADD will post a progress thermometer showing the percentage of students who sign the prom promise.

"The prom promise is for everyone to sign, not just upperclassmen," Coffee said.

The purpose of prom promise is to prevent accidents involving alcohol. Someone dies every thirty minutes from drinking and driving, and SADD wants to make people aware that it can happen to them or someone close to them. "With all our projects, we hope people will become more aware of the danger of drinking and drugs. We want people to know that ac-

cidents can happen to anyone," said sophomore SADD member Tina Hong.

The theme of the campaign is "Sign it, Mean it, Keep it." And if SADD can get a wrecked car, it will remind students of the consequences of their actions.

In a future display case, there will be a scene of a couple all dressed up, having a good time at prom with alcohol in their hands and a banner above them saying, "Dressed to Kill."

SADD members will pass out safety pins to students arriving in the morning to help promote awareness on April 6. Students wearing the safety pins will receive Lifesavers Lollipops to remind students to act responsibly.

There will be booths in the back of the assembly for the signing the prom promise. SADD also hopes to be visiting underclassmen gym classes and junior English classes on April 20 and 21. The seniors will attend an assembly in May to listen to guest speaker Kari Frazier tell her story

of drinking and driving and how it has affected her life.

"The whole point of prom

promise is to get the whole school involved," sophomore Carrie Cramer said.

Example 2-1. "Sign Prom Promise—Win a Chance to Dunk a Principal." Here's a story idea you'd expect to find after checking the school calendar of upcoming events. It's basically written in a straightforward style. Using the pledge as an illustration lets it speak for itself. From *The Highlander,* McLean H.S., McLean, VA.

Who is the firebug at PHS?

By SOO MI PARK and CORTNEY WALDORF

Two weeks ago, fourth period classes were interrupted by an announcement made by Mr. LaBarbiera, requesting that teachers report the names of all the students who left the classroom during that period. As it turned out, this request was made because a flower pot had been thrown into a classroom in the 200 corridor. However, the first thought that popped into many minds; "Was there another fire started by the unknown arsonist?"

School is not a safe haven for everyone anymore. In the past several weeks, three fires have occurred -- two set in wastepaper baskets (in bathrooms), and one set on papers on a bulletin board. Soon after the papers were set on fire, the flames were extinguished by the arsonist. Un-

fortunately, the culprit has not yet been caught, but Mr. Zanella said that, "there are possible suspects."

Even though nothing can be proved, one definite factor is that dire consequences await the arsonist; the student will be charged with a felony that will remain permanently on his/her record. The administration of PHS will be working closely with the police and fire departments to make the students more aware of the serious consequences that result from such "pranks."

Meanwhile, Zanella cautioned teachers, at the November 7 faculty meeting, to be aware of their students' whereabouts at all times. Students should not be walking in school hallways during class time, he stressed, unless they have a clear purpose.

Example 2-2. "Who is the firebug at PHS?" More a feature than straight news, this piece could have been inspired by the principal's announcement, or by its being the topic of so much talk. The result is a story that sets out to answer many of the reader's questions. From *Forum Press,* Paramus H.S., Paramus, NJ.

MOCTEZUMAN/Ryan Leary

AIDS testing— an inside report

by Michaela C. Fuller

Most of us have never given a second thought to the AIDS test, or what it is. I decided to see where the test was available in this area, and what the test is really like. Through the yellow pages, I found the Imperial Beach Community Clinic, at 600 Palm Avenue. The clinic offers free HIV tests on Wednesdays, by appointment only. When I called to schedule my appointment, all they asked for was my first name, they told me that the testing is completely confidential. I went under the name of 'Chris', just in case. I found out later that it is so confidential that your test and your name is never even entered into their computer files and no records are kept of your visit after you pick up your results.

When I got there I checked in, and within a few moments I was called into a room with a female doctor, who proceeded to ask me questions about my risk levels, according to things such as sex, drugs, and other possible factors. All the questions were optional- it was up to me to answer them or not. Nothing is demanded of you. Then, after explaining about the six month window period of the HIV virus, I was shown into a little cubicle where a guy took my blood. He didn't know what test he was taking my blood for, or why I was there. He was very nice, and *I was actually not terrified of him putting a needle in my arm, which is saying a lot.*

I was really nervous about taking the test. I was wondering things like how would they treat me, and how embarrassing would it be? I had to make up a story to tell them about why I was there. I didn't tell them I was there for an article in the newspaper. I was afraid they would treat me badly, because I was taking the AIDS test, but I was surprised when they treated me just great, very considerate and compassionate. The most embarrassing part of it was just walking in the door. I thought that as soon as I walked in the door, everyone there would know why I was there, and rumors would fly. Nothing like this happened, though. There were families and couples there, along with other teenagers and kids. The clinic offers a variety of services, and Wednesdays they offer regular services, along with the AIDS test, so you can't tell why people are there.

When I left, I was given a piece of paper with an eight digit serial number on it, to pick up my results. They don't use your name, only a number, it's added confidentiality. I was only at the Clinic for about fifteen minutes, including the test, a quick counseling, and the waiting.

When I went to pick up the results (negative, of course), the same woman gave me a short counseling session about what the results meant, and that if I have any doubts to be retested in six months. The clinic staff was wonderful, I recomend them.

Example 2-3. "AIDS testing—an inside report." This is participatory journalism by a courageous young reporter who dared to do what many would be afraid to venture. She invites the reader to share her feelings, but her story might also help someone who really needs the test to decide to take it. From *The Montezuman,* Montgomery H.S., San Diego, CA.

Increase in shoplifting plagues local merchants

by Melissa Hansen

Have you ever picked a grape or taken a piece of candy from the supermarket? Has a cashier ever given you too much change, which you didn't return? If you have, or if you have done something comparable, you are a thief, legally speaking.

This year, about 20 million Americans committed shoplifting or petty theft, which resulted in an annual retail loss of $9 billion in the U.S. Shoplifting is more significant than petty theft, which is the steal- ing of an item that is considered insignificant (e.g. one lipstick).

Shoplifting is one of the fastest growing larceny crimes in the United States. In Bergenfield, 45 cases were reported this year. "Compared to northern towns like Dumont and Tenafly, this is a high percentage of shoplifting cases," said Detective Thomas Hegele of the Bergenfield Police Department.

The most common items stolen by females are cosmetics, clothing, and jewelry. Alcohol, cigarettes, and women's clothing are most commonly shoplifted by males. The number one item taken from drug stores is Preparation H. According

to Mr. Matt Connell, owner of Betty Lee Drugs, the medication is used by drug addicts to reduce the swelling that follows sniffing cocaine. The two main items taken from grocery stores are cigarettes and aspirin. "Drug dealers steal these cigarettes and aspirin to sell or trade in New York," Hegele stated.

Many local merchants have felt the effects of shoplifting. "Here in the Florence Shop we consider shoplifting to be a big problem," stated owner Tom Eberhardt. Shoplifters are usually experienced professionals stealing for drug-related reasons. "We've had shoplifters as young as ten years old and as old as 70 plus," commented Eberhardt.

Stores take extra precautions during the holidays. The Florence Shop believes the best way to prevent shoplifting is through employee education. Locking up expensive items or storing them behind the counters are also effective measures. "We prosecute 99 percent of the criminals," said Eberhardt.

Shoplifting becomes a problem, especially when inventory is taken. "You may not see what everyone takes all of the time, but it adds up by inventory, which is every six months," said Ms. Karen Brown, assistant manager. The majority of offenders in Mandee's are adults. "We use Sensormatic Tags and electronic systems to try and prevent

the crime," stated Brown.

Why do these people steal? According to convicted shoplifters, they want something for nothing. Seldom is money, or the lack of it, a motivation. Others shoplift to articulate their behavior that proclaims "I need," or "I want." The high that comes with shoplifting temporarily forestalls their despair.

Other reasons for shoplifting can go back to childhood, when some people were deprived or mistreated. Some steal because of feelings of guilt for unpunished crimes. Shoplifting may spring from a subconscious wish to be caught, embarrassed, or punished.

Shoplifting is more than a serious crime. Some shoplifters become addicted to the thrill of the steal and are unable to stop stealing. Each haul has to be better and more daring than the last. For many, shoplifting is not just an adolescent phase - it's a disease.

The "typical" shoplifter does not exist. Some shoplifters wear voluminous clothing with dozens of pockets and two linings; other culprits wear jeans and a sweater just like an ordinary paying customer. There's no positive identification for a shoplifter.

There is also no geographical pattern for shoplifting. However, stores in or near major cities are hit hardest. The local "Mom and Pop"

stores (family owned general stores) are hurt the worst, since it is harder for them to replenish dwindling inventories. In Bergenfield, Pathmark and the newly closed Grand Union suffered 64 percent of the reported shoplifting cases.

Out of the 45 cases in Bergenfield, 62 percent were cleared, which means the merchandise was recovered or a complaint was filed. "I suggest to all merchants that they file complaints, especially against kids so we can get the necessary counseling for them," Hegele stated.

For adult offenders, penalties include:

First offense - a fine of not more than $500.

Second offense - a fine of no less than $100 and no more than $500.

Third offense - a fine of no less than $250 and no more than $1000. With the third offense the adult must serve a minimum term off thirty days in a county jail.

For juveniles, penalties could include:
Community service
Period of adjustment
Probation
Detention
Fine

Preventative Measures

Sensormatic Tags or electronic deterrents: clunky white tags which are attached to clothing and beep if passed through an electronic post.

Tell Tags: tags attached to merchandise that emit shrills up to an eighty-three decibel alarm.

Anne Droids: mannequins that have closed circuit cameras mounted behind the eyes and a microphone hidden in the nose.

Muzak: light elevator music with subliminal antitheft messages urging shoplifters to stay honest.

A well-trained and alert employee.

Art by Anthony Santiago
Infographic by Amy Chung

Example 2-4. "Increase in shoplifting plagues local merchants." Obviously based on a professional news item, although not naming the source of background facts and data, this piece of investigative reporting also shows extensive research in the community. Its findings are clearly and logically woven together, and the story makes effective use of sidebars. From *Bear Facts*, Bergenfield H.S., Bergenfield, NJ.

To tape or not to tape

Students should be discouraged from using tape recorders, especially when covering general news and feature stories. Far more important than having every word on tape is learning the necessity of listening intently and taking—more likely scribbling—careful, well-chosen notes.

Awareness of a running tape recorder often distracts both the person being interviewed and the reporter, who tends to be careless about jotting down all newsworthy points. And, because notes can help a reporter mentally organize a story before writing it, taped interviews may leave the reporter without a clear idea of how to proceed.

In addition, it usually takes longer to write a story from a taped interview. Playing the entire tape lasts just as long as the actual interview, and it is a tedious, frustrating task to alternately fast forward/rewind through a tape to find the snatch of comment needed to quote or check.

Using the tape recorder is a wise policy if a story has the potential to cause controversy, especially if the reporter plans to use extensive quotes and may want proof of their accuracy later. Of course, whenever a recorder is used, a reporter should first ask permission from the person interviewed.

Reporter guidelines: Techniques of successful interviewing

BEFORE YOU START OUT

1. Know as much background to your assignment as possible.
   a. Find out whom to interview and where.
   b. Read related stories, if available, in both your school and professional press.

2. List likely questions.
   a. Begin with the 5 W's and an H, at least Who, What, When and Where. Even though you know the answers, it never hurts to verify them—and it can help put you and your interviewee at ease.
   b. List additional questions that will allow you to write a major story or feature with more depth and detail.

3. Organize the questions in your notebook in a form that allows you to refer easily to them during the interview and readily decipher the answers when you start to write.

4. Make an appointment so that your news source can be prepared for the interview and set aside sufficient time to answer your questions fully.
   a. In school, set a time when neither reporter nor the interviewee has other classroom responsibilities. A school paper gets a bad reputation by continually seeking to get students excused from class for interviews or other purposes.
   b. Outside of school, you may phone first, identify yourself and state your purpose instead of scheduling the interview in person, as is usually more convenient in school.

5. Conduct important interviews in person rather than by phone, where the interview tends to develop less naturally, and it's difficult to interact.

FACE TO FACE: THE REPORTER AS INTERVIEWER

1. Even someone shy can become a good interviewer, for interviewing provides a clear purpose for speaking, not as yourself but as a representative of the press. In some

ways, it can be compared to acting, for many actors are known to be basically shy. And, reporters can also read from a script—a list of prepared questions.

2. To open the interview, introduce yourself and thank the other person for granting you time to research your story.

3. Throughout the interview, make a point of being polite, poised, alert and attentive.

   a. Listen carefully and don't hesitate to ask the other person to clarify anything you don't understand or want explained in greater detail.

   b. Ask the spelling of proper names and unfamiliar words, and also repeat numbers relating to statistics you may decide to quote in your story.

   c. Remember, both you and the person you're interviewing want to make this story as complete and accurate as possible. With time set aside for the interview, you can expect cooperation.

4. It's called "conducting" an interview because the reporter sets the pace and leads the way.

   a. Try to be businesslike but relaxed, to put the news source at his or her ease.

   b. When the news source is talking, show that you are listening by nodding your head or muttering agreement.

   c. To show understanding, some experts recommend recapping part of the speaker's comments before going to the next question.

   d. Avoid giving a list of questions to your news source and letting her or him fill in the answers. The word *interview,* by definition, is a meeting and one that allows personal interchange so that ideas of both reporter and interviewee can be clarified and refined.

5. Keep the need for quotable sentences and phrases in mind.

   a. Select words that are well-chosen and expressive.

   b. When you hear a likely quote, you may take advantage of a pause to say, "I like what you just said. May I quote that?"

   c. Take a few seconds to copy the statement carefully. You may want to read it aloud to make sure you've quoted accurately.

6. Be alert for leads to additional sidelights, features and details that will amplify your story.

   a. You need not stick strictly to your "script." Feel free to ask questions that develop other aspects of the story that sometimes become the most interesting.

   b. Near the end of the interview, you might want to ask if there's anything more the news source would like to add.

   c. Glance over your notes to see if any remaining questions need asking or details need clarification.

7. Before leaving, thank the news source for the interview and ask permission to check back, if need be, to verify details.

AFTER THE INTERVIEW

1. Glance over your notes while your memory is still fresh. Spell out any troublesome abbreviations, and fill in details that may seem unclear later.

2. If you are not under deadline pressure, try to "fix" the main points and, either mentally or on paper, pick out highlights of the interview, which will be the basis and strength of your story.

3. The next step: the interviewer becomes the reporter.

DEVELOPING A LINE OF QUESTIONING—School spirit? You better be for it. Extend the school day? No way!

There are some questions that hardly need asking because almost everyone knows most of the probable answers.

A good newspaper article or feature depends as much—and sometimes more—on the quality of the questions asked during the interview as it does on the writing. And, after a good interview, some stories almost seem to write themselves.

How can a school reporter learn to ask better questions?

First, when forming a question, try to anticipate the probable answer. If you already know what most people will say, such as, "I'm opposed to abortion because it's actually murder," or "I believe in a woman's right to have control over her own body," the question need not be asked.

When writing a story, especially a feature, the reporter makes an effort to get to the heart of the story, to present a rounded portrait of the subject, and to bring out inside information and lively details that make the subject—and story—come to life.

Reporter guidelines: Beyond the 5 W's and an H

When preparing for important interviews, try to think of eight to ten probing—not prying—questions to ask the person you're interviewing. These are in addition to the usual *Who, What, Why* type of information that will go into your nutgraph (or graf).

In regard to a student, information about the subject's class, course of study, and plans for the future are needed for the background, but the real interest—the "wow"—comes from the impression that the reader is getting a close-up view of the person's life, complete with telling anecdotes and unexpected insights.

And, if the story succeeds, much depends on the writer's preparation—as well as his or her genuine interest in getting and telling the story.

There are countless ways to cover any story. Some are commonplace and trite. Others lift the same assignment out of the ordinary. Consider these opening paragraphs of a follow-up story:

Homecoming queen commands herself to "keep smiling"

"I never expected to be so nervous," said Jenny Jeffries about the moment of her crowning as this year's homecoming queen.

"Everyone was staring at me . . . hundreds of people, maybe thousands. I felt like I ought to check my makeup, see if my hair was out of place," she explained. "But all I could do was try to keep smiling . . . and smiling."

THINKING UP QUESTIONS FOR "JENNY":—What could you ask? What questions will make a person think before answering, and then start the interview flowing freely and easily—possibly leading in a direction you never thought of?

Racking your brain first can make the interview go more smoothly. Here are some possibilities for the homecoming queen story.

1. How was it different from what you expected?

2. Were there any embarrassing or potentially embarrassing moments?

3. What advice would you give to future candidates? Future queens?

4. Since the event, has your becoming queen affected the way you're treated by classmates or teachers?

5. What do your parents think about your election as queen? Your brother or sisters?

6. What did you like best about the experience?

7. What did you like least?

8. What did you think when you found out you'd won?

9. Do you think of this as the high point in your high school career? Why or why not? If not, what is your high point, and why?

10. Why do you think crowning a homecoming queen is a tradition worth continuing?

Rounding out your interview: In addition to interviewing the queen herself, think of other sources to contact for interviews in order to give other perspectives and write a more telling story.

For features or issue-oriented stories, you should seek interviews with at least three sources.

NEWSWRITING WORKSHOP: Note to advisers

You may wish to use the following materials in one or more of the following ways:

1. as tune-up exercises for students who have specific problems with writing

2. as a journalism guide in situations where experienced staffers and novices meet in the same class

3. as part of regular beginning journalism or English courses

You may also wish to duplicate all or part of the Newswriting Workshop materials for students to include in their journalism notebooks or staff manuals.

For those exercises asking students to rewrite sentences or write original ones, answers given are suggested solutions. However, students who follow directions may write other versions that are equally acceptable if they are clearly and concisely written with precise word choices.

In addressing subjects that relate to grammar, the background material avoids formal terminology because of the many different forms used in its teaching. You may wish to restate grammatical rules, using terms that your students will find more familiar. As students work with grammatical errors, emphasize that readers often regard misuse of grammar and incorrect spelling as signs that a writer or paper may be just as careless with facts.

Forms and a guideline for preparation of copy, tracking stories, evaluating interviews and posting assignments (Figures 2-8 through 2-11), along with answers to workshop exercises, will be found at the end of this unit.

The clean, lean style of newswriting

Good reporters value words

They know that clarity comes from stating their ideas in the fewest words necessary. They choose words carefully, to give their readers a precise account of the story they are reporting.

Whether a news story or scholarly research paper, all types of well-written prose share a number of characteristics. Writers can't count on expression, gestures, tone of voice and the ability to ask and answer questions as ways to clear up misunderstanding and provide fuller explanation. Writing must stand on its own.

Writers have the responsibility to anticipate the questions their words plant in their readers' minds. They need to prune and shape each sentence to eliminate excess words, fuzzy thinking and muddled phrases.

Becoming your own editor

In your hurry to get your idea on paper, don't expect your first version to be your best. The next step is to assume the role of editor, critic and—most important—average reader, and question what you've said. With practice, you'll find that some of your greatest satisfaction as a writer can come from polishing and editing your own work—and making it shine.

Here are three techniques for improving your writing, whether it's for journalism or other classes.

1. Use the active voice of verbs, not the passive.

2. Tighten rambling sentences.

3. Say what you mean, mean what you say.

Name _____   Date _____

— EXERCISE 1A —
Be your own editor: Getting active

Use the **active voice** of verbs, not the passive.

Not all verbs have both active and passive voices. Those that do express the effect of one person or thing upon another.

    Active: The reporter interviewed the principal. (5 words)
                  Chess Club elected officers. (4 words)

    Passive: The principal was interviewed by the reporter. (7 words)
                  Officers were elected by Chess Club. (6 words)

The active voice uses fewer words, while the passive voice takes longer to say the same thing and lacks a sense of action. Some writing coaches advise students to eliminate the passive voice entirely. Others admit its value when the subject or actor is unimportant or unknown.

Note: Don't confuse the passive voice with linking and helping verbs in other verb phrases.

    Active: The reporter *finished* his story early.
    Passive: The story *was finished* early by the reporter.
    Linking: The reporter *was* Jerri McCullen.
    Active: Jerri *was looking* for our adviser. (*Was* = helping verb)

DIRECTIONS:

PART A.

Rewrite the following sentences to eliminate the passive voice. Some contain more than one passive verb phrase; others require a subject for the verb when changed into active voice. After each sentence, note the word count before and after.

1. Many questions are being asked by students about the new athletic code.

_____

_____

                  Word count: Before _____   After _____

2. Practice Quiz Bowl sessions are being offered to prospective members by Mr. Dale Swiggart, team adviser.

_____

_____

                  Word count: Before _____   After _____

— EXERCISE 1A —
Be your own editor: Getting active (cont'd)

3. The Blazers' first football game of the season was played on a day when a record high was reached by the temperature.

   _____

   _____

   Word count: Before _____ After _____

4. Twelve students—five male and seven females—will be offered parts in "Too Late or Too Little," this spring's Dramatics Club play.

   _____

   _____

   Word count: Before _____ After _____

5. Such extracurricular activities as athletics and music will be eliminated or cut by the Byrnehurst Board of Education if the upcoming school levy is not passed by voters.

   _____

   _____

   Word count: Before _____ After _____

PART B.

Another way to eliminate the passive voice is to rewrite the sentence, using a different approach and verb.

> **Passive:** A poll was taken recently by the staff of *The Torch* in which a decline was shown in the number of male student smokers. (22 words)
>
> **Improved:** A recent *Torch* poll shows a decline in the number of male student smokers. (14 words)
>
> - or - The number of male student smokers has declined, according to a recent *Torch* poll. (14 words)

DIRECTIONS:

Rewrite the following sentences to eliminate the passive voice. You may use the active voice of the verb given or rewrite the sentences with a different verb and approach. You may want to divide some sentences into several clearer, shorter ones.

1. The complaints that have been made by students about the school cafeteria food are being taken into serious consideration while the new menu is being planned by a committee, headed by cafeteria manager Mrs. Harriet Garvey.

   _____

   _____

   Word count: Before _____ After _____

— EXERCISE 1A —
Be your own editor: Getting active (cont'd)

2. Simulated air raid drills were held in Mr. Dale Dart's American history classes to show how students were made to take part in air raid drills during the Cold War with Russia so they would be prepared if enemy attacks were made on the U.S. mainland.

_____

_____

_____

Word count: Before _____ After _____

3. Socializing between classes must be targeted before efforts to control tardiness to class can be successful, states Mrs. Pamela Early, dean of students.

_____

_____

_____

Word count: Before _____ After _____

4. Elimination of senior courtyard privileges is being discussed by the administration because of accusations that the rights have been abused and complaints have been received about noise from teachers in nearby classrooms and discarded trash from school custodians.

_____

_____

_____

Word count: Before _____ After _____

5. Juanita Sanchez, Byrnehurst senior, has been selected to represent the school in a citywide seminar which will be Tuesday, March 5, when coordinating activities for the Summer Peace and Fun program will be discussed.

_____

_____

_____

Word count: Before _____ After _____

Name _____ Date _____

— EXERCISE 1B —
Be your own editor: Get to the point

PART A. Tighten rambling sentences

Poor: Be careful not to write sentences that are loosely constructed in a long-winded fashion and that have a tendency to ramble instead of getting right to the point.

Better: Get to the point. Don't be longwinded.

DIRECTIONS:

Edit the following sentences by cutting down wordy phrases and cutting out unnecessary repetitions. Be sure to retain essential information.

Example: The three Byrnehurst students who were arrested for allegedly setting a fire in the boys' locker room on Oct. 21 will be brought to trial on Nov. 24. Two of the students are held in the juvenile detention center and the other student is on home suspension.

Better: Three Byrnehurst students go on trial Nov. 24 for allegedly setting a fire in the boys' locker Oct. 21. Two are held in the juvenile detention center and the third is on home suspension.

Word count: Before <u>45</u>   After <u>35</u>

1. Shortly after 11 P.M., Byrnehurst Principal Kevin Claypoole was notified by police of the break-in and attempted arson which was then in progress.

_____

_____

_____

    Word count: Before _____   After _____

2. The break-in was first noticed when a group of Byrnehurst students passed by in a car and called 911 to report that they had noticed shadowy figures running from the building.

_____

_____

_____

    Word count: Before _____   After _____

— EXERCISE 1B —
Be your own editor: Get to the point (cont'd)

3. The students who sing in the Byrnehurst mixed ensemble, the HiNotes, which is comprised of 16 members, placed first against 12 other schools that were entered in the district vocal music competition at Sutter State University on March 31. This was the HiNotes' first time ever to take part in this competition.

_____

_____

_____

Word count: Before _____   After _____

4. Because the ensemble's performance won the top spot in the district vocal music contest, the group landed a spot in the state contest in which district winners from all over the state compete.

_____

_____

_____

Word count: Before _____   After _____

5. In preparation for this year's prom, Byrnehurst Sparkles, committees which are made up of both students and parents have been working for months to make this night a night that will be both safe and fun. Among other things they have been planning various types of games and contests which will go on all night long.

_____

_____

_____

Word count: Before _____   After _____

6. At the last board of education meeting, board members chose to adopt a new and different type of block scheduling which allows students to be enrolled in only four classes during each semester.

_____

_____

_____

Word count: Before _____   After _____

— EXERCISE 1B —
Be your own editor: Get to the point (cont'd)

PART B. Get a strong start

Opening words in a sentence or paragraph make the first impression—choose them carefully. Expletives are not just "dirty" words. They're *there* and *it*, too. Used as introductory words, *there* and *it* delay the real "meat" and subject of a sentence, and they frequently lead to wordiness and dullness.

Poor:	*There* will be a meeting of students wishing to . . .
Better:	Students wishing to explore the Internet can find . . .
Poor:	*It* will no longer be a policy to allow students coming late . . .
Better:	Students coming late to class will no longer . . .

DIRECTIONS:

Edit and rewrite the following sentences.

1. There has been an increase in enrollment at Byrnehurst each year for the past five years, and there have been nine new faculty and staff members added this year as a result.

   _____

   _____

   _____

        Word count: Before _____   After _____

2. It is only a few weeks until the official dedication of Byrnehurst's new gym when there will be a special ceremony and an opportunity for students and community members to inspect and admire its up-to-date facilities.

   _____

   _____

   _____

        Word count: Before _____   After _____

3. It is the first amendment that supports the belief that school papers should exist as an entity that does not fear censorship.

   _____

   _____

   _____

        Word count: Before _____   After _____

— EXERCISE 1B —
Be your own editor: Get to the point (cont'd)

4. There will be a cast of 36 in this year's school musical.

   _____

   _____

   _____

   Word count: Before _____   After _____

5. According to Ms. Jamie Fairchild, faculty director, it would be difficult to coach individual actors with such a big group so it has been decided that Mrs. Ellen Stuart will be faculty co-adviser.

   _____

   _____

   _____

   Word count: Before _____   After _____

Name _____   Date _____

— EXERCISE 1C —
Be your own editor: Make it right

PART A. Say what you mean, mean what you say

Poor: Hanging around the house all day, my room felt like a prison.

Your room was "hanging around the house"? Where does it generally spend its time? And your room can "feel"? Well, now!

The proper term for such lack of clarity is *ambiguity*. This means you could take a word or statement more than one way. You can only guess or assume you know what the person really means.

Better: After hanging around the house all day, I felt my room was like a prison.

DIRECTIONS:

Read the following statements and determine why each sentence is ambiguous. Then, write a new version that eliminates such ambiguity.

1. Mr. Theodore Kendricks, board president, suggested changes in staging the rally that the committee did not approve.

   _____

   _____

2. The originators of the campaign stress the fact that dropping out of school causes many kinds of future losses by providing a video on the topic.

   _____

   _____

3. Potential dropouts often refuse to listen to parents and teachers, and the video promises to help them.

   _____

   _____

4. It was Principal Kevin Claypoole who announced that Head Basketball Coach Andy Wilcox had submitted his resignation yesterday at an emotional pep rally in the gym.

   _____

   _____

5. Facing the need to choose a college, a big problem is finding the time and money to visit those that seem promising.

   _____

   _____

— EXERCISE 1C —
Be your own editor: Make it right (cont'd)

6. While researching Byrnehurst's history, the class discovered that Clyde Goodfellow was believed to be the oldest white man born in this county at the time of his death.

_____

_____

PART B. Choose the right word

The spell check won't help you choose between two words that sound similar or alike but have different spellings and meanings. Your only hopes: turn to the dictionary, ask someone who knows or choose another word.

DIRECTIONS:

Read the following sentences, then choose the correct word from the pair written in parentheses. You may need to consult the dictionary—and some errors result from a reporter's creatively hopeful attempt at spelling.
Write the correct form in the blank space or spaces before each example.

_____ 1. The committee rejected several comedies because they considered the dialogue too (risky, risqué) for a school play.

_____ 2. Students' complaints that they received a (plerifera, plethora) of homework need not be taken seriously, the speaker said.

_____ 3.

_____ 4. The track team ended (it's, its) season
by proving the truth of (their, there) motto:

_____ 5. No team is (to, too) powerful
for the Blazers (to, too) beat.

_____ 6.

_____ 7. Incoming freshmen find it hard to (accept, except) the fact that their high

_____ 8. school record seriously (affects, effects) their future.

_____ 9. This year, Student Council has all its plans in (sink, sync).

_____ 10. Not many students can claim to be a real-life (heroin, heroine), but Anne Zellers deserves the honor.

_____ 11. Most teens belong to some kind of (cliché, clique) or group.

_____ 12. Jay Jordan submitted a report on 15th-century (Sand script, Sanskrit) manuscripts.

Developing the newswriter's mindset

Objective: "not affected by personal feelings or prejudice; based on fact, unbiased; impartial, fair, impersonal . . ."

Approaches to writing differ noticeably, even in a newspaper. The chief difference between news stories and other types of writing found in newspapers—such as columns, editorials and reviews—is that newswriters try not to inject their own opinions. Their job is to avoid taking sides and to record the facts of what happened, from the evidence they gather through interviews and investigation.

The reporter's byword should be objectivity. Being objective means that reporters, unlike publicists, advertisers or propagandists, aren't trying to "sell" their readers anything. A news reporter should be able to tell readers, "I'm giving you the facts and details so you can form your own opinion from what you've read."

The importance of a byline

At one time, school and professional newspapers rarely gave bylines to reporters covering straight news. Bylines were reserved for personal opinion pieces like columns and reviews, or stories that deserved special recognition, such as front-page scoops or feature stories.

Since editors expected news reporters to keep their writing free of opinion, newspapers presented their stories as pure fact, unbiased and uncolored by an individual writer's point of view. The lack of a byline added a certain weight and authority. This was the news, not just one person's version of it, and the newspaper was bringing it to you.

The need for bylines

With the exception of editorials expressing the collective opinion of the paper itself or its editorial board, almost every story in today's newspapers carries a byline. The reason is not that today's reporters deserve more recognition. Rather, it's acceptance of the fact that no writer can be completely objective, no matter how hard he or she tries. Each decision a writer makes puts an individual slant on the story and may affect the reader's perception of the news.

What details should go first?

What sources will I cite?

Whose words should I quote directly?

Everything that goes into—or is left out of—a news story is a reflection of a writer's personal viewpoint.

Name _____   Date _____

— EXERCISE 2A —
How viewpoint affects reporting

DIRECTIONS:

Do this exercise at a set time and place, perhaps the first five to ten minutes of class or another time prescribed by your advisers. Do the exercise in the company of the class or other students, but do not work together or confer about your choices.

In the space below, write down five statements about the most important activities taking place around you in the given time period. Compare your answers when you have finished. The exercise is intended to show how individual viewpoint affects reportage, and how responses vary in the activities chosen, the order listed and manner of writing about them.

1. _____

2. _____

3. _____

4. _____

5. _____

Focus on newswriting

Even with bylines, the rules of newswriting have not changed.

1. Reporters of straight news strive for objectivity.

2. The byline is not a license permitting writers to express their opinions, attitudes and enthusiasms.

3. Good reporters pursue accuracy by double-checking facts and identifying their sources.

4. When issues have more than one side, the good reporter seeks to cover all views fairly.

5. Good reporters respect the meanings of words.

Shun overwriting

In an effort to make stories more exciting, guard against overwriting and wasting strong words such as *incredible, phenomenal* and *disaster.*

> *Example:* A tragedy struck Byrnehurst Jan. 5 when a blizzard caused cancellation of the Byrnehurst Invitational Basketball Tournament.

Is cancellation of a tournament a genuine *tragedy:* "a dreadful or fatal event or affair, a calamity"?

Did the snowfall qualify as a *blizzard:* "a violent windstorm with dry, driving snow and intense cold"?

Using the powerful word *tragedy* to label a less serious situation is inaccurate and misleading. Usage in this sense not only weakens its meaning but calls the reliability of the writer and paper into question.

Good reporters don't settle for other than precise nouns and verbs, the two types of words that convey meaning more exactly and directly than adjectives and adverbs, which color and modify them.

Reporting: In the third person

> *Not acceptable:* You're going to love the faculty talent show, with Coach Ray Kalopowski doing his stand-up comedy routine and the Active Voices, the English department vocal group.

Enthusiastic, yes. Good newswriting, no.

To maintain an objective tone, news reporters stick to the third-person viewpoint. To avoid intruding themselves or their opinions into a story, they do not use *I* or any of its forms: *me, my, mine, mine* or *myself.* Nor do they address the reader directly with any form of *you,* including *your, yours, yourself, yourselves* and *you* understood in commands.

Because *we* always includes *I* and someone else, possibly *you, we* and its variations *us, our, ours* and *ourselves* are not objective either.

In straight news stories, the ban against *I, you* and *we* does not extend to direct quotations, when the *I* stands for the person quoted and the words express the speaker's opinion, not the reporter's.

> *Okay:* "I know everyone is going to love the faculty talent show," said Mrs. Muriel Mayson, faculty talent show chairperson.

The case for bylines

Bylines on straight news stories do not free reporters from being objective. They remind readers that news stories may intentionally or unintentionally reflect their writer's opinions and that writers openly take both credit and responsibility for their words.

As you focus on newswriting, here are three key factors that contribute to bettering your newswriting style:

1. Make precise word choices.

2. Keep to the objective viewpoint.

3. Use quotes correctly.

Name _____   Date _____

— EXERCISE 3A —
Focus on making precise word choices

PART A. All synonyms are not the same

Don't make the mistake of thinking that all words in a list of synonyms are interchangeable. They aren't. For example, as synonyms for *stall*, as in "He stalled in giving his answer," a thesaurus lists *prevaricate, hesitate* and *procrastinate*. Compare their definitions.

   (1) *stall* (to delay, especially by evasion or deception)

   (2) *prevaricate* (to lie)

   (3) *hesitate* (to pause)

   (4) *procrastinate* (to put off to another time)

     You might *prevaricate* about the dog chewing up your homework, because you had *procrastinated* the night before. But, you'd hardly *procrastinate* about the dog chewing up your homework because you'd *prevaricated* the night before. You might try to *stall* the teacher, but not *hesitate* her.

     Don't use words from a thesaurus just because they sound good. Beware of words you aren't sure of. Check both spelling and meaning—and remember that it is the precision of a word that matters. Don't choose *conglomeration* when you mean *mess*.

DIRECTIONS:

Look up the following words in the dictionary and write a brief version of their definitions. Choose the sense that clarifies how each differs from, yet is related to, others in its group.

Comparative definitions

Group I.

   (1) discipline _____

   (2) punishment _____

   (3) drill _____

   (4) order _____

Group II.

   (1) meeting _____

   (2) appointment _____

   (3) conference _____

   (4) gathering _____

— EXERCISE 3A —
Focus on making precise word choices *(cont'd)*

Group III.

(1) organization _____

(2) assembly _____

(3) group _____

(4) union _____

Group IV.

(1) party _____

(2) celebration _____

(3) bash _____

(4) reception _____

Group V.

(1) accident _____

(2) blunder _____

(3) mishap _____

(4) disaster _____

Group VI.

(1) plan _____

(2) suggestion _____

(3) recommendation _____

(4) scheme _____

PART B. Using words precisely

Although some words in each group might serve as synonyms, they cannot be used interchangeably without thought. Practice precision by choosing two words from each group and writing an original sentence of at least 15 words to illustrate the correct meaning of each, as given in part A.

When you have finished, share your sentences with another student or students, either by exchanging papers or duplicating examples. Determine whether the chosen words express the right shades of meaning.

I.a. _____

_____

b. _____

_____

— EXERCISE 3A —
Focus on making precise word choices (cont'd)

II.a. _____

_____

b. _____

_____

III.a. _____

_____

b. _____

_____

IV.a. _____

_____

b. _____

_____

V.a. _____

_____

b. _____

_____

VI.a. _____

_____

b. _____

_____

Name _____   Date _____

— EXERCISE 3B —
Focus on avoiding redundancy

Don't say the same thing twice

Redundancy: unnecessary repetition in expressing an idea, often characterized by using two words with the same meaning as complements or in conjunction with each other.

Beginning writers are sometimes redundant in a mistaken attempt to be precise. They use one word to reinforce another or an extra word as an insurance policy, to guaranteeing understanding. They don't always realize when one word contains or implies another. Such redundancies make readers impatient and make writers seem unaware or uncertain about what they are saying.

> **Example:** My sister's new infant child is a baby girl, just three months old.
> *Infant:* a child in its earliest period of life, a baby.

While a *baby* could be a piglet or kitten, an *infant* is normally a child, especially if it belongs to one's sister.

> **Better:** My sister's baby girl is just three months old.

DIRECTIONS:

Underline the redundant words, then write an improved version of each sentence. If doubtful about precise meanings, check a dictionary. Some sentences may contain more than one redundancy.

1. Bill is such a prevaricating liar that you can never count on getting the true facts from him.

   _____

   _____

2. The Blazers' defensive tackle is a huge giant of enormous proportions who looks almost ready for the pros.

   _____

   _____

3. Macky, our furry little canine pup, is named after Mack the Knife because he likes to playfully bite us, just in fun.

   _____

   _____

— EXERCISE 3B —
Focus on avoiding redundancy (cont'd)

4. Macky is a bouncy bundle of energy whose sharp teeth have totally destroyed two of the family's sofa pillows on their couch.

_____

_____

5. It was a disappointing letdown to discover that disks for the two computers were not interchangeable with one another.

_____

_____

6. After becoming a famous celebrity he wrote a first-person autobiography of his life which became a popular bestseller.

_____

_____

7. The elementary school third grader received an unexpected surprise on her birthday when her mother treated everyone in the whole class to pizza.

_____

_____

8. The new innovation in dental care is supposed to be very unique.

_____

_____

9. Byrnehurst French teacher, Mrs. Marie Trudeau, who is a pregnant mother-to-be, begins a leave of absence in the coming month of April.

_____

_____

10. The debut performance Friday, Oct. 9, will be the first time the composition is presented to an audience of people.

_____

_____

Name _____   Date _____

— EXERCISE 3C —
Focus on being objective

PART A. Keep to the third person

When reporting the news, writers should stick to the third person, not using the pronouns *I*, *we*, *you* or any of their derivatives except in direct quotations.

> *No:* Remember this.

But, do remember that a sentence like the one above has *you* understood as its subject, and really says, "You remember," so it would not be objective.

> *Examples:* Be careful. *(Not objective—You [understood] subject)*
> Care is needed. *(Objective)*

DIRECTIONS:

In the blank space, write *OK* if written objectively in the third person and *NO* if not objective. In sentences that are not objective, underline the word or words that should not be used. If *you* is the understood subject, note this at the end.

_____ 1. Just as we have a larger enrollment at BHS this year, we also have a larger faculty with five new teachers.

_____ 2. After their first four games, our girls' volleyball team holds a 2-2 record, and you can be sure they're out to end up on the winning side.

_____ 3. You may have noticed a new piece of "found metal" sculpture on the cafeteria wall. We have Edvin Baker, Byrnehurst graduate and practicing artist, to thank for it.

_____ 4. No plans exist to discontinue open lunch, despite rumors to the contrary, Principal Kevin Claypoole declared.

_____ 5. The end of first semester is almost upon us, and you know what that means . . . a round of exams.

_____ 6. What you want to say on a T-shirt is our business, not the administration's.

_____ 7. Questions about administrators' rights to censor student T-shirts will come before the Byrnehurst Board of Education April 13.

_____ 8. Make it a point to support your team at our last home game before the league tourney.

_____ 9. "Plan to attend the spring carnival for a lot of fun and a chance to help a worthy cause," urged Bill Ludlow, Student Council president.

_____ 10. Students deal with pressures of exam time in various ways, from cramming all night to cramming on junk food, said BHS counselor Jim Wright.

— EXERCISE 3C —
Focus on being objective (cont'd)

PART B. Use accurate, informative adjectives

What is "pretty" to one person might be "gaudy" to another and "too plain" to someone else. *Good…bad…awful…beautiful…ugly:* All are examples of words that make value judgments, expressing the writer's opinion. Newswriters should avoid words that direct the reader to have a positive or negative attitude, unless they're part of direct quotations.

    Seek precise nouns and verbs. Use adjectives sparingly, and choose only those that are informative, not slanted.

DIRECTIONS:

From the following pairs of phrases, put an *X* in the black space before each one in which the adjective is informative, not slanted.

1. _____ a. worthwhile meeting
   _____ b. final meeting

2. _____ a. written statement
   _____ b. astonishing statement

3. _____ a. complex project
   _____ b. clever project

4. _____ a. excellent idea
   _____ b. prize-winning idea

5. _____ a. disgraceful grades
   _____ b. below-average grades

6. _____ a. sour expression
   _____ b. frowning expression

7. _____ a. rare, bluish-purple flower
   _____ b. rare, beautiful flower

8. _____ a. valuable course
   _____ b. innovative course

9. _____ a. near-capacity audience
   _____ b. big, enthusiastic audience

10. _____ a. entertaining speaker
    _____ b. well-known speaker

Focus on newswriting—Using quotes correctly

"I feel poor attendance is a symptom, not the disease," said Mr. Kevin Claypoole, Byrnehurst principal.

To reporters, the fact is what a speaker says, not that the speaker's opinion agrees with theirs.

Interviews form the basis for the majority of news stories, and the wise use of quotations helps bring the story to life, provides an authoritative source for information and adds a personal angle to its telling. When choosing quotes to include in your story, make sure they are accurately recorded or copied in your notes, and choose those that add dimension, meaning and insight to it. If in doubt about the accuracy of a quote, double-check to save grief later.

There are three ways to use quotations in a story.

1. **Direct quotation:** Use the speaker's exact words inside quotation marks with the *attribution*, or phrase identifying the speaker, outside them.

    Example: "The amount of participation in Campus Cleanup Day shows students' positive attitude toward school," said Principal Kevin Claypoole.

Attribution may come either at the beginning, middle or end of a quotation. If placed in the middle, attribution should not interrupt the sentence's flow. Check a grammar or style book for proper punctuation.

2. **Indirect quotation:** Using the speaker's words without quotation marks, an indirect quote is often introduced with a phrase such as: The speaker said that . . .

    Example: Mr. Claypoole said that plans for the event show students still have a positive attitude toward school.

It is sometimes necessary to change the form of pronouns and verbs to conform with third-person usage.

   Examples:
(Direct)	Mr. Claypoole said, "*I'm* eager to put the program into effect."
(Indirect)	Mr. Claypoole said *he is* eager to put . . .

3. **Partial quotation:** Reporters often pull out a few key words or telling phrases to highlight with quotation marks.

    Example: Mrs. Lucinda Hammersmith, geography teacher, said that students "just love" the group projects.

    Note: When writing attributions, you should regularly choose *said* as the verb. You may also identify speakers of either indirect or partial quotes with the phrase, "according to . . ."

    Example: According to the coach, the team adapted "without a lick of trouble" to the changes in rules.

117

Name _____   Date _____

— EXERCISE 4A —
Focus on quotes

DIRECTIONS:

Rewrite the following as direct, indirect or partial quotations, using the form given in parentheses.

    The sources interviewed were Bill Ludlow, Student Council president, and Ms. Sadie Lane, Council faculty adviser. When quoting a source for the first time, identify the speaker by full name and position or title. In subsequent quotes, use a synonym, pronoun or name such as Bill or Ms. Lane in accordance with your paper's style.

    Use correct punctuation.

1. The theme, "Teens in Touch," expresses the spirit of this year's conference. (Ludlow; direct quotation)

    _____

    _____

    _____

2. Council members are serving kids' favorites—pizza, and ice cream for lunch. (Lane, indirect)

    _____

    _____

    _____

3. The Byrnehurst Student Council originated the idea for the conference, and its members will serve as hosts. (Ludlow; indirect)

    _____

    _____

    _____

4. Teens everywhere share the same problems. This gives us all a chance to learn from each other. (Ludlow; direct quotation, attribution in middle)

    _____

    _____

    _____

— EXERCISE 4A —
Focus on quotes (cont'd)

5. Ten schools, compared with seven last year, are attending the conference, which shows it's a good idea getting better every year. (Lane, partial quote)

_____

_____

_____

For 6-10, write the type of quotation you think is best. If you think the statement should or need not be quoted, simply write: OK—factual.

6. Along with panel presentations and round table discussions, the conference will feature Dr. Byron Wilcox, psychologist and advice columnist, as keynote speaker. (Lane)

_____

_____

_____

7. Dr. Wilcox is a dynamic speaker, whose topic will be Facing the Future. He feels teens don't fully realize how much what we do while we're teens will affect us as adults. (Ludlow)

_____

_____

_____

8. Dr. Wilcox has an easy manner, and his advice makes good sense. One of his pet slogans is "Party today, pay later." (Lane)

_____

_____

_____

9. All of the topics of the day are timely and important. They include Council's Role in Student Discipline, Students as Peer Advisers, and Promoting School Safety.

_____

_____

_____

10. If the conference is as successful as last year's, everyone will come away with ideas we can put into practice in our own lives and at our own schools. (Ludlow)

_____

_____

_____

Name _____   Date _____

— EXERCISE 4B —
Focus on generalizations

Part A. Generalization

A broad or general conclusion, opinion or principle that may be based on:

1. facts, statistics or research

2. personal observation; meager, insufficient or inaccurate information

   Generalizations may be valid or invalid, depending upon their source and support.

   Invalid: Most students hate homework.

   How did the writer achieve such a sweeping conclusion? As a writer or reader, even if you agree or think it "ought to be so," you can't accept it as true without further proof. What students are involved? What steps were taken to gather needed evidence?

   Supported: Boys do 45% better than girls on standardized tests in math and science, according to results released by a national testing foundation.

   The good reporter will also provide specific data, including the source of the conclusion and details about the population sampled. Unsupported generalizations can spread false ideas, disguised as facts, and reporters must take care not to use them.

DIRECTIONS:

Read the following examples, and decide whether each makes an acceptable generalization. If unsupported, rewrite the sentence either to eliminate the opinion or to add the type of data that would support it. You may make up the additional information and source, if necessary. If supported, write *Valid,* and use the blank space to explain why.

1. Many students have been wondering how the construction of the new addition will affect our school, specifically regarding the physical education program.

   _____

   _____

   _____

2. When the work is completed, Byrnehurst will have the best gym in the state, according to Athletic Director Andy Dumont.

   _____

   _____

   _____

— EXERCISE 4B —
Focus on generalizations (cont'd)

3. Choosing whether to eat a healthful lunch or indulge in their favorite junk foods is a major problem to most teens.

_____

_____

_____

4. The majority of students feel that Byrnehurst's dress code needs revision.

_____

_____

_____

5. Computers promise to do more for education than most teachers can make them deliver.

_____

_____

_____

Part B. A cumulative effort

DIRECTIONS:

The following sentences contain an assortment of different types of errors. Identify and correct each.

1. The speaker stressed that students should set there own goals and strife for success to the best of their abilities.

_____

_____

_____

2. Another reason why Dennis Percy's win was surprising was that he was starting out as a new-comer to the tennis team.

_____

_____

_____

3. As his final conclusion, the speaker noted that a live well lived also involves honesty and integrity, too.

_____

_____

_____

— EXERCISE 4B —
Focus on generalizations (cont'd)

4. The Byrnehurst Lions Club is now excepting students nominations of teachers who will be considered as candidates for Teacher of the Year.

    _____

    _____

    _____

5. Buying a lottery ticket just for a lark, a big surprise came to the father of sophomore Ted Roberts, when he won $100,000.

    _____

    _____

    _____

6. There is a recent study which shows that American students' 9th grade reading skills are among the world's best.

    _____

    _____

    _____

7. Throughout the classrooms and hallways of BHS, students are not obeying some of the basic school rules of behavior.

    _____

    _____

    _____

8. One reason students ignore rules is because some of them are being broken by teachers themselves, such as eating and drinking in class.

    _____

    _____

    _____

9. This play is a story about ten guests, who were invited to a mysterious, spooky mansion for a weekend, and there host fails to make an appearance.

    _____

    _____

    _____

10. Researchers are trying to discover the reasons why there is such noticeable evident differences among girls and boys in their achievements in math and science.

    _____

    _____

    _____

Write it right—Obeying the rules

What good is grammar? It's not just a way to make your writing "correct" by following someone else's fussy rules. Grammar is actually an agreed-upon system of putting words and sentences together to make it easier to grasp one another's meaning.

Without communication difficult rules be of grammar would or impossible.

Even word order makes a difference, as you can see. In English, the subject of a sentence usually comes first, followed by its verb. Jumbled up, a simple statement such as "Communication would be difficult or impossible without rules of grammar" makes little or no sense. Yet even the rules allow freedom of choice, for consider the following:

Communication without rules of grammar would be difficult or impossible.

Without rules of grammar, communication would be difficult or impossible.

Good writers should know the rules of grammar and also be aware of the flexibility they provide. Knowledge of grammatical rules gives you the ability to express yourself freely and confidently. To write effectively, you must know the rules before breaking them—then know how and why you chose to do so.

Even though reporters have a good, working knowledge of grammar and its rules, certain areas consistently cause problems. These are the ones discussed in newswriting handbooks and workshops. If you lack a basic understanding of grammar, many guides and textbooks cover the subject thoroughly. You can find a variety of choices in your school and local library and bookstores.

Language on the move

Some elements of language are subject to change, and good writers try to keep up with new words added by technological and social changes. Yet they avoid using slang and word fads, which soon become dated.

Journalists often must communicate with the widest possible audience, and this influences their choice of words. A school newspaper's editorial board must decide whether to appeal mainly to students—perhaps adopting a liberal approach to slang and profanity—or to address all of its readers, who include a range—students, parents, teachers, advertisers and community members—as wide or wider than that of many professional papers.

Getting in style

In addition to grammar, use of language offers a variety of choices in such matters as punctuation, capitalization, forms of address and use of abbreviations. In contrast to the rules of grammar, these are questions of style. In fact, as users of Internet know, the symbols of punctuation on the World Wide Web combine to form a system of their own.

Although the basic rules of punctuation and capitalization still hold for print journalism, newspapers enjoy a certain latitude in developing certain details. One of the "bibles" of style is the *Associated Press Stylebook and Libel Manual,* available from most booksellers, while many school papers develop their own style manual because of their special population and needs.

Rule 1 for style: Be consistent

Because forms of address and symbols of punctuation convey their own messages, staffers must learn and follow the chosen style. Mistakes in usage cause writers to lose credibility with readers who feel that slovenly language shows a lack of professionalism. It also sets a bad example for student readers and forms habits that could affect future employment.

Write it right—Who's who and what's that

Make your references clear

The purpose of a pronoun is to take the place of a noun—or call for a noun as an answer.

In well-written sentences, readers should find it easy to identify the reference or *antecedent* of any pronoun used. They can usually assume that pronouns replace the most logical choice, generally the one that most closely precedes it and matches the pronoun in person and number.

Example: The adviser asked the twins if they would model in the show.

No doubt about it—"they" are the twins, but the reference becomes confusing in sentences like this:

Example: The principal told the student editor he didn't understand him.

Who's "he"? Who's "him"? It could logically be either. Sometimes the only way out is to rewrite the sentence entirely:

Correct: The principal accused the student editor of misunderstanding him.

Or, using a direct quotation:

Correct: The principal told the student editor, "I don't understand you."

Writers must accept the blame if sentences are ambiguous because of faulty or illogical pronoun references. Always check their usage from the innocent reader's viewpoint.

Name _____ Date _____

— EXERCISE 6A —
Write it right—Checking references

DIRECTIONS:

Read the following sentences carefully. If clear, simply list each underlined pronoun and its antecedent. If one or more pronoun references are unclear, rewrite and improve the sentence.

1. Board members are considering a raise in teachers' pay, <u>which many</u> feel isn't high enough.

   _____

   _____

2. The Blazers meet the Panthers Friday, Sept. 21, at 9 P.M. After three straight victories, <u>they</u>'re out for another.

   _____

   _____

3. The teacher cleared <u>his</u> throat so often <u>it</u> distracted the student <u>who</u> began to count <u>them</u>.

   _____

   _____

4. This year's track team boasts a field of 39 candidates and six returning letter men, <u>whose</u> goal is to repeat last year's championship season.

   _____

   _____

5. In a recent <u>Torch</u> poll, a majority of students expressed <u>their</u> views about a change in the dress code <u>that</u> <u>they</u> did not like.

   _____

   _____

6. The students who originated the plan told <u>their</u> opponents that <u>their</u> proposal was the better one.

   _____

   _____

— EXERCISE 6A —
Write it right—Checking references (cont'd)

7. Jeff enjoys a variety of rummy played on the computer <u>that</u> one of his friends sent <u>him</u>.

   _____

   _____

8. If an error occurs, *The Torch* will print <u>its</u> retraction in the following edition on the same page <u>that</u> the error occurred.

   _____

   _____

9. The session will feature a panel of speakers <u>that</u> includes a judge, a member of Alanon-Teen and an adolescent center drug counselor, who will share <u>their</u> experiences and encourage audience input.

   _____

   _____

10. Newcomer Leonard Washington will try to rebuild both the boys' and girls' tennis teams, <u>which</u> is a demanding job for one person.

   _____

   _____

Write it right—Little words, big problems

PART A. About personal pronouns

They're little words, but choosing the right one can be tricky. That's because they change their form, depending upon their usage in a sentence.

When you use them singly, they rarely cause trouble.

Examples: *She* is the business manager.
The adviser asked *her* about the account.

Yet, combining them often results in confusion.
First, here's the entire "family."

Personal pronouns:			
Used as subject or its equal	As object of verb, prep.	Showing possession	Possessive pronoun
I	me	my	mine
you	you	your	yours
he, she, it	his, her, it	his, her, it	his, hers, it
we	us	our	ours
you	you	your	yours
they	them	their	theirs

Back to baby talk

Me want that. Give it to I.

Almost everyone knows better than to make the kind of errors made above, yet they are similar to those that often occur when two personal pronouns—or a noun and a pronoun—are joined together by *and, or,* or *nor.*

Examples: Lisa and (I, me) will co-edit next year's literary magazine.
Our adviser asked (she, her) and (I, me) to plan the ad campaign.

The easiest way to be sure of the correct choice is to break the sentences down into two ideas:

Lisa will be co-editor.   =   The choice: Lisa and I
I will be co-editor.

In the same way, the correct version is "Our adviser asked her and me to plan the ad campaign."

PART B. Noting relationships

Check the chart of personal pronouns and notice the similarity of most words in the same row. Some also resemble others in the same column. If your spelling is right but your choice is wrong, computer spell checks can't catch errors in pronoun usage. But, awareness of the similarity of words in each group can make it easier to choose correctly.

Is it *there* or *their*?

Notice that *their* is another form of *they*, when you read across. *There, where, here*—all words that point out places—are look-alikes, too.

> ***Examples:***   *Where* should I put it? *Here*? Or *there*?
> Both of *their* cars are Fords, but *her* car is red, *his* is blue.

Is it *its* or *it's*?

Check the third and fourth columns. None of the words, including *its,* has an apostrophe when showing possession.

> ***Example:***   It has *its* good points. She has *hers*. He has *his.*

On the other hand, just as you say, "*He's* going," you also say "*It's* gone." Add to your list of look-alike words: *we're, you're, they're*—meaning *we are, you are, they are.*

> ***Example:***   *They're* wrong, *you're* right. *Your* turn is next, not *hers.*

Note: The subject form is used in sentences like these:

a. *She* is the award-winning composer.
b. The award-winning composer is *she.*

Name _____   Date _____

— EXERCISE 7A —
Problem pronouns

PART A. Directions:

In the following sentences, choose the correct pronouns from the words given in parentheses.

_____ 1. The coach singled out Jeff and (he, him) as the game's most valuable players.

_____ 2. A run-off vote between (he, him) and (she, her) decided the election for Council president.

_____ 3. The final tally showed that (he, him) won, but (she, her) was only a few votes behind.

_____ 4. The school's Spanish teachers are (she, her) and Mr. Alfred Lopez.

_____ 5. Both Mr. Lopez and (she, her) have excellent accents.

_____ 6. The scholarships given Sandra and (he, him) are awarded yearly.

_____ 7. Of all the schools in the league, (they, them) and (we, us) have the most intense rivalry.

_____ 8. The teacher wants you and (I, me) to take attendance.

_____ 9. Rumors are circulating that the Wilkersons and (they, them) are planning a surprise party for Mr. Claypoole.

_____ 10. The source of the rumor is (he, him) and Scott.

Part B. Directions:

Choose the correct word.

_____ 1. Where (they're, there, their) is smoke, (your, you're) likely to find Greg, *The Torch*'s star reporter.

_____ 2. (They're, There, Their) suggestion was not good as hers.

_____ 3. When (you're, your) near a deadline, panic may set in.

_____ 4. Advertising has (it's, its) own deadline, and (it's, its) earlier than the deadline for news.

_____ 5. After (they're, there, their) interviews, beginning reporters sometimes can't decipher (they're, there, their) notes.

_____ 6. During a press conference, (you're, your) scribbling so fast that some of (you're, your) handwriting is almost illegible.

_____ 7. If you can't read (you're, your) notes, (they're, there, their) almost useless.

_____ 8. (It's, Its) unwise to rely upon memory, especially if (you're, your) story will include quotes.

_____ 9. A news story loses (it's, its) credibility if (it's, its) not based on a reliable interview.

_____ 10. Being (they're, there, their) isn't enough; a reporter's story is only as solid as (it's, its) facts and information.

Write it right—A theory of relativity

Choose the right relative pronouns

that	who	where
which	whom	when

Relative pronouns don't just take the place of a noun—they also join the noun they replace to the words that follow and show the relationship between them.

> *Example:* Claire has an idea that should revitalize the feature page.

Stated as two sentences, this would read:

> Claire has an idea. Her idea should revitalize the feature page.

Using the relative pronoun *that* makes the meaning clearer.

Each of the relative pronouns has its own use and sense:

> *that:* takes the place of a noun naming a person, place or thing; used only when what follows is necessary to meaning

> *which:* should take the place of a noun naming only a thing or place, never a person; usually what follows is not essential to meaning

> *when, where:* used respectively for nouns meaning a place or a time

> *who, whom:* used to take the place of a noun naming only a person

Use *who* when you would use *I, she, he, we, they* in a separate sentence.
Use *whom* when you would use *me, her, him, us, them.*
Again, note the similarity in forms.

Name _____ Date _____

— EXERCISE 8A —
Write it right—A theory of relativity

A. DIRECTIONS:

Working from the chart, assess the relative pronouns used in the following sentences. If there is a choice between *which* and *that,* choose *which* if a comma sets off the preceding part of the sentence. This means what follows is not essential to meaning.

Underline each incorrectly used relative pronoun, state why it is the wrong choice and give the correct form. Although some sentences contain more than one relative pronoun, no more than one per sentence is used incorrectly.

1. The group that forms the prom steering committee has seven members, of which five are seniors.

   Reason incorrect _____ Should be _____

2. They have proposed a plan that the entire Council will vote upon at next Thursday's full Council meeting, that begins right after school.

   Reason incorrect _____ Should be _____

3. The annual Fall Sports Banquet, which takes place Dec. 4, will feature a talk by a former pro football star who Coach Grady knew in college.

   Reason incorrect _____ Should be _____

4. Former tight end Reggie Logan will speak on the days where he played with the pros and relate some of the incidents that taught him the most.

   Reason incorrect _____ Should be _____

5. Logan says he gained much from pro ball and considers himself a person whom needs to give back part of the good that he's received.

   Reason incorrect _____ Should be _____

B. DIRECTIONS:

In the blank spaces in each sentence, supply the appropriate relative pronouns. In some cases, more than one correct choice is possible.

1. A delegation of *Torch* staff members recently returned from a journalism conference in New York City, _____ lasted three days.

2. Although the time _____ they were free to sightsee was limited, *Torch* editor Paula Pen said it was a thrill just to be in New York, _____ so much news happens.

— EXERCISE 8A —
Write it right—A theory of relativity (cont'd)

3. The group attended workshops _____ covered topics ranging from headline writing to the latest innovations in technology.

4. News professionals and school paper advisers, one of _____ was *Torch* adviser Mrs. Adrian Adams, conducted the sessions.

5. Her topic, _____ was "Designing pages for better readership," attracted an audience _____ wanted to keep going after the session officially ended.

6. *Torch* staffers, _____ attended the workshops _____ interested them most, attended Mrs. Adams's session en masse.

7. Staff members, _____ Mrs. Adams asked to come as confidence builders and cheerleaders, said they felt lucky and proud to have her as adviser.

8. Byrnehurst's paper, *The Torch*, three issues of _____ were submitted to judging, won top honors among papers _____ came from all over the nation.

9. Cindy Kenyon, _____ was one of Byrnehurst's winners, said, "Winning was good, but just being there, _____ you could meet so many kids with the same interests you have, that was even better."

10. After the conference, Mrs. Adams said, "There's a kind of pressure _____ comes from putting out a paper and another _____ comes from speaking to a large audience, both of _____ can prove intimidating and rewarding."

Write it right—Making difficult choices

How many are one?

It seems like a silly question, yet pronouns such as *one, everyone, each, anyone, someone* and *no one*, which mean only a single person or thing, are some of the hardest words for writers to use satisfactorily. It's less a matter of being grammatically correct than deciding whom to please.

One is one, clearly, but how many is *everyone?* Generally, it's one as well: *Everyone* is going. *Anyone* is welcome. *Each* of the contestants is ready. All of them naturally take the singular verb *is*. The problem comes when *her, his, its* or *their* refers to one of these pronouns.

> *Example:*   Each problem has *its* own solution. Each of the girls has *her* own book, not every boy has *his*.

It's all right so far. The difficulty comes from dealing with a mixed group. It would be odd to hear someone say, "One is in their seats." Yet hearing "Everyone is in their seats" is common—common, but grammatically wrong.

There are five possible ways to go, none very good.

    A. Everyone has *their* own opinion. (A group possession?)

    B. Everyone has *an* opinion. (Any opinion?)

    C. Everyone has *her* own opinion. (All females?)

    D. Everyone has *her* or *his* own opinion. (Not sure?)

    E. Everyone has *his* own opinion. (All males?)

None satisfies everyone. The last is the form traditionally taught as including both genders, while the first comes naturally to many. There are arguments for and against each version. Sometimes it's easier to change to a plural. Instead of writing "Everyone will do as (he, she, he or she, or they) pleases," change the sentence to "All of the students will do as they please."

Of utmost importance—be consistent. Choose one form, make it part of your style manual and carry this style through every story and issue. It may be helpful to know that the *Associated Press Stylebook and Libel Manual* follows traditional usage, opting for the choice of *he* to stand for either gender.

Name _____ Date _____

— EXERCISE 9A —
Write it right—Making difficult choices

PART A. Directions:

In the following sentences, fill in the blank spaces with your staff manual's approved choice of *his, her, his or her, its,* or *their.* If you feel a revision is in order, rewrite the sentence, making the subject plural.

1. The poll invited each of the students to express _____ opinion of Byrnehurst cafeteria food.

2. Everyone agreed that _____ favorite choice was pizza.

3. Anyone who buys _____ lunch can get a nutritional meal at a reasonable price, said Mrs. Harriet Garvey, cafeteria manager.

4. No one admits basing _____ choice on taste rather than nutrition.

5. Someone who brings _____ own lunch may find cafeteria food looks better, now that tacos and peanut butter sandwiches are offered, too.

PART B. Playing the numbers game

Some, all, most, none, more: Words like these may be singular or plural, depending upon the noun to which they relate. Your choice depends upon whether the pronoun refers to a group of individual items, which requires plural, or parts of a whole, which require singular. Both of the following examples are correct.

> **Example:** *Some* of the cake *is* left.
> *Some* of the pieces *are* left.

DIRECTIONS:

In the blank space, write the correct choice.

_____ 1. Most of the action (takes, take) place at a resort hotel in New England.

_____ 2. Most of the actors (has, have) already learned their lines.

_____ 3. According to student director Pam Pryor, some of the scenes still (needs, need) work.

_____ 4. Some of the rehearsals (lasts, last) till after ten.

_____ 5. All of the play (presents, present) a challenge to direct and perform, said Pam.

_____ 6. All of the characters have (his, her, his or her, their) own quirks and personality traits that make them funny.

_____ 7. Most of the suspects claim (his, her, his or her, their) alibis are airtight.

_____ 8. None of the suspects (is, are) likely villains.

_____ 9. Most of the suspense (comes, come) from the classic question, "Who done it?"

_____ 10. All of the characters (is, are) prime suspects at one point or another.

Write it right—Words for the wise

Certain word choices show that writers are knowledgeable and professional, while others raise doubts about their competency. Here are 25 fine points of usage that can refine your writing to a higher level.

1. **and, but, or:** Use to join two matching elements.

   Correct: He takes *Latin* and *French*. (Joins two words)
   Vacation starts tomorrow, and *I'm glad.* (Joins two clauses)
   She is either *doing her homework* or *watching TV.* (Joins two phrases)

   Incorrect: She looks forward *to going to New York* and *to see some plays.*
   To going . . . does not match *to see . . .*

2. **And, But:** Avoid using these linking words at the beginning of a sentence. Restrict usage to sentences in which you want to indicate a strong pause between two related ideas, yet call attention to what comes next.

   Correct: But, here's a word of warning

3. **different from:** This is the only acceptable phrase.

   Correct: School is different from vacation.
   From and *than* do not have the same meaning. *Than* implies a comparison; *different from* is purely contrast.

   Correct: School is more fun than vacation.

4. **either/or; both/and; neither/nor:** Make sure their placement correctly sets off matching elements.

   Correct: They compared answers on both the third and the fifth problems.
   The third and *the fifth* are matching elements.

   Incorrect: They compared answers *both* on the third and the fifth problems.
   On the third and *the fifth* do not match.

5. **alright, alot:** *All right* should always be written as two words, just like its opposite, *all wrong*. (*All ready* and *already* have different spellings and different meanings, as do *always* and *all ways*.)

   Correct: According to school rules, it is *all right* to tape a class, if the teacher approves.

   a lot: If you didn't mean, "I have a lot of homework," you couldn't sometimes add "a whole lot." A lot is always two words when it means a great deal.

6. **fun time:** Some nouns work with others, such as *desk lamp, dog collar, ocean views. Fun,* used this way, is strictly informal and also expresses the writer's opinion.

7. **great:** So overworked in sports stories and reviews, it has lost all impact and become virtually meaningless.

   The track team finished a great season with a great win over . . . The pageant was a great success . . . The movie was . . . You get the idea.

   Replace *great* with a word that's more precise, not more extravagant.

8. **just recently:** In news stories, a reporter uses *recently* as a way to answer the question "when" yet not call undue attention to a past date. The addition of "just" emphasizes the time and is therefore worse than useless. **Omit it.** If recent enough to qualify as "just" so, use the actual date.

9. **less, fewer:** Both refer to quantity, but *fewer* refers to items that can be numbered, *less* to part of a total amount.

    Example: Jeff has *fewer* computer games than Ramon, who has *less* free time than Jeff has.

10. **may, might, can:** For clarity, use these words with distinct senses.

    may (permission):   Students *may* not park in the school lot without permits.

    might (possibility):   The renovation *might* be finished in time for graduation.

    can (ability):   Gwen *can* run faster than anyone else on the team.

11. **men's, women's:** Pity the poor apostrophe. Lately, it's been abandoned in such phrases as "teachers' meeting" and "girls' team" that were once seen as possessives. Because teachers and girls both end in "s" as plural modifiers, this works. However, you wouldn't say "The mens are playing," so "mens and womens teams" can't be right either. Use the apostrophe or avoid the form entirely.

    Correct: Men's basketball rules are different from *women's.*

12. **mostly juniors or seniors:** Not clear! What are "mostly juniors and seniors"? Be specific or write "a majority of . . ." (*Mostly* is an adverb, as in "That expression is used *mostly* in Great Britain.")

13. **not bad, not so good:** *The novel was not bad.* What does that mean? Was it good? Or was it not good either, which makes it mediocre or boring? Instead of using this kind of negative expression, state precisely what you mean.

14. **over, more than:** *Over* refers to where; *more than* refers to how much or how many.

    Correct: Ken Kesey wrote *One Flew* Over *the Cuckoo's Nest.*
    The poll shows *more than* 75 per cent favor the amendment.

15. **plan to:** Just as you wouldn't be "hoping on going" so you should not say you're "planning on going."

    Correct: He plans to go to Florida and hopes to leave Friday.

16. **plus:** Careful writers avoid using *plus* to link similar ideas, as it turns the final element into an afterthought.

    Avoid: Libbee did her French and algebra homework, plus wrote her theme for English.

    Better: After doing her French and algebra homework, Libbee wrote her theme for English.

17. **pretty easy:** Meaning quite or to a degree, *pretty* is common in everyday speech, but not precise enough to sound professional. It's best to omit the qualifier and just write, "It's easy."

18. **real, really:** *Real* describes a person, place or thing. *That is a real diamond. Really* is used for emphasis. *It is really real and really expensive.*

    Caution: Like *pretty*, the word *really* sometimes creates the effect that the writer isn't professional enough to trust his or her choice of words and is trying too hard to convince.

19. **sort of, kind of:** Both phrases really mean the same as "type of." Test for correctness by using this phrase in their place. If you wouldn't write, "It's type of cool today," don't use *sort* or *kind* either. However, since "I like that type of film" is correct, *sort* or *kind* will work there, too.

20. **students of Byrnehurst, members of the choir:** This kind of phrase wastes words. Write Byrnehurst students, choir members, the choir.

21. **couple weeks, type person, graduated school:** Everyday speech often slurs or skips over words and parts of words that are essential when writing.

    Correct: couple of weeks, type of person, graduated from school
    Be on the look out for these and other, similar omissions of needed words.

22. **will be going, plan to be attending:** Shun long verb phrases like these and pick the shortest form possible.

    Better: will go, plan to attend
    In some cases, recast the verb for brevity and clarity.

    Wordy: They *would have liked to have seen* a play.

    Better: They *had hoped to see* a play.

23. **would of, could of:** Such forms result from an attempt to spell contracted words like "would've" and "could've" according to their sound. With verbs such as these, write out *would have* and *could have,* and avoid overuse of other contracted forms, such as *doesn't* and *can't.*

24. **too, to, two . . . also:** *Too* and *also* both have the meaning of "in addition."

    Example: Meg will come *also.* You can come, *too.*
    However, *too* has another meaning that *also* lacks. *Too* also means excessively.

    Example: It's *too* hot. (*Note:* When deciding between *too* and *to,* remember the extra "o" is a way of drawing the word out and showing its stress. *Two* is the number 2 of this sound-alike trio.)

25. **well, good:** A word pair that causes natural confusion because of their similar meanings. Both *good* and *well* describe a person, place or thing that meets with approval, but *well* has the added meaning of not sick or ill.

    Correct: He looks *well.* (not sick)
    He looks *good.* (rates approval)

    Well also serves as the adverb form of good.

    Correct: He does *good* work. (adjective)
    He does the work *well.* (adverb)

Name _____   Date _____

— EXERCISE 10A —
Write it right: Words for the wise

PART A. Directions:

In the blank space, write the correct choice.

_____ 1. Time-tested ways to encourage sleep include drinking warm milk, thinking kind thoughts (and, plus) counting sheep.

_____ 2. In college, students have (fewer, less) restrictions and

_____ 3.   (fewer, less) pressure from adults to keep at their homework.

_____ 4. The audience numbered (more than, over) 2,000.

_____ 5. Only a few bands perform (good, well) enough to rate an invitation to perform in the annual parade, the band director said.

_____ 6. The juniors' winning homecoming float featured a (real, really) colorful papier-mâché clown.

_____ 7. Jonas Taylor (would have been marching, would have marched) with

_____ 8.   the band in the New Year's parade if it (would not have, had not) been for a collision between two tubas.

_____ 9. Although some onlookers laughed, the mishap (could have, could of, could've) caused serious injuries

_____ 10. The collision between the (to, too, two) bandsmen took place when

_____ 11.   one turned (to, too, two) the right instead of the left during a maneuver.

_____ 12. Tuba Stewart Lytle was injured (to, too, two) but not seriously

_____ 13.   enough (to, too, two) prevent his performing.

_____ 14. BHS students took part in a national survey to determine what (kind of, type) teenager is most likely to smoke.

_____ 15. At the PTA carnival, the (dunking booth of Booster Club, Booster Club dunking booth) was the center of attraction.

_____ 16. Although the distance was only a (couple, couple of) miles, it seemed longer because of the hazardous road.

_____ 17. The Blazer (men, mens, men's) tennis team has a 4-0 record while

_____ 18.   the (women, womens, women's) have split their tennis meets.

— EXERCISE 10A —
Write it right: Words for the wise (cont'd)

_____ 19. In college, students must decide (either to, to either) accept responsibility for studying or face the probability of failure.

_____ 20. Students shouldn't expect their freshman year in college to be (fun time, a time for fun) and nothing else.

PART B. Directions:

Write effective, original sentences of at least ten words correctly using each of the following:

might (as a helping verb)	plan (as a verb showing intention)
more than	kind of
less	too
different (showing contrast)	plus
both/and	amount of

1. _____

_____

2. _____

_____

3. _____

_____

4. _____

_____

5. _____

_____

6. _____

_____

7. _____

_____

8. _____

_____

9. _____

_____

10. _____

_____

Name _____   Date _____

— EXERCISE 10B —
Write it right: Words for the wise

PART A. Directions:

In the blank space, write the correct choice of the words in parentheses. If you have a better replacement or feel the word should be omitted entirely, indicate this.

_____ 1. Byrnehurst's annual faculty talent review (is set to take place, takes place) Friday, April 12, at 7:30 P.M.

_____ 2. The (winners of the contest, contest winners) will each receive

_____ 3. a savings bond (plus, in addition to, and) a medal.

_____ 4. According to the coach, this year's football team shows (real, really) special promise.

_____ 5. It is (sort of, type, quite) unusual for a star basketball player to have knitting for a hobby.

_____ 6. After (graduating, graduating from) high school, Tammy Pearson enrolled in summer school to get a head start in college.

_____ 7. Len put a large (amount, number) of hours and an impressive

_____ 8. amount, number) of effort into his project, according to his father.

_____ 9. In a *Torch* poll taken (recently, just recently), the majority of girls who smoke said fear of getting fat affected their decision to continue smoking.

_____ 10. To them looking (good, well) is more important than

_____ 11. staying (good, well).

_____ 12. An attempt to do homework (and, plus) the distraction of TV equals carelessly done assignments.

_____ 13. A small (amount, number) of students cause the greatest

_____ 14. (amount, number) of trouble.

_____ 15. Returning graduates told seniors that college is different (from, than) high school in many ways.

_____ 16. (Alot, A lot) of high school students think it's

_____ 17. (Alright, all right) just to get by.

— EXERCISE 10B —
Write it right: Words for the wise (cont'd)

_____ 18. Students who (plan on attending, plan to attend) college can do much preliminary research via the Internet.

_____ 19. Seniors (can, may, might) have excused absences to visit

_____ 20.   campuses that they (can, may, might) attend next year.

PART B. Directions:

First, underline the errors, and then write corrected versions of the following sentences. You may find more than one error per sentence.

1. Since he failed one course and wanting to start college this fall, Andrew's summer plans are different than most seniors'.

   _____

   _____

2. When asked to sing "The Star Spangled Banner," alot of students looked sort of embarrassed and had to hum part of it.

   _____

   _____

3. A psychologist says teens need to understand its alright to be different than the so-called ideal, which doesn't really exist.

   _____

   _____

4. According to Dr. Alexis Stuber, teens who seek a fun future are pretty much chasing an illusion.

   _____

   _____

5. A couple professions that have the appearance of promising real fun are professional sports and entertainment, she said.

   _____

   _____

— EXERCISE 10B —
Write it right: Words for the wise (cont'd)

6. Womens and mens professional sports offer less chances than fields of science, such as engineering, chemistry, plus computer technology.

   _____

   _____

7. Viewers of television could of been able to have seen Dr. Stuber just recently when she appeared on the *Talking with Teens* show.

   _____

   _____

8. According to Dr. Stuber, it is pretty normal for teens to feel real confused about what they plan on doing with their futures.

   _____

   _____

9. Over half probably will not have had made a definite decision, plus even college students often might change majors to.

   _____

   _____

10. The show offers a real great opportunity for teens to discover there problems are pretty similar to one and other.

    _____

    _____

News stories—Putting first things first

Get to the point

News stories don't try to keep a reader in suspense. They first recap the story's main points, then go into details later for those readers who want fuller information.

The lead—telling it as it is

Unlike some kinds of writing, the *lead* or first paragraph of a news story doesn't just tell what the piece is going to be about; it tries to answer the reader's most pressing questions in the story's first few words.

Who?   What?   When?   Where?   Why?   How?

To a good reporter, these questions—the 5 W's and an H—come to mind automatically. *Did you hear what happened today? Well, I was sitting in chemistry class, and the teacher was . . .*

Get to the point! *A fire broke out in the chem lab this morning, causing . . .*

When writing a lead, think of the 5 W's and an H in the following way:

Who:	The "actor," the one making the news.
What:	The action, also answering "did or will do what?"
When:	The time that something did or will take place. In an advance story, include the day and date. In a follow-up, choose the date nearest to the story's publication date; the day is usually unnecessary. With past dates of little importance, "recently" can provide this reference.
Where:	In a school paper, the school's name is sufficient for a local story.
	Example: Parents of Byrnehurst students will soon receive positive news about the school, according to . . .
Why:	May be stated or implied, but the answer should relate to specifics in the lead.
How:	Also a stated or implied answer, directly related to the lead.

Name _____   Date _____

— EXERCISE 11A —
Identifying the 5 W's and an H

DIRECTIONS:

Read the following professionally written leads, and identify the Who, What, When, Where, Why, How. If one of these questions is not answered, write N/A in the space.

Note: The answer to "who," or the actor, may at times be something other than a person.

1. To give his students a feel for the Cold War, Hartford Public High School teacher Robert Abate is sending them on a trip: to the long-neglected fallout shelter in the basement. (32 words)

Kalpana Srevasin, Associated Press
Dateline: Hartford, Conn.

Who _____

What _____

When _____   Where _____

Why _____

How _____

2. Hurricane Bertha churned toward the Atlantic seaboard with 100 mph winds yesterday and barely a hint of making its predicted turn toward the north. Nearly 1 million residents and tourists were urged to pack up and leave. (37 words)

The Blade, Toledo, Ohio
Dateline: Jacksonville, Fla.

Who _____

What _____

When _____   Where _____

Why _____

How _____

3. A devastating wildfire, costliest in Alaska history, raged out of control today as crews fought to protect more homes and a main road. (23 words)

Adam Weintraub, *USA Today*

Who _____

What _____

© 1998 by John Wiley & Sons, Inc

— EXERCISE 11A —
Identifying the 5 W's and an H (cont'd)

When _____ Where _____

Why _____

How _____

4. To make way for the latest addition to the updated Times Square—a 25-screen movie complex a developer plans to literally pick up a historic 42nd Street burlesque house and move it 30 feet down the street. (38 words)

New York Times, New York City

Who _____

What _____

When _____ Where _____

Why _____

How _____

Getting a good start

The lead is the most important paragraph of a news story (Figure 2-3). The 5 W's and an H help the writer to ask himself: What is the heart of this story? What will people want and need to know first? How can I get its importance across in the clearest, most effective possible way?

A well-written lead allows the rest of the story to unfold naturally and logically. A poorly written one causes a reporter to stumble around wondering what should come next.

The lead: A summary needn't be dull

A check of professional papers shows that the majority of news stories still feature summary leads—the Who, What, When, Where, Why, How—condensed in a readable, fact-packed sentence or two.

Lengths of leads vary by paper.

Front page leads in *USA Today,* of which five of six were summaries, average 25 words while the *New York Times,* with six of seven summaries, had leads averaging 43 words each.

In *The Blade* of Toledo, Ohio, five of five front page stories had summary leads. Their average length was 30 words.

Setting standards

Counting words doesn't ensure a good lead, but paying attention to word count helps a reporter realize the importance of individual words. One standard is the 28-30 word lead, which is appropriate for school newspapers. The shorter word count equates to greater readability, yet 28-30 words allows for the inclusion of the essential 5W's and an H.

Keeping leads brief also calls attention to the impact of precise, forceful words. In Exercise 11A, compare the reporters' choices with the following:

a. Hurricane Bertha *headed* toward the Atlantic seaboard—vs. "churned."

b. An *enormous* wildfire *burned* out of control—vs. "devastating" and "raged."

Get the essentials in every summary lead

1. Start from the 5 W's and an H.

   Who }
     } *State these*
   What } *four elements*   Why} *Give fuller dimension*
     } *in every*   } *to story—either*
   When } *summary*   How } *stated or implied*
     } *lead*
   Where }

2. Avoid beginning stories with a date or time, especially a past one.

3. Seek compelling words as openers.

   • Beware of overused phrases, such as *Byrnehurst High School . . .* that make all leads sound alike.

   • Avoid starting with weak words like *The, A,* or *An.*

4. Select strong verbs in the active voice, if possible.

5. Shun long, drawn-out verb phrases such as "will be going" in favor of "will go" or even "goes."

6. Limit your lead to approximately 30 words.

7. Choose facts and details to sum up the entire story and give it direction.

8. Identify the people named in the lead, but avoid long, complicated titles.

9. Do not use the words *I, you, me* or their derivatives outside quotation marks, or expressions such as "Do it now" with *you* implied as subject.

10. Polish and edit to make every word count.

Name _____   Date _____

— EXERCISE 12A —
The lead: Checking examples

DIRECTIONS:

Find and cut out clippings of three summary leads from your local paper, *USA Today,* or other professional newspaper. Attach a copy of each to this exercise, then complete the following.

Lead 1: Headline _____

Source _____

Identify the 5 W's and an H:

    Who   _____

    What   _____

    When _____   Where _____

    Why   _____

    How   _____

With which of the six elements did the reporter begin the summary?

_____

_____

What questions, raised by the lead, give direction to the rest of the story?

_____

_____

               No. of words in lead _____

Lead 2: Headline _____

Source _____

Identify the 5 W's and an H:

    Who   _____

    What   _____

    When _____   Where _____

    Why   _____

    How   _____

— EXERCISE 12A —
The lead: Checking examples (cont'd)

With which of the six elements did the reporter begin the summary?

_____

_____

What questions, raised by the lead, give direction to the rest of the story?

_____

_____

No. of words in lead _____

Lead 3: Headline _____

Source _____

Identify the 5 W's and an H:

Who _____

What _____

When _____   Where _____

Why _____

How _____

With which of the six elements did the reporter begin the summary?

_____

_____

What questions, raised by the lead, give direction to the rest of the story?

_____

_____

No. of words in lead _____

Writing the lead

Putting your focus on the lead—and its 5 W's and an H—enables the rest to fall into place. After gathering the facts, and often in the process, the news reporter begins to envision where to begin. Even with the facts, there is often more than one satisfactory approach. Consider the following:

The Facts

1. Weather-related closings this winter exceed state limits.
2. Byrnehurst Board of Education adopts revised schedule for rest of year.
3. Students must make up time and attend school on two days originally scheduled as spring break.

Who is who?

In writing the lead, the reporter must first choose between two possible "Who's"—students or the board of education. One way to decide is by checking the qualities often credited with making some stories more newsworthy than others.

7 Newsworthy qualities

1. *Prominence:* Someone with a well-known name attracts more interest than someone who's unknown.
2. *Magnitude:* The larger the size, the more people involved, the greater the price, the bigger the news.
3. *Proximity:* The nearer it happens, the more likely to affect the reader, the more the reader cares.
4. *Uniqueness:* A singular or rare incident outshines the usual.
5. *Timeliness:* The time is now, the recent past or coming up.
6. *Significance:* Full of meaning or promising meaningful results.
7. *Human interest:* Touching readers' feelings, emotions or sense of humor, or arousing empathy.

In this story, "students" seems the best "who" because of proximity and significance. You might also add timeliness, magnitude and almost everyone would hopefully add, uniqueness.

Who:	Students
What:	must make up two additional days
When:	during time originally scheduled for Spring Break
Where:	at Byrnehurst
Why:	because this year's weather-related closings exceed state limits
How:	by attending school

Put this way, the lead can almost write itself.

Version 1: Students must spend two additional days in school during time originally devoted to Spring Break. The schedule change results from weather-related school closings that exceeded state limits.   (28 words)

You could even change the focus slightly.

Version 2: Students will lose two days of Spring Break because of a Board of Education schedule revision, forced by state regulations limiting the number of allowable weather-related school closings.   (29 words)

Or, you could start with "Why?"

Version 3: To satisfy state requirements, students must attend school during two days originally scheduled for Spring Break in order to make up days lost because of weather-related closings.   (28 words)

Can you think of another effective way to write this same lead?

The best lead is the one that says the most in the required number of words, yet makes its points clearly and doesn't confuse the reader.

What details, if any, were left out of each example? Such omissions are valid, and often provide reporters with a natural way to develop the rest of the story.

Name _____   Date _____

— EXERCISE 13A —
The Lead: Getting the basics

DIRECTIONS:

Using the following facts, first outline the 5 W's and H. Then write at least two versions of each lead, beginning with a different element, if possible. Avoid beginning with a date.

Remember, you do not have to use a person as the subject of your sentence—it can be a thing, such as a "wildfire" or a "hurricane."

Background facts:

Results of *Torch* survey—10% of Byrnehurst freshman class surveyed. More than 65% call it "unfair and unnecessary" to force freshmen to eat in a separate space from upperclassmen. Approximately 25% felt it made it easier to make friends with others in their class. The rest, no opinion. Administration adopted the policy this year to give freshmen a chance to get acquainted and prevent upperclassmen from hazing.

Who _____

What _____

When _____   Where _____

Why _____

How _____

Newsworthy quality or qualities _____

_____

Summary lead, Version 1:

_____

_____

_____   Word count _____

Version 2:

_____

_____

_____   Word count _____

Name _____   Date _____

— EXERCISE 13B —
The Lead: Practice your skills

DIRECTIONS:

Using the following facts, first outline the 5 W's and H. Then write at least two versions of each lead, beginning with a different element, if possible. Avoid beginning with a date.

Remember, you do not have to use a person as the subject of your sentence; it can be a thing, such as a "wildfire" or a "hurricane."

Background facts:

Environmental Club to sponsor Awareness Week, March 5-9. Goal is to make students aware of how much everything they do—from smoking cigarettes to casual littering—contributes to making our environment livable or unlivable.

Activities: poster contest for clubs and individuals; campus cleanup; candy sale—hope to raise enough to buy a tree to plant on Byrnehurst campus.

Who _____

What _____

When _____   Where _____

Why _____

How _____

Newsworthy quality or qualities _____

_____

Summary lead, Version 1:

_____

_____

_____   Word count _____

Version 2:

_____

_____

_____   Word count _____

The new newswriting

Television has its "sound bites"—flashing the most dramatic segments of a story, then racing on. The Internet provides a myriad of sites, inviting the browser to select or ignore. The newspaper offers an overview of the news, spread out for the reader in one convenient package—offering fuller coverage than TV and usually directed to a particular audience: a city, a special interest group, a school, or even a country, as is *USA Today*.

Competition has in some ways changed the way newspapers present themselves, but it has not eliminated the way straight news with a summary lead should be written.

The famous inverted pyramid

It's called the inverted pyramid, and to some ways of thinking it's an upside down way to write a story. (See Figure 2-4.)

Instead of working to a grand conclusion, the news reporter tries to pack the vital details into the very first paragraph—the summary lead, the five W's and an H. Next come the second most important points, answering the questions raised by the first paragraph. The third most important points follow and so on, with the least significant left till last.

The "Why" of the inverted pyramid

Readers can get an overview of the news by reading only headlines and leads. They can also decide exactly how much more they want to know. And when they stop reading, they can be sure they haven't missed anything more newsworthy.

Another reason for the inverted pyramid is the cutoff test. In journalism, this isn't a type of fashion statement; it means that the last paragraphs should contribute to the story yet are dispensable, so the reader won't be left hanging if they are cut off.

Writing to pass the cutoff test makes it easier for an editor to tailor a story to fit available space. In theory, a well-written story could be cut back from the end, paragraph by paragraph, and still sound complete if run after every cut. In fact, the summary lead itself should be able to stand alone as a news brief.

Which comes first?

With modular design, editors may allot space in advance and assign reporters to write their stories to fit. Having awareness of the cutoff test, however, provides more leeway for flowing copy into a given space, without need for adjustments in leading and headline size when making up a page. It also enables the reporter to concentrate on content and effective organization, instead of writing "to order" to plug a specific space.

Organizing straight news, inverted pyramid style

1. Rank and write facts, details and events from the most to least important.

2. Keep to the 3rd person—with no *I's, we's, you's* unless as part of quotes.

3. Keep lead to about 30 words.

4. Break up paragraphs with meaningful quotes.

5. Vary quoted material by presenting it as direct, indirect and partial quotations.

6. Insert factual statements and exposition amid a series of quotes to direct reader to newsworthy points.

7. On first reference, identify an individual with his or her title and position (coach, senior, Mrs.) and generally write out the full name of an organization (Blazers Against Drunk Driving—not BADD). See staff manual for exact style.

8. Be aware of time. Start with the most contemporary past, current or future date and work backward.

9. Put details of greatest importance and interest as near to beginning as possible.

10. Have more than one source for major stories.

11. Remember, your reader wants news, not history, opinion, flowery writing or chitchat.

12. Have a specific order for lists of names: higher to lesser prizes; seniors to freshmen; alphabetical and so on. If extensive, list in sidebar or separate column with its own heading.

13. Vary paragraph lengths. Narrow newspaper columns make paragraphs stretch longer than an equal number of words in books.

14. To pass cutoff test, include brief paragraphs at end that contain valuable but not essential information.

15. Avoid using more words than you really need. Better said: avoid wordiness.

Name _____   Date _____

— EXERCISE 14A —
Analyzing an inverted pyramid story

DIRECTIONS:

Read Example 2-14A, "No end in sight," published in *USA Today*. Then analyze its organization to discover how reporter Adam Weintraub used the inverted pyramid style to write his story on an Alaskan wildfire.

To guide your analysis, write your answers to the questions that follow.

1. List in order the five specific mentions of time in the story, label each as present, future or past in relation to the published date, and explain why the reporter placed them in this relative order of importance.

   (a) _____

   (b) _____

   (c) _____

   (d) _____

   (e) _____

2. Note and list three examples of persons or places that the reporter names and the phrases with which he identifies them.

   (a) _____

   (b) _____

   (c) _____

3. Consider the following version, joining the first two paragraphs:

   > A devastating wildfire . . . raged out of control today as crews fought to protect more homes and a main road, and they hope there is no wind shift that . . . (43 words)

   The reporter evidently considered it more effective to begin the second paragraph with *And*.

   Name two problems that might result from the revised version and make it weaker than the original.

   _____

   _____

   _____

   _____

— EXERCISE 14A —
Analyzing an inverted pyramid story (cont'd)

4. The second paragraph could begin "They hope . . ." instead of "And they hope . . ." How does the antecedent of "they" affect this decision?

   _____

   _____

   _____

   _____

5. Note the strong verb forms used throughout the story. List the more precise synonyms used for each of the following:

   (a) put out   _____

   (b) turned (into) _____

   (c) sending   _____

   (d) caused   _____

   (e) caused   _____

6. Would the story have sounded complete if the last paragraph were omitted? _____ The last two? _____

   Explain _____

   _____

   _____

   _____

By Bill Roth, Anchorage Daily News via AP

Struggle: Dan Govoni shovels dirt in the path of flames near his home in Houston, Alaska. The wildfire has forced evacuations in Houston, a settlement of about 900, and Big Lake, home to about 1,500.

No end in sight for Alaska blaze

By Adam Weintraub
USA TODAY

A devastating wildfire, costliest in Alaska history, raged out of control today as crews fought to protect more homes and a main road.

And they hope there is no wind shift that would endanger Wasilla, a town of 4,800 north of Anchorage.

Officials say unless the weather turns it will be impossible to quench the blaze. No rain is forecast until Sunday.

Since Monday, winds whipped what was a 65-acre fire into 200-foot plumes of flame, flinging embers a half-mile into tinder-dry forest.

"The fire is moving so rapidly it's defying traditional fire-fighting methods," said Bob King, spokesman for Gov. Tony Knowles. "It's jumping rivers. It ignited a cabin on an island in a lake."

Fireworks may have sparked the blaze Sunday near Big Lake, 60 miles north of Anchorage.

The fire has burned more than 37,500 acres and 150 homes, caused $40 million in damage and forced evacuation of more than 1,000 people and a minimum-security work farm. Nearly 1,300 firefighters were on the scene.

For a time Wednesday, flames threatened the Parks Highway, main road from Anchorage to Fairbanks, and stopped southbound trains.

Example 2-14A. "No end in sight for Alaska blaze," by Adam Weintraub, *USA Today*.

News briefs—Sharpening your skills

News briefs offer excellent opportunities to practice getting away from dull, ineffective leads that begin *The this club . . ., The that club . . .,* and on to *The next club. . . .* Turn news briefs into a mental game by trying to discover different, yet effective ways to begin your leads. Vary your choices of the 5W's and an H, while avoiding past dates. Once in a while, you might even add a note of humor or surprise. But it's not wise to be too "cute" too often. Cuteness can grow old fast and seem not clever, but strained.

Here are the facts:

Byrnehurst jazz band members selling boxed chocolates and chocolate bars. Their fund-raising drive began Oct. 24 and continues until Thanksgiving. Orders will go in every two weeks; all deliveries made before Christmas. Their goal: $2000, enough for professional-type bandstands with Blazer Jazz emblems and matching vests in Byrnehurst's colors of red and gold for band members. Jerome "Louie" Lewis, student leader, said, "It's a sweet deal." Candy, wrapped in red and gold, comes in various sizes and prices.

Version 1: With a goal of raising $2000 for professional-type bandstands, Blazer jazz band members have begun a boxed chocolate and chocolate bar sale that continues until Thanksgiving vacation.   (28 words)

Version 2: A campaign to raise money for new professional-style stands for the Blazer jazz band is now underway. Members are selling boxed chocolates and chocolate bars for delivery before Christmas.   (30 words)

Version 3: BHS students can enjoy a sweet treat and help the Blazer Jazz band, too, by buying boxed chocolates and chocolate bars during the group's fund-raising drive, going on now. (30 words)

Version 4: By selling specially-wrapped boxed chocolates and chocolate bars, now till Thanksgiving, Blazer jazz band members seek to sweet-talk their way to new, professional-type bandstands.   (28 words)

Version 5: Jazz can be sweet or hot, and Blazer jazz band members are taking the sweet route by selling boxed chocolates and chocolate bars during their current fund-raising drive. (29 words)

Completed news brief, with lead version 1:

With a goal of raising $2000 for professional-type bandstands, Blazer jazz band members have begun a boxed chocolate and chocolate bar sale that continues until Thanksgiving vacation.

Jerome "Louis" Lewis, student leader, calls the sale "a sweet deal." The candy, which will be delivered before Christmas, comes in various sizes and prices.

The band also hopes to raise enough money for matching vests in Blazer colors of red and gold.

Name _____   Date _____

— EXERCISE 15A —
News briefs: Sharpening your skills

DIRECTIONS:

Below are facts gathered for a news brief. First, pick out the main facts, based on the 5 W's and an H. Then, write three different versions of the lead, each beginning in a different way. Finally, choose one, and write a complete story of two to three paragraphs.

The facts: Travis Logan, senior, first-place winner in visual merchandising at district DECA competition held at Union College two weeks ago (with reference to date of issue). As winner, will go to state contest in April. Says, "My goal is taking a first at state so I qualify for the nationals in Florida." Other Byrnehurst winners: DeDee Contreras, junior, second in written test; Duncan Pfieffer, honorable mention in role playing.

Note: You may identify DECA as Distributive Education Clubs of America in a paragraph other than the lead.

Who _____

What _____

When _____   Where _____

Why _____

How _____

Summary lead, Version 1:

_____

_____

_____   Word count _____

Version 2:

_____

_____

_____   Word count _____

Version 3:

_____

_____

_____   Word count _____

— EXERCISE 15A —
News briefs: Sharpening your skills *(cont'd)*

Completed story:

_____

_____

_____

_____

_____

_____

_____

_____

_____

_____

_____

_____

_____

_____

_____

_____

_____

_____

_____

_____

_____

Name _____   Date _____

— EXERCISE 15B —
News briefs: Sharpening your skills

DIRECTIONS:

Below are facts gathered for a news brief. First, pick out the main facts, based on the 5 W's and an H. Then, write three different versions of the lead, each beginning in a different way. Finally, choose one, and write a complete story of two to three paragraphs.

Background facts:

Color Guard tryouts to be held Tuesday, May 25, to Thursday, May 27, on school campus at west side of parking lot. Girls in grades 10-12 can compete for 16 positions. Skills needed: dance, coordination, rhythm, flag-twirling ability. Those chosen join marching band in fall. Squad performs choreographed routines at football and basketball halftimes, parades. Last year, 68 girls came to first sessions. If necessary, second round will take place the following week. For applications: Mrs. Cindy Barker, Color Guard adviser, room 103.

Who _____

What _____

When _____   Where _____

Why _____

How _____

Summary lead, Version 1:

_____

_____

_____ Word count _____

Version 2:

_____

_____

_____ Word count _____

Version 3:

_____

_____

_____ Word count _____

— EXERCISE 15B —
News briefs: Sharpening your skills *(cont'd)*

Completed story:

_____

_____

_____

_____

_____

_____

_____

_____

_____

_____

_____

_____

_____

_____

_____

_____

_____

_____

_____

_____

_____

_____

_____

_____

Name _____   Date _____

— EXERCISE 15C —
News briefs: Sharpening your skills

DIRECTIONS:

Below are facts gathered for a news brief. First, pick out the main facts, based on the 5 W's and an H. Then, write three different versions of the lead, each beginning in a different way. Finally, choose one, and write a complete story of two to three paragraphs.

Background facts:

Drama teacher Ms. Linda Parker has received a grant to study in England this summer. She will spend six weeks, taking a course at Oxford University and participating in a dramatics workshop in London, where she will attend both Shakespearean and modern plays, participate in theater seminars and meet both directors and actors. "It's a dream come true," she said. This will be Ms. Parker's first trip across the Atlantic.

Who _____

What _____

When _____   Where _____

Why _____

How _____

Summary lead, Version 1:

_____

_____

_____ Word count _____

Version 2:

_____

_____

_____ Word count _____

Version 3:

_____

_____

_____ Word count _____

— EXERCISE 15C —
News briefs: Sharpening your skills (cont'd)

Completed story:

_____

_____

_____

_____

_____

_____

_____

_____

_____

_____

_____

_____

_____

_____

_____

_____

_____

_____

_____

_____

_____

_____

The time is now

The summary lead has traditionally offered a way for busy readers to skim the newspaper and receive a digest of what's happening without reading every inch of every story. In fact, each news story provides three different versions of the news.

1. In the headline:

Generally written from the lead alone, without regard to the rest of the story, the headline provides a summary of the summary. Headlines offer an immediate overview of the news to both casual and careful readers.

2. In the lead:

The 5 W's and an H equal the essential factors in a news story.

3. In the body:

The rest of the story should begin by answering the questions raised by the lead, and continue with the most important and current events coming first. The background is filled in later. Remember, news is not history, it is *now*—or as close to now as deadline permits. Keep your stories as timely as possible by ranking equal details as more important when closer to the present.

  The lead comes first, but as you write your lead, pay attention to where your story is going—for only the right lead will take you there.

Name _____   Date _____

— EXERCISE 16A —
Writing the news story

Step one: Ranking facts

DIRECTIONS:

Below is information you might have amassed in covering an assignment. Rank the seven most news-worthy details in order from most to less important, numbered in order from 1 to 7. Remember the significance of time and the seven newsworthy qualities (Workshop 13) that arouse special interest.

Items not numbered may come later in your story or serve as identification or description.

Story on Jeanay DeMars, Byrnehurst graduate

_____   Was graduated from Byrnehurst 11 years ago; parents still live in town.

_____   Has role in Emmy-winning soap opera, *Thirst for Life.*

_____   In TV show, plays Adrianna, whom Doreen accuses of taking her boyfriend, Jeb.

_____   According to storyline, Adrianna has mysteriously disappeared.

_____   Disappearance leaves Jeanay free for several weeks while written out of the script.

_____   Bill Ludlow, Student Council president, contacted Jeanay's parents for her address.

_____   SC president wrote Jeanay in New York to invite her to take part in Homecoming festivities.

_____   She accepted, saying, "I'll be delighted to see my old school again. I missed my 10th reunion last year, and I'm glad for the chance to come now."

_____   Jeanay will be introduced to the student body at the Pep Rally Friday, Oct. 11.

_____   Will visit drama class of former teacher, Ms. Linda Parker, and speak with students about her career and answer their questions.

_____   Jeanay is a former Byrnehurst homecoming queen.

_____   Will crown this year's queen at halftime ceremonies of Homecoming Game Saturday, Oct. 12.

_____   Game begins at 2 P.M.

_____   Last year's queen Lisa Sessions can't attend.

_____   "I want to see my former teachers and thank them," Jeanay said.

_____   Ms. Parker said, "I remember Jeanay as bright and sweet, not the conniving type she plays on TV—but that's what you call acting."

_____   Bill said, "It was a lucky break that she's free. I expected her to say 'no,' but then I'd still have her autograph, if she even bothered to answer."

_____   While in Byrnehurst, Jeanay will make several other personal appearances and inter-views, but says she mostly looks forward to spending time with her family and friends.

Name _____   Date _____

— EXERCISE 16B —
Writing the news story

Step one:

Working from your ranking of the most important elements, identify the 5 W's and an H, which you will use in writing your story about Jeanay DeMars's visit to Byrnehurst.

Who _____

What _____

When _____   Where _____

Why _____

How _____

Step two:

Write three versions of the story's lead.

Lead, Version 1:

_____

_____

_____   Word count _____

Version 2:

_____

_____

_____   Word count _____

Version 3:

_____

_____

_____   Word count _____

Name _____   Date _____

— EXERCISE 16C —
Writing the news story

Step three:

Write the completed story on Jeanay DeMars's visit, being sure to follow the steps for writing straight news, inverted pyramid style. If requested, have your adviser's or editor's approval before proceeding.

Step four:

Check your work for errors before handing it in for editing.

_____

_____

_____

_____

_____

_____

_____

_____

_____

_____

_____

_____

_____

_____

_____

_____

_____

_____

_____

_____

_____

Name _____   Date _____

— EXERCISE 16D —
The news story: On your own

DIRECTIONS:

Assume you have amassed the details below for a story in the forthcoming issue. Write the completed story, following the steps given.

Step one:

To engage the reader's interest, rank the major points in order, paying close regard to importance and time. Also identify the 5 W's and an H.

Step two:

Write a summary lead that captures the pith of the story. If requested, have your adviser's or editor's approval before proceeding.

Step three:

Write the completed story, being sure to follow the steps for writing straight news, inverted pyramid style.

Step four:

Check your work for errors before handing it in for editing.

Background facts: Blazer symbol returns home

Fifteen years ago members of shop classes created a symbol for the Byrnehurst Blazers—a 3-1/2 foot Olympic-style torch with a silver handle and a carved wooden flame, painted gold. The symbol was mounted over the front entrance to the school along with a sign, "BHS Blazers—Keepers of the Flame." Torch and sign were dedicated Monday of Homecoming Week that year—and stolen or kidnapped two days later.

The Blazers' homecoming opponents, the Rockport Rangers, were chief suspects. Their guilt was never established, but the torch mysteriously reappeared a few weeks after the Blazer-Ranger game, which Byrnehurst lost.

Symbol reinstalled and shone proudly for more than a year, when it disappeared again.

Whereabouts remained unknown until about three weeks ago when found, wrapped up in newspaper and plastic garbage bags, blocking front entrance. After police made sure contents were not explosive or dangerous, the torch was found inside, slightly battered but reparable.

Along with the torch was a note saying, "Having the torch isn't fun anymore, and I'm tired of feeling guilty. A former BHS prankster"

Principal Kevin Claypoole said, "We have no plans to pursue the identity of the thief, who apparently has learned his lesson."

"We'll redo it so it's good as new, maybe even better," said Mr. Lyle Burke, shop teacher.

Plans are in the making to create an honors wall in main hall near administrative offices. There, the renovated torch will be displayed on a bracket, inside where it is safe yet available for use in parades and on other ceremonial occasions. Alongside will hang an official school flag and plaques honoring students with unique academic honors and achievements.

Rededication will take place *(supply time and place)*.

Note to advisers

The adviser's role in editing

The unit on copy editing comes amid the section on newswriting, instead of separately, so that student journalists will realize that editing and revision are parts of a whole and integral to good writing.

Student reporters must understand that no form of written self-expression is successful unless its meaning and purpose are clear to someone else. They should find it easier to accept the concept behind editing and revision when they expect their work's publication. By starting out at once to edit, be edited and revise their work, student writers more readily begin to appreciate these steps as natural parts of the journalistic process.

ADVISER OR EDITOR?—There is an important distinction between the role an editor plays in forming and expressing opinions and the function performed in polishing copy to its most communicative level. The first involves ideas and opinions; the second, skill, techniques and modes of expression.

In fact, a good editor can help a writer perfect the vehicle of expression, even while disagreeing with the ideas the writer expresses. In this sense, all editors serve as advisers, for a good editor does not attempt to sway a writer from stating a desired point, but only advises how to state it more effectively.

The ideal way for a beginning writer to learn from an adviser/editor is for the two to sit down side by side, so the writer discovers the actual thought processes of a perceptive reader. In the fragmented time of school newspaper production, this opportunity rarely presents itself, yet, one-on-one sessions with the adviser as coach remain the most effective method.

MEANINGFUL ALTERNATIVES—Peer editing can be a viable substitute for the adviser/coach and can be approached in a number of ways.

1. Assign an experienced reporter to serve as mentor. The interchange will help both students develop an awareness of techniques involved in effective communication.

2. Make copies of a student's paper, keeping the writer's name anonymous, if possible. Have novice reporters copy-edit the paper, then go over it as a group led by an editor or adviser. This allows both the writer and group to grasp the process of polishing work for publication and gain skill in copy editing for clarity and style.

3. Pair novice writers and have them exchange papers to engage in peer editing and discussion of their work. Emphasize that they are helping, not being hypercritical, when they point out weaknesses.

4. After a writing exercise is finished, provide a copy of an approved version of a story so that students can compare their own work with the "textbook" version. This method will, of course, be more effective with skills and copy-editing exercises than with newswriting assignments, which may validly have a variety of approaches.

By learning copy-editing techniques early in the game, students will realize that editing and revision are not punishment but a way of lifting their work to a higher level, not only fitting it for publication in the school paper but also grooming them for any profession where written communication matters.

All writers—even professionals—expect to be edited. Because they're meant for a reader, no writer can be completely sure of the impact of his or her words until they're tested on someone else. No one really enjoys facing criticism, but professional writers know the value of editing, and they profit from what they learn. Even the best writers, like Ernest Hemingway, went through the process.

Good editors, who don't request changes for the fun of it or enjoy being critical, help writers by pointing out where they've wasted words or need a supporting example. Editing not only strengthens and smoothes the story at hand, but can also heighten awareness and help create better writers. Under the pressures of deadline, it may sometimes seem that editors overlook all writer's efforts and seek only to find fault. It's important for both writer and editor to remember that the process of improving a story is a professional, not a personal one.

FROM FIRST TO FINAL DRAFTS—Each completed version of a story is called a draft, and reporters should write, self-edit and revise their stories before submitting their first official draft. At times, a consultation with an editor, more seasoned reporter or adviser may precede this step.

The first draft will likely not prove the final one. Next comes copy editing. The term *copy editing* assumes a manuscript is not yet ready to appear in print but needs further editing to correct and improve its wording, spelling, punctuation, grammar and style— as well as catch other problems, such as factual errors, lack of clarity, faulty attribution of quotations and missing identification. (See Figure 2-5.)

If the story requires only minor corrections, the copy editor's marked copy or hard copy plus disk can go directly to the staffer responsible for word processing the final copy. If considerable revision is needed, the edited hard copy goes back to the reporter for the necessary rewriting. Novice reporters may need to write repeated drafts to make their stories publishable.

THE FINAL STEP—Before the paper is ready to print, it requires a final reading to catch those sly errors that impishly slip by the most careful editing. Those include spelling errors that steak bye—oops! sneak by—a computer spell check because the problem is meaning, not spelling. Then, there are words and phrases the delete key may zap by mistake—and so much more.

Although reporters should proofread the final drafts of their own stories, proof-reading should also be done by someone less familiar and less likely to skim through the story and miss remaining slips.

Copy editing via symbols

The professional way to edit is by having a copy editor find errors, mark them and expect the reporter to make the changes indicated. The classic symbols shown here are used in copy editing and proofreading. Both reporters and editors should memorize and use these marks.

Symbol	Meaning
¶	- Indent for paragraph
The leading scorer	- Begin new paragraph
the Council's plan.	- No paragraph—run in
Credit goes to Jess. . .	
Byrnehurst School High	- Transpose
fifty	- Change to numerals
50	- Spell out
December 25	- Abbreviate
Dec. weather	- Don't abbreviate
united states of America	- Uppercase
The Teacher requires	- Lowercase
the Bla zers	- Remove space
seniorgirl	- Insert space
the copy editor stet	- Retain (means "let it stand")
The ruling an example is	- Insert word
example	- Insert
examnple	- Delete and close up
Mrs. Lane who	- Insert comma
the mens team	- Insert apostrophe
Who said that?	- Insert quotation marks
⊙ or ⊗	- Period
=	- Hyphen
⊢⊣	- Dash
]The title [	- Center
by Ellen Godie]	- Flush right
[Example	- Flush left
# or 30 -	- End sign
MORE - or - Add 1, etc.	- Mark hard copy of more than one page
Heading	- Put in boldface type

Name _____   Date _____

— EXERCISE 17A —
Revising edited copy

DIRECTIONS:

Rewrite the following copy, making marked changes. Because parts of this story need extensive revision, the editor or adviser has written notes in the margin to call attention to sections that need careful rewriting.

Byrnehurst girl crowned Junior Fair Queen

(Senior)

Jenny Day reigned as Byrnehurst county junior fair Queen during the last week of August after the annual competition on the Fair ground stage. *(winning)*

Among the twenty-five contestants were 5 girls from Byrnehurst. *(a)* They were Kerry Kerwin, Stephanie Quinn, finalist Emmie Finch, second runner-up Debbie Yates, and first runner-up Robin Sterling. About *Put names with higher ranks first* her win Jenny said, "The other girls all were so nice, so friendly, and so talented that i just feel lucky to have won."

Among her prizes for winning, Jenny received a one hundred dollar U.S. savings bond, a free out fit from the Fashion Place, and a dinner for four at Regency restaurant.

(#)

Revised version: Rewrite the story, making the indicated changes.

_____

_____

_____

_____

_____

_____

_____

_____

_____

_____

Name _____   Date _____

— EXERCISE 17B —
Practice copy editing

DIRECTIONS:

Use the correct proofreading symbols to mark all of the errors you find in the story below. It is preferable to mark the corrections in blue pencil or pen so that they will show up more easily. In fact, the term *blue-penciling* is sometimes used as a synonym for editing.

Check your newspaper's style manual or a dictionary if you have any questions about correctness.

Books to read, books for sale

A new book is one you havent read yet, said Del Hanford presidant of the Byrnehurst creative writting club which is sponsering a used book sale which will take place Wed. and Thurs., March 12 and 13.

The entire english department is participatting in the campain and books can be dropped of in any english classroom.

Think of them as being preread books that somebody else would like to read, to, Del said. He urgged studnets and members of the faculty to scour there shelfs home. The book colection begins Mon. February 17, and last through Fri. February 28.

Club members will sort the books acording to subject, science ficcion, fantasy, romance, mystrey, nonficciont, ect. All catagories accept so-called adult ficcion will be excepted.

Proceeds from the sale will go tward purchasing a new Oxford unabbridged dictionery for the library and perhaps new video types for the english dept.

#

Paragraphs in transition

In a well-written news story, one idea leads naturally and logically to the next. This doesn't just happen. It is the result of careful planning and writing. (See Figure 2-6.) You have already practiced two ways to achieve this goal.

1. By writing a lead that forecasts and directs how the story will unfold.

2. By having a definite timeline—working from the most current development and basing succeeding paragraphs on reverse chronology and/or relative importance, from most to least.

The third way to make stories read logically is to have clear transitions between paragraphs.

Linking paragraphs together

Professional reporters and writers do not lean upon formal transitional words and phrases such as *nevertheless, furthermore, on the other hand* and *however* to bridge sentences and paragraphs. Words like these tend to interrupt the flow of ideas and serve only to patch paragraphs together, not lead logically from one to the next.

Analyze stories in professional newspapers and magazines, and note the techniques these media writers use.

1. *Repeating of key words or their synonyms*

Examples:

| Paragraph 1: | "Blithe Spirit" by Noel Coward, this year's junior-senior *play,* debuts . . . |
| Paragraph 2: | The *play* centers on . . . |

* * *

| Paragraph 1: | The annual United Appeal *campaign* has set . . . |
| Paragraph 2: | According to Dean Scarlotti, student chairman, the *drive* will . . . |

* * *

Paragraph 1:	*Mr. Kevin Claypoole,* Byrnehurst *principal,* announced . . .
Paragraph 2:	*Mr. Claypoole* said, "The problem concerning us is . . ."
Paragraph 3:	In response to students' questions, the *principal* explained . . .

2. *Replacing or emphasizing key words with pronouns or pronoun forms*

| Paragraph 1: | *Two candidates* tied for the Council presidency . . . |
| Paragraph 2: | *They* will face each other . . . |

Paragraph 1:   Special classes to prepare *students* for taking . . .

Paragraph 2:   *Those* interested should sign up in . . .

● ● ●

Paragraph 1:   *Ms. Lee Klein,* head counselor said, "This will help prepare . . .

Paragraph 2:   *She* emphasized the importance of . . .

3. *Using phrases or clauses that tie paragraphs together*

Paragraph 1:   Changes in this year's exam schedule will provide . . .

Paragraph 2:   *In addition,* students should expect . . .

● ● ●

Paragraph 1:   The constitutional amendment will no longer allow . . .

Paragraph 2:   *Before the final vote,* protesters . . .

● ● ●

Paragraph 1:   Senior Travis Logan won two first-place awards . . .

Paragraph 2:   *Also singled out for honors* were . . .

Steps for organizing complex news stories

1. Rank major points in order with relation to news value and timeliness.

2. Judge whether a part of the story should run as sidebars. (Workshop 20)

3. Write a lead that encompasses the various elements and gives clear direction to the story, preparing the reader for what will come.

4. *Always* take up the elements in the same order as given in the lead when writing the rest of the story.

   Examples:

   First places in editorials, newswriting and photography, along with a superior in its overall newspaper category, were among honors won by *The Torch* at the Union District Journalism Contest, April 19.

   Winning firsts were Paula Pen, editorial; Bonnie Burke, newswriting; and Pete Cannon, photography.

5. *Always* list names, awards and other items in a specific order.

   - Most to less important, unusual or newsworthy—first prize first; then second, and so on.
   - Highest to lowest rankings—seniors first, then juniors, sophomores, freshmen.
   - With equal-ranked students, put names in alphabetical order.

6. Lists of names, such as casts of characters, team rosters, or students winning music awards, are often effective sidebars.

   Note: Be sure to include clear identification and choose a specific order.

   Example: **Power Puff football team members**

   Pink Panthers

   Seniors: Debbie Blake
   Sue Evans
   Midge Gordon
   Gail Howell, and so on

   Juniors: Joellen Able
   Della Brent

   Artful Dodgers

   Seniors: Liz Cummins . . .

7. Complete the story in inverted pyramid style. (See Figure 2-4 on page 155.)

Name _____   Date _____

— EXERCISE 18A —
Analyzing a complex news story

DIRECTIONS:

Read and analyze the story, "Holiday songs ring out," Example 2-18A, to answer the following questions.

1. Identify the 5 W's and an H in the lead paragraph of the main story.

   Who _____

   What _____

   When _____   Where _____

   Why _____

   How _____

2. With so much material, what probably dictated the reporter's choice of details in paragraphs two and three?

   _____

   _____

   _____

   _____

   _____

3. What two factors or qualities that make a story newsworthy probably dictated the writer's choice of the annual holiday concert as the first event to describe more fully? Explain why.

   A: (factor) _____

   _____

   (reason) _____

   _____

   B: (factor) _____

   _____

   (reason) _____

   _____

179

— EXERCISE 18A —
Analyzing a complex news story (cont'd)

4. How many of the final paragraphs could pass the cutoff test and be eliminated? _____
   Even though nonessential, why do they round out the story?

   _____

   _____

   _____

   _____

   _____

5. What are the two sidebars used with this story? Why is each more effective used this way than as a part of the story?

   (1) Sidebar _____

   Reason _____

   _____

   (2) Sidebar _____

   Reason _____

   _____

6. Identify the 5 W's and an H in the lead paragraph of "Music to go."

   Who _____

   What _____

   When _____   Where _____

   Why _____

   How _____

— EXAMPLE 2-18A —
Holiday songs ring out as annual concerts near

Rehearsals of "Here Comes Santa Claus" echo through the Byrnehurst music wing as vocal and instrumental groups prepare for a busy schedule of holiday programs.

In addition to the annual combined holiday concerts, Blazer musicians will present more than 25 special performances for local groups and organizations.

The concert choir, BeSharp vocal ensemble, Blazer jazz band, orchestra and chamber groups will perform throughout the community, and the band will take part in the annual Welcome Santa parade Saturday, Nov. 29, according to music department chairman, Mr. Kent Frazier.

Mr. Frazier said the combined concerts on the evening of Dec. 18 and during school Dec. 20 will feature several new twists, but details remain secret.

"Surprises are the best part of the holidays, aren't they?" he said. "I don't want to spoil the fun." But he added that he "wouldn't dream" of cutting out favorites like "White Christmas" and the traditional carol sing.

In addition to the combined concerts, a highlight of the holiday season for the choir is the opportunity to sing in the Choral Gala Dec. 21 at Byrnehurst civic auditorium.

The annual concert includes individual selections by each participating choir: the Gospel Singers, the citywide Symphonic Choir, Unified Church Chorus and the Byrnehurst High School Choir.

"Then we'll all join for the grand finale, 'The Hallelujah Chorus' from *The Messiah*," said Mrs. Madeline Jones, Blazer choir director. "It will be a thrill for our kids to sing in a choir that big . . . and a thrill to listen to, as well."

According to Mrs. Jones, the BeSharp vocal ensemble is working up all new routines for this year's holiday engagements. The 16-member group sings, choreographs and stages its songs—and livens its act with costumed, novelty numbers.

"We've had so many bids for the holiday season, we had to turn some down because of scheduling conflicts," Mrs. Jones said.

The instrumental department faces a busy schedule, as well. Also director of Byrnehurst's bands, Mr. Frazier said, "We're ready for the holidays, if they're ready for us."

He added, "Seriously, the jazz band has been practicing some swinging arrangements of holiday standards, while the chamber ensemble is working up some lovely versions of early classics and well-loved tunes like 'Greensleeves' and 'Amazing Grace.'"

The jazz band will play for the Holiday Hop, Dec. 13, in the cafeteria, and both groups have numerous other engagements during the season.

At the annual Welcome Santa parade, the Byrnehurst band will have its usual place of honor, right before Mr. Claus himself, coming to town in his vehicle of choice.

"Last year, it was a fire truck. Who knows what it will be this year?" Mr. Frazier said. "But you can be sure, the band will be there, leading him past the bandstand to the tune of 'Here Comes Santa Claus.'"

Byrnehurst choir and band members also plan to go caroling and present special programs to those in nursing homes during the holiday season.

According to both Mrs. Jones and Mr. Frazier, this is Byrnehurst musicians' busiest time of year.

"We welcome the chance to let our kids show the community their talents and do what they love," Mr. Frazier said.

— EXAMPLE 2-18A —
Holiday songs ring out as annual concerts near (cont'd)

Sidebar:

Holiday Concert Schedule

Nov. 29	Welcome Santa Parade	Band
Dec. 4	Lions Club luncheon	BeSharp
Dec. 5	Citywide PTA dinner	Chamber

. . . et cetera

Sidebar:

Music to go

Although most holiday dates are filled, Byrnehurst musical groups accept engagements throughout the school year to perform at various functions, according to music department head, Mr. Kent Frazier.

Sponsoring groups generally offer an honorarium or donation, which goes toward expenses and the purchase of music and equipment not included in the board of education budget.

The Byrnehurst groups do not perform for organizations that seek to profit from their appearances.

Name _____   Date _____

— EXERCISE 18B —
Analyzing Transitions and Quotes

DIRECTIONS:

Analyze the first fifteen paragraphs of Example 2-18A, "Holiday songs ring out as annual concerts near."

Part A. Fill out the chart below, listing the following:

   (1) The linking word or words joining it to the preceding paragraph. (For the first paragraph, this does not apply.)

   (2) The type of transition (Workshop 18)

	Linking words	Words relating to previous paragraph	Type of transition
1.			
2.			
3.			
4.			
5.			
6.			
7.			
8.			
9.			
10.			
11.			
12.			
13.			
14.			
15.			

Part B. List the kinds of paragraphs: direct quote, indirect quote, partial quote or expository.

1. _____	6. _____	11. _____
2. _____	7. _____	12. _____
3. _____	8. _____	13. _____
4. _____	9. _____	14. _____
5. _____	10. _____	15. _____

Name _____   Date _____

— EXERCISE 18C —
Analyzing Transitions and Quotes

DIRECTIONS:

Analyze the first fifteen paragraphs of Example 2-18B, "Seniors with perfect attendance…" by T. J. Ward, published in *Sound to Sea.*

Part A. Fill out the chart below, listing the following:

(1) The linking word or words joining it to the preceding paragraph. (For the first paragraph, this does not apply.)

(2) The type of transition

Linking words	Words relating to previous paragraph	Type of transition
1. _____	_____	_____
2. _____	_____	_____
3. _____	_____	_____
4. _____	_____	_____
5. _____	_____	_____
6. _____	_____	_____
7. _____	_____	_____
8. _____	_____	_____
9. _____	_____	_____
10. _____	_____	_____
11. _____	_____	_____
12. _____	_____	_____
13. _____	_____	_____
14. _____	_____	_____
15. _____	_____	_____

Part B. List the kinds of paragraphs: direct quote, indirect quote, partial quote or expository.

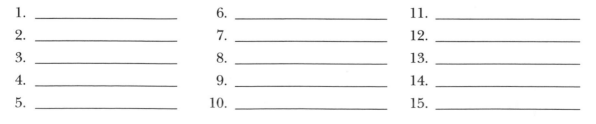

1. _____   6. _____   11. _____
2. _____   7. _____   12. _____
3. _____   8. _____   13. _____
4. _____   9. _____   14. _____
5. _____   10. _____   15. _____

6 ———— **N** ———— **E** ———— **W** ———— **S**   **Manteo High School**
Thursday, Feb. 29, 1996

Seniors with perfect attendance last semester earn off-campus lunch privileges

Pilot program enacted to test plan for next year.

By T.J. Ward
Copy Editor

A war was officially won on Friday, Feb. 8 when assistant principal Carmen Melito briefed 62 seniors on their emancipation for the lunch hour. After several years of petitioning, '96 seniors with perfect attendance, for either of the nine-week periods in the fall semester, received cards granting them off-campus lunch.

The program, instituted on the day of announcement, parallels the perfect attendance incentive written into the new attendance policy which gives juniors opportunity to earn off-campus lunch for next semester. Principal Everette Walterhouse grandfathered the program, making the incentive retroactive in order to include this year's seniors.

"I took the liberty to do that and start a trial program," said Walterhouse. "It is something students have wanted for a long time and I think it is time to give it to them."

Passes for off-campus lunch last through the third nine-week grading period and were based on attendance of either the first or second nine weeks of the fall semester.

"I think what were looking for is to be fair to everyone," said Melito. "It was just a natural to include the seniors for the last nine weeks and then we thought of the first nine weeks."

The decision to include seniors stemmed from what Walterhouse called a "trust factor" as well as the administration's desire to be fair.

"We expect our students to act like adults so we need to give them some of these choices and responsibilities," said Walterhouse. "I believe in them and that they can handle that responsibility."

Time between decision and execution of the pilot program remained short, as only a day after a final decision, made without approval from the school board, the announcement went out to teachers and seniors were briefed on the regulations of the privilege.

"We put it together as fast as we could in order to get it going," said Walterhouse.

Taking advantage of his freedom, Matt Featherstone buys lunch at McDonald's. He is one of 62 seniors to test off-campus lunch. *(Photo by Chris Puma)*

"We went out on a limb for this. We don't have approval from the school board," Melito told seniors at the meeting. "We have the approval of the superintendent but this is a pilot program."

Students that currently hold the privilege serve as a prototype to illustrate that the program will work. Both Walterhouse and Melito expressed confidence about the pilot and the example seniors will set for future classes.

"I don't foresee any real problems," said Melito. "Letting students off campus involves some dangers, maybe accidents,

Summary of off-campus lunch policy

Seniors have the opportunity to earn off-campus lunch by maintaining perfect attendance for this nine-week grading period. One tardy following lunch will cause a one-week suspension of the privilege. After the second tardy that student's off campus pass will be revoked. The administration initiated this program to improve attendance.

maybe some students deciding not to come back. But I think the students who have this now know it's a pilot program and that the whole school is watching them. I think this will prove to the school board that this will work with our students."

While administrators expect the incentive program to improve attendance they also emphasized the educational value of allowing seniors off campus for lunch. By not requiring parental consent for students to leave campus, the administration has left the decision up to the students.

"It's our job to teach students how to function in the outside world. Making decisions is part of that," said Melito. "All of the students involved are over 16. We felt that asking the parents would be counterproductive to the learning experience."

The institution of the program has left seniors with an appreciation for the administration.

"I think it's great for seniors," said Nichole Reams. "It's a big step for Mr. Walterhouse to go out on a limb for us like this without the school board. I've enjoyed going off campus and getting a break."

While seniors are happy with the new privilege some want a few changes in the program.

"I like it," said Brandy Lawrentz. "Sometimes I just go to someone's house and eat lunch. It's good just to get away from school. I think they should try opening it to all seniors and only have two lunches. It would make it easier and we'd have more time."

The general feeling of the program is positive. "I don't see this as creating any difficulties," said Walterhouse. "This is a positive thing, it is an opportunity."

Example 2-18B. "Seniors with perfect attendance last semester earn off-campus lunch privileges," by T. J. Ward, *Sound to Sea,* Manteo H.S., Manteo, NC.

The whens, hows, and whys of using quotes

Almost all of the facts and information a reporter uses in a typical news story come from interviews—and, of course, interviews are also the reporter's main source of quotes. Other sources include speeches, an author's writings and press releases.

Much of a story's factual data comes from someone's saying, "We've set Friday and Saturday, March ninth and tenth as the play's dates," yet it's unlikely a paper would carry such a quote. As a reporter, the choice is yours. You can base your decisions on the following considerations.

1. Too much of a good thing is deadly. A string of factual statements and exposition, or paragraph after paragraph of fully quoted statements has a sameness that risks boring the reader.

   Too many quotes make readers ask, "What are the facts of this story?" Too much straight exposition makes them ask, "Who's the authority for this? What does *that person* say?"

   A major or complex story needs more than one quoted source.

2. Information that contains facts (who, what, when, where, how or specific whys) can run as straight prose. You also do not need to quote fully supported details or provable data.

3. Use a variety of direct, indirect and partial quotes.

4. Make sure the speaker of all quotations is properly identified, preferably with "said" as the attribution of direct quotes.

5. Many quotations suit either the direct or indirect form.

Direct:	"I expect a better turnout this year than last," the director said.
Indirect:	The director said she expects a better turnout this year than last.

6. Use quotations to express a speaker's opinion. Beware of using *thinks* or *believes* in place of *says*, since you can't be sure what the speaker is truly thinking.

Poor:	The lawyer thinks the jury will find his client not guilty. (Is this true or hype or wishful thinking?)
Better:	The lawyer said, "I think the jury will find my client not guilty."
-or-	The lawyer said she thinks the jury will find her client not guilty.

7. Use direct quotations to give the reader a sense of the speaker's unique point of view, personality or manner of speaking.

Example:	The speaker said, "Too often kids get into trouble by losing their tempers without using their heads."

8. Use partial quotes to make colorful or memorable words stand out. But be careful: overuse makes the writing seem jumpy and straining for cuteness.

Example:	Mr. Frazier said there'll be plenty of "toe-tappin', finger-snappin'" rhythm in store when the jazz band plays the blues.

9. When writing direct quotations, do not rephrase the speaker's statements nor rewrite to correct grammatical errors. However, do not use abnormal spellings, such as "gunna" or "coulda," in an attempt to reproduce someone's speech pattern.

   In a school newspaper, you may wish to use partial quotes instead of full ones to avoid this problem.

   An ellipsis—three dots (. . .)—showing an omission may sometimes be used, but care must be taken not to overuse it.

Name _____   Date _____

— EXERCISE 19A —
Analyzing Transitions and Quotes

DIRECTIONS:

Clip a straight news story of at least ten paragraphs from your local newspaper or a national daily such as *USA Today*. Glue or otherwise affix it to this exercise, indicating its source and date of publication.

Source of clipping: _____   **Date** _____

Part A. Analyze the first seven to ten paragraphs, and fill out the chart below, listing the following:

(1) The linking word or words joining it to the preceding paragraph. (For the first paragraph, this does not apply.)

(2) The type of transition

	Linking words	Words relating to previous paragraph	Type of transition
1.	_____	_____	_____
2.	_____	_____	_____
3.	_____	_____	_____
4.	_____	_____	_____
5.	_____	_____	_____
6.	_____	_____	_____
7.	_____	_____	_____
8.	_____	_____	_____
9.	_____	_____	_____
10.	_____	_____	_____

Part B. List the kinds of paragraphs: direct quote, indirect quote, partial quote or expository.

1.	_____	6.	_____
2.	_____	7.	_____
3.	_____	8.	_____
4.	_____	9.	_____
5.	_____	10.	_____

— EXERCISE 19A —

Analyzing Transitions and Quotes (cont'd)

Part C. Answer the following questions concerning the reporter's use of quotations.

1. Does the story quote more than one source of information? _____ List the sources of direct, indirect and partial quotes used in the article. Include their names and full identification.

   _____

   _____

   _____

   _____

   _____

   _____

2. Does the story strike an effective balance between types of quotes? _____ Between quotes and exposition? _____ Why or why not? _____

   _____

3. Do the quotes help the reader understand the story better or provide special insight? _____ Why or why not? _____

   _____

4. Based on your answers to the foregoing questions and the guidelines given in Workshop 19, write a paragraph analyzing the strengths and weaknesses of the reporter's use of quotations in the story.

   _____

   _____

   _____

   _____

   _____

   _____

   _____

   _____

   _____

   _____

Choosing the sidebar route

A sidebar is a short, related story or graphic, that fills in details of a complex story or in-depth report—and adds visual interest and punch to a page.

For the reader, sidebars provide valuable information and insight in easier-to-grasp form than if buried within a longer story. Sidebars tend to draw readers' attention and, after they have read the sidebar, interest them in the rest.

Types of material suitable for sidebars

- Brief, related stories
- Lists: names, schedules, requirements, etc.
- Quotes or excerpts
- Glossaries of unfamiliar words
- Quickie quizzes and checklists
- Illustrative anecdotes
- Fact boxes, step-by-step guides
- Helpful background data
- Sources for further information
- Infographs: numerical data, such as survey and test results, presented as computer-generated charts and diagrams that permit easier comprehension and add eye appeal to pages

Pull quotes

Another way to liven your pages and awaken readers' interest in a story is the use of pull quotes.

The reporter or editor "pulls" a short, catchy and intriguing quote from the story to print in its midst, such as, "Surprises are the best part of the holidays, aren't they?"

Pull quotes help arouse readers' curiosity and serve as art elements that break up long, gray stretches of type. With direct quotations, include the speaker's identification.

When using pull quotes, develop a special format to use throughout the year but, like any eye-attracting element, be careful not to overuse with every story on every page. (See "Newspaper layouts: Setting attractive standards" in Unit 3.)

A suggested pull quote to use with a major story may be submitted by the reporter as part of each story assignment's tracking form.

Variations on the lead

The summary lead does the best job as the opening paragraph of most straight news, yet some stories seem to cry out for a lead to call attention to a worthwhile story that readers might avoid if the lead summarizes it. It may seem too technical, too far removed from anything that affects the reader personally.

How much interest could a reporter arouse with a lead such as this?

> *Example:*   Health officials have warned doctors to watch for bites from the small hobo spider, a Pacific Northwest arachnid recently placed on the venomous insect list.

With a summary lead, the bare facts have little effect, but, Doug Levy, a reporter from *USA Today*, began the story like this: "Beware the hobo spider." (See Example 2-21A.)

Carrying this lead, the story is almost certain to attract readers' attention.

Variations on the traditional lead are also effective on human interest stories, features and news features.

> *Here is another example:*   Prepare yourself for the ultimate good news story: Most people say they are happy. (From *USA Today* [See Example 2-21B].)

Introducing the nutgraph

Because this type of variation on the lead fails to answer the majority of the 5W's and an H, this essential information must come within the first few paragraphs of the story. It's called a *nutgraph* because it's a paragraph that gives the needed information "in a nutshell." You might also think of it as the essential kernel or "nut" planted within the story itself. Nutgraphs are required elements with this type of lead.

In the "good news story," the third paragraph supplies the nutgraph: "This assessment appears in *Psychological Science,* a journal of the American Psychological Society." Could anyone resist reading the whole story, which might serve as the basis for a survey and feature for your high school paper?

Variations on leads may do any of the following:

1. **Generalize** - Draw a general conclusion based on given data, as the "good news" story does.

2. **Personalize** - Choose one individual's experience, and let it stand for similar situations that others also face.

   > *Example:*   Jane Jeffreys knows what it means to have her hopes dashed by the "numbers game" of academic testing.

   Although others may have suffered the same type of disappointment, readers find it easier to share one person's feelings than to sympathize with an anonymous group.

   A word of caution: Avoid naming a student if the story concerns a potentially embarrassing revelation.

3. **Question** - This method is dangerously tempting to overuse. Use it with no more than one story per issue, if that often.

Hobo spider now on venomous list

By Doug Levy
USA TODAY

Beware the hobo spider.

The little arachnid, found in the Pacific Northwest, has been placed on the venomous spider list, health officials said Thursday.

It joins the black widow and the brown recluse in the poisonous category. Experts at the Centers for Disease Control and Prevention are telling doctors to watch for possible bites.

The hobo is about ¼- to ½-inch long, brown with gray markings. Its bite, which until now had been blamed on the brown recluse, is usually painless but can cause headaches, nausea and blurry vision.

"It's not unheard of to have a fatal reaction, but it's not the most common," says epidemiologist Michael Heumann of the Oregon Health Division in Portland. "In most people, it will cause a local reaction. In some people, the symptoms last for months." Examples:

► A Spokane, Wash., woman died from internal bleeding two months after being bitten.

► A 10-year-old boy in Portland, Ore., was bitten on the leg while sleeping and found his entire leg swollen a week later.

► A woman in Bingham County, Idaho, who was bitten on the ankle developed a deep black ulcer at the bite site. It left her unable to work.

Hobo spiders build funnel-shaped webs in dark, moist areas such as wood piles and crawl spaces. They bite when provoked. CDC's advice: Cover your skin when in areas they're likely to live.

Studies reveal a happy America

By Karen S. Peterson
USA TODAY

Prepare yourself for the ultimate good news story: Most people say they are happy.

That includes most blacks and whites, men and women, rich and poor (except the very poor), the unemployed, the disabled and the elderly, says a review of research.

This upbeat assessment appears in *Psychological Science*, a journal of the American Psychological Society.

In every national survey, most Americans report positively about what experts call "subjective well-being" — their level of happiness — writes psychologist Ed Diener, University of Illinois, Champaign.

But nobody seems to know it, Diener says, including psychology majors in college. His own study found 79% incorrectly think poor blacks are mostly unhappy; 95%, unemployed men; 50%, the elderly.

One longitudinal study of the years 1946 to 1992 found that Americans consistently rate their life satisfaction at least a 7 on a scale of 1 to 10. Studies show people tend to think positive thoughts more often than negative ones and are more likely to recall positive events.

A 1991 study found "that all socioeconomic groups, and both whites and African Americans, scored well above the neutral point of life satisfaction," Diener finds.

Most Americans are amazed that the disabled are happy, he says. A 1995 study found 93% of quadriplegics are happy to be alive; 84% call their quality of life average or above.

The findings don't mean people are continuously elated, Diener says; rather, they are "resilient" and become happy again after adversity.

His earlier research shows that people with close relationships and religious faith and who are absorbed at work and pursue achievable goals are happier than those who do not.

Researcher and psychologist David Myers of Hope College, Holland, Mich., notes some people may "put on a good face" when interviewed. But even if their happiness self-reports are exaggerated by "say, 20%," Diener's results are still valid, Myers says.

Self-reports also are often backed up by family and friends, Myers says. Diener's work is "a stunning finding, given all that has been written by mental-health workers, who spend their hours with miserable people" and make generalizations from what they hear.

Example 2-21A. "Hobo spider now on venomous list," by Doug Levy, *USA Today.*
Example 2-21B. "Studies reveal a happy America," by Karen S. Peterson, *USA Today.*

Example : What do bananas, romance novels, 24 new U.S. citizens and a 113-year-old Portuguese fishing vessel have in common?

They were all part of Philadelphia's first Marine Day . . .

The Philadelphia Inquirer

4. **Intrigue, create suspense** - Some leads "tease" the reader to read on.

Example: An off-duty police officer grabbed his shoes, radio, and not much else before dashing to the rescue of a 7-year-old boy trapped in a sinking car.

The Blade, Toledo, OH

5. **Offer Factoids** - A conclusion such as this might come from a reported study.

Example: Stopping smoking and staying on a diet are two daunting challenges the average American faces in achieving good health.

6. **Give samples, listings** - The following lead, a preview of a children's weekday television show, gives an example of why a mother has a love-hate relationship with some wild but too familiar creatures.

Example: The deer walk right up on Linda Kratt's deck and eat the flowers she has carefully planted in pots.

The Philadelphia Inquirer

Another lead for this type of story might be the listing.

Example: A mother's love-hate relationship with tame deer, an elephant that paints pictures, and a monkey that likes to take photos . . .

7. **Focus on the reader**

Example: Beware the hobo spider.

A word of warning: Used sparingly, variations on the summary lead can lift an ordinary story into an extraordinary one. It's overuse, however, can trivialize the news and make it seem that the paper and its reporters are straining too hard to be clever, cute and entertaining. The response then becomes: Get to the point. Just report the news, please!

Remember, the majority of front page stories of professional papers sampled had summary leads. And, in your attempts to personalize stories, remember that the illustration given should be factual and true, not imaginary. A reporter lost a Pulitzer prize, her reputation and her position with the revelation that she had made up the central figure in her award-winning story.

Variation or summary—making your decision

Before settling on a variation of the summary lead, a reporter should have the basic 5 W's and an H of the story fixed in mind. It also helps to sketch out a possible summary lead, either on paper or as a mental note. This is not wasted effort, for it helps you focus on the essence of the story and delineates the factors that need to go in a nutgraph.

To avoid overuse of this type of lead, the paper might well adopt a policy of having reporters first discuss this option with the page editor whenever the variant lead seems an attractive possibility. This step can ensure that certain variations, such as beginning stories with a question, do not become dulled by repetition.

Name _____   Date _____

— EXERCISE 21A —
Home paper improvement project

I. Variations on the lead

DIRECTIONS:

From a past issue of your paper or an exchange paper, choose a story that you can improve by using one of the variations on the traditional summary lead. If it is not present in the story as published, explain what additional information you would need to gather to write this type of lead and how you would obtain it.

    If it is contained in the story, name the paragraph where it is found. Attach a copy of the story and indicate its source.

1. Story headline _____

   Source _____   Date _____   Page _____

2. Answer one of the following: (a) If the information is provided by the published story, state which paragraph contains it. (b) If not, explain what additional information you need and how you'd obtain it.

   _____

   _____

   _____

   _____

3. Assuming you have the needed information, either from the published story or additional research, rewrite the first paragraphs with a variation on the summary lead and continuing up to and including the nutgraph.

   _____

   _____

   _____

   _____

   _____

   _____

   _____

   _____

   _____

— EXERCISE 21A —
Home paper improvement project (cont'd)

II. Adding sidebars

DIRECTIONS:

From a past issue of your paper or an exchange paper, choose a story that would benefit from a sidebar or sidebars.

Attach a copy of the story and indicate its source.

1. Story headline _____

    Source _____ Date _____ Page _____

2. List and describe the type or types of sidebars that you would add.

    (a) _____

    (b) _____

    (c) _____

3. Answer one of the following: (a) If the information is provided by the published story, briefly describe it and indicate which paragraph(s) contains it. (b) If not, explain what additional information you need and how you'd obtain it.

    _____
    _____
    _____
    _____
    _____
    _____
    _____
    _____
    _____
    _____
    _____
    _____
    _____

Wheeling In The Cameras

by **Stephanie Huang**
and **Christina Han**

The Chinese Tianjin TV Station filmed an eight part docudrama titled *American Passport and Chinese Heart* on the MV campus April 10-14. The script is about 21-year old MV alumnus Patrick Chang, who at age thirteen was injured in a diving accident and was paralyzed from the chest down.

"Everyone has a handicap," says Chang's father. "For some it may be a language barrier, for others, a physical one. But Patrick has always shown a positive attitude. Even though the accident should never have happened, he has made the best of his situation."

Chang graduated from MV in three years, completing a college preparatory program and receiving a Presidential Academic Fitness Award. He is the only paraplegic who has attended MV. At nineteen, Chang completed his undergraduate program in Economics with distinction and entered Stanford's Ph.D. program. In addition, he donated $200,000 on his eighteenth birthday to establish a scholarship foundation in his grandfather's hometown, Beilun, Nongbo, China.

Chang's sister, Michelle, co-authored the script. Michelle and Patrick graduated together from MV in June 1990. Her goal for the series is to simply "do my brother justice. He has a lot of dedication, strength, and inspiration. I hope this can accurately show his spirit." Michelle would like to "thank the MV students for being so well behaved and the staff, teachers, and many actors and actresses for their contributions."

At a press conference April 13, the production manager, on behalf of Tianjin TV, presented MV with a traditional Chinese Opera mask that will be on display in the MV office. Upon acceptance of the gift, Assistant Principal Joanne Laird said, "We are now part of a big family. We will hang this gift in the main office so that it will be the first thing people see when they come to MV."

continued on pg. 20

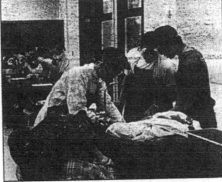

The film crew records student activities, such as Chemistry students working on their labs, for *American Passport and Chinese Heart.*

Photo by John Kaczorowski

Analyzing a news story

Carefully read examples 2-21C through 2-21G to see how they handle essential elements of the news story such as:

1. Lead—summary or variation
2. The 5 W's and an H
3. Inverted pyramid style
4. Varying quotations/exposition
5. Transitions
6. Multiple primary sources
7. Sidebars

TV Station Documents Life Of Paraplegic MV Alumnus

cont. from page 1

In addition to the twenty original cast members, some MV staff and students with speaking roles in the film are Drama Teacher Marjorie Forester as Patrick's girlfriend; Chemistry Teacher Mike Ivanitsky as himself; Assistant Principal Joanne Laird as herself; junior Tony Kinkela as Lucas, a paraplegic; junior Neel Murarka as Chris, a teen tutored by Patrick; and Senior Eugene Hong as Jeffery, Patrick's younger brother. "They gave me 24 hours to draw up a list of students, so I just listed a few that I know have participated in our drama department or have been in front of cameras," said Laird. Homan Igehy, a friend of Chang's since the eighth grade, also took time off from Stanford where he is pursuing a Ph.D. in Computer Science to help.

American Passport and Chinese Heart will be released in June. "I hope that through this TV series, relations between China and the U.S. will be strengthened," said Michelle. "We'll have a screening night and sell tickets," suggested Laird.

Example 2-21C. "Wheeling in the cameras," by Stephanie Huang and Christina Han, *El Estoque*, Monta Vista H.S., Cupertino, CA.

Multimedia class gives students creative outlet

When most students are still hitting their snooze buttons, a group of 13 students is at school, hitting computer keys in a new multimedia class.

The class is a pilot program taught in the zero period by Technology Coordinator Rick Kidwell and Spanish Teacher Lisa Snook.

Multimedia is a general description for computer programs that combine elements such as text, graphics, video and sounds into presentations called stacks.

"It teaches how to animate on computers and how to take pictures(using a digital camera), and change them around to show what you see.

"You can do what you want so it's very creative and unique, it's a form of expression," Senior Ray Abraham said.

By the end of the year, the class will be editing video, and making such things as computerized slide shows and overhead transparencies.

"There are advantages to using multimedia; you can do graphs and animation to show what you learned about your subject.

"For instance you can see how it changes with time, and it's something different, so it isn't boring, the way a regular paper sometimes is," Abraham said.

As part of the class work, the students will offer their talents to help teachers put together multimedia presentations.

This type of work will require students to work together and have a basic knowledge of the applications.

"I like the team orientation, people getting together with technology as a group to form ideas and improve upon each others' efforts."

Senior Bart Kelsey said.

Although the teachers taught some basics on computers, in a typical class they only get involved when someone has a problem.

"The teachers aren't there to teach, they are there to guide, you do most of the work, the teachers just help you along with that," Abraham said.

Because multimedia applications can play sounds and videos, they must be used on computers with a lot of RAM (memory), which are expensive.

The computers are part of a technology recommendation. A group of teachers was involved in the decision to form a basic lab.

"What we were really headed towards was allowing other classes to work using Hypercard. Mr. Bell has expressed interest in using the lab for his history classes," Kidwell said.

The classroom is now equipped with six computers, a color scanner and a printer. By the end of the year there will be 19 computers, and by the beginning of next year, there will be 30.

This "starter set", which will cost about $45,000, is designed for use by any class that wants to use the facility.

"We knew with our limited funds we couldn't buy unlimited supplies, but we've exceeded our expectations in implementation," Kidwell said.

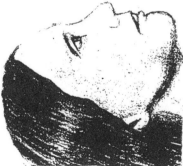

Example 2-21D. "Multimedia class gives students creative outlet," (*Blue & Gold*), Findlay H.S., Findlay, OH.

SMOKING AREA'S FUTURE CLOUDED AGAIN

By SOO MI PARK

The PHS smoking area has always been controversial, having been moved, abolished, and reestablished several times. Now, for two reasons, another campaign to close it down seems on the verge of success:

■ Although the Board of Education approved the area provided users kept it clean, there have been complaints about dirty conditions.

■ And there are complaints that the school, which teaches ninth- and tenth-graders that smoking is harmful and often fatal, isn't practicing what it preaches by permitting smoking.

Beyond catering to smokers, the smoking area has helped ease another longtime problem: smoking in the bathrooms. The administration notes that smoking in bathrooms was bad before the smoking area was opened; since then, it has decreased significantly.

Nonetheless, the Student Senate debated the smoking area question for two weeks. At its second meeting, it overwhelming adopted a resolution to close the smoking area at all times, and presented it to the Administration. The Administration recommended that the smoking area be closed during school hours, 7:30 a.m. to 4 p.m., since it would be impossible to post guards 24 hours a day to prevent smoking.

Principal Richard Zanella presented the proposal to the Superintendent, who in turn presented it to the Board of Education. The issue is planned to be discussed at the board meeting January 3.

If the board adopts the resolution, Zanella said that it will take "vigilance on our part" to enforce the school-hours ban. He said he would recommend using more aides and rearranging work schedules to help patrol more efficiently.

Also, penalties will be enforced if a student is caught smoking. On the first offense, parents are notified and a conference is held with the student, his or her parents, and the vice principal. The student will also receive one day of in-school suspension.

On the second offense, the student cannot return to school until a parent conference is held and the student will be subject to a two day in-school suspension and a mandatory meeting with the student assistance coordinator.

On the third offense, there is a parent conference and a five day out-of-school suspension. This last suspension may be avoided if the student enrolls in a smoke cessation program with his or her own money.

Some students, of course, oppose the closing of the smoking area.

"I don't think the smoking section should be closed down, because I will just smoke even more in the bathrooms no matter how much 'security' the school gets to try to stop me and my friends," said one student.

Many students fear increased bathroom smoking. "If the smoking section stays closed, then smokers will just resort to empty stairwells and bathrooms," said senior Bernadette So. "I think one of the only solutions to this problem is to put the smoking area somewhere else, where not many people occupy that space.

"Where the smoking section is now is an inconvenience to people who drive to school, and if smokers have to have a section, it should not inconvenience non-smokers," So said.

No one knows what the board will decide. But whatever the decision, it will be another in a long list of changes in the status of the PHS smoking area.

Example 2-21E. "Smoling Area's Future Clouded Again" by Soo Mi Park, *The Forum Press*, Paramus H.S., Paramus, NJ.

Detroit Pistons gaurd Allan Houston speaks to eighth grade students on the importance of a good education.

Piston Star Visits MJHS
Allan Houston urges students to excel

by Nancy Flemming

Detroit Pistons guard Allan Houston visited MJHS on Thursday, March 9 as a part of the Detroit Pistons Stay in School program, which is sponsored by First of America bank and Chrysler.

He stressed the importance of getting a good education, and setting goals for yourself. "You can't let anyone distract you from what your goals are," Houston explained.

The Stay in School program is an attendance based initiative open to sixth, seventh, and eighth graders attending public school in nine counties across southeastern Michigan. The program emphasizes the three "A's": attendance, attitude, and achievement.

The Pistons contacted Mrs. Weeks, eighth grade principal, and wanted to send him here. "The Pistons then sent Allan Houston here as a part of the Stay in School program," Mrs. Weeks stated.

For the most part, the students who attended the assembly treated Houston with respect. At first, they were a little shy in asking questions, but once the ball got rolling, they kept it rolling.

Some students were a little disappointed. For instance, Janell Comment explained,"It was okay, but I think we should have gotten to talk to him more, and should have gotten to meet him in person."

Houston, a 1993 graduate of the University of Tennessee, stated, "It's very important that students have someone that they're familiar with coming in. It has to be someone they can identify with or else it goes in one ear and out the other. Tomorrow I'll be gone, but hopefully they'll remember my message."

Gerry J. Smith, Community Bank President of First of America bank in Monroe commented, "Basically, we support education because these kids will be our employees someday and our customers someday."

Houston, who maintained a 2.9 GPA throughout high school, told the students that his biggest influences growing up were his father, who coached him in high school and college, and Muhammad Ali.

Example 2-21F. "Piston Star Visits MJHS," by Nancy Flemming, *The Declaration,* Monroe Junior High, Monroe, MI.

Sitting in a school bus, Carol Bratton, bus driver, waits for students to board so she can complete her route. Mrs. Bratton is one of the 80 contracted bus drivers within the Lodi Unified School District who may be subjected to random drug tests.

photo by Thao Ha

Drug tests weed out bus drivers

by Rebecca Merkel

No longer will "loaded" bus drivers be picking up loads of students in the Lodi Unified School District.

According to Jay Zimmerman, transportation director, within two months, 50 percent of LUSD employees sporting a commercial driver's license will be randomly tested for drug use. Another 25 percent of the 80 contracted LUSD bus drivers will be tested for alcohol use.

Mr. Zimmerman said drug and alcohol testing was made into a federal regulation about five years ago for employees operating in safety sensitive areas, but wasn't approved until after four years of negotiations.

"This is the final step of this law," said Mr. Zimmerman. "We're just conforming to federal regulations."

However, Mr. Zimmerman thinks that the testing, which will be done by private companies, is a good idea.

"It's pretty important to be drug and alcohol free. I totally support it, and most of the drivers do too," explained Mr. Zimmerman.

Though there has only been a minimal occurrence of drugs and alcohol among LUSD bus drivers, Elliott Grauman, classified personnel director, is in favor of the policy that was approved April 4.

"Zero tolerance is the approach we have toward students, and I think employees ought to set the examples for students," said Mr. Grauman, who would ideally like to see all LUSD employees tested.

Currently, many different testing is exercised. These tests include pre-employment, post-accident, reasonable suspicion, and return to duty. Mr. Grauman believes that only two employees left because of suspicious circumstances last year.

However, the new testing procedure is expected to cost more than some possible workers. According to Mr. Grauman, the projection of costs for drug and alcohol testing will be about $10,000 annually. Also, costs could fluctuate because of follow-up tests and other unusual circumstances.

At this point, negotiations with the California State Employee's Association over the effects of the policy have still not been worked out. Effects of the policy include details such as what action would be taken if an employee tests positive for drug or alcohol use.

Mary Parkins, bus driver and job steward for the union, thinks the policy is sound as long as drivers are protected.

"I just want to make sure that the drivers are protected and that the rules and regulations are followed to the letter," said Mrs. Parkins, who fears manipulation of the tests at the administrative level. "I don't want anybody to get screwed."

Mrs. Parkins, who has been driving buses for about 15 years, believes that after a driver has been tested they should be allowed to see a copy of the results.

Mrs. Parkins thinks this is important because of a situation that occurred previously where a driver, who was returning to duty, ate a poppyseed muffin before her drug test. Because of the opiate in the poppyseed muffin, her test results were positive. She wouldn't have known what had happened if she wasn't able to see a copy of the readout.

But what would make Mrs. Parkins even more comfortable with the testing policy is a visual explanation of the process.

"I'd like to see the whole process that they go through," said Mrs. Parkins. "I would feel more comfortable because I've seen some really hairy things go down."

Overall, Mrs. Parkins thinks the testing should be done.

"I'm a real advocate of drug testing. We have an important job," said Mrs. Parkins, who doesn't think the new policy will eliminate any drivers.

Junior Jamaal Jefferson shares Mrs. Parkins belief about the policy being a good idea.

"It's for a good purpose, but if there are complaints about invasion of privacy I can understand that also," said Jefferson.

However, Jefferson is glad to see the district taking action against bus drivers under the influence.

"We can't have drunk people driving the students of the district," said Jefferson. "If there's a problem, the district shouldn't hesitate to take action."

Example 2-21G. "Drug tests weed out bus drivers," by Rebecca Merkel, *Tokay Press,* Tokay H.S., Lodi, CA.

Name _____   Date _____

— EXERCISE 21B —
Writing a news analysis

DIRECTIONS:

The following questions are tools for analyzing others' newswriting and your own. Use one of the examples given or another story, assigned by your adviser.

Example No. (If applicable) _____   Publication _____

1. Headline _____

_____

2. Identify the type of lead: summary or variation. _____

A. For a summary lead:

(1) List the 5 W's and an H. Who _____

What _____   When _____   Where _____

Why _____   How _____

(2) Which of the 5 W's and an H do the opening words emphasize?

_____

(3) Is the headline written from the lead? _____

B. For a lead variation:

(1) What type of variation is used? _____

(2) In what paragraph is the nutgraph?_____ Write its first five and last five words.

_____

_____

(3) Why does a variation suit this type of story? _____

_____

_____

— EXERCISE 21B —
Writing a news analysis (cont'd)

3. Identify two or three news sources the reporter must have used for this story, including name and position.

   _____

   _____

   _____

4. Which newsworthy qualities make this story of special interest to its targeted readers? (List the qualities and explain why.)

   _____

   _____

   _____

5. Determine whether the writer achieves an appropriate balance of quotations and expository paragraphs. Indicate the number of paragraphs of each type.

   (1) Direct quotation _____   (3) Indirect quotation _____

   (2) Partial quotation _____   (4) Expository paragraph _____

   Is any one type overused in a string of successive paragraphs? _____

6. Following the lead or nutgraph, does the story keep to the inverted pyramid style? _____ Give at least two examples to support your decisions.

   _____

   _____

   _____

7. Although some paragraphs might already have been cut, could the story still pass the cutoff test? _____ Explain your answer. _____

   _____

   _____

   _____

8. What transitional devices link paragraphs 2 through 5 to the one preceding each? List the type, along with the linking words or phrases from each pair of paragraphs.

   (2) _____

— EXERCISE 21B —
Writing a news analysis (cont'd)

(3) _____

(4) _____

(5) _____

9. What sidebars, if any, are used? List type and caption or heading.

_____

_____

_____

_____

_____

10. What weaknesses, if any, do you find in this story? Be precise, giving examples.

_____

_____

_____

_____

_____

11. Briefly sum up your overall opinion of this news story.

_____

_____

_____

_____

_____

Featuring features

One definition of the word *feature* that closely relates to a newspaper feature is "special attraction." For many readers, feature stories are the "treat," promising what is interesting, enjoyable and helpful to know, although lacking the immediacy or significance of straight news.

THE ACTIVE ROLE OF FEATURE WRITERS

Unlike a straight news story, for which the facts may be evident and organization structured to an inverted pyramid, the feature story depends upon the writer's ability to capture the attraction of a subject—from idea to research to writing. Because of the relatively long interval between issues, school papers can count on well-done features to awaken interest and increase readership.

Ideas for features are everywhere and anywhere. But an idea is nothing without a special angle, a curious reporter determined to get the whole story and the kind of writing that makes the pieces fit together in a readable, informative whole. (See Figure 2-7.)

Types of features

1. **Personality**—a hobbyist, award winner, student or faculty member, anyone with an interesting story to tell. Don't just skim the surface. Make your readers feel they know this person well.

2. **News features**—an "insider's" up-close slant on a story in the news.

3. **Human interest**—stories with a heartwarming twist, a unique turn, a subject that most readers care about.

4. **Occasional pieces**—based on holidays or special events, yet taking an unfamiliar slant on the familiar details.

5. **Historical feature**—maybe as simple as how your school got its mascot, how your town got its name or what Native American tribes claimed the land first. Base such stories on interviews and quotes, not just written research.

6. **Informative feature**—what your readers need to know—researched and written so the story serves up practical knowledge in an interesting way.

7. **Shared-experience feature**—from the first time on rollerblades to a visit to traffic court, the reporter writes a firsthand account of how it was.

8. **How-to article**—tells readers what they need to know to do, or start doing, something. Use examples and expert quotes to keep it from reading like an instruction manual.

9. **Consumer report**—investigates a product, such as diet pills or a new clothing fad, to discover what local experts say, how student consumers react. Compare their pros and cons, availability, prices.

10. **Background**—gives an "insider's, behind-the-scenes" account by exploring a subject of interest that individual readers couldn't or wouldn't explore on their own.

Choosing an angle

Unlike news stories, features don't fit the inverted pyramid structure; they focus on an angle or theme carried through from beginning to end. Features don't need to take the cutoff test. Instead, they build to a pointed ending or example that leaves the reader with an illustrative quote, anecdote or observation—something to think about.

An angle for a feature story on a student athlete might concern "overcoming adversity" or "the importance of parental support." A feature on teenage fads and fashions of the past might make the point that things haven't changed so much as some kids might think.

Focusing in on your topic

One of the hardest articles to write is a feature assignment like "something about Christmas." It's relatively easy to fill up space. Just gush out several hundred trite words on why we've lost the spirit of Christmas or how the best gifts of all are free. But features are not personal essays or opinion pieces or creative expression; they are reported stories—gathered by research and interviews.

The example of Christmas comes to mind first because it's a topic that looks deceptively easy yet is one—if not *the* one—most rarely done well. This is the place for word association . . . or even a thinking cap. Christmas—Santa Claus—how about putting on a red suit and white whiskers to see what it's like to be a sidewalk Santa? Christmas is a time for charity—how about students who do volunteer work with children? What have they learned about kids and Christmas?

Ideas for features should be original—and have a personalized angle. They should be worth exploring, and the reporter should strive to get an insider's view of the story—show what it's really like, from more than one source. A feature story can only be as good as the effort that goes into gathering it. The enthusiasm of an alert and interested reporter can lead to a wealth of anecdotes, examples and details that make a feature stand out.

Feature no-nos

There are certain kinds of features and columns, found in professional newspapers, that student papers should ban. True, they take up space, but they do little or nothing to advance the skills of student writers, and they tend to trivialize the paper, both in the eyes of staff members and readers, whether faculty or students.

Stay away from publishing:

Crosswords, find-a-words and similar games or puzzles. Devising them may be fun, but they are nothing more than fillers. Staffers' ingenuity is better spent elsewhere.

Advice columns, horoscopes. Student writers do not have the credentials to write these kinds of columns. Regardless of your opinion of professional astrologers, you should consider it a deceptive practice to publish a student's forecast of the future, without qualifying it as baseless. Some students take them seriously.

Advice columns can expose the identity of a troubled student or delay someone's seeking qualified help. Students, wisely, may hesitate to respond to a would-be advice columnist's call for letters—and student writers may even stoop to both writing and answering the letters themselves. This, of course, is unethical.

In rare instances, a uniquely talented columnist might come up with a version that is technically an advice column but does not deserve pigeonholing, as in "Ask Andrew," Example 2-24B, page 231. Welcome it, if it comes.

Gossip—never! While some professional papers may still have society columns, any piece of writing that verges on gossip is strictly taboo in a school paper. Gossip promotes cliquishness, causes divisiveness and results in hurt feelings—from omissions as well as intentional or unintentional barbs.

Reporting by participation

The personal experience feature

Although the majority of true features are objective, readers can also get a firsthand account of an experience that seems adventurous, worrisome or fun if a feature writer takes part first. This type of feature allows the reader to view the sights, sounds and scenes through the writer's eyes and share or compare reactions.

High school reporters have gone behind the scenes at a circus, ridden as a backseat driver in a drivers' ed car, even taken an HIV test—just for the sake of reporting on it. The possibilities are endless.

The key to a good personal experience feature is for the reporter to keep every sense alert—and describe his sensations with fresh eyes. As with all feature stories, the personal experience feature should not be written from imagination or opinion, and it's vital to show—not tell. Since the personal experience story, unlike other features, is generally written in the first person, the writer must make a special effort to avoid the overuse of "I" or to overemphasize the importance of self.

Getting your features in focus

1. Your feature may be assigned—or suggest your own. You can start from a topic, such as sibling rivalry, an angle or a feature-worthy person, place, thing or event.

2. Try to gather more material than you can use, and be ready to write your story to the facts, not make the facts fit your preconceived ideas.

3. Encourage your subjects to talk, and listen for anecdotes, incidents, examples and quotes that add depth and vitality.

4. After gathering material, choose details and meaningful quotations that allow your story to unfold interestingly and logically. Features are not written in descending order of importance.

5. Write an intriguing lead paragraph that conforms with your angle. You may choose a story-telling lead or another lead variation, but don't make a habit of specializing in any one.

6. "Show, don't tell." Use precise descriptions that enable readers to picture a scene, share the writer's experience and draw their own conclusions.

7. Concentrate on facts, background details and examples that contribute to the story's theme.

8. Avoid repetition, such as a string of quotes from several people saying virtually the same thing.

9. Vary direct quotations, indirect or partial quotes with factual statements and expository paragraphs.

10. Build to a strong ending that reemphasizes the theme. It may be a telling quote, but it should not be a moralizing message or direct suggestion from the writer, such as "Remember, you too can make a difference, if you try."

Analyzing a feature story

The following are outstanding examples of student-written feature stories that have appeared in school newspapers throughout the country. (See examples 2-22A–2-22E.)

Read them carefully to discover how they have handled essential elements of the feature story such as:

1. Theme or angle

2. Writing that shows, instead of tells

3. Varying quotations/exposition

4. Transitions

5. Multiple primary sources

6. Sidebars

COMPARING Night and Day

By Meghann Brock

The hallways are bright and airy, the colors of the walls neutral and soothing. *This quality alone provides a sharp contrast with Alameda High's questionable color scheme of blue, yellow and orange.* School has not started yet and most students are sitting in small clusters talking quietly. My jaw drops when I realize that most of the students are...studying!!!

Trapped in the throes of a teacher's dream- come-true? Not quite. This is the world of Head Royce, an exclusive private school in the Oakland hills. I spent a day there to get a feel for this private institution, and here's what my day was like:

Head Royce has a rotating schedule similar to one of those the faculty was considering having here next year. Today Art History is the first class on the agenda. I'm surprised to see that, although the teacher is nowhere in sight, the door is unlocked and a couple of students have dropped off their backpacks (untouched) ahead of time.

Five other people seat themselves and are ready to work by the time the teacher comes in. As the teacher shows slides of Michelangelo's work, I look around wondering where the rest of the class is. There is nothing to look for. There are only six people in this class.

The teacher shows slides and lectures passionately about the art. I am impressed with her interest in the subject she is teaching and with the way everyone gives her respect and attention.

On our way to the next class I notice that there are numerous paintings, pictures and other art projects on the walls; they are completely unprotected, but not one of them has been harmed or desecrated in any way. As I look at the neatly potted and undisturbed plants in the hallway I realize that students are not stopping to gossip with one another. A simple nod and they are off to class with a deadly straightforward attitude. No one is late! I begin to hum the Twilight Zone

to myself.

All of the teachers are extremely interested in what they are teaching and—though they only lecture and there are no class discussions or other forms of participation—it is hard to become bored with something that the teachers are so passionate about.

There are Morning Assemblies on Mondays, Tuesdays, and Thursdays. Everyone sits down on the floor in the gym and people casually announce club meetings and school events. Amazingly, all the students listen politely and clap when each person finishes talking. These announcement assemblies are meant to foster school unity, and they seem to do just that.

More classes go by, each one as personal and comfortable as the next. The open, informal atmosphere does not allow for sleeping in class. Due to the small class sizes and close proximity of the teacher, it would be very rude to not pay attention.

I have not heard or seen a single person talk in class. There is no time wasted on disciplining, because every-

Meghann Brock

one hear is eager to learn. Well, maybe not eager, but willing.

At lunch students share the microwave oven to heat their lunches, or they buy something from one of the

parents are paying this much a year, you pay attention in classes," she replied.

Touche.

I asked one Head Royce junior

vending machines. Needless to say, the machines are in good condition. I wonder how well they would work if we installed them at Alameda High.

I mentioned to one student that I was with that everyone seemed to do so well in their classes. "When your

about her opinion of public schools. "I think public schools are much more diverse," she said, "but it seems that since the 70's they've gone downhill. You have to work much harder for your education [there], because it's too easy to slip through the cracks.

"I love the fact that there are more people at public schools and that you can choose from a wide variety of friends instead of being stuck with people you've been friends with forever," she continued. "I feel that I've made very strong friendships, but it's also made me feel trapped and claustrophobic at times. I think that I wouldn't be as motivated in public school because of the peer pressure to go out and party instead. Partying doesn't fit in to the high-strung life of Head Royce."

Besides the obvious fact that there is more real life experiences to be had in public schools, I have realized that trying to compare the two is like comparing night and day. Each school has its good points and bad points.

And I became aware that people at Alameda High have a lot to be grateful for, as well as some things to improve on.

My special glimpse into the other side has helped motivate me more, because I realize it is possible to focus. Hopefully it will do the same for you.

Example 2-22A. "Comparing night and day," by Meghann Brock, *The Oak Leaf,* Alameda H.S., Alameda, CA.

The smiling guy in Room 249

By Monika Moore

He stands 6 feet 4 inches in Room 249 every day, first through fifth periods. He wears bright, wacky shirts and his safety goggles are made of neon plastic. His lab coat is a holey, burned rag, and if you break his one strict rule, you'd better brush up on your singing voice for a rendition of the infamous "Goggle Song."

"He's my favorite teacher. He makes everything really fun and I'm always laughing in his class. Even when we do the hard labs, he makes learning easy and enjoyable," sophomore Heather Joy said with a smile. She is in his first period Chemistry class.

Richards teaches both AP Biology and Chemistry. His chemistry students cringe at the assignments listed on the board because many of them appear long and complicated.

But senior Jesse Sedillo, who is in his AP Biology class fourth period, had this to say about Richards and the class:

"Yeah, some of the things are hard to do, but he explains things well and we can always figure it out and learn something. He really relates to the kids and says things that we can understand."

Judging from his way with students, it may seem that Richards has been teaching for years. But this is only his third year as a teacher at Alameda High.

Prior to teaching, Richards worked as a cancer researcher at UC Berkeley for twenty years. When asked if he discovered anything incredible during those years, he replied, "Nothing that would make any sense to you."

Perhaps his prestige and intellect was passed down from his father, whom he modestly calls "no one you would know."

We may not know him by name, but John Richards was the head of a program that sent the first satellite into space. He was pictured in Life Magazine and some of his original satellite technology is still used in those that transmit our phone conversations today.

No one important, right?

Even more fascinating, Richards is dyslexic. Sometimes he writes letters backwards, and reading is a long, trying task. But he spends whatever extra time he needs to do these things and doesn't let it get in the way of learning or teaching.

Richards says he wanted to be-

come a teacher because he wanted to be "poor, haggard, and get no respect."

But seriously, Richards realized that he should begin teaching while he

Monika Moore

was coaching his son's little league team. He discovered that he really enjoyed working with young people, and that education is an important part of a young person's life. He wanted a challenge and a change from his familiar occupation.

The result: a well-rounded scientist teaching students about the fundamentals of chemistry and biology and, more importantly, the role they play in our lives.

"He brings real-life situations into the classroom. You do assignments that help you understand the world. He has a positive attitude and tries to help

everyone, and makes sure you can do things on your own because you can't be baby-sat all your life," said senior Antonio Proctor.

As for his personal life, Richards is married and has two sons, Evan and Lyle. Many students have seen him after school bike riding: helmet, fluorescent clothing and all. He also fly-fishes, goes backpacking, and builds furniture for fun. He used to race cars, and has told many students about a "hot" red and white Mustang he used to

Reflecting on his own career, Richards said, "Teaching is very worthwhile, but the bureaucracy is disturbing. People have good intentions, but the mechanism sucks. No success, no money. It's a problem that needs solving, and it's frustrating. But I love the students. A lot of them have good things to say and are smart and hard-working."

Richards doesn't like to think of the students doing their work for him just because they were assigned to do. so. He would prefer that he is thought

of as working for the students; a tool they can use to learn and be guided by.

Richards wanted to know why he was being interviewed for this story. When told that he was among students' favorite teachers, he again wanted to know why. Richards believes it's more important for people to know why a teacher is so well-liked than to know who that teacher is. He says that there is a lack of communication between students and teachers; only by building a bridge of communication would teachers be able to know which teaching techniques work.

"He lets us do things that make us think," said one junior chemistry student. "Like the lab we're doing now. It's not a book lab. It's a lab that makes us use our creativity and figure out things on our own. When you figure stuff out on your own, it's fun. Also, his stupid jokes make us laugh, and that always helps."

> **The Goggle Song**
> Goggles, you'll love your
> goggles,
> They will keep your eyes
> from [stomp] burning out.
> So wear your goggles, upon
> your eyeballs,
> If you don't, you must stay
> out.

Example 2-22B. "The smiling guy in Room 249," by Monika Moore, *The Oak Leaf,* Alameda H.S., Alameda, CA.

They spent their Friday nights at the rink, while their friends were at football games. They munched on salad, as others enjoyed french fries. And the competitions didn't always bring gold medals; but sometimes broken bones.

Two Lakota seniors sacrificed it all to go for the gold.

Anne Means and Gretchen Boerup have been ice skating since they were nine years-old.

"I used to watch Dorothy Hamill skate," Means says. "We had one of those slick floors and I used to skate around in my socks. Then they opened a rink in Lexington where I used to live. So my mom let me take lessons there."

Boerup began young too.

"I did a little pond skating in Wooster, Ohio," Boerup says. "Then we moved to Memphis and they had an Ice Capades rink. So, I took group lessons there."

Both girls began competing in their second year of training . They started with the Ice Skating Institute of America (ISA). Then the seniors switched and joined the United States Figure Skating Association (USFSA).

Boerup explained the difference between the two.

"You have to join the USFSA to go to Nationals or the Olympics," she says. "ISA is more for the skater who just wants to go out and have fun."

For some skaters, it's more serious.

"This one time this girl took her competitor's skates and ground them into the concrete so she couldn't skate," Means claims.

Boerup says that's nothing.

"I know some of the skater's parents have jumped judges and started beating them if they don't give their kids a good score," Boerup says. "And you just don't do that to a judge. You are supposed to show the greatest respect to a judge."

Competitions for Nationals begin with Regionals. The top four skaters compete at the Midwestern Championships, the four best from that advance to Nationals.

There are six levels in competition: Pre-Juvenile, Juvenile, Intermediate, Novice, Junior, and Senior. Boerup competed at Nationals last year and placed seventh out of the 250 competitors in the Junior level.

Means retired from competitive skating this summer. Her decision to quit was a result of numerous injuries and the stress of

the intense training schedule.

"I got injuries year after year," Means says. "I still went, but you can't skate up to level when you have so many injuries."

"(Skating) has taught me a lot, like time management and responsibility, but at the same time I missed out on so much," she explains. "I really wanted to see what life was all about."

Means began to miss skating, so she landed a job skating at the Cincinnati Zoo.

"Since I quit, I can get paid for skating,"

■ Anne Means ice skated competetively for nine years.

Means says. "I'm doing a show called Ice Ages at the Cincinnati Zoo. I have a show every night but Tuesday. It's really a lot of fun."

She came back for the skating.

"I miss stupid things," Means explains. "I don't miss jumping because of falling. I miss the sound of the ice and the wind blowing my hair back. That's why I'm doing the show because I was starting to miss skating a lot."

Boerup also cut down on practice time.

"I backed off a little this year so I could go to the football games, parties and stuff," Boerup says. "For a while I only skated five days a week, but then I made Mids (Midwestern Championship), so I started

"You can never quite separate yourself from the skater."

-- Gretchen Boerup

back up again."

Stephanie Miller, Boerup's coach at the All Seasons Ice Center in Crescentville, Kentucky, believes that ice skating is a sport for only a few.

"To be a skater you need concentration, dedication, and articulation," Miller says. "You have to give some things up to come in and skate. Gretchen comes in six days a week. She is usually on the ice by 2:30 and she stays until at least 6 p.m."

Grades could suffer for some skaters, but these skaters have maintained high grades.

"When you are a skater you're expected to get good grades," Means explains. "If you get C's you're looked down upon and you're not allowed to skate as much."

Boerup agrees.

"Anne and I are both getting good grades," Boerup says. "We are both in National Honor Society. I don't know any skaters who are flunking out. (Skating) doesn't really hinder our grades, it's more our social life."

And sometimes, they say, the sport isn't taken seriously.

"Most people don't realize how much time and money we spend, and how many things we sacrifice," Means states. "It really makes me mad when people don't think that it's a sport."

But it definitely is to Means.

"I love (skating)," Means exclaims. "I want to coach when I get older."

Boerup doesn't plan on quitting, either.

"I don't want to stop skating," Boerup says. "I'll probably coach or judge later."

Skating is more than just a sport for Means and Boerup; it's a life-style.

"It depends on if you are willing to commit your whole life to skating," Boerup says. "You can never quite separate yourself from the skater. From the first time you start competing, you are a skater and that's who you're going to be for the rest of your life."

Means agrees.

"Once you start you're either a skater or you're not; there's no in between," Means says.✱

Example 2-22C. "On the rink," by Shannon Galloway, *Spark*, Lakota H.S., West Chester, OH.

All bets are off

Evidence indicates teen gambling is a growing problem

by Mike Becker

I t happens every day. Students gather to put their own money on the line. They face the prospect of an easy profit or a complete loss. It may seem unreasonable to the casual observer, but gambling does exist among the students of Central. It is a definite presence.

Many students gamble, but the debate continues as to whether gambling is just entertainment or a destructive addiction.

It's no secret that students gamble. Each day money changes hands in the cafeteria between students playing Liars' Poker or people talking about the cash they have riding on the Monday Night Football Game. Students have even organized football pools where everyone pays to get in and the winner takes home a sizable prize.

Some might wonder why gambling is being marked as such a bad thing. It is legal in countless institutions across the country from casinos to racetracks to the local convenience stores selling lottery tickets.

"I don't think most people who gamble are very serious," said Martin Miller '95. "A few might have gone over the edge, but it's really not that big a deal."

Matt Hufford '96 said, "It doesn't seem like a real problem, and those who do gamble know they're doing it at their own risk anyway."

Pete Kuhn '95 took a more practical look at the issue and said, "Most kids around here have so much money that it doesn't even matter."

Students seemed to mostly disagree with the notion that gambling is a problem. Counselor Jim Eickhoff, Guidance dept., doesn't feel it is a serious threat at Central either. "As far as I know, there haven't been any major difficulties here. I haven't heard much talk about it."

Despite these viewpoints from within the school, national statistics indicate otherwise. Recently, results published in *U.S. News & World Report* estimated that there are 1 million gamblers who are in their teens. Out of this number, approximately five percent also meet the criteria for being compulsive gamblers. An even higher percentage are marked as "potential compulsive gamblers." A volunteer counselor of the Gamblers Anonymous (GA) program, defines compulsive gambling as bets being made for gambling's sake rather than for fun. "Instead of being a one time thing just for entertainment, the gambling becomes a real addiction. Just like an alcoholic who needs another drink or a druggie who needs another hit, a compulsive gambler needs to make another bet. He can't stop. He needs his action."

Just like the negative connotations that drugs and alcohol have, gambling, simply another form of addiction, has its dark side as well. *U.S. News & World Report* also reported that more than ten percent of teenage gamblers are believed to have committed crimes in order to finance their illegal endeavors, while problem gamblers are predicted to be more than twice as likely to abuse drugs or alcohol later on. The most obvious consequence is that large sums of money are more easily lost than won.

All of these new statistics indicate one definite thing. Youth gambling does exist in full force

continued on page A4

Bets off

continued from A1

and numbers may be increasing at an alarming rate.

"The situation is getting worse and worse," said the same GA representative. "More establishments [for gambling] are popping up everywhere. Gambling is being accepted. Because it exists in so many forms, it is becoming more widespread and teenagers have greater access to it." He is most worried that kids who start will unwittingly make the transition from casual to compulsive gambling.

"At first they'll just be in it to make a quick buck. Something for nothing. But when they lose, it doesn't worry them. The problems start when the losses start affecting their social lives or school work. The gambling becomes a real emotional problem, a hidden illness."

Technically, gambling shouldn't even have to be considered a problem at Central. The School Discipline Policy of the

Student Handbook lists gambling as unacceptable behavior that is punishable by detention, suspension or expulsion.

"We hope that students will realize gambling isn't something they should be doing at all, but espe-

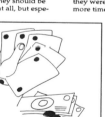

cially here," said Dean Dave Franson. "But just like there are always people who will drive 50 in a 40 miles per hour zone, there are people who will still [gamble] anyway."

Despite the school's official policy, it is not easy to tell if the regulation is being strictly enforced.

"We do look out for gambling," added Dean Franson, "and right now there are a couple individuals who have been seriously warned about it. There was a definite problem because they were spending more time on their gambling than on their homework."

While these isolated cases have been found and dealt with, it is impossible to know how many other students with gambling problems exist at Central, or even how severe the problem might be. However, students who have gambled themselves still didn't see it as a problem.

"I've gambled, but I know when to stop, too," said Jim Dziewior '95.

Some students receive parental support or permission to gamble.

One teenager even had an adult with him and his friends at the racetrack to place their bets on the horses. "Everyone can use some extra money. It's not fun to just go and watch the horses," said Josh Cartwright '95. "But I was willing to lose the money I bet. The track is not a good place for people who can't handle their money or who can't afford to lose what they bet."

While Central is equipped to deal with students who develop drug or alcohol problems, programs for those with gambling addictions are virtually nonexistent. There are other options for students who have crossed the line from gambling casually to compulsively.

Many private psychiatrists can help people through counseling and therapy. GA is

**"I've gambled, but I know when to stop, too."
- Jim Dziewior '95**

one of the largest organizations that deals exclusively with the problem.

"GA really is one of the best places to get help," said the GA counselor, "but first the gambler has to be able to admit it to himself. Once he does that, he can get suggestions from others on what to do next. My impression is that schools are doing very little about gambling, so its up to the kids and parents to get the help they need." Information on locations and times of meetings can be obtained through the GA Hotline, (312) 346-1588.

Gambling has quietly become a nationwide problem. All over the country, incidents of teens harming themselves through gambling are becoming more and more visible. Gambling has truly become the newest disease to inflict the youth of America.

Example 2-22D. "All bets are off," by Mike Becker, *Devils' Advocate*, Hinsdale Central H.S., Hinsdale, IL.

La Cueva dropout surviving on his own with job

Barbara Tapp
Features Staff

Confident and secure, Brian Romero leads the way into his domain, a well-kept apartment in the Northeast Heights. He stops to casually lay his coat on a chair at his dining table.

The apartment is well-furnished with an old sofa, a wooden chair upon which he sits, some lamps that don't work - they're "simply there for looks," and a four chair dinner table. Brian's apartment reflects his lifestyle, that of freedom.

Brian has taken on the pressures of independent life without completing high school.

"I felt I wasn't going to finish. I wouldn't graduate with my class," Brian states matter-of-factly.

He dropped out of La Cueva last fall, during the first semester of his senior year, and he did not waste any time getting on with his life.

"The day I quit, I went to Dion's and asked for more hours," Brian says. "I basically started working my brain out."

Through his intense work and time put in at Dion's on Academy and Wyoming, Brian has worked his way into a position where he can become a general manager.

His future doesn't solely lie within the walls of the pizzaria. Brian wants to get his General Equivelancy Diploma [GED]. That is, when he gets the time.

"I hope to become general manager there [Dion's], and that's not entirely out of my reach. But if that doesn't go, I fully intend to get my GED," he states.

Brian's decision to begin life without the completion of high school centered around his feelings of school in general, not just La Cueva, he said. He explains he disliked the entire school environment, saying simply, "It's not for me."

"It was frustraing, like trying something over and over again and never succeeding," Brian expresses.

When asked if this feeling would interfere with any possible plans for higher education after a GED, he admits it would. But he won't let it overcome him.

Hesitantly, Brian expresses that the decision was his; however, his parents have changed their behavior toward him as a result of his choice. He says, though, that his relationship with them has actually improved, due to his no longer needing encouragement to finish homework or maintain grades.

"They treat me a lot differently, a lot better. My high school [experience] was like a burden on them; I never did well," he comments.

> "[High school] was frustrating, like trying something over and over again and never succeeding."
>
> -Brian Romero,
> LC dropout

Brian says he still sees his parents about once a week, but being so involved at Dion's and living alone leaves little time for his family.

While contemplating whether or not he'd make the same decision to drop out over if given another chance, Brian shifts positions in his chair uncomfortably.

"It's hard to say. I guess if I knew then what I know now, I wouldn't have quit," Brian states.

Regarding other students feeling the same pressures he did in school, Brian emphasizes the difficulties of independent life.

"If you think you're going to do better at something else, then do it," Brian states. "I did, and I'm having a blast."

Factors he lists to consider include the paying of bills on your own, dealing with income taxes, and other general budget work. Often taken for granted that parents undertake these responsibilities, it takes some getting used to, Brian explains.

"It's made me a lot smarter, a lot wiser..."

He pauses a moment.

"There are times when I'm really confident of my decision, and times when I'm really unsure." He sighs heavily.

Having taken on no new hobbies or pastimes, Brian says one of the biggest parts of living alone is being lonely.

"The thing is, though, I'm at work most of the time and when I'm not, I think I'm sleeping."

He questions himself. "Yeah, I'm sleeping."

Example 2-22E. "La Cueva dropout surviving. . . ," by Barbara Tapp, *The Edition*, La Cueva H.S., Albuquerque, NM.

Name _____ Date _____

— EXERCISE 22A —
Writing your feature analysis

DIRECTIONS:

The following questions are tools for analyzing others' feature writing and your own. Use one of the examples given or another story, assigned by your adviser.

Example No. (If applicable) _____ Publication _____

1. Headline _____

2. What type of feature is this example? _____

3. What theme or angle does the writer emphasize throughout the story?

   _____

   _____

4. Explain how the final paragraph echoes or reemphasizes this theme.

   _____

   _____

5. Identify two or three sources the reporter must have had for this story, including name and position.

   _____

   _____

   _____

   _____

6. Which qualities make this story interesting and unusual? (List the quality and explain why.)

   _____

   _____

7. Determine whether the writer achieves an appropriate balance of quotations and expository paragraphs. Indicate the number of paragraphs of each type.

   (a) Direct quotation _____   (c) Indirect quotation _____

   (b) Partial quotation _____   (d) Expository paragraph _____

   Is any one type overused in a string of successive paragraphs? _____

— EXERCISE 22A —
Writing your feature analysis (cont'd)

8. What transitional devices link paragraphs 2 through 5 to the one preceding each? List the type, along with the linking words or phrases from each pair of paragraphs.

   (2) _____

   (3) _____

   (4) _____

   (5) _____

9. What sidebars, if any, are used? List type and caption or heading.

   _____

   _____

10. What weaknesses, if any, do you find in this story? Be precise, giving examples.

    _____

    _____

    _____

    _____

    _____

    _____

    _____

    _____

    _____

11. Briefly sum up your overall opinion of this feature.

    _____

    _____

    _____

    _____

    _____

    _____

    _____

    _____

    _____

— EXERCISE 22B —
Researching and writing a feature story

DIRECTIONS:

Do an interview feature on someone—not a member of your newspaper staff, a close friend or member of your family. Either plan a focus in advance or develop an angle in the course of your interview. Then, encourage your subject by seeking examples, incidents and details that will show, not just tell, what makes your subject worth your reader's interest. Be alert for quotable statements.

Also, interview at least two, preferably three, others who know this person. Seek comments directly related to your angle but not limited to it, as this might inhibit their speaking freely. Using your notes and other background information, write a finished feature.

Note: If you wish to write another type of feature, first seek permission from your adviser. It should be based, however, upon at least three pieces of research, including two or more interviews. Do not write a seasonal or occasional piece for this assignment.

Story

(Write at least 500 but not more than 900 words. Your story may be submitted as typed copy or handwritten, as your adviser requests.)

Notes

_____

_____

_____

_____

_____

_____

_____

_____

_____

_____

_____

_____

_____

_____

In-depth reporting—Covering all angles

It's there—spread out before you. Unfolded, the center sheet of the paper invites you to treat it as one, double-size page, not as two. Be creative! Dig deep! Do investigative reporting that tells the real story, the whole story.

Because of its promise and possibilities, the center spread—pages 4 and 5 in an eight-page paper (also called the *double truck*)—has become the space reserved for regular in-depth reports by many school papers. It offers space for dramatic layouts, artwork and attention-getting head-lines-for related stories, sidebars and infographs on a subject of dominant interest.

The investigative or in-depth report must be a team effort. It requires careful planning and thorough follow-through. The editor assigning the story must acquire sufficient knowledge to brief reporters adequately beforehand. Reporters must research such sources as print media, the Internet and expert opinions before conducting interviews in the school and local community.

The in-depth report can provide a splendid opportunity for student reporters to exercise their abilities full-out. Yet, if reporters are not dedicated to getting the entire story, the eye-catching headlines and artwork only call attention to an empty shell.

Going for the story behind the story

Step one: Preplanning Investigative report topics must pass editorial board approval, but ideas may come from any staff member, who may then request to write the lead article. Otherwise, the section editor may choose to write the main article or the report's comprehensive introduction.

Other major stories should go to individual writers, who may also provide short, related side-bars and data needed for graphics. Several shorter stories may be a combined assignment. All articles should be objective, although an editorial expressing the paper's viewpoint can run on the editorial page or be clearly labeled and set off within the report itself.

Step two: Planning The more precise the planning, the better the chances of a well-done in-depth report.

In-depth reports often begin with an umbrella topic, for example, teens' money problems, which is then both narrowed into specific stories and expanded to include different facets of the subject. Ideas often come from studies reported in the national media, such as one stating that students need to learn how to control their spending and that debit cards, which work like credit cards but have a spending limit, can help them do so.

With "money" as the umbrella, the editor can preplan, then refine when working with the reporting team.

Tentative umbrella head: Where does the money go?

1. Working teens
   - how does work affect grades
   - how many hours, for what purposes
   - possible poll, also expert sources

2. Allowances
   - how much, how many follow budgets
   - do they cause family problems
   - could include student poll, professional sources

3. Spending habits
   - clothes, entertainment, personal needs, in-school expenses—what does school cost, including bus fare, lunches, lab fees, supplies, etc.

4. Credit, savings, etc.   – how students handle credit; whether, how much and how regularly they save

5. Sidebars   – poll results, charts of percentage with jobs
         – informational items on taxes, college costs, etc.

6. Explore other possibilities

Step three: Research and writing   A purpose of the in-depth report is to uncover helpful facts that readers need and want to know—in a story that strikes closer to student interests than professional media coverage can or does. In-depth, investigative reports should be tailored and written especially for the paper's readership, enlarging upon what they know or could readily find out for themselves.

Like a feature story, the in-depth report should have a definite theme or purpose and contain anecdotes, examples, incidents, details and quotations as well as facts to make its point interestingly, fully and effectively.

Pitfalls of in-depth reporting

Sex, teen pregnancy, abortion, gun control, gang violence, crime, AIDS, terrorism—these powerful topics have the danger of becoming mere catchwords, sensationalism devoid of substance, in the hands of school editors and reporters unwilling to go beyond the obvious.

An in-depth report should be local. It should not quote secondhand comments from a local source or sources that merely repeat other media reports without offering firsthand knowledge and examples. It should not be an inquiring reporter piece with expected answers, many repetitious, from students whose main purpose is getting their names in the paper. It should not rehash other stories.

Bringing current concerns home

The in-depth report requires more extensive research and planning than the straight news story. Therefore, it needs a more elastic deadline than the paper's usual one, notwithstanding a reporter's tendency to leave assignments till the last minute.

Teams can work during "down" time, while technical production goes on. Several in-depth reporting teams may be working under different "umbrella" topics at the same time. Teams should meet weekly to discuss problems and progress, and reporters should show definite evidence of their work to date, according to an announced schedule.

Topics for in-depth reports should be scheduled in advance and filed in the future book. However, topics can be switched if a more timely or relevant subject comes up in time for the substitution. Since the stories are written on separate deadlines, those that do not come up to standard should be postponed or killed.

Besides the front page, the center spread is the most prominent showcase for stories in the paper. There is no law saying the entirety of both pages need be devoted to a single topic. In-depth reports can be designed or redesigned to a single right hand page, or a page and a vertical half page with stories or ads alongside. Otherwise, center spreads are often designed with no ads, like the front and editorial pages.

Careless, insensitive investigative reporting on a controversial subject can hurt people—those involved in the story and also the staff and its adviser, through possible libel suits and official action.

Analyzing an in-depth report

Examples 2-23A–2-23D are outstanding examples of student-researched and written in-depth reports that have appeared in school newspapers throughout the country. Read them carefully to discover how they have handled essential elements of the in-depth report such as:

1. Topic of sufficient significance
2. Primary sources
3. Thorough and intensive coverage
4. Effective presentation
5. Correct journalistic style
6. Informative sidebars

This student demonstrates a technique students use to shoplift, despite a warning sign in the background. Timesphoto by Katie Piotrowski.

Focus

Shoplifting

For some it is a way to get things they cannot afford. Others do it for the thrill

by Meghan Gordon

First it was a candy bar here, a lipstick there.

Then it got bigger and better until Marie* got caught her freshman year shoplifting after years of stealing.

"I thought I had become invincible, and no one would ever catch me. I thought the people deserved for me to steal from them because they made the prices so high, and I couldn't afford it. Later on, I found out the reason the prices were so high was because of people like me that stole from them," Marie said.

"I went to Drug Mart knowing I was going to steal, and we went in and started grabbing stuff. When we finished with our 'shopping,' we went to leave and an undercover security lady stopped us and said to my friend 'Miss, I would kindly like you to empty whatever is in your pockets out.' My friend tried to deny it, but the lady claimed she saw us," Marie said.

Marie said she was then escorted to a storage room and had to give up everything she and her friend had tried to steal.

"My friend, the one that got caught, only had one thing, but when they searched me, they found $36 worth of stuff ranging from makeup to magazines to books.

"I was escorted home in a police car, the policeman came to my door and talked to my parents, and as I stood there crying, I realized how disappointed I was in myself and the humiliation I felt beyond belief," Marie said.

Jim Lakatos, assistant manager at Drug Mart, said the store's main shoplifting problem is just juveniles and young adults getting what they want and not paying for it.

Lakatos said once someone has been caught stealing in the store, he or she is not allowed back in any Drug Mart store again unless he or she is a minor, and is with a parent or guardian.

If anyone tries to come back in after he or she has been caught and prohibited from the store, it is then

Shoplifter tells of experiences

by Duane Tysiak.

Stealing was all one Lakewood High School sophomore could think about.

"I can't even count the number of times I've shoplifted," the student said.

The student, who has never been caught, says he steals because it's fun and he doesn't have any money to pay for it.

"I've stolen $2000 at least from malls, grocery stores, drug stores but never anyone's house; that's not cool," the student said.

All you have to do is outsmart the employees, which is not hard, the student said.

"Those electronic sensors are a joke," the student said, "All you have to do is rip off the sensor or demagnetize it," he added.

Stores that have cameras are the biggest deterrent, the student said.

"Avoid them. You will be caught," he said.

It is hard to get caught, the student said, "if you have any brains."

The biggest mistake, he said, is going to the same store in the same day.

"Let's say there's a guy named Fred who steals three pairs of pants. Fred goes back later to steal a shirt. Security is going crazy looking for shoplifters, and Fred gets busted," he said.

The student said the more you steal, the better chances you have of being caught because you get overconfident.

"Most of the stuff I steal, I keep. Some I sell," he said

The student said he hasn't shoplifted for three months because he

Example 2-23A. "Shoplifting," by Meghan Gordon, *The Times*, Lakewood H.S., Lakewood, OH.

Focus

up to the employees to recognize and keep in mind the faces, Lakatos said.

Drug Mart has taken precautions to derail shoplifting , such as increasing security cameras and security personnel, he said.

"We also have sensormatic devices, which are little electronic strips. It's on some products so if you go out the door without being demagnetized, it sets off alarms," Lakatos said.

Rini-Rego's grocery store also has problems with shoplifting but is working on minimizing the problem, one of the assistant managers said.

He said on a scale of 1 to 10, the shoplifting problem at Rego's is a three or four, based partly on how efficient the Lakewood police are when called in.

"It's somewhat of a deterrent that the cop will be here in short period of time after we've called, and we do prosecute," he said.

He said the store is not allowed to so any search procedures, unless the actual consumption of the item is seen.

Rego's hired a security agency that sends in plain clothes people at random hours of the day to give a surveillance check of the store, the assistant manager said.

"We used to have sensors on the doors, but it wasn't cost efficient to have them up," he said.

Even though its not always possible, Lakatos said, Drug Mart tries to stop the shoplifter outside of the store.

"After they get stopped, we just take them in back, the police are called and then (the shoplifter) is realized into the custody of the police," Lakatos said.

Juveniles are caught more than any other age group, Lakatos said.

"At least they are usually the ones that get caught. I don't really know, everyone is probably stealing, but we just seem to catch more kids than anyone else," Lakatos said.

Cosmetics and toys are the top two items stolen the most frequently from Drug Mart, Lakatos said.

"Cosmetics are really up there—it may be the price, people just cannot afford it," Lakatos said.

The most stolen item at Rego's, the assistant manager said, is cigarettes. He said they feel this is because the item is a valuable commodity. The store is in the process of relocating the item to make it harder to steal.

Mike Moblay, the assistant man-

' thought the people deserved for me to steal from them because they made the prices so high, and I couldn't afford it. Later on, I found out the reason the prices were so high was because of people like me who stole from them'-Marie

ager of Revco, said shoplifting is not a immense problem at the store, although it does occur.

Candy and gum are items among the most often stolen at Revco.

"Anything can be stolen, but the smaller the item, the bigger the chance of it being stolen. The impulse items at the front of the store or at any door would be the things that are stolen the most," Moblay said.

A shoplifter may find it easier to steal from stores when it is a certain season, Lakatos said.

"In the wintertime, it is easier because of bulky winter coats, more chance to hide stuff, but as far as the rate goes, I think its pretty much steady all year round. I hate to pin point kids, but the availability of kids being out of school is up in the summer and might have a lot to do with it," Lakatos said.

Like the rise or fall of the amount of shoplifting in the different seasons, the assistant manager of Rego's said he felt the approach of a holi-

day brings on more shoplifters also.

"During a holiday time, shoplifting increases because there is an extra traffic flow in the store, and it's a lot easier to steal things when you have a higher traffic flow. The holidays is also a time when people are in a pinch for money, and then there is an increase of theft," he said.

Drug Mart is trying to make a conscious effort to show it is being aware of who is in the store and what is going on at the store, Lakatos said.

"We just want people to be aware that we are keeping an eye on them. We also train our employees, and they do notify security if they see anything suspicious," Lakatos said.

Revco employees are trained to watch out for anyone who looks suspicious, Moblay said.

"With a watchful eye, we can just try to keep things to a minimum in the store," Moblay said.

Julie*, a sophomore, says she usually shoplifts about three times a month, and when she does she takes large quantities of items.

"I like Dillard's because it is really open, people don't watch and they don't count their items. When I'm stealing clothes, I usually just stuff

Continued on page 15

Revco loses $50,000 yearly to shoplifters

by Duane Tysiak

Stealing a candy bar here and there may not seem expensive, but the cost adds up, Mark O'Brien, Revco manager, said.

"We lose about $40-50,000 a year to shoplifters. To make up for this, we must sell an extra $250,000," O'Brien said.

The store uses product sensors and security cameras on occasion.

"Some customers find the cameras offensive," O'Brien said.

The store has a limit of two students at a time. This is normally enforced after school and when summer vacation starts, O'Brien said.

"Ninety percent of students who come in are nice and well mannered," he said.

Once a student is caught shoplifting, O'Brien says the best thing to do is call the parents and the police. The

student can come in and work off the fine or he or she can do community service.

O'Brien says he wants students to realize what they think is a harmless prank can hurt them in later life. If a person gets a reputation for being dishonest, it is very hard to get rid of that reputation.

Finast has security cameras and plain clothes detectives, Banae Gholston, a store detective, said.

We catch about five students a week, he said.

"They normally don't steal by themselves. They always say they were going to pay," Gholston said.

Half the students get probation or community service. The other half pay a fine, Gholston said.

Only about one percent of the students who walk through the door shoplift, he added.

Example 2-23A. *(continued)*

Example 2-23B. "Crescent City—a tribute to New Orleans," *Bear Facts*, Alief Hastings H.S., Houston, TX.

Example 2-23C. "Out of mainstream education," by Barbara Tapp, *The Edition*, La Cueva H.S., Albuquerque, NM.

Example 2-23D. "DRUGS . . . HERE," by Melanie Kain, *The Chronicle*, Harvard-Westlake School, North Hollywood, CA.

Name _____   Date _____

— EXERCISE 23A —
Writing your in-depth report analysis

DIRECTIONS:

The following questions are tools for analyzing an in-depth report. Use one of the examples given or another report, assigned by your adviser.

Example No. (If applicable) _____   Publication _____

1. Overall headline _____

2. Why is (or is not) this subject of sufficient interest and significance to students to rate an in-depth report? _____

   _____

   _____

3. Why does (or doesn't) the report provide students with better information on this subject than other sources do? _____

   _____

   _____

4. List the headlines and subject of the major stories covered.

   (a) _____

   (b) _____

   (c) _____

5. What sidebars, if any, highlight special aspects of the report? List the caption, type of sidebar (infograph, factoids, glossary, etc.), and subject of sidebar.

   (a) _____

   _____

   (b) If not, what type of sidebars would prove effective? Include suggestion for content.

   _____

   _____

6. Is the report effectively presented with photos, drawings and other graphics? _____
   Explain your answer. _____

   _____

   _____

— EXERCISE 23A —
Writing your in-depth report analysis (cont'd)

7. What weaknesses, if any, do you find in this report? Be precise, giving examples.

_____

_____

_____

_____

_____

_____

_____

_____

_____

8. Briefly sum up your overall opinion of this in-depth report.

_____

_____

_____

_____

_____

_____

_____

_____

_____

_____

_____

_____

Name _____   Date _____

— EXERCISE 23B —
Planning an in-depth report

DIRECTIONS:

Work from one of the following topics or a topic of your own. Then plan how you would conduct an in-depth report if you were the editor or team leader. Topics: politics, censorship, student rights and responsibilities, the environment, technology, college, stress, education, ethics, parenting.

Step one:

Limit your topic by focusing on a definite theme or purpose. Then, do preliminary research and write a summary of what you have learned and why you think it a good choice for an in-depth report, including the benefits it offers to readers.

_____

_____

_____

_____

_____

_____

_____

_____

_____

_____

_____

_____

_____

Step two:

Write a suggested, overall headline or umbrella title.

_____

_____

— EXERCISE 23B —
Planning an in-depth report (cont'd)

Step three:

List at least three major related stories, including sources, for interviews and the type of information needed for each.

_____

_____

_____

_____

_____

_____

Step four:

List four possible infographs or sidebar items related to the topic, and explain what each would contain.

_____

_____

_____

_____

_____

_____

_____

_____

_____

_____

_____

_____

_____

_____

Original approaches to columns and humor

A newspaper column is actually two different things. With reference to layouts, it's one of the vertical sections of printed matter on a newspaper page. But, of most interest to many writers, a column is also a type of feature article that appears regularly in a newspaper or magazine. It is generally set apart in some way, either by carrying a standing head or kicker, such as "For what it's worth" that runs over its headline, by using a thumbnail portrait of the writer, by having a byline or by all of the foregoing.

Columns often have the same page placement in every issue, for readers who turn to their favorites first. Professional papers run various types of columns: editorial, advice, food, nutrition, sports, financial, personal viewpoint—the list encompasses almost every section and kind of subject found in the paper.

Many school papers lack clearly identified columns. Others have stories with content that properly fit the definition of column but are labeled "feature" or "opinion." Columns combine elements of both, yet bunched together they create the impression that the newspaper staff is primarily centered on its own interests and issues. To make columns seem more special, set them off with standing heads or icons, and run them according to their type of coverage—on editorial, entertainment, feature or sports pages.

The columnist's voice

Newspaper readers turn to a column because of two expectations:

1. They're familiar with the columnist's voice and, to a degree, they know what to expect. In the case of a political column in a professional paper, they know which way the writer leans, to the right or the left, so they know which side the writer is likely to take on a controversial topic, such as capital punishment. From a humor column, they expect a smile and a chuckle. From a column called "Money Talks," they expect advice on how to save, spend and perhaps make money through investing.

2. Readers also expect their favorite columnists to present them with surprises. Columnists gain popularity because of their unique and personal slant on their subjects, plus their deft manner of writing. Of greatest importance is their ability to "tune in" on a subject and make it their own while, at the same time, opening readers' eyes to a fresh and stimulating viewpoint that, ideally, both delights and enlightens.

Columns: A vehicle for self-expression

For newspaper writers, a column is considered a prize—a tribute to writing ability, journalistic know-how and a unique vision. Although most news stories also carry a byline, a column means not only a byline and possible mug shot, but also newfound freedoms—the freedom to choose your own topic and to inject more of your personality into your work.

Sounds like fun?

With a column comes greater responsibility. A columnist can, and does, touch on the same subjects that features, editorials and even news stories do. Like a feature, a column can contain anecdote, example, incident and quotes. Yet its subject must also have a point to make, something that causes the columnist to single it out and to feel that it needs airing or exposure from his or her special point of view.

Space to fill or something to say

In too many school newspaper columns, it's obvious that the writer's concern was filling up space or doing enough just to "get by," not get across an idea or viewpoint.

No credit should go to a columnist who's willing to crow, "I have nothing to say." Readers will recognize the bluff and find it unfunny. Anyone willing to take on a column must take the responsibility to try—no excuses acceptable for results that anyone with a modest flair for words could easily attain.

News editors and advisers should have a contingency plan for just such an occurrence—the rewrite of a news release, perhaps, a story-telling photo or a timely schedule of events.

Should the columnist have a second chance? One more, at most. Once it becomes clear that the paper seeks quality work, not just space-filling quantity, the lesson should not need frequent repetition, nor should columns remain wishy-washy swamps of idle thoughts and runaway words.

Columns with a plus

Ideas for columns rarely pop out on command. Columnists must actively seek them. The majority of good columns in a school paper express a personal or humorous slant on subjects of student interest, including those devoted specifically to sports.

Here are ways to stimulate your brain cells:

1. *Observation*—Look, and you'll find inspiration all around you—from why people (including teachers) dress as they do—to why kids spend so much on "heroic" sport shoes (Is that why they prop their feet up on chairs?)—to reporting how students deal with their overstuffed lockers (Ever see someone kick one shut?)

2. *Listening*—Listen in the hallways—not just to your friends but to the general student body. What are their interests, their complaints, their way of talking? Listen in classrooms—not just to subject matter but to the kinds of questions asked and answered by both students and teachers.

3. *Incidents*—Slipping and falling on your way to your table in the cafeteria—having someone treat you patronizingly because of your age—an act of kindness—your feelings of stage fright getting up in front of class or dating someone new.

4. *Talking with others*—If you were treated rudely, others probably have been, too. Talk with other students, but don't turn it into an inquiring reporter column. Get two or three choice incidents to use as anecdotes.

5. *Seeking new experiences*—Make a point of doing three acts of kindness and report on the response. First dress sloppily, go to the mall and ask passersby for a quarter for a phone call; then dress nicely and do the same; see if there's a difference. Stop people in the school halls or mall and offer them a dollar, no strings attached (if you can get the paper to invest in the experiment)—and note the responses.

   Do something you've never done before: make a trial visit to a fitness center; go to a symphony concert or a wrestling match; try ice skating or a hair-raising roller coaster. Describe what you saw, heard, tasted, smelled and felt, along with incidents involving other people there at the same time.

6. *The news*—Reports in newspapers, on TV, the Internet, your own paper can be a springboard for columns as well. Take an idea, bring it home to your readers from a student's viewpoint and draw the conclusions that seem obvious to you.

Seriously now: A columnist need not be unfailingly lighthearted, bubbly and humorous. But no school columnist should make the mistake of appearing nothing more than a carping critic—someone who comes across as a petty, fault-finding nag who feels superior to the common crowd.

Many engaging and successful columnists place themselves alongside the majority, yet aren't afraid to admit insecurities, embarrassments and shortcomings that others share but try to hide. In fact, columnists sometimes adopt a persona that sounds more insecure and klutzy than they actually seem in person.

A columnist should not hesitate to make a serious or necessary point, such as to deplore casual disrespect for others' person or property, if that conclusion is rightfully drawn from the observation and incidents making up the column.

A one-of-a-kind thing

A good column depends upon the unique personality and viewpoint of its author. For a school newspaper, that means it lasts only a few years at most. No writer should try to take up where another has left off. A column should be retired after its writer's graduation, like a star player's jersey.

Columns are, for sure, a prize for a talented writer, but they must also be tailored to the writer's unique outlook, interests and abilities. Columnists must take full responsibility for their work, actively seek ideas and nurture them with care. Columns are not a spot for egoists who think their readers hardly matter and reporting is beneath them. Good columnists are hardworking reporters themselves who have taken on the extra job of responding to what they report from their own special viewpoint.

Along with the byline comes the byword: Keep it short. A column should be one column, generally around 450 to 650 words—although exceptions come with every rule. If a columnist has nothing to say, say nothing.

Analyzing a column

Examples 2-24A–2-24D are outstanding examples of student-written column material that has appeared in school newspapers throughout the country. Read them carefully to discover how each author has mastered essential elements such as:

1. Has an original perspective
2. Written to make a point
3. Goes beyond the surface
4. Uses sources other than random thoughts
5. Has relevance for student readers
6. Shows, does not just tell
7. Exhibits a high level of writing

Excavating the Wintergreen graveyard

Under-desk gum deposits more than just an inconvenience

By Benn Howard
Computer Editor

Every once in a while, my knee bumps up against the bottom of my desk. And every once in a while, I feel a slight squish as my patella hits the artificial wood.

"Crumpets 'n' Entrails!" I think to myself, "Have I just ended the pitiful life of some fat, bloated insect? Has the top of my knee melted into a fleshy goo?"

No - an inconsiderate cretin has left his/her gum, still warm and moist, under my desk, strategically placed just where my pant leg contacts the surface. Lucky me. Now I have the ever-so-fun task of picking

out every single molecule of gray Doublemint from the fabric. *Just* how I wanted to spend sixth hour.

I did a quick check in my fifth hour Government

class and discovered an average of three globs per desk. What are these people think-

ing? Are they just acting extra-nice and leaving their own gum for the less fortunate who can't always afford a rubbery substance to busy their jaws? Or do they believe that some Bubble-Gum Fairy flutters around the school, whisking the discarded pink blobs away to a magical land full of Wintergreen happiness and Tutti-Frutti joy? Apparently, more students believe in the Gum Fairy than Santa Claus, because almost every classroom has at least one desk-underbelly covered

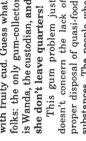

with fruity cud. Guess what, folks: the only gum-collector is Wanda, the custodian, and she don't leave quarters!

This gum problem just doesn't concern the lack of proper disposal of quasi-food substances. The people who carelessly stick their gum wherever-they-darn-well-please have no consideration for the next person who encounters it. Their actions boldly state "As long as I don't have to deal with it any more, I can do what ever I want, and I *don't* care what happens to anybody else."

After asking around, I found a few gum-chewers who claimed they discreetly hid wads to act "rebellious." Fine -

act rebellious, but break the big, important rules, not the tiny, logical, unimportant ones. Sticking gum in inconvenient places is just lazy, impolite, and petty — *not an oh-so-dangerous action of a* James Dean-esque bad boy (or girl.) Daringly shoving Bubble-licious under desks *doesn't* attract members of the opposite sex or give one a rugged appeal.

Maybe we should force students caught performing this unappetizing action to chew *all* the gum wads under their desk.

This solves two problems at once - punishing the offender and disposing of the under-desk blobs.

Example 2-24A. "Excavating the Wintergreen graveyard," by Benn Howard, *The Goal Post*, Bedford H.S., Temperance, MI.

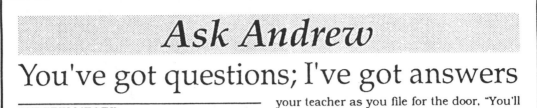

Ask Andrew

You've got questions; I've got answers

ANDREW MEGER
Copy Editor

There you are. You've been sitting in class for the past half-hour, still not understanding what the teacher is getting at in comparing World War I to the cosine of an acute angle in an equilateral triangle.

Knowing your teacher is a sick sadist and will place all this information on your test tomorrow, you raise your hand to ask a question.

The minutes tick by, the teacher is still talking, and your arm is still raised.

You begin to give up hope that any of your questions will ever be answered just as the lecture from Hell stops, and your teacher asks, "Any questions?"

Then the bell rings.

"Good luck on your test tomorrow," says your teacher as you file for the door, "You'll need it."

It's at times like these that you want honest, straight answers. Well, now is your chance.

If you have a question that you never wanted to ask but always wanted to know the answer to, write it down on a piece of paper and drop it off in the newsroom (F119) or into Ms. Trimnal's mailbox.

A signature is required for the question to be printed.

No question is too weird or too obscure for me to try to answer, but please make the question of a printable nature.

So if you've ever wanted to know the secret ingredient that makes those Fiestadas so delectable, or simply just what the capital of Wyoming is, write it down and send it in.

I'll see what I can do for you.

Example 2-24B. "Ask Andrew: You've got questions; I've got answers," by Andrew Meger, *The Spectrum*, Arundel Senior H.S., Gambrills, MD.

ASK ANDREW

Students ponder M&M's, Metro system, Tupperware

ANDREW MEGER
Copy Editor

When asked, the school populace turned out letters numbering in the hundreds (well, seven), each asking a question that has puzzled a student for sometime.

Each received careful consideration and only the hardest and most bizarre questions were chosen (actually, they were picked at random).

Explain how the Metro system works. Do the trains reverse? Do the lines go in a circle? What's going on?

-**Adria Erwin**, senior

Well, I couldn't figure that one out off the top of my head, so I decided to call the Metro Transit Authority.

After a mere 45 minutes on hold (for those of you who are interested, Mel Torme and Frank Sinatra are *in* on the muzac scene), I got a chance to talk with a helpful, if hostile, operator.

It took five minutes for her to grasp the question, despite the fact I spoke very slowly.

When she finally came back to me with an answer (after leaving me in muzac-hell for 15 more minutes), she told me that the trains run forward *and* backward on the same track.

Trains go from point A to point B, then backwards through the tunnels to point A.

Why doesn't Tupperware melt in the microwave? And if it does melt, at what temperature?

-**Mark Koch**, senior

I got in touch with a very sweet operator named Margie at the Tupperware Inc. headquarters hidden deep in Florida.

As it turns out, Tupperware *can* melt in the microwave, especially if it is of the non-microwave safe variety. Even the types tempered against microwave usage will melt if taken above 180 degrees Fahrenheit.

"Always check your Tupperware," Margie said, with concern in her voice. "If it's of the wrong type, it could damage your microwave. We've even heard a rumor that one [microwave] exploded two years ago."

This worries me. In a day and age when we have to fear our mail for package bombs, post offices for disgruntled employees, and federal buildings for Ryder trucks, we also must fear our own Tupperware.

If M&Ms melt in your mouth and not in your hand, what do they do in your armpit?

-**Courtney Davis**, sophomore

The two main factors governing why and where M&M's melt are heat and moisture. If

you are an average youth and your palms are relatively dry, then the candy will not melt unless your hands are extremely warm. Your mouth is normally wet with warm saliva, so the M&M will melt.

Now, if you have just been out exercising and then you place an M&M in your armpit, it will melt because the pit is both hot and covered with sweat.

If your pits are cool, the only effect will be that you'll look pretty silly.

WHERE IS WYOMING??

-**Craig Odar**, senior

There is no such place as Wyoming, at least according to our local 1-800 operator. When I asked for the number of the Wyoming Tourist Information Center, she said that there was no such agency.

The reason for this is that the place we know as "Wyoming" is actually a secret government base where such things as Bigfoot, Jimmy Hoffa, Amelia Earhart, and crashed flying saucers are kept.

All people who live in "Wyoming are in fact government agents. They are required to keep their place of residence a secret as it falls under the realm of national security. For example, how many people do you know from Wyoming? Not many.

If the human body is primarily carbon-based, when it is compressed at a high pressure, would it turn into a diamond?

-**Aaron Mills**, senior

Unfortunately, no. The reason is that while we do have a large amount of carbon in our cellular structures, it is usually chemically combined with other elements like oxygen, nitrogen, and so on.

Because a compound does not necessarily possess the same traits as its parent elements, you won't be able to crush your little brother and get rich in the process.

If everything that goes up must come down, what happens to a bullet that is fired into the air from a starting pistol?

-**Natalie Edwards**, senior

In truth, most starting pistols use blanks, so there is little danger of being hit by a bullet from above.

But in the case of actual weapons using actual bullets, there is a risk of being hit by a falling projectile.

The average bullet leaves the barrel of a hand gun traveling at a certain constant rate of speed. This rate of speed depends on the make of the gun, type of ammunition, and other such factors.

Gravity affects the bullet as

it travels upward, causing it to slow, and, eventually, plummet to the earth.

Where the bullet lands is a function of the angle at which it was initially fired, the more angle, the longer the flight path.

The chances of being hit by a falling bullet are quite slim, unless of course, you live in a gun intensive area, like Texas or Detroit, where any opportunity to fire a gun into the air is taken.

How much would it cost to buy all that stuff listed in "The Twelve Days of Christmas"?

-**Chuck Steele**, senior

About $51,764. That is, of course, if you give your true love all 364 presents. That's about 12 partridges, 40 golden rings, and a whopping 36 calling birds among the multitude of presents given at Christmas.

If, on the other hand, you're stingy and only give your true love one set of each, from 12 drummers drumming to that rascally partridge and his tree, the price would only be about $12,481 (and 65 cents).

It probably wouldn't surprise anyone that a bunch of bored economists at **PNC Bank** have been keeping a record of the price since 1984 as a joke.

Oh, those economists and their wacky sense of humor!

Example 2-24C. "Students ponder M & M's . . . ," by Andrew Meger, *The Spectrum*, Arundel Senior H.S., Gambrills, MD.

8 • The Chronicle

Learning your are, bee, cues

Upon my mom's insistence, a few weeks ago I made my "21 days in advance" reservations for that all-important college-visiting this spring. However, while on the phone with United Airlines, something really started to annoy me—even more than the corny music they play while you are on hold.

I was epessially irritated by the use of a phonetic used with every letter in my confirmation number, such as "F as in Frank."

Whoa There!
Seth Familian

Although this may seem like something which is really stupid to get angry about, I had a lot of free time that day, so I called my sister in angst. The result of that call was our touché to the world of phonetic spellings—the non-phonetic alphabet. (Just stay with me, folks, this is, in fact, funny.)

This "alphabet" can be used to truly aggravate anyone who asks for the spelling of a word, or in my case, a confirmation number. Simply follow the chart below to trick any of your fellow confounded spellers:

A as in are	B as in (stinging/spelling) bee
C as in cue	D as in double-u
E as in eye	F as in Fa–a long, long way to run
G as in gnome	H as in huh?
I as in that is (i.e.)	J as in jalapeño
K as in know	L as in Lladro
M as in mnemonic	N as in take note (n.b.)
O as in Oui	P as in phat
Q as in Qué	R as in prescription (R_x)
S as in sea	T as in tsar
U as in uh...	W as in why
X as in xerox	Y as in yawp

Well, there you have it folks! I realize that the letters O and Q are in other languages and letters such as B, F, N, U and Y are a little far-fetched, but what do you expect? We were just trying to be creative!

Well, that's the end of my c as in cue, o as in oui, l as in Lladro, u as in uh..., m as in mnemonic, n as in take note!

Example 2-24D. "Whoa there: Learning your are, bee, cues," by Seth Familian, *The Chronicle,* Harvard-Westlake School, North Hollywood, CA.

Name _____   Date _____

— EXERCISE 24A —
Writing your column analysis

DIRECTIONS:

The following questions are tools for analyzing a column. Use one of the examples given or another column, assigned by your adviser.

Example No. (If applicable) _____   Publication _____

1. Headline _____

2. Why is (or is not) this topic of sufficient interest to students to rate a column?

   _____

   _____

   _____

3. What probably inspired the columnist? Name the type of factor (news, observation, personal experience, etc.) and the specific source.

   _____

   _____

4. What point is the columnist making?

   _____

   _____

   _____

5. Besides his or her ideas, from what sources has the writer gained material for the column?

   _____

   _____

   _____

6. Analyze the level of writing. Consider such factors as word choice, style, use of quotes, grammatical usage, transitions, etc.

   _____

   _____

   _____

— EXERCISE 24A —
Writing your column analysis (cont'd)

7. What weaknesses, if any, do you find in this column? Be precise, giving examples.

_____

_____

_____

_____

_____

_____

_____

_____

_____

_____

8. Briefly sum up your overall opinion of this column.

_____

_____

_____

_____

_____

_____

_____

_____

_____

_____

_____

_____

_____

_____

Name _____   Date _____

— EXERCISE 24B —
Expressing yourself as a columnist

DIRECTIONS:

Choose a topic, based on your observation of incidents at your school or a personal experience especially planned for this assignment. Use examples, details, and techniques of "show, don't tell" to express your views about it. Keep to approximately 450-600 words.

Accent on entertainment

More and more pages of school newspapers feature entertainment. In fact, one carried entertainment on 6 of its 24 pages—the same number devoted to news. Of course, some entertainment stories do qualify as straight news—the upcoming school carnival, for example. The annual school band concert qualifies, too, although some don't think of such shows as entertainment but as command performances for family and friends.

Many profiles and feature stories also fit the entertainment category: the student dancer who won a coveted role in a community ballet or a background story on set building and prop gathering for the drama club play. The possibilities are many, yet most school papers almost entirely overlook the school itself as a source of entertainment stories. Instead, they rely on reviews of CDs, movies, television, restaurants, concerts and sometimes books—and therein lies the danger.

The temptation of reviewing

In professional newspapers, the review is a column in which a writer knowledgeable in a chosen field criticizes a piece of entertainment for the reader's enlightenment. It's a prize assignment that calls for taste and judgment.

Writing reviews presents many potential pitfalls for inexperienced writers. The most noticeable is the temptation to fill up space with empty words or "borrow" from professional reviewers.

Lengthy reviews solve the shortage of story ideas but, in spite of the apparent lure of entertainment, add little to readership appeal. An entertainment page carrying just two long reviews and streams of gray type—can hardly look lively and entertaining.

Remember the rule: Primary sources!

It's a given that any review expresses its writer's opinion. But it's also assumed that the writer has been there, done that . . . has used his or her eyes, ears and other senses, as well as having a ready vocabulary of aptly chosen words to share those reactions with someone just as interested.

In well-done reviews, readers share the experience and reaction of the writer—and see the reason for the reviewer's enthusiasm or lack of it. Reviewers, like other columnists, can just spout words, but they are really reporters, who should accurately describe what they hear and/or see as well as express their impressions and reactions.

"I think so-and-so did a really good job . . . the album was one of the group's greatest so far . . . the third cut has some especially good lyrics . . . all in all, the album was really not bad."

Such an example, the type found in too many school papers, leaves a reader wondering, "What was the album really like? Who's fooling whom?"

To the other extreme

The professional reviewer or critic needs broad and deep experience, as well as a background that assures valid comparisons and often a specialized vocabulary. Lacking such background, many student reviewers lean on jacket covers, liner notes and professional reviews instead of their own understanding, vocabulary and opinion. At times they sound lame, as in the previous example. Some sound as if they were striving to get the professional jargon right but not quite making it.

Others simply sound too good for student work. The ugly word *plagiarism* becomes unavoidable, though the accusation needs proof. Unless the source is known, comparison of the suspected work with writing done on other work can provide a clue.

The real question

By publishing long reviews of music and films, does our school paper try to provide an original and valid source of information for its readers? Or are reviews just an easy way to fill pages? Are reviews better and more timely in magazines, professional papers and on TV?

Entertainment well done

Entertainment stories in school papers can be lively, original, informative . . . and entertaining, too. Page editors or editors and reporters should be on the alert for ideas and plan to originate the following types of stories:

1. *Behind-the-scenes reports:* Eyewitness accounts of backstage life after a concert, a committee decorating its homecoming float or rehearsals of a class play—with the reporter being the eyes and ears plus other senses of the reader.

2. *Profiles of students or teachers engaged in one of the lively arts:* Music, literature, drama, dance, creative arts—what it takes and what it gives, what they hope and dream. A feature portrait in which a person comes to life is entertaining in itself.

3. *Reviews of student plays, performances:* Written to make those who attended nod in agreement and those who didn't go wish that they had gone, if positively reviewed. Try to accent the good, yet report honestly on student work.

4. *Entertainment features:* Human interest, historical, informative—any feature format, all with close attention to details, examples, incidents, anecdotes and quotes, written firsthand from primary sources and personal interviews.

5. *Focus on reviewing:* A series of short reviews, giving the reader choices, is preferable to wordy recitals listing names, titles, a plethora of details, just to fill space.

Rated reviews: A quick, eye-catching way to get across the reviewer's opinion is by developing a rating system for each type of review. The classic symbol is the star, ☆☆☆☆—4 or 5 for tops, down to 0 or 1 for flops.

In school, the A+ to F scale is a natural, but you can create original symbols, such as one diamond to four ◇◇◇ for eating places, or a musical symbol such as ♪♪♪ for records.

Make use of sidebars: Instead of cluttering reviews with lists of names, titles and other data, create boxed sidebars with information like restaurant hours, lists of performers, ticket charges and price ranges, and other helpful facts.

Develop creative approaches to all types of reviews

1. *Restaurants:* Feature different kinds of ethnic restaurants each issue or pick another special purpose for the choices made.

   Focus on the treatment of students dining unaccompanied by adults, the kind of food that would appeal most to students and their budgets. You might conduct experiments, such as the difference in managements' attitudes toward someone dressed up or down. As a reviewer, do nothing, however, to call undue attention to yourself. A restaurant reviewer, by definition, is supposed to be anonymous—just another patron.

One school featured a pair of reviewers on the restaurant beat, two boys who reported on their findings in dialogue form. Tossing their comments back and forth, they created a witty and informative column.

2. *CDs, music, videos:* Professionals almost always get there first—with review copies sent out to magazines and stations, often well before they're available in local stores. It's hard for school papers to compete and easy to echo the pros' opinions, if not outright "lift" them.

   Try new approaches. Do album reviews inquiring reporter style. Ask students to name their favorite and newest disc, why they like it and what cuts they prefer. Avoid repetition, but alert students whose favorite was already taken. Keep a list of names to avoid repeating.

   If a staffer writes the reviews, cover more than one and keep them short, to the point and clearly rated.

3. *Movies:* As with CDs, the professionals review them first. Unlike music reviews, a movie may have neared the end of its run and been seen by most fans before the paper gets to it.

   Do a switch. Instead of movies already seen in the multiplexes or shown on TV, write reviews of classic movies, perhaps as "The Video Kid." Choose classic comedies such as Buster Keaton's *The Great Train Robbery, The Gods Must be Crazy,* or anything by Laurel and Hardy or the Marx Brothers.

   Do a series of reviews on films starring legends like Marilyn Monroe, John Wayne or Sidney Poitier. Review foreign-language films that have an educational tie-in: *Das Boot,* the German U-boat film, or *Like Water for Chocolate,* originally in Spanish.

4. *The threat of television:* Because of its universal popularity, it's tempting to turn to television, but with TV it's even harder to find an angle that hasn't been taken, not once but many times before, than with movies or music. Avoid tackling the subject unless you have something really new to say.

5. *The Internet, computer games:* If you like to browse, report on Web sites of special interest to students. Pick a special topic, the fan club of a favorite movie star, for example, and report on what you find. Include sample tidbits from each site—and its address.

   When reviewing computer games, keep them brief, go the inquiring reporter route, and avoid the temptation of taking your lead from other sources. Both the Internet and computer games offer the possibility, through a poll or survey, of answering such questions as how many students regularly devote time to either, how many hours they average daily or weekly and so on. Also interview students and thread significant quotes, along with the opinions of experts and teacher, concerning the impact of technology in your school.

6. *Local concerts, performances:* Without a special "inside" story, an event several weeks past is hard to cover effectively. It doesn't hurt to overlook it.

Analyzing an entertainment story

Examples 2-25A–2-25D illustrate the variety of outstanding student-written entertainment stories that have appeared in school newspapers throughout the country. Read them carefully to discover how each author has mastered essential elements such as:

1. Has an original approach

2. Uses primary sources

3. Offers information, not just opinion

4. Keeps to the point—does not waste words

5. Seems knowledgeable, enthusiastic

6. Shows awareness of reader's interests

Offbeat author describes Gen X

His books reflect the typical youth of the 90s with a message that is timeless.

Whitney Kee Dane
Entertainment Editor

Divorce, post-college angst, yuppie-busting, hippie parents and an unclassified generation are predominant topics penetrating the works of author Douglas Coupland.

In the style of J.D. Salinger, Coupland produces modern-day companions to "Catcher in the Rye," using uniquely fresh vocabulary and reflecting the self-consciousness of the 90s' youth.

A Canadian native, Coupland's first three novels, "Life After God," "Generation X" and "Shampoo Planet," not only accurately convey the essence of the 20-something crowd, but also catechize their wall street, media-produced predecessors.

Witty and honestly-observant, Coupland successfully captures the listlessness of today's info-laden culture, and defines the idiosyncrasies of the generation familiar to him, without being preachy or morose.

Not altering his opinions or style for the sake of being in the mainstream, like many aspiring writers today, Coupland discloses social criticisms with an arresting eye for satire, irony and humor, ultimately mastering the generational experience.

Coupland's novels offer something new and exciting for the youth today. Like "Oedipus Rex," the message is timeless while the characters remain typical of the 90s.

"Shampoo Planet" cover courtesy of Pocket Books Fiction.

Example 2-25A "Offbeat author describes Gen X," by Whitney Kee Dane, *Sound to Sea*, Manteo H.S., Manteo, NC.

RENTAL REVIEW

Making the best of Le Bad Cinema

Straying from the norm of A-list movies, B-list movies offer flying saucers, stupid cavemen and lots of laughs

Eric Hsieh
Michelle Yung
Staff Writers

Tired of watching four-star movies filled with too much theme acted out by fine thespians? No. Getting weary of magnificent special effects and great make-up? Not really.

If so, then whip out the movie rental card and be prepared to watch such great masterpieces with rhetorical titles such as, Hollywood Hot Tubs: Educating Cystal, Attack of the Body Snatchers and The Invasion of the Zombies from Mars who killed George Washington. Luckily enough, we did not subject ourselves to such horrible movies, but instead as dignified reporters, we chose to review slightly more palatable movies titled (we're not kidding) Attack of the Killer Tomatoes, Eegah!, and Plan 9 From Outer Space.

EEGAH!
zero-stars
(pretty good for a bad movie)

With a name like *Eegah!*, the first movie we reviewed could belong nowhere else but with its similarly

crude peers. *Eegah!* is named after the grunt made by the loveable caveman Richard Kiel, who starred as *Jaws* of 007 fame. The plot is simple: Neanderthal captures babe; babe escapes; Neanderthal comes looking for babe; Neanderthal gets shot by cops. *Eegah!* will earn no bonus points for the acting; the cast's speech gave the impression of a prolonged episode of "Leave It to Beaver." However, watching the naturally tanned guitar virtuoso Tom exchanging punches with his friend over bodacious babe Roxy was exciting enough to merit a break from perpetual fast forward.

Although it appeared that director Nicholas Merriwether filmed *Eegah!* in the act of walking to his cave for two minutes on end just to fill the 95 minutes, we did somewhat enjoy the movie. After all, we could make fun of it. What other movies would have great lines such as, "Gee, Roxy! I swear on all my Elvis albums that I wrote that song!" ?

ATTACK OF THE KILLER TOMATOES
one and one half stars
(This belongs in the LeBad section? Hm. Quite good, actually.)

Just from reading the title of this movie, it is easily ascertained that viewers are in for a good 90 minutes of unparalleled idiocy. We expected this and we certainly got it … with a lot of laughs to go with it as well.

Killer Tomatoes proved to be rather hilarious with its march-like theme song which opened up the movie with a big bang of slapstick.

In the tradition of the Zucker brothers who gave us *The Naked Gun* series, *Killer Tomatoes* showcased a rather funny cast, including a troop of tomatoes which made gurgling noises closely resembling to what Eewoks on helium may sound like.

PLAN 9 FROM OUTER SPACE
negative four stars
(The Mutha of all LeBads)

Sitting through *Plan 9* was a pure nightmare, even though the movie was only 78 minutes long. Unlike *Eegah!*, we could not even push fast forward because there was a plot, albeit very poorly executed. The spectacular visual effects drove us to the edge of our seats as we watched the strings holding up the space saucers which oh-so-gently cascaded across an over-used painting of fluffy clouds.

Not surprisingly, this movie spawned right from the creative womb of the king of all bad movies, Edward D. Wood, Jr. himself. Wood made it fashionable to use stock footage and clips from other

films which he would unabashedly insert into his own works of art. These scenes are quite easy to spot; let's just say that Mr. Wood had no chance of filming a myriad of tanks and soldiers storm across desert land to shoot down a few flying saucers.

Wood is as bad as a writer as he is a director. *Plan 9* gives the writers of the kid-adored television favorite "Power Rangers" a lot of hope. We don't know if Wood was trying to build up suspense or if he was just plain stupid. Take the cemetery scene for example: a group of officers and an inspector hover above a corpse. After a few minutes of examining the corpse, the inspector finally declares, "Well it's obvious that he's dead. And it's obvious that he's been killed … murdered. That means there's *got* to be somebody responsible for it." No, really … we're smarter than laboratory mice.

> "Not surprisingly, this movie (Plan 9) spawned right from the creative womb of the king of all bad movies, Edward D. Wood, Jr. himself. Wood made it fashionable to use stock footage and clips from other films which he would unabashedly insert into his own works of art."

Example 2-25B. "Making the best of Le Bad Cinema," by Eric Hsieh, Michelle Yung, *The Prospector,* Cupertino H.S., Cupertino, CA.

TokyoDen no Tabemono wa Ooishi desu
Tokyo Den offers authentic Japanese settings, good tasting food

BY SUZY KRATZIG

Like most typical Japanese restaurants, Tokyo Den has beautiful aquariums, fountains, and a tatami that can be sectioned off with sliding Japanese doors. The journalism students ate in two of these tatami rooms after first kicking off their shoes and sitting down on cushion "chairs" that can slide up to a long black table. On the table were not forks and knives, but chopsticks, and everyone on the staff became proficient chopstick users by the end of the meal.

After much deliberation over what to order, they decided to get several different dishes and share so that everyone could try a little bit of everything. They ordered gyoza, chicken yaki tori, and many other Japanese dishes.

Junior Anthony Pizzini, a frequent Japanese food eater, ordered sushi in addition to the other dishes. "The sushi comes in a variety of raw and cooked sea life," he said. Pizzini ordered cooked octopus and shrimp sushi.

Newspaper and yearbook adviser Candis Brinegar tried sushi for the first time. "The octopus is firm," she said. "It's good."

Each meal comes with misu soup (a watery, tangy soup), a salad, steamed rice, and an orange.

In the tatami room, a Japanese waitress teaches seniors Joaquin Herrera and Staci Cooper how to prepare shabu-shabu at their table. *Photo by Daniel Davis*

Different sauces compliment each dish. "The sauces were really hot," senior Joaquin Herrera said.

Seaweed, avocado, cucumber, and crab legs surrounded by a layer of rice are the ingredients of the California roll. Gyoza are beef dumplings and taste like mexican beef, according to junior Monica Davila. Yaki tori is grilled chicken served with vegetables and covered with teriyaki sauce.

"If I could live on just vegetables, beef teriyaki, and chicken teriyaki, I would live in Japan," sophomore Josephine Corpus said.

Misako Cummins, a waitress originally from Yokohama, Japan, brought us shabu shabu, a winter dish that the customers cook themselves. Shabu shabu comes with a strange looking cooking instrument, donut-shaped with hot water in the donut part, and an enormous plate covered with carrots, cabbage, spinach, onions, Japanese mushrooms, rib-eye steak (cut paper thin), and fishcake (fish ground fine and then steamed).

The Japanese waitress taught us how to cook the food in the water, and the few journalists (who still had room left in their stomachs) enjoyed the shabu shabu. "I've had so much food, and it tastes so good, just like authentic Japanese food," said junior Clarissa Gonzales, who spent last summer in Japan.

Tokyo Garden offers Japanese ice cream as well. We sampled two of the three kinds, the green tea ice cream and the red bean ice cream. "The [green tea] ice cream tastes like lipstick," Brinegar said.

The red bean ice cream actually has red beans in it, thus the name. "It's a heavier texture with a fruity taste," sophomore Sarah Wisian said.

Overall, the 13 students enjoyed the $290 meal (keep in mind the number of people and the great amount of food). "It's a good place," senior Daniel Davis said. "It's worth the money. The Japanese cabbage is especially good."

Seniors Vilma Gonzalez and Suzy Kratzig enjoy a varity of traditional Japanese food at Tokyo Den. Gonzalez is familar with *eating* with chopsticks, because she visited Japan last summer with the *Sister City* Program. Kratzig, however, struggled eating with the Japanese utensils. *Photo by Daniel Davis*

Japanese Factoids

• Rice, the main crop of Japan, used to be part of every meal; however, lately, the Japanese have begun eating bread at one or two of the meals.

• A Japanese diet has typically used little fat, and obesity has never been a big problem. Since food chains from the United States have been coming to Japan, however, the Sumo wrestlers have not been the only overweight Japanese.

• Slurping noodles, eating fast, and shoveling food into your mouth is considered good manners.

• Fish and soybean products, in the form of tofu or miso, provide the protein in the Japanese diet.

• Japanese people sometimes eat live shrimp in a ritual called *odori*, which means dance, because the shrimp wiggle and dance while being consumed.

• Before almost every meal the Japanese say, "Itadaki masu," pronounced ee-tah-dah-kee mahss which is equivalent to the American grace, and they do not eat until they say it.

• Okonomi-yaki, "Japanese pizza," is something the customers cook themselves on a grill at the table. It is composed of a stiff batter, a raw egg, chopped vegetables and fish or meat, and spiced up with flaked fish and seaweed.

• A typical feature of a traditional Japanese breakfast is seaweed.

Example 2-25C. "Tokyo Den offers authentic. . . ," by Suzy Kratzig, *El Tejano*, W. B. Ray H.S., Corpus Christi, TX.

Put a Little Mystery in Your Life

by Suzyn Smith

Spring Break is just around the corner, and whether you'll be lying on the beach, or just hanging around in McLean, there is no better reading than a mystery serial. Whether your favorite detective is Miss Marple or Sam Spade, there is certainly a mystery serial to suit your fancy....

Continental Op
by Dashell Hammet

Continental Op is about a detective by the same name and his adventures solving several cases. This book is one of three *Continental Op* books, all of which contain about half a dozen short stories. The various stories keep it interesting, and it's a fast paced, enjoyable book.

My only complaint is its lack of character. *Continental Op* seems to have no life outside of detective work. It doesn't appear that he eats, sleeps, or exists outside of his cases. *Continental Op* is a good book, but the Sam Spade series by the same author is even better.

A is for Alibi
by Sue Grafton

This was by far the best of the books I reviewed. Kinsey Millhone, a private eye and general tough chick, is searching for the killer of her client's Don Juan husband.

Kinsey is a joy to read about. She is an interesting person and you find yourself caring about her as well as being slightly in awe of her. The characters are described well and the action is fast paced.

The book has a complicated plot and sharply written dialogue, but it's not so heavy that it doesn't make a good beach read.

There are eleven books in this series, from *A is for Alibi* to *K is for Killer.* If the other 10 are anywhere near as good as this one, I recommend them all.

The Mystery of the Cold Hands
by Erle Stanley Gardener

If you are an insomniac like myself, you are accustomed to waking up at three in the morning and watching Perry Mason on FOX. It's a decent show, and there's a decent line of books behind it.

The detective in this series is actually a lawyer (this is better than Matlock, I swear.) He and his faithful secretary/girlfriend Della solve the murder of a man who had accused Perry's client of embezzlement.

It's an easy read and enjoyable. It's an older series, but it's nice way to spend a Sunday afternoon.

The Cat Who Saw Red
by Lillian Jackson Braun

A popular theme in mysteries is having people not normally associated with crime solving the mysteries. But this trend reached a new level with the introduction of this series, where the detectives are cats. One of the interesting things about this book is that one is never sure if Koko and Yum Yum really know what is going on or if they are just incredibly lucky, since their owner narrates.

In *The Cat Who Saw Red*, the cats solve the murder of their owner's high school sweetheart. It's entertaining, but if you're looking for a hardboiled mystery thriller, you'll have to look elsewhere. This book is lighthearted and a good beach read, but not worthy of great scrutiny.

Example 2-25D. "Put a little mystery in your life," by Suzyn Smith, *The Highlander,* McLean H.S., McLean, VA.

Name _____ Date _____

— EXERCISE 25A —
Analyzing an entertainment piece

DIRECTIONS:

The following questions are tools for analyzing the examples given and others similar in type, assigned by your adviser. Since some stories about entertainment are also news or features, use the appropriate analysis for these types of articles.

Example No. (If applicable) _____ Publication _____

1. Headline _____

2. Why does (or does not) this story offer information not readily found in professional media?

   _____

   _____

   _____

3. What primary sources did the writer or writers use?

   _____

   _____

   _____

4. Why does (or doesn't) the writer or writers seem knowledgeable and enthusiastic?

   _____

   _____

   _____

5. Does the article seem to make good use of space or primarily serve as a space filler? Explain your choice. _____

   _____

   _____

6. Analyze the level of writing. Consider such factors as word choice, style, use of quotes, grammatical usage, transitions, etc.

   _____

   _____

   _____

— EXERCISE 25A —
Analyzing an entertainment piece *(cont'd)*

7. What weaknesses, if any, do you find in this article? Be precise, giving examples.

_____

_____

_____

_____

_____

_____

_____

_____

_____

8. Briefly sum up your overall opinion of this piece.

_____

_____

_____

_____

_____

_____

_____

_____

_____

_____

_____

_____

_____

_____

Name _____   Date _____

— EXERCISE 25B —
Covering entertainment . . . Expressing yourself as a reviewer

DIRECTIONS:

Choose one type of entertainment story, then select a topic and write an article suitable for your school paper. Remember the importance of primary sources and an informative, original viewpoint.

_____

_____

_____

_____

_____

_____

_____

_____

_____

_____

_____

_____

_____

_____

_____

_____

_____

_____

_____

_____

_____

_____

Room for opinion—Editorials

Speaking for the paper

Like all items in a newspaper—news stories, features, columns and even sidebars—editorials require substance. When readers get the idea that the purpose is to fill up space or writers are parroting others' opinions, the paper gets the reputation of not being worth reading.

Because they represent the opinion of the paper itself, editorials should excel in both content and quality. Unlike most articles, editorials carry no bylines. This anonymity does not equate with insignificance, for editorials represent the official stance of the paper's editor, editorial board and publisher toward the issue in question.

The problem for school papers

Who is publisher of a school paper? The answer, debatable, deserves consideration. To school administrations, the answer is obvious. The administration is responsible for the paper's existence, therefore is its publisher by definition. This becomes more certain in direct relation to the support it contributes, and a Supreme Court decree upholds its legal right to censor a school paper.

Unlike a professional paper in which editorials may champion certain sides of political issues because of its owner's or publisher's views, the school administration and school newspaper staff often see their shared situation from very different perspectives. To staff and adviser alike, the school paper is not a newsletter, not a propaganda device. It is the voice of the students, and it needs to be editorially free to express student views.

Allowing for differences

Just as the administration may have a narrow concept of its and students' roles in schools, so may editorial board and staff have an agenda of their own—a "we vs. they" attitude. But the question is, who are "we" and who are "they"? Under administrative pressure, the answer may become, "We are the besieged newspaper staff." The resultant editorials tend to speak privately to this condition, not to and for the general student body.

Remember, no matter what your purpose or topic, an editorial is no place to indulge in personal attacks. One aim of editorials is to win their readers to your side. This means not only those who are already with you but those who haven't yet made up their minds. A good editorial tries to present its views with logic, a sense of balance and supporting proof that impress all readers with the merit and reasonableness of its opinion, causing them to reweigh their views, if not winning them to yours.

Before an editorial topic is decided upon, the editorial board should discuss its validity and its ramifications.

Editorial angles

Pointing out what's wrong is easier than contributing to a problem's solution—and a good editorial's concern should be to better a situation, not to bludgeon it. Starting points for good editorials range far beyond the problem type. Look around, and decide what interests and concerns of your student body, school, community—or even the country and world—could be the basis of an editorial or series of editorials.

Many editorials are directly related to the news—giving the paper an opportunity to express ideas editorially that objective reporting makes off limits in newswriting. Editorials are sometimes based on "news pegs" or related stories that appear in the same issue.

Because an editorial speaks for the paper and its editorial board, the pronoun "we," known as the "editorial we," takes the place of the singular "I" when the writer openly expresses an opinion. "We believe the students and administration can find grounds for uniting and solving this problem. . . ."

Focusing on your goal

Editorial writers set out to accomplish one or more of these goals for their readers:

1. *Interpret:* The situation is complicated; the rumors and hall talk make it worse. A good editorial can provide the necessary background and promote understanding.

   Such topics as a change in graduation requirements, new laws concerning parents' legal liability for their offsprings' behavior, and students' unawareness of the effects of new products and fads can provide grounds for research and editorial interpretation.

2. *Criticize:* It needn't always be negative. One synonym for *criticize* is to judge, and judges award blue ribbons as well as hand out prison sentences.

   Look for student efforts that have turned out well and administration initiatives that hold promise. Don't concentrate only on sore spots that need fixing, although don't hesitate to turn a bright spotlight where attention is needed.

3. *Persuade:* A call for action, for understanding, for agreement. Many editorials set out to convince their readers—whether it is the wisdom of 18-year-olds' registering to vote or signing the Prom Promise.

   Editorials are not lectures, sermons nor cheerleading exercises. They need to go beyond what "everyone knows" and is "supposed to think." Because such topics seem ripe and ready, they are easy to pick, but they can be hard to write in a way that invokes a thoughtful response.

4. *Inform:* It's not news, but few students know about it, and they ought to know. It may be students who contribute their time and efforts to a worthy cause. Or provisions to make the school more livable for those with disabilities—and how able-bodied students can do their share to help.

5. *Entertain:* Humor and a lighthearted approach can provide a fresh way of seeing familiar places and situations. For example, how would a visitor from outer space—or the distant past—"see" the crowded hallways or student fashions?

Instead of negatively criticizing certain types of behavior, devise a new set of standards, making them the norm. What if kids were graded on desktop graffiti? Beware of satire, which often slips into sarcasm and cruelty, only seeming fun to someone who wrote it or is out of its range.

Editing the editorial

It's been said that it's more difficult to prepare a ten-minute speech than make an hour one. It's harder, if not more time consuming, to write a good short story or poem than a novel. And someone who likes to talk a lot often says less than a person of few words. The care taken in choosing those words matters, and in writing editorially, every word matters greatly.

Keep to the point

Keeping track of words keeps writers focused on what they're trying to say. It's especially important for those who are fluent with language and can fill up a page, while hardly pausing for breath.

Lead editorials in high school papers should run approximately 350 to 500 words long. Editorials that grow longer tend to lose readers—not because readers are mindless or even uncaring about major issues, but because the writer got so carried away with the sound of his or her own words that the editorial lost its focus and wandered into mushy vagueness or purposeless repetition.

Three parts of a whole editorial

1. *The lead:* No formula exists for writing the first paragraph of an editorial. The subject dictates how you begin; however, don't start an editorial with a hard sell. Don't imply that your views are right and anyone who disagrees is a blind fool. Such attitudes close the mind of anyone who believes differently, no matter how persuasive your proof. Don't begin with a question, such as "Do you believe capital punishment is murder?" You'll invite your readers to answer, and begin thinking of their own views, not yours.

   Do approach your lead with interest, enthusiasm and purpose, concentrating on how you can best share your opinions with your readers, making your outlook theirs.

2. *Body:* Center on supporting details, evidence and examples that prove your point and will help your readers reconsider theirs, if different. In editorials, as well as other types of writing, showing is more effective than telling someone what or how to think. If the topic involves controversy or conflict, don't adopt a fighting stance. Accept the sincerity of the others' views and seek a common ground that will clarify the validity of yours.

3. *Conclusion:* The final paragraph of an editorial should leave your reader with something to think over, act upon, agree with, and/or smile about. Ideally, every sentence and paragraph should point toward this conclusion. If it doesn't, perhaps you didn't have the purpose clearly enough in mind or allowed yourself to become sidetracked.

The editorial page: The paper's home page

Traditionally free of advertising, the editorial page expresses the paper's convictions. In many papers, it's found on page 2, but it would be equally valid directly after the paper's successive news pages, especially if editorial issues take up more than one page.

Contents of the editorial page all relate to the paper, its staff policy and opinions. These include:

1. *Editorials.*

2. *Mini-editorials:* A few short paragraphs, offering tokens of praise for something well done or brief comments on areas needing attention. If they express the paper's view, they need no byline.

   Mini-editorials may also fit as a column, identified with an icon or standing head such as "Pluses & Minuses," which briefly touches on positive and negative examples of school concerns.

3. *Letters to the editor:* Comments from students, plus statement of policy for acceptance. The forum editor should screen for factual accuracy, advise contributors of needed changes, keep a list of those published to avoid repetition or favoritism, consult with editors about Editor's Notes, if needed, and be careful not to belittle contributors' opinions if varying from paper's. Staff members may not participate—the paper is theirs.

4. *Editorial cartoon:* An editorial statement in itself, the editorial cartoon may illustrate an editorial or stand alone. If a separate editorial, the cartoon may take a standing head and/or caption.

5. *Photo editorial:* A picture can speak volumes, perhaps as an editorial statement on vandalism or as a graphic warning against drunken driving. If used as an editorial, a photo should be clearly boxed and have caption, cutline and credit.

6. *Editorial columns:* Not the official opinion of the paper but of the writer, who is identified with byline and perhaps thumbnail portrait and standing head. Editorial columns may tackle the same topics as other editorials but reflect only the writer's personal views.

Going overboard on opinion

One or two pages provide a sufficiency of space for opinion in a school paper. More create the impression that the paper has centered itself on its staff members' interests and egos, instead of seeking news and features of interest to everyone in the school.

Instead of running numerous pages of opinion, it is preferable that pages carry specific folio lines reading *Features, Entertainment, Lifestyle* and so forth. Since columns generally fit one or another of these headings, they can be parceled one to a page and spark the entire issue.

Analyzing an editorial

Examples 2-26A–2-26C are outstanding examples of student-written editorials that have appeared in school newspapers throughout the country. Read them carefully to discover how they have handled essential elements of the editorial such as:

1. Clear purpose or goal

2. Effective introduction or lead

3. Broad, analytical point of view

4. Supporting evidence

5. Coherent organization

6. Thought-provoking conclusion

STAFF EDITORIAL

Choosing to serve

4.0 credits of physical education, 1.0 credit of fine arts, 1.0 credit of applied arts, 0.5 credit of consumer education and 50 hours of community service. Fifty hours of community service?!

As graduation requirements continue to restrict students' choices, proponents of mandatory community service have gone too far.

Recently a committee of faculty and staff discussed a mandatory community service requirement for graduation. Whether or not it will be implemented, and the conditions under which it may be implemented are still being debated.

First of all, we are all for community service. Spending time to better the community and become more socially conscious and responsible is commendable. We would encourage all who have not enjoyed this experience to seriously consider it. Undoubtedly, many of us students would greatly benefit from the opportunity to serve others whether it is voluntary or it merely fulfills a requirement. Not only would we learn valuable lessons in service, we

would gain a valuable experience in helping others.

The spirit of volunteerism has always been alive in America. Making it mandatory, however, eliminates the "volunteer" aspect of volunteerism. Many students have already chosen to take part in voluntary community service, and we applaud them for it. However, the key word here is "chosen." Once this choice is taken away, a probable outcome is that some students will serve with the wrong attitude.

Volunteer work should be done by people with an eagerness to donate their time and services to those who need it, not by kids who would rather be elsewhere. Instilling this attitude in students defeats the whole purpose of the service requirement.

Also, creating this extra requirement for graduation goes beyond the school's rights. In all respect and fairness to the students at Central, the establishment of graduation requirements should remain within the realm of courses taken during school. It should not extend to the time outside of school known to most as "free" time. An infringement of this free time is unfair and insensitive to students' rights.

Who will end up deciding whether we will have this requirement or not? Since the affected parties involve the students, the entire student body should have a voice. Unless the proposition passes by vote, it should not be considered.

Community service is great. The freedom to choose to serve or not to serve is even better. Many worthwhile opportunities exist for high school students. However, the decision about which opportunities to pursue should be up to each individual.

Let's keep it that way.

Example 2-26A. "Choosing to serve," *Devils' Advocate*, Hinsdale Central H.S., Hinsdale, IL.

Rudeness runs rampant recently

A monster named Rudeness is running rampant through the halls of WCHS. This monster claws at the innocent and robs people of their common sense.

To be fair, only a small number of us have been bitten by this nasty little bug, but those who have managed to cause enough havoc and temper flare-ups among us sane people to make us all feel a bit mean.

The following are some profiles of the most common types of rudeness in WCHS.

The Careless Lane Charger

Many a time, while fighting our way through a cramped, sweaty hallway, we get clubbed in the face by a huge backpack mounted on the back of a student. For whatever reason, this person has suddenly stopped, cut in front of us or swung around-knocking us into walls, other people, etc.

The main problem with this person is a lack of awareness.

Completely oblivious to the fact that he shares the hallway with 200 other people, he is totally clueless as to why the wild-eyed person behind him is stepping on the backs of his heels with a vengeance.

The Lunch Line Hopper

This is the rude person who cruises by all of us relatively nice people waiting in a single file line to obtain food.

This person not only has the audacity to constantly cut in line but to also yell, "I'm just getting Nachos! I'm just getting Nachos!" to the rest of us, who he must believe are blind or stupid.

The Immature Gum Chewer

This is the rude person without a face. A wolf in sheep's clothing, he looks more like a member of the herd than the predator he is.

This is the person who never learned how to dispose of his chewing gum properly. No, these people feel compelled to spit their gum on to the floor or into the drinking fountains.

So all of us relatively nice people come along and become grossed out after coming away from a fountain with a mouthful of someone else's spit or not moving at all because one of our shoes is stuck to a wad of Bubble Yum on the floor.

The Locker Space Hog

Everyone has had to deal with this type of rude person. This is the person who opens their locker door soooo wide that there is no way we can possibly see our combination lock, let alone open the darn thing.

These people do not respond to pleas, bribes or dirty looks because they, like the Careless Lane Charger, are oblivious to the face that there's anyone else in the hallway but THEM.

Alright, to be completely fair and honest everyone is a capable of committing these rude acts from time to time. Hey, we're only human.

The main difference, however, between a truly rude person doing these things and a relatively nice person doing them is this: A nice person smiles and says, "Sorry!"

Guys, we're all stuck in this place together. Were all tired, sick, bored and praying Spring Break gets here *very soon*, so let's all be a little more courteous to one another.

In the words of a certain wise man we all know and love, "Be nice to each other." Just do it. It's even easier than it sounds.

Example 2-26B. "Rudeness runs rampant recently," *Tracks*, Warsaw Community H.S., Warsaw, IN.

THE CATALYST ADDRESSES ISSUES IMPORTANT TO STUDENTS

Value of speakers questioned

Talk isn't cheap when it comes to motivational speakers. This year students have been subjected to three such speakers, and the results were less than outstanding.

Exclusively for the freshmen, Adam Robinson spoke about being a better student and unlocking their potential. In front of the whole school, Bruce Buguski shared his wit concerning respect and the power of positive thinking, and Anne Anzalonie spoke about individual learning skills.

Having Robinson as a speaker cost $1,000. The Student Senate helped with the cost as well as The Academic Excellence foundation and other organizations. Buguski (who Southview shared with McCord) was partially paid for by the Council of Clubs. Anzalonie cost the school $400 plus a contribution from the Academic Boosters for $300. So, assuming that Buguski makes an average speakers salary of $900, that's a total of $2, 600 spent for speakers.

Some could argue that the money is worth it if the students are learning and growing from the experience, but the problem is, they aren't.

Most students don't pay any attention to the speaker. They talk amongst themselves and don't catch a minute of what the person is trying to say. Even if the students do listen though, they don't usually take the message to heart.

The intentions were good. The school hoped to help students with their study skills, and increase respect in the building, but motivational speakers aren't getting the job done.

Teaching the students respect and good study skills should happen in the classroom. Whenever students attend a motivational assembly, they lose class time. That class time is being used as a social hour in the gym by most students. Therefore, they aren't learning what they need to learn either way.

Motivational speakers cost precious money that could be used for other purposes such as new lab equipment or badly needed textbooks. Therefore, they hurt the students more than they help them. If we stopped meeting in the gym to listen to them, we might learn what we need to know.

Example 2-26C. "Value of speakers questioned," *The Catalyst*, Sylvania Southview H.S., Sylvania, OH.

Name _____   Date _____

— EXERCISE 26A —
Writing your editorial analysis

DIRECTIONS:

The following questions are tools for analyzing an editorial. Use one of the examples given or another editorial, assigned by your adviser.

Example No. (If applicable) _____   Publication _____

1. Headline _____

2. What probably inspired the editorial? Name the factor (news, school problem, personal observation, etc.) and the specific source.

   _____

   _____

   _____

3. What point is the editorial making?

   _____

   _____

   _____

4. From what sources has the writer gained proof and examples?

   _____

   _____

   _____

5. Why does (or doesn't) the editorial have an effective introduction?

   _____

   _____

   _____

6. Why does (or doesn't) the editorial stick to the point and reach a thought-provoking conclusion?

   _____

   _____

   _____

— EXERCISE 26A —
Writing your editorial analysis (cont'd)

7. What weaknesses, if any, do you find in this column? Be precise, giving examples.

    _____

    _____

    _____

    _____

    _____

    _____

    _____

    _____

    _____

8. Briefly sum up your overall opinion of this column

    _____

    _____

    _____

    _____

    _____

    _____

    _____

    _____

    _____

    _____

    _____

    _____

    _____

Name _____   Date _____

— EXERCISE 26B —
Expressing yourself in an editorial

DIRECTIONS:

Choose a topic, and write an editorial or editorial column, basing it on solid facts and supporting evidence. Indicate the type of editorial you have chosen.

_____

_____

_____

_____

_____

_____

_____

_____

_____

_____

_____

_____

_____

_____

_____

_____

_____

_____

_____

Problem or promise—School sports writing

Sports equal action and excitement

Sports pump up the adrenaline, both of athletes and fans, and cause a natural high. The problem for the school paper: how to communicate that action and excitement in its sports pages. The operative words are "FOCUS ON ACTION."

1. Transmit ACTION through variety.

   Sports news, features, profiles, sports briefs, columns, in-depth reports, sidebars and infographs; vary the types of stories on every page and every issue.

2. Transmit ACTION through photographs.

   Run story-telling photos plus cutlines that capture the spirit of a sport or an athlete and give a lift to your pages.

3. Transmit ACTION through writing.

   Look forward, not back to past games and past glories. Favor active verbs in the active voice to sharpen your stories.

4. Transmit ACTION by broadening coverage.

   Include intramural play, women's sports, individual participation sports, even offbeat competition as well as varsity-level coverage.

The special league of sports writers

Good sports writers must exercise the same skills as all good reporters, yet readers expect even more from them. Fans expect sports writers to be more knowledgeable about the game and its players than their readers are. In the case of school papers, the real fans have most likely attended the game, read about it in the local paper, and/or seen TV coverage. Those with only a passing interest hunt stories that capture a sport's flair and flavor.

Good journalism is good journalism, and—whether it's an advance or follow-up on a game, match or other sporting event, a feature or in-depth report, a profile or column—the sportswriter should apply the appropriate techniques for that type of story. Good sports writing gets its readers involved in all aspects of the game—from the particular challenges of each sport and rules governing its play to the team's place in standings and fine points of the game that rate more attention.

Going for active, accurate sports coverage

1. Strive to look forward, not back in time.

   Examples

   Poor: After disappointing losses for its first four games, Blazer varsity football found a winning formula Oct. 16 with two touche down passes from QB Brand Post to End Jim Wagner as it edged Storyville 14–13.

   Note: Save the losses till a later paragraph.

© 1998 by John Wiley & Sons, Inc

Poor: On their way to repeat the success of last year's team, Byrnehurst girls' team shut out its first five opponents, winning 2–0 against Mayfair April 11.

Better: After its 2–0 win against Mayfair April 11, the Byrnehurst girls' soccer team has posted shutouts against its first five opponents and looks ready to win a second successive league championship.

2. Stick to third person, except in quotes.

   Examples

   Poor: Our varsity basketball team fought to the finish . . .

   Better: The Blazer varsity basketball team fought . . .

3. Keep stories free of strictly one-sided reporting.

   Examples

   Poor: A highly deserved win over the Storyville Knights Feb. 29 proved again that Blazer basketball is best.

   Better: A 79-58 win over the Storyville Knights Feb. 29 strengthened Blazer's standing in the league basketball championship race.

4. Know the sports you write about.

   a. Correctly use and spell the specialized terms of each sport. Not all sports events are games; some are matches or contests.

   b. Know the rules, the strategies, the records and the schedules, but avoid becoming too technical for less learned readers.

5. Keep your writing moving forward.

   a. Use strong verbs and precise nouns.

   b. Avoid using trite expressions that strain to be striking and colorful, but only sound clichéd.

6. Seek informative quotes that tell the inside story.

   Examples

   Poor: When the coach was asked how he felt about future games, after the lopsided win over Mayfair, he replied, "We always try to be ready for every game we play because everyone's aching to topple us, and as a team we know that it's best to take it one game at a time."

   Solution: Ask follow-up questions, but if you can't get a usable full quote from an uncommunicative person, try a partial one.

   Better: Looking forward to future games after the lopsided win over Mayfair, the coach said, "Everyone's aching to topple us." He called it "best to take it one game at a time."

7. Look for the inside story.

   a. Attend practices—listen, look and learn. Attending practice can help you put the team's efforts in clearer focus, make you acquainted with coaches and players and provide material for features and profiles as well.

   b. Talk with and quote athletes as well as coaches for valuable insights and telling opinions.

8. Be fair to the opposition, but show your enthusiasm.

   a. Strive for balanced coverage that offers valid evaluation of both your team's and your opponent's strengths and weaknesses.

   b. Even local, professional papers promote the home team. Don't belittle your opponents, but remember which side you're on. Such little details as putting your school first when giving scores (Byrnehurst 13, Mayfair 21 or Blazers 13, Titans 21) do matter.

      Note: Match up school name/school name or mascot/mascot.

   c. Concentrate on highlights for your teams and its players after a close game or win. Mention the pluses—the good moves or smart plays after a loss. Don't ignore the opposition or downplay their ability, but don't downplay your team by building up the other side.

9. Keep the game and the entire season in perspective.

   a. Know the records and standings of the home team, its individual players and its opponents.

   b. Evaluate and interpret key plays, strategies and the overall situation with statistics, background information and facts.

   c. At games, remember you are a reporter, not "merely" a fan. Keep track of statistics, key plays and players; think of your story as you watch.

Time for sports

For school papers, sports coverage is complicated by the time lapse between an event and the nearest date its account can appear in an issue. As a result, many school papers have cut game stories to a minimum, briefly covering the most recent one available, limiting the rest to infographs charting scores and standings, in a section you might call "The Scoreboard."

In writing an abbreviated story, the reporter should concentrate on the following questions, in addition to the basic 5 W's and an H:

1. Who won?

2. What are the game highlights?

3. Did anyone set or nearly set a record?

4. Why is the game important in standings or for one or more players?

5. What other elements stand out?

6. What consequences, if any, are likely?

Seeking an advance

Time limitations also have an effect on the practicality of advance sports stories. The big game with the school's number-one rival may happen two weeks after the issue comes out. Leaping over the intervening ones does not take account of their possible effect on the "big one" nor the difficulty of getting information from coaches whose motto is "one game at a time."

Solutions:

1. An overview, perhaps by a sports columnist, of what the rest of the season looks like in the light of the team's record so far.

2. Concise paragraphs about upcoming games, concentrating on what to watch for in each and grouped under a single heading like "Sports briefs," with a longer paragraph about the major rivalry.

Going to magazine-type coverage

Whether published in 8-1/2″ × 11″ or 11″ × 17″ formats, many of the best-reading school sports pages across the country make good use of their space and the possibilities of desktop publishing.

School sports look more exciting when presented with plentiful action pictures, infographs, sports briefs and behind-the-scenes stories. Since it's impossible to compete with television and the local daily or weekly, go with what works and wins.

When you quit devoting multiple-paragraph stories to detailed accounts of individual games, you free space for coverage of a greater number and variety of boys' and girls' sports—and even nontraditional forms of athletic endeavor—that appeal to a wider readership.

Don't desert the traditional high-profile sports like football and basketball. There are a lot of features, news features and columns in them as well—but don't limit yourself to them.

Sports especially lend themselves to:

1. Analysis

2. Interpretation

3. Overview

4. Background

5. Interview

6. Feature

Sports editors and writers need all the necessary journalism skills, plus a vision that brings the spirit, intensity and variety of sports to the pages of their school paper.

Analyzing a sports story

Examples 2-27A–2-27E are outstanding examples of student-written sports stories that have appeared in school newspapers throughout the country.

> In many ways, sport pages are actually a mini-paper within a paper—devoted to a single subject—Sports.

After reading the examples carefully, choose one or analyze another story, assigned by your adviser. Judge its effectiveness on the basis of its appropriate type: news, feature, column, etc.

While cheerleaders Teresa Pizzillo, Missy Pohorence, Char Novotony, Liz Miller, Maria Epifanio, Trisha Belski, and Holly Eklund are shown remaining relatively stationary during the Cleveland Heights game, several have reported injuries during the year. A USA Today report shows cheerleading injuries have increased throughout the country. Timesphoto by Pat Slife.

Cheerleading injuries on increase, report shows

'You have the state rules for the tournaments: no mounts. You have the local rules which say you can go one high, and cheerleading competitions which have their own set of rules'

—Athletic Director Dan Gerome

by Russell Fritz

During the last 13 years, injuries in chearleading has increased a considerable amount, USA Today recently reported. Minor injuries such as sprains have always been there, but a 68.2 percent increase of emergency room visits were reported by USA Today.

Junior cheerleader Tanya Dissell was performing a round-off back handspring and tore a ligament in her knee. A torn ligament is typically compared to a football injury that would come about if the athlete was tackled from the side of her knee.

Freshman basketball cheerleader Corey Bowen was one of the cheerleaders from Lakewood who had to go to the emergency room.

"I was doing a mount and I was thrown up to do a cradle. I wasn't caught entirely and I fell," Bowen said. She spent the evening in the emergency room and had serious difficulty walking the next several days.

"There have been minor injuries that come with the sport, but we have been lucky. We try to be safe and when we begin to practice a new stunt

we use up to 20 spotters," cheerleading head coach Patty Rice said.

The cheerleaders had not been using floor pads until the accident.

There is also no consistency in rules regarding mounts and gymnastic tricks in cheerleading.

"You have the state rules for the tournaments: no mounts. You have the local rules which say you can go one high, and cheerleading competions which have their own

set of rules," Athletic Director Dan Gerome said.

The official rule in the LEL is cheerleading mounts are not to be more than one person high.

"We save our mounts, which are dangerous, for competitions. There is talk about removing mounting from cheerleading in this school. The mounts are Lakewood's only chance for competing," Rice said.

Some schools are even more preventive concerning injuries. Shaker Heights is an example.

"At Shaker we don't mount or tumble. Our squad doesn't do anything to cause a knee injury," Shaker Heights High School cheerleading adviser Elaine Patrick told the Times.

"I think coaches from other schools may have little or no cheerleading background but are hired because they have support for the activity. With this lack of knowledge they don't use proper spotting and preventative injury techniques," Rice said.

Rice said she has had 15 years experience of participating or coaching cheerleading.

Example 2-27A. "Cheerleading injuries on increase, report shows," by Russell Fritz, *The Times*, Lakewood H.S., Lakewood, OH.

PLAY BY PLAY

1,360 steps.

1,500 meters on an ergometer.

20 minutes of simulated rowing.

75 minutes of intense physical conditioning five days a week.

Then comes Saturday, with more steps and a longer workout.

All this every week for five months without setting foot in a boat.

For two Lakota High School juniors and about 65 other Cincinnati-area high-school students, this is fun.

Tori Smiley started with the Cincinnati Rowing Center when she heard about it from a friend and Jenny Tacosik joined a few weeks ago.

Smiley quit the Lakota swim team to devote more time to rowing.

"I was really getting burnt out on swimming and so I was like 'Hey, I could do that.' It sounded like really hard work."

And it has been.

A typical after-school practice begins with a five-minute run and a series of warm-up exercises. The crew then goes on a 20-minute run to Sawyer Point, around Riverfront Stadium, and back to the Montgomery Inn Boathouse, where training takes place. The rowers do weight circuits and work out for about 20 minutes on either ergometers (rowing machines) or in the center's tank. The tank resembles a swimming pool with two islands in the middle that the crew sits on to row.

"Cincinnati high-school kids are very lucky that this facility is here with this indoor tank where you can actually row. It's a real benefit for novice rowers to come in here and be able to row, said CRC Women's Varsity Coach Jamie Snider. "It teaches technique and all the demands of what's entailed when you actually do get out on the water in a real boat. You're at least three weeks ahead of yourself with this tank. If it wasn't here, you'd have to go through all that out on the Ohio River."

Once a week, the crew runs stairs at Riverfront Coliseum and takes an erg test, which requires the rowers to go 1,500 meters in as short a time as possible.

"You have to perfect your technique; you're always working on that, and you have to build strength; you're always working on that," said Smiley.

Saturday mornings, the CRC team trains with the University of Cincinnati crew at Nippert Stadium.

"That is awesome," Smiley said. "You have people who are a little bit stronger than you and so you have a goal. You have that person that they just edge you out and you have to catch them."

She acknowldedges that it takes a unique kind of person to make a good rower.

"Rowing is not for everyone. To be a good rower, you really really have to be dedicated. It's a team thing. If you've got eight people in a boat and one person's not pulling their weight, the boat won't be level. You totally have to work together," Smiley said.

Snider agrees.

"It's a real team sport. I always tell the kids 'If you have an ego, you really shouldn't be in the rowing program.' There's no stars. Nobody has any greater responsibility than anybody else."

The long months of training finally come

Due to sports, Tori Smiley and Jenny Tacosik are experiencing

BY KERRY FLYNN

Different Strokes

Photo by Kerry Flynn

■ Tori Smiley, second from right, in the training tank at the Cincinnati Rowing Center.

together during the fall season, from the start of the school year through November, and the spring season, which lasts from April through June.

That's when the crew climbs into a boat just a foot and a half wide, and half an inch thick, riding an inch above the surface of the water, and puts its skills to the test.

"A rowing race is 2,000 meters long from start to finish. There's no place to hide. Once that gun goes, you have to go

▼ continued on page 19

Example 2-27B. "Different strokes," by Kerry Flynn, *Spark*, Lakota H.S., West Chester, OH.

Jellyfish persevere despite loss of seniors, All-American

By Elisabeth Tomlinson

For years, the name Jordan Jellyfish has been synonymous with state championships. But, when the swimming and diving team lost nine seniors at the end of last season, members were concerned that this year's team would not continue the winning tradition.

They have since changed their minds.

The loss of the seniors, and the decision of senior All-American swimmer Rob Masten not to swim for the Jellyfish this season, were major blows for the team.

"It's been pretty tough. We've really missed not having the depth we did last year. Last year we had a massive growth [of top swimmers]; this year we just have a nucleus," said senior Kevin Jinks, co-captain of the men's team.

However, the team members have surpassed their own expectations.

"When I was coming into the season, I didn't know what to expect. I was afraid it was going to be a bad year," said senior David Myers, co-captain of the men's team. "I think we've all surprised ourselves."

Coach Jim Maxwell believes that the legacy of past teams has helped this year's team carry on the winning tradition.

"Success breeds success," said Maxwell. "The team is used to winning. The senior class passes [winning] down to the freshmen and sophomores every year. Nobody wants to be on the team that does not finish as well as the others have in the past," Maxwell said.

The swim team's only loss this season has come against its rival Chapel Hill. The men's team

lost the meet by 11 points, and the women's team lost by 27.

Many members of the team blame the loss on not being able to practice for six days before the meet because health inspectors had closed the NCCU pool, where the team practices.

"We're convinced we could have done better if we hadn't stayed out of the water," said Myers.

Even so, just coming that close to beating Chapel Hill was a victory in itself for the men's team, said Jinks.

The loss was more disappointing for the women's team, which is looking for a state championship.

Senior Annie Bowers, co-captain of the women's team, said that the loss gave the Jellyfish a feel for how tough its competition is. "We knew [Chapel Hill] was strong at the top, but I never realized how strong [before the meet]," she said.

She added, "We're definitely one of the top three teams in the state. The only competition we've had so far this season is Chapel Hill."

The women's team is well on its way to a state title if early results are any indication. So far, the team already has a record of more than 100 regional qualifying times.

"This season is different from any other year because we've had so many people qualify for regionals," said senior Becky Sanford, co-captain of the women's team.

While members of the men's team do not expect to win at states, they are hoping to finish near the top.

"With the resources we have

this year, to pull off a top five finish would be a victory for us," said Jinks.

Part of the credit for the team's success so far this season goes to its freshmen, said many team members.

"We knew coming into [the season] that the freshmen would be good, but we did not know exactly how good. They are definitely better than we thought they would be. . . .They're beating seniors from other teams," said senior Jenny Karpinski, co-captain of the women's team.

Maxwell added, "The freshmen and sophomores are really pushing the seniors. The seniors would not have been swimming like this two months ago."

But, as in every year, the swim team does not compete at meets alone, because the diving team's

Photo by Elisabeth Tomlinson

There's a fungus among us: Mold takes over the NCCU pool, causing health inspectors to temporarily close the facility.

score is added to the swim team's score.

This year's diving team is young, with only three sophomores. Rebecca Fitz, the only returning diver, said that she has had to help teammates Tim Hooker and Julie Lane get better, while she concentrates on improving her diving as well.

Fitz added that since Hooker and Lane are beginning divers, she has had to become the team's leader. "Last year, I was the only freshman on the team and there

was a returning state champion diver. There really wasn't any pressure on me to dive well. . . .Then I came back this year and now I'm supposed to be the one to score all the points. It's been hard on me," she said.

Fitz has placed first at two of the three meets the diving team has competed in so far this season. At the third meet in Chattanooga, Tenn., she placed ninth. Hooker has placed first in one meet so far.
—*Stephen Chaney contributed to this article.*

Photo by Elisabeth Tomlinson

On your mark: Members of the men's team prepare to swim. The Jellyfish have lost only to arch rival Chapel Hill this year

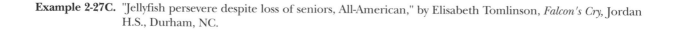

Example 2-27C. "Jellyfish persevere despite loss of seniors, All-American," by Elisabeth Tomlinson, *Falcon's Cry*, Jordan H.S., Durham, NC.

One win's all they have, one win's all they need

Men's basketball hopes end to losing streak will come in tournament

by Shawn Batten
Sports Editor

One win.

That's all the men's basketball team will need in districts to advance to another regional tournament and have a chance to prove a statement which it has been trying to make all season: its record doesn't reflect its talent.

"We are a good team, no matter what our record shows," Head Coach Cliff Gates said. "We've had to go up against the toughest teams in the region, but the margins of our losses show that we can be competitive."

Because the team has only one district win, it will probably have to face either the second or third place team in the district in a must-win contest for a regional berth. Although the team hasn't been able to earn a victory against the Concorde's top teams, its players feel that the district's parity will aid in making a win possible.

"It seems as though everyone's beaten everyone," senior Eamonn Lanigan said. "We've lost our last few games by just a few points, so it looks as though our time has come."

Senior Eamonn Lanigan reaches for the ball as a Woodson defender tries to swipe it away. Lanigan is one of just three seniors on the team this year. *Photo by Josh Levine.*

Gates feels that the team's recent resurgence may actually give it an advantage in the playoff game. "I'd hate to have to play us in the first round," he said. "We've really been getting better and we now know, after having gone through the district twice, that we can really stack up against just about anyone."

As the season began, several players who had been members of last year's JV or varsity teams chose not to return for this year's campaign. Lanigan said that those whom he personally knew of chose to leave because they didn't agree with the team's gameplans. "There seemed to be some conflicts with the coaches about not getting enough playing time or about the team's style of play," he said.

Gates feels that those on the team comprise the best combination of players that he could hope for. "Sure, there are some people who, speaking on a personal level, I wouldn't mind having," he said. "As far as basketball goes, though, I think that what we have now is as good or better than anything we could have had."

The team features only three seniors, all of whom start. Gates, however, views his team's youth as an asset rather than a liability.

"It's an ideal class mix," he said. "I was still worried at the start of the season about whether or not the underclassmen could play at the varsity level, but they really have matured and shown that they can. The fact that we've had closer losses in the last few weeks proves that they've been contributing."

Freshman Noah Kramer-Dover said that he doesn't see any real difference between his level of play and those of his opponents. "Whenever I played in rec[reational] leagues, I'd always play a couple of years up anyway," he said. "When the game starts, it really doesn't matter what class you are in. I don't think the other guy ever notices it."

Example 2-27D. "One win's all they have. . . ," by Shawn Batten, *TJ Today*, Thomas Jefferson High School for Science & Technology, Alexandria, VA.

Offensive woes continue for football team

John Tracy
Harbinger managing editor

photo Mark Benotti

RUNAWAY! – Quarterback Trevor McCormick eludes a Milford defender.

| Milford 28 | |
| Algonquin 0 | |

With only twenty-four players in uniform, the football team fell to Milford 28-0 in the homecoming game.

The offense was shut out for the second game in a row despite another strong showing by sophomore fullback Evan Berte (8 carries, 54 yards), who took a breather late in the second half with a twisted ankle.

"We gave this game away," said Coach Mike Harpin.

"When Berte had big runs, we couldn't capitalize. We had no momentum the entire game."

Milford took a 21-0 lead early in the second quarter and was encroaching on Algonquin territory again as time was winding down in the half. However, the defensive line continued its strong play against the rush.

Lineman George Karrat forced a Scarlet Hawk fumble behind the line of scrimmage and recovered deep in Milford territory.

"Our D was out there for the entire game," said Karrat. "Our offense just couldn't control the ball."

After a failed run and incomplete pass, the team tried to get on the board with :03 remaining. However, a low field goal attempt was blocked as the half expired.

The team began a spirited second half as Brian Choi returned the opening kickoff to midfield.

Two consecutive outside runs resulted in first downs, but attempts to run between the tackles were stuffed and the team was forced to punt.

Again on Algonquin's next drive, they failed to capitalize and their punt snap was fumbled at the 1 yard line. Milford upped the score to 28-0 on the next play, a Matt Taraborelli dive.

"We're struggling through it," said Harpin. "Physically, we're doing all right, we're hitting them hard. Our defense has been good, especially Jim Ebrecht and Rich Waldo."

| Nashoba 33 | |
| Algonquin 0 | |

Unbeaten Nashoba's balanced offensive attack was too much for the young football squad as the Chieftans cruised to a 33-0 victory.

Once again the running game moved the ball well, but the endzone remained out of reach.

Nashoba racked up 26 points in the first half, relying on strong-armed quarterback Gregg Newton's one touchdown pass and crafty tailback Jeff Kerrigan's two scoring runs for most of the offensive load.

| Shrewsbury 13 | |
| Algonquin 7 | |

The football team held its first lead of the season, but could not keep it as Shrewsbury scored two unanswered touchdowns to take the victory 13-7.

In the first quarter, the offense managed to push the Shrewsbury defense to the goal line where quarterback Trevor McCormick plunged into the endzone on a keeper for the first score of the game.

Shrewsbury rallied back with two scores in the second and fourth quarter to take the game.

Example 2-27E. "Offensive woes continue for football team," by John Tracy, *The Harbinger,* Algonquin Regional H.S., Northboro, MA.

Name _____   Date _____

— EXERCISE 27A —
Writing your sports analysis

DIRECTIONS:

The following questions are tools for analyzing a sports story. Use one of the examples given or another report, assigned by your adviser.

Example No. (If applicable) _____   Publication _____

1. Headline _____

2. Briefly explain why the story does or doesn't rate highly with respect to the following factors. Supply supporting details.

   (a) Timeliness—does not dwell on old news.

   _____

   _____

   _____

   (b) Newsworthiness—contains "inside" or new information.

   _____

   _____

   _____

   (c) Primary sources—based on multiple interviews, sources.

   _____

   _____

   _____

   (d) Positive approach—does not needlessly emphasize past events or team losses.

   _____

   _____

   _____

   (e) Makes effective use of space—including graphics, infographs.

   _____

   _____

   _____

— EXERCISE 27A —
Writing your sports analysis *(cont'd)*

3. What weaknesses, if any, do you find in this example? Be precise, giving examples.

_____

_____

_____

_____

_____

_____

4. Briefly sum up your overall opinion of this example.

_____

_____

_____

_____

_____

_____

_____

_____

_____

_____

_____

Note: You may also use another type of analysis, such as news or feature, to complete this assignment.

Name _____   Date _____

— EXERCISE 27B —
Writing for the sports page

DIRECTIONS:

Choose a topic, and write a sports story, basing it on solid facts and supporting evidence. Indicate
type of article: _____

List sources: _____

_____

_____

_____

_____

_____

_____

_____

_____

_____

_____

_____

_____

_____

_____

_____

_____

_____

_____

_____

Preparation of copy

1. Insert or write header in upper left corner of page—to include the following:

   (a) Slug: a brief, single word to identify story, such as LUNCH for story on new cafeteria policy

   (b) Reporter's last name

   (c) Section or page assignment—for example, News, Features, Sports, Entertainment, etc.

   Example: LUNCH
                PEARSON
                NEWS

2. All rough drafts should be double-spaced for easier editing and revising.

3. Process all copy in consistent font, size and style, such as:

Standard body copy	9 Melior or 10 pt. New York
Staff editorials, if run in wider columns	11 pt. Melior or 12 pt. New York

4. Set copy to standard width.

5. Indent three spaces for all paragraphs.
   Greater indentations create awkward gaps that distract and slow readers down.

6. Set byline at beginning of story according to paper's style.
   Include name and identification.

   Example: B. D. Pearson, features editor

7. Headline should not appear as part of rough drafts, but be added when copy is processed and placed on page.

8. If printout to hard copy is a single page, hand mark with # or -30- at end.

9. If printout runs to more than one page, indicate this by writing "more" at bottom of first and following pages, up to final # or - 30 -.

10. Write "add 1" on upper right-hand corner of first additional (or second) page, "add 2" to the following page, and so on.
    Note: The first page should not be numbered.

11. Be sure that every page has a cover or tracking sheet attached to it.

Tracking sheet

Slug _____   Reporter _____   Section _____

Length in inches (basic column width)_____

Completed drafts	Date submitted	Editor's initials
First	_____	_____
Revise 1	_____	_____
	_____	_____
Final draft	_____	_____
Edited copy		
Returned for revision	_____	_____
	_____	_____
Final OK'd	_____	_____
Placed in page	_____	_____
Suggested headline		
Style (if assigned)	_____	
Main head	_____	
	_____	
Subhead (if desired)	_____	
	_____	
Suggested pull quote	_____	
	_____	
	_____	
Sidebars (If applicable, include with story.)		
1. Type	_____	
Heading	_____	
2. Type	_____	
Heading	_____	

Interview evaluation request

Date: _____

To: _____   Room or office: _____

You recently served as a source for the following story. It will help us improve both our coverage and our accuracy if you will answer the questions below. Thank you very much for your cooperation.

Story _____

Student reporter _____

Did the student reporter treat you politely?	Yes	No
Was the reporter prepared for this interview?	Yes	No
Were the facts reported accurately?	Yes	No
Were direct quotations accurate?	Yes	No
Did the published story clearly report your views?	Yes	No

If you have further comments, please write them below. Please return your response to the adviser, editor, staff office or mail box.

Your signature _____

Date _____

Comments: _____

_____

_____

_____

_____

_____

_____

_____

_____

_____

_____

Reporter's assignment sheet

Date of publication _____   General deadline _____

Story Slug	Reporter	Length	Section

NEWSWRITING WORKSHOP: Answer key

Note to Advisers

Exercises that require writing or ask students to express their opinions may have a variety of valid answers. The most important factors are correct journalistic style and acceptable grammar.

Exercise 1A, Part A.

1. Students are asking many questions about the new athletic code.

   Words: Before 12, After 10

2. Adviser Dale Swiggart is offering practice Quiz Bowl sessions to prospective members.

   Words: Before 15, After 13

3. Temperatures reached a record high on the day of the season's first Blazer football game.

   Words: Before 22, After 15

4. "Too Late or Too Little," this spring's Dramatic Club play, offers roles for twelve students—five male and seven female.

   Words: Before 22, After 20

5. Extracurricular activities such as athletics and music face cuts or elimination if voters reject the upcoming school levy.

   Words: Before 28, After 18

Exercise 1A, Part B.

1. In planning the new cafeteria menu, a committee headed by Cafeteria Manager Mrs. Harriet Garvey is seriously considering student complaints about the food.

   Words: Before 39, After 23

2. Simulated air raid drills let members of Mrs. Dale Dart's American history classes experience how schools prepared students for enemy attacks on the U.S. mainland during the Cold War with Russia.

   Words: Before 46, After 31

3. Efforts to control tardiness to class won't succeed unless they target socializing between class, said Mrs. Pamela Early, dean of students.

   Words: Before 23, After 21

4. Senior courtyard privileges face possible elimination as a result of administration discussions about students' abuse of this right. Teachers in nearby classrooms have complained about noise, and custodians about discarded trash.

   Words: Before 39, After 31

5. Juanita Sanchez, senior, will represent Byrnehurst in a citywide seminar Tuesday, March 5. Participants will discuss coordinating activities for the Summer Peace and Fun program.

    Words: Before 34, After 25

Exercise 1B, Part A.

1. Police notified Byrnehurst Principal Kevin Claypoole shortly after 11 P.M. of the break-in and attempted arson then in progress.

    Words: Before 23, After 19

2. A group of Byrnehurst students, who drove by and noticed shadowy figures running from the building, called 911 to make the first report .

    Words: Before 31, After 23

3. The HiNotes, Byrnehurst's 16-member mixed ensemble, placed first against 12 other schools when the group participated for the first time ever in the district vocal music competition at Sutter State University, March 31.

    Words: Before 52, After 34

4. Winning first place in the district makes the ensemble eligible to compete at the state level.

    Words: Before 33, After 16

5. A committee of both students and parents has worked for months to make this year's prom, Byrnehurst Sparkles, both safe and fun. Planned activities include games and contests continuing all night long.

    Words: Before 56, After 32

6. Block scheduling, which the board of education adopted at their last meeting, allows students to enroll in only four classes per semester.

    Words: Before 33, After 22

Exercise 1B, Part B.

1. Increased enrollment each of the past five years has resulted in the addition of nine new faculty and staff members this year at Byrnehurst.

    - or -

    Nine new members have joined the Byrnehurst staff and faculty this year as a result of increased enrollments each of the past five years.

    Words: Before 32, After 24

2. The official dedication ceremony of Byrnehurst's new gym takes place in several weeks, offering students and community members an opportunity to inspect its up-to-date facilities.

    Words: Before 36, After 25

3. The first amendment supports the right of school papers to exist free of censorship.

    Words: Before 23, After 14

4. This year's school musical has a cast of 36.

    Words: Before 12, After 9

5. Mrs. Ellen Stuart will serve as co-adviser because the big cast makes coaching individual actors difficult, according to Ms. Jamie Fairchild, faculty director.

    Words: Before 33, After 23

Exercise 1C, Part A.

1. The committee did not approve of Board President Theodore Kendricks' proposed changes in staging the rally.

    - or -

    Because the committee did not approve the rally, Mr. Theodore Kendricks, board president, suggested changes in its staging.

2. To stress the fact that dropping out of school causes many kinds of future losses, the originators of the campaign are providing a video on the topic.

3. The video promises to help dropouts, who often refuse to listen to parents and teachers.

    - or -

    The video promises to help parents and teachers, who find dropouts often refuse to listen to them.

4. At an emotional pep rally in the gym, Principal Kevin Claypoole announced that Head Basketball Coach Andy Wilcox had submitted his resignation the day before.

5. Facing the need to choose a college, students have trouble finding the time and money to visit those that seem promising.

6. While researching Byrnehurst's history, the class discovered that, at the time of Clyde Goodfellow's death, records credited him with being the oldest white man born in this county.

Exercise 1C, Part B.

1. risqué; **2.** plethora; **3-6.** its, their, too, to; **7-8.** accept, affects; **9.** sync; **10.** heroine; **11.** clique; **12.** Sanskrit.

Exercise 3A, Part A.

I. (1) discipline—training that develops self-control; (2) punishment—the penalty imposed; (3) drill—the method of teaching by repeated exercises; (4) order—a definite plan, a command, a state of peace.

II. (1) meeting—a coming together for any purpose; (2) appointment—an engagement to meet at a set time and place; (3) conference—a formal meeting for discussion; (4) gathering—a group not necessarily together because of its other members.

III. (1) organization—a group with an established structure or system; (2) assembly—a gathering to make a whole; (3) group—a number of persons or things, gathered or classified together; (4) union—a group officially joined together for a specific purpose.

IV. (1) party—a gathering for social entertainment; (2) celebration—a festive event to honor someone or something; (3) bash—an all-out party, slam-bang fun; (4) reception—a social function for receiving guests, often to meet an honored person.

V. (1) accident—an unintended happening; (2) blunder—a foolish mistake; (3) mishap—an unlucky or unfortunate minor accident; (4) disaster—a happening that causes great harm or damage.

VI. (1) plan—a thought-out program for making, doing or arranging something; (2) suggestion—an idea proposed as a possibility; (3) recommendation—an idea favorably presented as suitable; (4) scheme—a way for doing something, usually clever, systematic and sometimes secret.

Exercise 3B. Part B, Original sentences

1. Bill is such a liar that you can't count on him for facts.

2. The Blazers' giant defensive tackle looks almost ready for the pros.

3. Macky, our furry little pup, is named after Mack the Knife because he likes to playfully bite us.

4. Macky is a bouncy bundle of energy whose sharp teeth destroyed two of the family's sofa pillows.

5. It was a disappointment to discover that disks for the two computers were not interchangeable.

6. After becoming a celebrity, he wrote a best-selling autobiography.

7. The third-grader's mother surprised her by treating her class to pizza.

8. The innovation in dental care is considered unique.

9. Byrnehurst French teacher, Mrs. Marie Trudeau, who is a mother-to-be, begins a leave of absence in April.

10. The debut performance of the composition will be Friday, Oct. 9.

Exercise 3C, Part A.

1. NO—we, we; 2. NO—our, you; 3. NO—you, we; 4. OK; 5. NO—us, you; 6. NO—you, our; 7. OK; 8. NO—you, our, (you—understood subject); 9. OK; 10. OK.

Exercise 3C, Part B.

l. b;   **2.** a;   **3.** a;   **4.** b;   **5.** b;   **6.** b;   **7.** a;   **8.** b;   **9.** a;   **10.** b.

Exercise 4A.

Allows various options. No. 6 is factual.

Exercise 4B, Part A.

Part A allows various options. Only No. 2 is valid.

Exercise 4B, Part B.

1.   The speaker stressed that students should set their own goals and strive for success to the best of their abilities.

2.   Dennis Percy's win was also surprising because he was a newcomer to the team.

3.   As his conclusion, the speaker noted that a life well lived involves honesty and integrity.

4.   The Byrnehurst Lions Club is now accepting student nominations for Teacher of the Year.

5.   Winning $100,000 in the lottery was a big surprise to sophomore Ted Roberts' father, who bought the ticket for a lark.

6.   A recent study shows American students' 9th grade reading skills rank among the best.

7.   BHS students do not obey some basic school rules.

8.   Some teachers, as well as students, ignore rules such as those that forbid eating and drinking in class.

9.   The play concerns ten guests, who are invited for a weekend in a mysterious mansion, only to find their host absent.

10. Researchers are seeking reasons for the evident differences between the achievements of girls and boys in math and science.

Exercise 6A.

1.   Many teachers feel the pay raise that board members are considering isn't high enough.

- or -

Board members are considering a pay raise for teachers, who many feel are underpaid.

2.   After three straight victories, the Blazers are out for another win when they meet the Panthers Friday, Sept. 21, at 7:30 P.M.

3. The teacher cleared his throat so often that the distracted student began keeping count.

4. This year's track team boasts a field of 39 candidates plus six returning lettermen, whose goal is to repeat last year's championship season.

5. In a recent *Torch* poll, a majority of students expressed their dislike of a change in the dress code.

   - or -

   In a recent *Torch* poll, a majority of students expressed their desire to change the unpopular dress code.

6. Council members reminded their opponents that they needed to cooperate to make the plan work.

7. Jeff enjoys a computer variety of rummy that one of his friends sent him.

8. *The Torch* will print retractions on the same page where an error occurred in the previous edition.

9. Clear: that = panel; their = judge, member of Alanon-Teen, counselor

10. Newcomer Leonard Washington has the task of rebuilding both the boys and girls tennis teams, which is a demanding job for one person.

Exercise 7A, Part A.

1. him;   **2.** him, her;   **3.** he, she;   **4.** she;   **5.** she;   **6.** him;   **7.** they, we;   **8.** me;
9. they;   **10.** he.

Exercise 7A, Part B.

1. there, you're;   **2.** Their;   **3.** you're;   **4.** its, it's;   **5.** their, their;   **6.** you're, your;
7. your, they're;   **8.** It's, your;   **9.** its, it's;   **10.** there, its.

Exercise 8A, Part A.

1. *which,* doesn't name people, should be *whom*

2. *that,* not essential, should be *which*

3. *who,* used as object, should be *whom*

4. *where,* relates to time, should be *when* (or *that*)

5. *whom,* used as subject, should be *who*

Exercise 8A, Part B.

1. which;   **2.** when or that, where;   **3.** that;   **4.** whom;   **5.** which, that (who);
6. who, that;   **7.** whom;   **8.** which, that;   **9.** who, where;   **10.** that, that, which

Exercise 9A, Part A.

Answer according to staff style.

Exercise 9A, Part B.

1. takes;   **2.** have;   **3.** need;   **4.** last;   **5.** presents;   **6.** their;   **7.** their;   **8.** are;
9. comes;   **10.** are

Exercise 10A, Part A.

1. and;   **2.** fewer;   **3.** less;   **4.** more than;   **5.** well;   **6.** really (or omit);   **7.** would
have marched;   **8.** had not;   **9.** could have;   **10.** two;   **11.** to;   **12.** too;   **13.** to;
14. kind of;   **15.** Booster Club dunking booth;   **16.** couple of;   **17.** men's;
18. women;   **19.** to either;   **20.** a time for fun.

Exercise 10A, Part B. Original sentences

Exercise 10B, Part A.

1. takes place;   **2.** contest winners;   **3.** and;   **4.** really (or omit);   **5.** quite (or omit);
6. graduating from;   **7.** number;   **8.** amount;   **9.** recently;   **10.** good;   **11.** well;
12. plus;   **13.** number;   **14.** amount;   **15.** from;   **16.** a lot;   **17.** all right;   **18.** plan to
attend;   **19.** may;   **20.** might

Exercise 10B, Part B.

1. Since he failed one course and wants to start college this fall, Andrew's summer plans are different from those of most seniors.

2. When asked to sing "The Star Spangled Banner," many students looked embarrassed and had to hum part of it. ("a lot" also permissible)

3. A psychologist says teens need to realize it's all right to be different from the so-called ideal, which doesn't exist.

4. According to Dr. Alexis Stuber, teens who seek a fun-filled future are chasing an illusion.

5. Two professions that appear to promise real fun are professional sports and entertainment, she said.

6. Women's and men's professional sports offer fewer chances than fields of science, such as engineering, chemistry and computer technology.

7. Viewers of television could have seen Dr. Stuber recently on the *Talking with Teens* show.

8. According to Dr. Stuber, it is normal for teens to feel confused about their plans for the future.

9. More than half have probably not made a definite decision, and college students often change majors, too.

10. The show offers an excellent opportunity for teens to discover how similar their problems are.

Exercise 11A.

1. *Who:* Robert Abate; *What:* is sending his students to fallout shelter; *When:* "is sending" implies currently or soon; *Where:* Hartford H.S. basement; *Why:* to give students a feel for Cold War; *How:* implies on foot

2. *Who:* Hurricane Bertha; *What:* heading toward populated land; *When:* yesterday; *Where:* Atlantic seaboard; *Why:* because of 100 mph winds; *How:* power of wind

3. *Who:* wildfire; *What:* raged out of control; *When:* today; *Where:* Alaska; *Why:* out of control; *How:* implied-devastatingly huge, unable to be stopped

4. *Who:* developer; *What:* plans to move burlesque house; *When:* has plans now; *Where:* New York City Times Square; *Why:* to make room for new addition; *How:* by literally picking it up

Exercise 13B.

Who: Approx. 65% of Byrnehurst freshmen; *What:* feel cafeteria policy "unfair and unnecessary"; *When:* currently; *Where:* at school; *Why:* they're forced to eat in a separate place; *How:* by this year's school policy

Summary lead: Approximately 65% of Byrnehurst freshmen call the new cafeteria policy, which separates them from upperclassmen, "unfair and unnecessary," according to a recent *Torch* poll.
Word count: 24

Students may have various other acceptable versions. If a number do this exercise, compare to determine which are more effective and why.

Exercise 13C.

Who: Environmental Club; *What:* sponsoring Awareness Week; *When:* March 5-9; *Where:* school; *Why:* to make students aware of their effect on environment; *How:* by sponsoring a variety of activities, including campus cleanup.
Summary lead: To emphasize how students can affect the environment, the Environmental Club's Awareness Week March 6-9 will focus on a variety of activities, including a campus clean-up.
Word count: 27

Exercise 15A.

1. (a) today—present—the biggest news, what's happening now

(b) Sunday—future—what may happen next

(c) Monday—past—when fire first became dangerous

(d) Sunday—past—earlier time than when fire began

(e) Wednesday—past—closer in time but less important; didn't happen

2. (a) Wasilla—a town north of Anchorage

(b) Bob King—spokesman for Gov. Tony Knowles

(c) Parks Highway—main road from Anchorage to Fairbanks

3. If joined, the lead would become too long, about 43 words. The two "and's," the first joining *home* and *road,* and the second joining the two parts of the sentence are so close together that it becomes hard to determine exactly what they join.

4. *They* refers to *crew* so the *and* more clearly links the word *they* to the preceding sentence. *They* could have been changed to *firefighters,* but this word would distract from the more important factor, the wind.

5. (a) put out—quench

(b) turned (into)—whipped

(c) sending—flinging

(d) caused—sparked/

(e) caused—forced

6. Most students should agree that both of the last two paragraphs could be omitted. *Explain:* Although both are worthwhile, the article does not leave the reader with a question in mind if either or both are missing.

Newspaper layout: THE SENSE BEHIND THE STYLE

Getting attention

Newspaper design is a matter of style. No matter what the approach or how much computer capability you possess, it's essential to remember that a good layout has two major purposes:

1. to call readers' attention to the stories and features in your paper, and
2. to increase and enhance the paper's readability.

Layouts that are all flash and flourish may distract the reader and trivialize the paper's content. No matter how compelling a layout, it must present stories and features of substance—or the result is an even greater letdown for the reader.

Choosing style

As with any type of fashion, the "do's" concerning newspaper layout are subject to change. The style you follow in laying out your paper must suit both your taste and needs. What's best hinges not only on appearance but also on many other factors, such as:

1. the adequacy of your technological resources,
2. the number of computer whizzes on your staff, and, far from last,
3. your willingness to be drawn by the seductive lure of computer wizardry
4. and the amount of time you will allow yourself to spend.

MODULAR DESIGN: THE LOOK IN A NUTSHELL—In place of standard-width columns ranked evenly on a page, modular layouts bring flexibility to newspaper design—and also new challenges. Modular layout simply means that all elements of a newspaper story are designed as a whole and placed as a single unit. The modular unit consists of:

- the story
- its headline
- photo and captions
- subheads, graphics, pull quotes, sidebars
- any other design elements chosen

283

With modular layouts, as in Example 3-1, the number of columns on a single page often varies. Perhaps the top module may have the equivalent of four columns with a photo taking up two, while the lower portion is divided into five—and subdivided as well.

For school papers, modular units are designed on a grid suitable for an 8-1/2″ × 11″ or an 11″ × 17″ or other tabloid-size paper. A popular and professional method of design is to sketch out trial layouts on a reduced size grid. The version chosen for publication becomes the dummy layout that serves as a guide for writing headlines and a model for placing all elements in the desktop publishing program. You can duplicate the grid you prefer from Example 3-2 or create your own grid and print copies via your computer. Printing grids in blue makes designing easier by providing a contrast to pencil-sketched dummies. Although unnecessary, adding horizontal lines to the grid may help with alignment.

COLUMNED FOR READABILITY—In lieu of modular design, the typical number of columns per page is three for 8-1/2″ × 11″ papers and five for 11″ × 17″ tabloids. Although these may serve for designing basic modular units, you may attain greater design flexibility by working from grids with seven to ten columns.

Additional columns turn the focus away from standardized columns, encourage creative design and make it easier to vary column widths. Multicolumn grids also provide a spot for inventive placement of cutlines, pull quotes, icons and teasers. When working with seven to ten columns, it's important to remember that narrow columns are not a readable width for lengthy copy—and that not every inch need be filled. The wise use of white space is a vital element of good design—whether you choose a basic three- or five-column layout, or experiment with innovative trends.

This above all: CONTENT

As with many forms of fashion, the latest laws of newspaper design are frequently matters of individual taste and not scientific discoveries.

Much is possible, but much that you could do—thanks to the amazing capacities of computer publishing—does not make an indispensable contribution to the quality of your school paper, to the growth of the students on the staff nor to the value received from the time, money and effort expended by you and your staff.

In fact, students sometimes become so swept away by the possibilities of computer design that the resulting layouts obscure content instead of emphasizing it. See Figure 3-3 for help in designing reader-friendly copy blocks.

KEEP FOCUSED ON CONTENT—Newspaper layout is merely a means to an end—and the end is making the paper more readable and its stories more accessible. With desktop publishing programs, type can be easily warped, wrapped and twisted—sometimes by deliriously happy computer fanatics who fail to notice or care that it can't be read. A good layout draws the reader into the page—ideally at a series of entry points such as:

• headlines	• pull quotes	• graphics	• subheads
• icons	• photos	• bullets	• initial caps

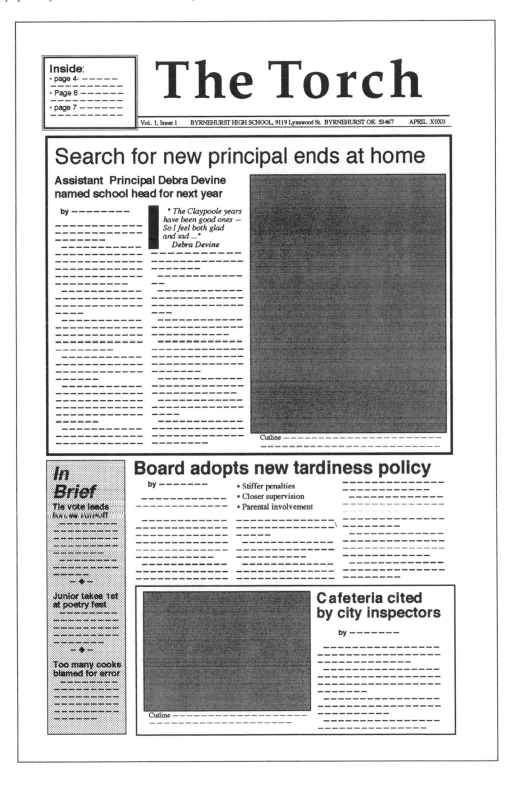

Example 3-1. Sample modular layout.

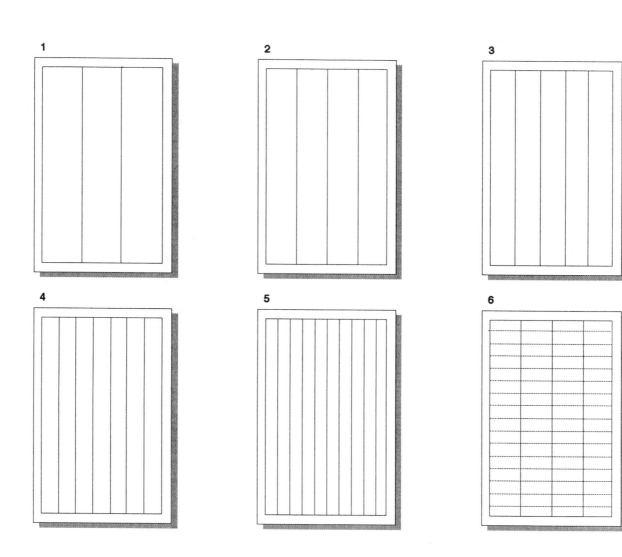

Example 3-2. Grids for dummy layouts.

Designing reader-friendly copy blocks

When designing pages, remember the following:

1. Avoid crowding type against rules or boxes.

2. Allow sufficient contrast when reversing type to white against a dark ground or black over a shaded or color background.

3. Overprinting a photo or other graphic often makes type difficult to read.

4. Wrapping type around a graphic may create nasty gaps and awkward spaces that slow readers down.

5. Paragraph indentations of newspaper columns should be no greater than three to five spaces.

6. Do not run extended body copy or text units in single columns when using 7-10 column grids.

7. Do not stretch copy across too wide a space. Too much means the full width of an 8-1/2″ × 11″ paper or across more than three columns of a five-column, tabloid-size page.

8. Printed on newsprint, both typographical tricks and photographs lose a certain degree of sharpness and clarity—something that deserves a layout artist's consideration.

Name _____   Date _____

— EXERCISE 3-3A —
How design affects readability

DIRECTIONS:

Read each of the following copy blocks which illustrate how layout affects readability. Then rank each, with 1 as the most readable and 6 as the least.

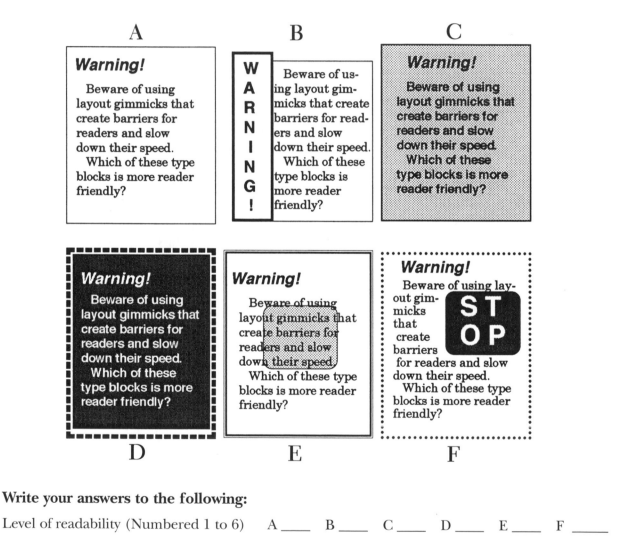

Write your answers to the following:

Level of readability (Numbered 1 to 6)   A ____   B ____   C ____   D ____   E ____   F ____

What factors create problems in reading the least reader friendly?

_____

_____

_____

— EXERCISE 3-3A —
How design affects readability (cont'd)

What factors create problems in reading the next to the least?

_____

_____

_____

_____

What other problems do you find in layouts you did not choose as numbers 5 and 6?

_____

_____

_____

_____

What qualities in your first choice make it most reader—friendly?

_____

_____

_____

_____

Once a reader yields to the attraction, the rest of the article should be designed for reading at the individual's fastest rate of comprehension. Irregular-width lines that provoke the reader with wide gaps between words, spacing that causes erratic eye shifts, odd leaps or jumps of copy over graphics or from one column to another—anything that forces the reader to search for a story's continuation—is a source of annoyance.

CONTENT MATTERS MOST—That message should remain in every layout artist's mind while designing the paper's pages. In making up a paper, the computer's capacity for experimentation should not be confused with the message. The byword should not be "What can I make the computer do now?" but "What can I do to make the story more reader friendly?" It's the writer's responsibility to make the story good; it's the layout artist's responsibility to draw the reader into it and insure its accessibility.

THE DOMINANT FACTOR—A primary rule for effective layout calls for one strong element to dominate each page, capturing the reader because of its large size and compelling message. It may be a photo full of action, emotion or human interest; a dramatic drawing or other type of graphic; a headline powerful in both design and message. It's an element that has an immediate impact on the reader. It's a technique borrowed from the newspapers and magazine vying for attention at newsstands, but it's a practice that—well used with effective photos and graphics—can activate school papers, too.

Note how a number of school papers (Examples 3-4–3-12) have successfully created front-page layouts that both are visually attractive and draw readers to their content.

Recreating a dummy

Example 3-4 shows the effective front-page layout created for the 11″ × 17″ tabloid *TJ Today* of Thomas Jefferson High School. Example 3-5 shows a dummy layout that might have served as a guide for the page's compositor.

Whether a layout designer, page editor or someone else completes the final computer version, anyone computer literate and familiar with a few simple symbols should be able to read and reproduce the dummy layout in the desktop publishing program.

In a school setting, especially, with its danger of unexpected absences, a carefully drawn final copy of the dummy may prove a necessity. For students, working from a dummy with horizontal lines spaced one inch (or 6 picas) apart can make life easier when completing the page.

Although there are various methods of marking dummy layouts, plan to use a set of consistent symbols ("Guidelines for marking dummy layouts," Figure 3-13) so all staff members understand one another's intentions.

Example 3-4. *TJ Today*, 11″ × 17″, Thomas Jefferson High School for Science & Technology, Alexandria, VA.

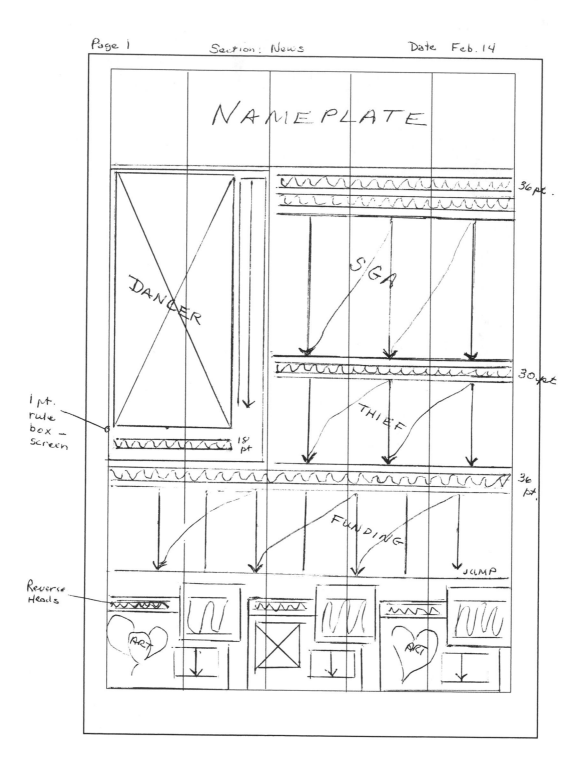

Example 3-5. Dummy layout for *TJ Today*.

Example 3-6. *Falcon's Cry,* 11″ × 14″, Jordan H.S., Durham, NC.

Example 3-7. *The Declaration,* 8-1/2″ × 11″, Monroe Junior High, Monroe, MI.

Example 3-8. *The Spectrum,* 11″ × 15″, Arundel H.S., Gambrills, MD.

Example 3-9. *Spartan Spectrum,* 11″ × 17″, Chula Vista H.S., Chula Vista, CA.

Example 3-10. *Newshawk*, 8-1/2" × 11", Fairborn H.S., Fairborn, OH.

Example 3-11. *Devils' Advocate*, 8-1/2" × 11", Hinsdale Central H.S., Hinsdale, IL.

Example 3-12. *The Claw*, 11" × 15", Blairsville Senior H.S., Blairsville, PA.

Guidelines for marking dummy layouts

1. Set off and label all permanent elements, such as datelines.

2. Block off spaces for photos or other graphics, and mark each with an X that stretches from corner to corner.

3. Rule off individual spaces for ads, and mark with a diagonal line that runs from the lower left to the upper corner.

4. Set off spaces for headlines with a wavy or squiggly line that varies in depth to show approximate type size.

5. Indicate—and label—space and position for bylines, pull quotes, cutlines, sidebars and similar elements.

6. Block off body copy, running an arrow to the bottom of each portion used in any one column, then indicating its continuation, if any, into additional columns. Clearly indicate if the rest of a story jumps to another page.

7. Briefly but clearly identify all elements with a word or two, such as story slug, name of advertiser, content of graphic or photo.

8. Mark desired size of headlines, boxes, rules and similarly variable elements.

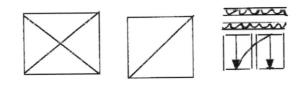

(2) Photo   (3) Ad   (4) Headline
                                                            & (6) copy

See example 3-5 for sample.

Name _____ Date _____

— EXERCISE 3-13A —
Recreating a dummy layout

DIRECTIONS:

Choose a front page from one of the examples given (3-4–3-12), an exchange paper, or another that your adviser provides.

Step 1:

Decide the number of columns on which the layout was based, and work from a dummy layout with a matching grid (Example 3-2).

Step 2:

Recreate the page as a dummy that might serve for setting the page in your desktop publishing program.

Take care to do the work neatly, indicating correct spacing and clearly marking and labeling all elements.

THE POINT OF PICAS—Some advisers prefer to set computer rules to measure layout space in picas rather than inches. It is not only the professional measurement, but also allows greater use of whole numbers instead of ungainly decimal points.

The pica/point system works like this:

1 point	=	1/72 of an inch

The height of type is measured in points.

72 pt. type is basically one inch high

36 pt. type equals 1/2 inch

18 pt. type equals 1/4 inch . . . and so on.

1 pica	=	12 points *or*
		1/6 of an inch

One pica is a recommended setting for the gutter between columns of type, as well as between a headline and its story. A space of 1-1/2 or 1.5 picas serves to separate the end of one story from headline, rule or graphic directly beneath it. Consistent use of white space provides a professional polish—and makes your paper more readable.

When boxing stories, photos or graphics, do not crowd or cram the type or art within its box. Set columns to a reduced width, allowing a margin of at least 1 pica—some say 1.5—in addition to the regular 1-pica gutter.

ADVANTAGES AND DISADVANTAGES OF USING PICAS—When the computer calls for a number, one clear advantage of picas is the simplicity of indicating "1" or "1.5" instead of changing a fraction to a decimal. The disadvantage is the possibility of confusion—and the necessity of teaching a new system of measurement to kids who can't find their way between centimeters and inches.

A POSSIBLE SOLUTION—Translate picas into inches, and list the resulting figures as the standard. Use these figures for setting styles in your computers and include them in your staff manual.

Gutter space between column:	0.167 inches
	1 pica
Between headline and story:	0.167 inches
	1 pica
Between end of story and head or item beneath:	0. 25 inches
	1.5 picas
Margin within boxes:	0.25 inches
	1.5 picas

WHERE DO YOU BEGIN?—Which comes first—designing the layout or writing the story? Even though a paper is content-driven, the question deserves consideration. One approach begins by assigning reporters to write stories to a given length based on their relative importance, to fit a preconceived layout design. The opposite way is to create the layout from completed stories, fitting them together as in a jigsaw puzzle—though one without any predetermined design.

A third way utilizes elements of both methods. If a story is too long, the compositor of the page can take advantage of the cutoff test and either lop off a few paragraphs or jump the end of the story to a succeeding page. (The problem with the latter is that it may disrupt the layout of another page.)

Do not attempt to make stories fit by increasing or decreasing the size of body copy or substantially altering the leading between lines. Such tricks may seem to work, but the results inevitably look amateurish.

Setting attractive standards

Headlines, bylines, datelines, cutlines, folio lines—not to mention lines of type and deadlines. Have you ever noticed journalism's concentration on lines? Then there are the nameplate or logo, masthead, captions, standing heads and icons. Many of these are repeated—often running every issue on the same page and sometimes in the same position. Well designed and placed, they add consistency and polish to a paper. They also serve as the foundation for newspaper design and can be placed as templates in a desktop publishing program.

Templates are simply model pages that provide the general structure of a given page. Composition begins from these typical elements although all are readily changed. Once a new version is completed, it can be "saved" for publication, leaving the template intact as before, for use the following issue.

DON'T BE LED ASTRAY—One of many temptations of the computer age and its multiplicity of choices is that of sampling all the type styles that come with your basic programs—and even of dabbling with the scores of new ones coming your way.

A number of mottoes have been coined to forestall such urges. A classic is KISS—an acronym for *Keep it simple, stupid!*—a rather rude reminder that too much clutter cancels the chances of any single element to stand out.

Another version, better suited for school papers, might be KICK—*Keep it clean, kids!* In other words, clean up your pages with sufficient, well-planned white space and clean, readable type.

An introduction to popular type families

As a prelude to designing standing elements, begin by choosing typefaces for body copy and headlines. It's best to limit your choices to two main families. Typographically speaking, a *family* consists of one particular style or design of type in all its sizes, weights, widths and variations. (A font is the complete set of a given size and style.)

As body copy, it's best to stick to a serif or Roman type, one with hooks or crosshatches on ends of letters for greater readability. Serif types available with many basic word-processing programs include New Century Schoolbook, New York and Times.

Limit body copy to two basic sizes at most: one for standard stories and features; one size larger for editorials or lead paragraphs to major stories, if set on extra-width columns. When choosing type, remember that point size may be deceptive. Although the ultimate depth may be the same, such factors as risers make some types seem smaller—and therefore look more crowded and harder to read—than others that are nominally the same size.

Example:

> This is 12 point New Century Schoolbook.
>
> This is 12 point Helvetica.
>
> This is 12 point Times.

Even while limiting yourself to one family, you still have much to choose from, for the computer readily changes styles from plain text to bold, italic, condensed, extended or a combination of these.

TYPE: A KEY ELEMENT IN DESIGN—Having chosen your body copy, you may use variations of it to design standing elements such as the following:

1. As **bylines:** the identification of a story's writer, appearing centered below the headline or, in some papers, at a story's end.

   Example:

by Mary Kelly,	plain italic
copy editor	bold italic
BY **MARY KELLY,**	caps/small caps; bold name
COPY EDITOR	smaller size, all caps
^{by} **Mary Kelly,** copy editor	super/subscripts; plain text and bold

2. As **cutlines:** description and identification printed beneath or alongside photographs.

   Example:

   > ***The cheers must go on.*** *In spite of a downpour, cheerleaders Carla Evans, Suzie Slade, and Bruce Bell try to whip up enthusiasm of rain-drenched fans at . . .*

   > **THE CHEERS MUST GO ON.** *In spite of a downpour, cheerleaders Carla Evans, Suzie Slade, and Bruce Bell try to whip up enthusiasm of rain-drenched fans at . . .*

   > | THE CHEERS MUST GO ON. | *In spite of a downpour, cheerleaders*

   Carla *Evans, Suzie Slade, and Bruce Bell try to whip up enthusiasm of rain-drenched fans at . . .*

3. As **subheads:** boldface lines of type used to break up the gray monotony of many-paragraphed stories.

   Example:

   Say it in a few words

   Since the purpose of subheads is to provide entry points and relieve readers' eyes, they provide more white space if not filling the entire column.

A boldface lead-in highlighting the first words or phrases, plus white space between paragraphs, is an alternate to subheads.

However, the desired emphasis is lost when the technique is varied to put words in **boldface** in the middle of a paragraph.

4. As **initial caps:** a large display type letter at the beginning of a paragraph.

Examples:

T hey may rise above the first line of type or be set down, within the paragraph. Some schools use them only with first paragraphs of major stories.

A nother use is to break the monotony of long, gray columns of type on a page and provide an entry point, similar to that of a subhead. Initial caps are easy to create in most desktop publishing programs.

5. As **pull quotes:** the same family as body copy, often in larger-size italics, serves as a teaser to entice readers to the rest of the story. Pull quotes need not be placed near their actual spot in a story.

Example:

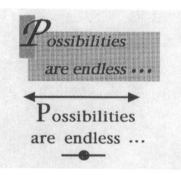

Because the possibilities are endless, devote time in your late spring, preschool or early fall planning sessions to create a set of compatible designs—one for each category. Then use them throughout the year.

It's a way to give your paper a definite character. And, having agreed-upon design elements also saves time—especially if you define them as custom styles and include them in your style menu for easy selection.

HEADLINES THAT STAND OUT—Headlines can scream—or they can concisely report. Whatever purpose they serve with regard to a particular story, they are always an important element of design.

Whether it's serif or sans-serif, it's well to choose a functional family that offers a range of options. One possibility: the Helvetica family, a workmanlike type that includes **Helvetica** (bold), Helvetica (plain) and even Helvetica Narrow.

For headlines, a type family with serifs, such as Bodoni bold or plain, tends to give a more formal look and may be more readable.

Types not included with word-processing or publishing programs are readily purchased and installed. As with all phases of layout and design, remember—don't overdo. Offbeat or novelty types may call attention to themselves but often do nothing to enhance the story they accompany.

Once chosen, a single family of headline type can provide abundant variety when incorporated in your layouts.

What's in a nameplate?

Appearing at or near the top of the front page, a nameplate introduces the newspaper to its readers in more than one way. Also called the logo, the nameplate not only announces the paper's name but also reflects its character. Here again it's true that less is often better than more. Distorted type and nameplate clutter may indicate that a staff is obsessed with nonessentials and is wasting time on trivialities, instead of concentrating on the production of first-class, well-written stories.

The well-designed nameplate may effectively use a different, but compatible typeface from the chosen headline and body type. It is almost unfailingly the largest size type used in the paper and can be easily created, even in a basic word-processing program. Each of the following could be sized larger in a tabloid-size paper. With a desktop publishing program, it is easy to create custom sizes in the size menu. You can even kern or vary spaces between individual letters to create the look you prefer.

72 pt. Palatino extended

72 pt. Monaco bold extended

Chicago bold italic extended

Nameplates are often centered in a space that runs the full width of the page, sometimes accompanied by the school crest or a symbol that represents the paper's name or school mascot. Nameplates may also be boxed in a space shy of the paper's full width to allow room for a menu listing a preview of inside pages, or for another type of message or slogan. A word of warning: This kind of nameplate is easily cluttered and can distract readers' attention from the "main events" on the rest of the page.

ADD COMPLETE IDENTIFICATION—In conjunction with the nameplate, completely identify your publication. Usually set in a single line under the logo and set off by rules, this information should include:

Flush left (Aligned from the left margin)

Volume—the number of years your paper has been published, including the current one, plus

Issue—the number of issues this school year (**Example:** Volume 1, Number 3)

Centered

School address—school name, if not elsewhere in the nameplate; street address, city, state and ZIP Code.

Flush right (Aligned at right)

Date of issue—including month and year, along with the day and date if pertinent.

DESIGNING FOR HARMONY—A well-designed nameplate can also serve as the basis for other standing element in your layouts.

Folio lines are identifications on inside pages, which include the section's name, date of issue, name of paper, and page number. The page numbers should go to the outside corner of the page—to the left on page 2, the right on page 3, and so on. A folio line usually heads each inside page, although some papers utilize the bottom margins for part of this information.

Example:

| Page 2 | Byrnehurst High School | THE TORCH *Opinion* |

A reduced version of the nameplate can also introduce the masthead, which lists the paper's vital statistics, including school name and address, staff members and other pertinent data, such as editorial policy.

USING ICONS FOR DESIGN HARMONY—In newspaper terminology, an *icon* is simply a symbol or image that serves as an identifier, through shape and design as well as wordage. Instead of standing heads on columns or features run every issue, a series of icons carries out the paper's unified design theme and works as additional entry points.

A further use of the nameplate design could be as an icon for a column, which might include a thumbnail portrait.

Example:

Laying out pages: From the beginning

The blank layout—where to begin? Start with standing or known elements. On page 1, this might be the nameplate, space for news briefs and a menu of inside stories already placed on the layout grid or template.

You'll also want a list of scheduled stories with other items to be included in each module. For the typical tabloid front page, three stories are plenty if the page also carries news briefs. Your goal is not to overload the front page—or any page—with rivers of gray type, but to allow enough space to display each story effectively.

Know the count of each story, either in characters or in a basic length in inches, which you can convert to fit into variable-width columns, according to a chart devised for your paper.

Since modular scheduling is based on a series of rectangles and squares, begin with the major story, including its headline, graphics, cutlines, sidebars, pull quotes, and so on.

As an example, start with a story 11″ long to fit in a five-column rectangle at the top of the page, right under the nameplate.

Here are the possibilities for the body copy:

- Run it divided into two equal columns 5-1/2″ long.
- Run it in U-shape, with pull quote, sidebar or graphic in its loop.
- Run it in an L-shape, divided into one long and two or three shorter columns running under a graphic.

Important to remember: Don't cut off part of a column from its continuation. Any element, such as a picture or pull quote, that separates the story and makes the reader hunt for the next word or paragraph causes an irritating stoppage.

LEAVE SUFFICIENT SPACE FOR A HEADLINE—In current terminology, each part of a headline in a single font, whether one or more lines, is called a deck.

The following guidelines, headline schedule and exercises (3-14 to 3-18) will help your staff write more effective headlines.

Example 1:

Headlines attract
Second deck adds to message, draws reader further into story

Deck 1: 30 pt. Helvetica bold, one line
Deck 2: 18 pt. Helvetica plain extended, two lines

Example 2:

Headlines attract
Second deck adds to message, helps draw reader into story

Deck 1: 36 pt. Helvetica bold, one line
Deck 2: 18 pt. Times plain, two lines

Example 3:

Headlines attract
Second deck adds to message, helps draw reader into story

Deck 1: 30 pt. Times bold , one line
Deck 2: 18 pt. Times plain, two lines

The typeface and sizes you choose become part of your newspaper's style, and this too should be consistent from page to page and issue to issue, making it part of the paper's character—and as distinctive as a signature.

SOME GENERAL ADVICE

1. Headlines that run across the width of a tabloid should be large enough to make an impression.

2. Don't be wordy. Headlines lead readers to a story they don't try to tell it.

3. Headlines more than three columns wide rarely benefit from a second line.

4. If the first deck runs above both graphic and story, it is often effective to run the second deck above the story alone or above only its first column.

5. Headlines generally are set flush left (aligned to the left).

6. Strive for professionalism. Too much gimmicky type makes a paper look amateurish.

USE VARIETY HEADS SPARINGLY, FOR EFFECT—The following types of headlines can add emphasis to special news stories and features, if not overused.

1. **Kicker:** A shorter first deck serving as a lead-in to a large-point headline, perhaps in all caps

School board shortens spring vacation:

NOT A LUCKY BREAK

2. **Tripod:** A word or so in large-point caps with two lines in smaller size to the side

ON LINE
Have students deserted the phone to search for friends via Internet?

3. **Hammerhead:** The opposite of a kicker

WARNING:

Board institutes no-tolerance policy
with regard to smoking on campus

Writing effective headlines

1. Use downstyle, limiting capital letters to the first letter of a headline and all proper nouns.

2. All headlines should contain either a verb or verb form.

    Example: **Thoughts of prom prompt**
                              dreams, doubts, dieting

                              Two senior golfers rank
                              among top 10 in state

3. Do not split up closely related words and phrases between two lines of a headline.

    NO: **Two golfers rank among**
                        top 10 players in state

                        First prize goes to Ken
                        Danielson in art show

    Better: **Ken Danielson takes**
                        first prize in art show

4. Avoid using weak words, such as *a, an, the*—and *is, are* or other forms of *to be*. Generally use a comma in place of *and*.

5. Use only single quotes in headlines. Write 'Macbeth', not "Macbeth."

6. It is usually redundant to include the name of the school or its initials in a headline in a school's paper.

7. Concentrate on the lead paragraph or nutgraph as your source of information for the head-line, but be familiar with the rest of the story's contents.

8. Use clear, direct, concise language—and remember, it's more important to be informative than cute or clever.

9. To make headlines fit, replace long words with short synonyms or vice versa.

10. As far as possible, write headlines to count. Don't rely on the computer to make size adjust-ments.

Newspaper headline schedule

The following counts are based on columns 12 picas or 2 inches wide. Counts can be adjusted to fit varying column widths.

Helvetica Bold:

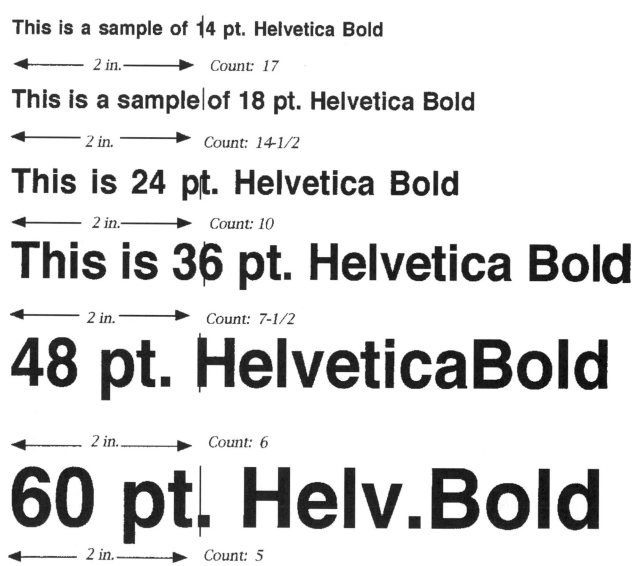

This is a sample of 14 pt. Helvetica Bold

← 2 in. → *Count: 17*

This is a sample of 18 pt. Helvetica Bold

← 2 in. → *Count: 14-1/2*

This is 24 pt. Helvetica Bold

← 2 in. → *Count: 10*

This is 36 pt. Helvetica Bold

← 2 in. → *Count: 7-1/2*

48 pt. HelveticaBold

← 2 in. → *Count: 6*

60 pt. Helv.Bold

← 2 in. → *Count: 5*

New York Bold:

This is a sample of 14 pt. New York Bold

⟵———— *2 in.* ————⟶   *Count: 16*

This is a sample of 18 pt. New York Bold

⟵———— *2 in.* ————⟶   *Count: 11-1/2*

This is a sample, 24 pt. New York

⟵———— *2 in.* ————⟶   *Count: 9 1/2*

This is 36 pt. New York

⟵———— *2 in.* ————⟶   *Count: 6-1/2*

48 pt. N.Y.Bold

⟵———— *2 in.* ————⟶   *Count:: 5*

60 pt.N.Y.Bold

⟵———— *2 in.* ————⟶   *Count: 4-1/2*

Helvetica Plain:

This is a sample of 14 pt. Helvetica Plain

←——— 2 in.———→   *Count: 19-1/2*

This is a sample of 18 pt. Helvetica Plain

←——— 2 in.———→   *Count: 15-1/2*

This is a sample of 24 pt. Helvetica Plain

←——— 2 in.———→   *Count: 12*

36 pt.Helvetica Plain

←——— 2 in.———→   *Count: 8-1/2*

48 pt. Helvetica Plain

←——— 2 in.———→   *Count:: 6*

60 pt. Helv. Plain

←——— 2 in.———→   *Count: 5*

New York Plain:

This is a sample of 14 pt. New York Plain

←——— 2 in.———→ *Count: 17*

This is a sample of 18 pt. New York Plain

←——— 2 in.———→ *Count: 13*

This is 24 pt. New York Plain

←——— 2 in.———→ *Count: 10-1/2*

36 pt. New York Plain

←——— 2 in.———→ *Count: 7*

48 pt. New York Plain

←——— 2 in.———→ *Count: 5-1/2*

60 pt. New York

←——— 2 in.———→ *Count: 4-1/2*

Character count chart for
writing headlines

Work from the column width of the assigned story. If the headline runs across more than one column, remember to include the space allotted to the gutter as part of your measurement.

Determine the count, based on your paper's headline schedule, or figure the character count from another sample. Unless assigned a specialty head, all lines of a multiline deck should be closely matched in length and fill at least 7/8 of the assigned width, if possible. Tinker with wording and substitute synonyms to make the headline both read well and look good.

Headline count system:

All lowercase letters	=	1 count
EXCEPT j-i-l-t and f	=	1/2 count
AND		
lowercase m and w	=	1-1/2 count

All uppercase letters	=	1-1/2 count
EXCEPT capital I	=	1 count
AND		
capital M, W, O	=	2 count

Other figures		
Spaces	=	1/2 count
Individual numerals	=	1 count
EXCEPT numeral 1	=	1/2 count
Question mark, dash	=	1 count
All other punctuation	=	1/2 count

Name _____ Date _____

— EXERCISE 3-17 —
Practice working with headlines

DIRECTIONS:

Using the count system chart as your guide, determine the character count of each of the following headlines.

1. # Teen Life program seeks
   # more community support

   24 pt. Helvetica plain, 2 lines   Character count: Line 1 _____, Line 2_____

2. # Debaters take on curfews
   ## Team members prepare for coming state tourney

   Primary deck, 24 pt. Helvetica bold, 1 line   Character count _____
   Secondary deck, 18 pt. Times plain, 1 line   Character count _____

3. # QUESTION:
   ## How will gym construction affect athletics?

   Primary deck, 48 pt. Helvetica bold, CAPS   Character count _____
   Secondary deck, 18 pt. Helvetica plain extended, 1 line   Character count _____

4. ## Girls volleyball schedule winds up
   ## with two post-season tournaments

   14 pt. Helvetica bold, 2 lines   Character count: Line 1 _____, Line 2_____

5. # AP English class
   # sees Shakespeare
   # in Stratford, Ont.

   ## Where there's a Will, there's a way
   ## to raise money for Canada weekend

   Primary deck, 24 pt. Times bold,   Character count: Line 1 _____, Line 2_____
       3 lines   Line 3_____

   Secondary deck, 14 pt. Helvetica bold,   Character count: Line 1 _____, Line 2_____
       2 lines

311

— EXERCISE 3-18 —
Correcting problem headlines

DIRECTIONS:

Each of the following headlines contains one or more flaws. First, determine the character count
of the headline as written. Second, identify the error or errors. Then, write an improved headline
to the same count and in the same style.

1. # BHS boys track team is aiming for 3rd straight league championship

(a) 24 pt. Helvetica bold, 2 lines   Character count: Line 1_____, Line 2_____

(b) Briefly list the error(s)_____

_____

_____

_____

(c) Write an improved version below. (You may wish to include some of the following information: Has 6 returning seniors, biggest-ever turnout for practice, date of first meet.)

_____

_____

2. # The colleges and universities in state seek uniform system in state grading
They are asking for every high school to use 1 system

(a) Primary deck, 24 pt. Helvetica plain, 2 lines   Character count: Line 1_____,
                                                                        Line 2_____

Secondary deck, 14 pt. Helvetica bold, 1 line   Character count _____

(b) Briefly list the error(s): _____

_____

_____

_____

(c) Write an improved version. (You may wish to include some of the following information:
Aim for conversion in two years; goal is for easier comparison of students applying for
entrance; plan now under consideration.)

Primary deck:

_____

_____

Secondary deck:

_____

_____

3\. # Judge Palmer Guest Speaker

Byrnehurst Students To Hear Speech
"What Teens Should Know About Law"

(a) Primary deck, 48 pt. Helvetica bold, 2 lines   Character count: Line 1_____,
Line 2_____

     Secondary deck, 18 pt. Times plain, 2 lines   Character count. Line 1_____,
Line 2_____

(b) Briefly list the error(s): _____

_____

_____

(c) Write an improved version below. (You may wish to include some of the following information: Speech will be part of Law Day, Palmer is juvenile court judge.)

Primary deck:

_____

_____

Secondary deck:

_____

_____

ABOUT HEADLINE WRITING—Headlines may go to an editor, the reporter who wrote the story or someone especially assigned to write them. There is an advantage to each method. The editor, especially one who also laid out the page, best knows the headline's desired effect; however, an editor may lack time to give a headline the attention it deserves. The reporter is most familiar with the story and perhaps has also written a suggested headline that is adaptable to the given format and character count. Yet, it's also true that some students have a special talent for working with character counts and juggling words to create effective headlines in the least possible time.

You may wish to use one method or a combination of them. While writing headlines is good practice for everyone on the staff, the pressure of deadlines may make it best to count upon a reliable few. Provide each writer with a headline assignment sheet (Figure 3-19) clearly indicating all requirements.

Refining the method

Depending upon the experience and training of your staff, you may wish to create a complete headline chart, covering a wide range of possibilities. Instead of having students work from a basic count, this chart could indicate in a kind of shorthand both type and character specifications.

Example: HB36-2/5-35ct could represent 36 pt. Helvetica bold in a 2-column headline, based on a 5-column page, with each line having a count of 35 characters. For inexperienced staffers, learning such terminology may needlessly complicate matters. For some, absorbing the principle of variable width letters may be quite enough.

If your goal is to save time and manage as efficiently as possible, remember to avoid complications and keep directions simple. If your paper uses variable columns, it is easier to measure widths and count headlines from a basic standard, such as 2 inches or 12 picas.

A note about body copy

Word-processing and publishing programs include a feature that allows you to set up body copy in one of four ways.

1. **Justified**

   Set justified, copy is balanced out to stretch from margin to margin, so that it's aligned evenly on both outer edges. This is the preferred choice for straight news and other writing that needs a professional finish. When justified type is set in extremely narrow columns or with type wrap, it sometimes results in strange gaps that create annoyingly spaced passages that are difficult to read.

2. **Flush left**

   Setting paragraphs flush left results in what is simply called a "ragged edge" on the right. Words are printed out at an evenly spaced distance from one another—not spaced out to fill the entire line. Flush left works best with columns and features that benefit from a casual look. It's important to use auto hyphenation—especially with narrow columns.

3. **Flush right**

   Just the opposite, setting copy flush right results in a jagged left edge, which most people find difficult to read. It is best used sparingly. One good use: a photo caption set to the left of the picture.

4. **Centered**

   More useful for advertisements and announcements than for regular text. Awkward hyphenation.

YOUR PAPER'S
LOGO

Headline assignment form

Story slug _____ Page no. _____

Primary deck: Typeface _____ Type point size _____

No. of lines _____ No. of columns _____ Count per line _____

Check: Down style _____ All caps _____

_____

_____

_____

Second deck, if needed: Typeface _____ Type point size _____

No. of lines _____ No. of columns _____ Count per line _____

Check: Down style _____ All caps _____

_____

_____

_____

Type of head or special directions, if any:

_____

_____

_____

Story by _____

Headline assigned to _____ DUE: ASAP

Date of issue _____ Page editor _____

Name _____   Date _____

— EXERCISE 3-20 —
Laying out a lead story

DIRECTIONS:

Work on the 5-column grids below, created for an 11″ × 17″ tabloid, or use another format assigned by your adviser.

Step 1. Place all standing elements, such as nameplate, teasers and briefs, found on the paper's front page.

Step 2. Use the facts given below to create at least three possible versions of a modular layout for the lead article. Assume it will share the page with two other stories.

Experiment with both headline styles and placement of the story's parts. Remember, no one way is necessarily best. One goal of a layout artist is to achieve variety while maintaining the paper's basic personality.

Facts included in lead:

A watchdog committee, Minding Our Schools, last week demanded removal of five books from the Byrnehurst English curriculum and more than a dozen others from the library.

Modular elements:

9″ story—SLUG: Censor

Photo—to run horizontally as landscape. (See glossary)

Possible pull quote:

"Grapes of Wrath has got to go!"
John Blakemore, committee spokesman

Possible sidebar:

List of 10 books, most often targeted for censorship in U.S. public schools

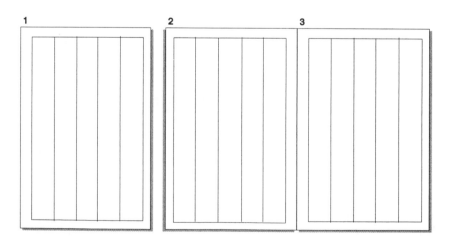

Page layouts: The total effect

Good layouts begin at the beginning: with the story that should make the major impact—plus a dominant element, photo, art or headline—to focus the reader's attention.

What next? Since the reader's roving eye may flit from item to item, deciding which to read first or even read at all, it's important to make each module as tempting as possible, yet part of a harmonious whole. On every page, the main stories and features will rise to the top; but it's important not to forget the lower half of the page and let it go gray below a real or imaginary fold. On inside pages, even advertisements can add contrast and appeal to a layout's design.

Sometimes it seems that rules for designing layouts offer more don'ts than do's. "Guidelines for avoiding layout pitfall," Figure 3-21, offers positive ways to improve your layouts.

SUPERIOR LAYOUTS: COMBINING SENSE AND THE STYLE—Every layout that you do presents its own special problems, and each layout also offers an infinite variety of ways to solve them. Study Examples (3-22–3-31) to discover the routes that school layout designers throughout the country have taken to create outstanding inside news, feature, entertainment and sports pages; then design a modular layout. (Exercise 3-32)

Like professionals, you need not hesitate to gather inspiration and ideas from what others have done. It is not plagiarism to analyze someone else's solution to a problem and then adapt it to suit your own needs. It is only dishonest to steal or copy what someone else has done, and then claim it as your own.

Guidelines for avoiding layout pitfalls

1. **Modular units help make the entire page interesting.**

   a. Give thought to laying out shorter stories as well as major ones.

   b. Avoid clutter and undirected busyness.

   c. Include at least two to three stories per page.

2. **Direct the reader's eye.**

   a. Box all elements in some stories and set the copy to a narrower width.

   b. Allow a margin of at least one pica between rule and printed matter or art.

   c. Use hairline, 1 pt. or 2 pt. rules—and occasionally 3 pt. or Harvard rules of 2 pts. outlined by 1 pt. on some modules.

3. **Make it clear what elements belong together.**

   a. Allow extra breathing space between stacked stories, such as news briefs.

   b. Use 1.5 picas (or 1/4 in.) between the end of one story and the headline or rule of the one directly beneath it.

   c. One pica (or 0.167 in.) is sufficient for elements within a single story.

4. **Separate elements that may prove confusing if side by side.**

   a. Steer clear of tombstone headlines.

   Junior's science project   **Quiz Bowl team gets set**
   captures highest rating   **for championship match**

   _____ _____   _____ _____

   _____ _____   _____ _____

   _____ _____   _____ _____

   _____ _____   _____ _____

   _____ _____   _____ _____

   Separate such stories with a photo, or put one in a box so they don't seem to run together.

b. Make it obvious which elements go together.

Confusing:

Junior's science project captures highest rating

PHOTO

—————— ——————
—————— ——————
—————— ——————
—————— ——————
—————— ——————

Quiz Bowl team gets set for championship match

—————— ——————
—————— ——————
—————— ——————
—————— ——————
—————— ——————

Which story goes
with the picture?
It's hard to tell.

Clear: Resize and box the story that doesn't belong with the picture.

Junior's science project captures highest rating

PHOTO

—————— ——————
—————— ——————
—————— ——————
—————— ——————
—————— ——————

Quiz Team seeks championship

—————— ——————
—————— ——————
—————— ——————
—————— ——————

5. **Establish consistent margins within all pages.**

   a. Avoid toying with leading and horizontal spacing to fill columns.

   b. Maintain alignment of rules and type across columns and at lower edge of stories and pages. Align elements vertically, as well.

6. **Strive for both horizontal and vertical movement on a page.**

   a. Stories stretching the length of a column tend to look dull and gray, and the resulting pages look rigid.

   b. Cutting a column in two with a photo or pull quote will not achieve horizontal movement and causes an unnatural, awkward break.

7. **Emphasize horizontal movement by spreading stories across columns.**

   a. Break stories 10″ or longer into two or more parts. Stories under 7″ long may run vertically.

   b. When dividing type blocks, avoid widows—the term for a partial line of type running alone at the top of a column.

   c. Vary your placement of body copy. Along with multicolumn rectangles, place text in L-shaped and U-shaped units around graphics, photos.

   d. Two inches should be the minimum length for a single "leg" or column of type in multiple-column settings.

   e. Use subheads and pull quotes as entry points and breaks in longer stories.

8. **Headlines should draw readers to stories, not seek attention for themselves.**

   a. Assign typefaces in proportion to both page size and length of story.

   b. Wordy, overly small headlines defeat their purpose.

   c. Be sure fancy effects, such as overprinting on gray or color backgrounds, will be legible when printed on newsprint.

   d. Allow sufficient space between items and select large-enough type sizes so overprints don't go gray.

9. **Take advantage of effective white space as a design element.**

   a. With seven- to ten-column formats, the "extra" columns provide a clean, uncluttered look when used for placement of cutlines, pull quotes or bulleted factoids.

   b. Be sure that white space adds and does not distract by forming a "river of white" that draws attention away from the paper's content.

10. **Pay attention to facing pages.**

    a. The double truck—pages 4 and 5 in an 8-page paper—is often designed as one unit. Remember to allow for the fold, which may create a distracting crease in a photo or story.

    b. Be aware of facing pages, such as page 2s and 3, and design their layouts to complement each other.

11. **Make limited use of stories jumped to other pages.**

    a. Too many leftover continuations of stories make inside pages turn gray and wishy-washy.

    b. Design a jump-line for end of story, usually containing just one or two words, such as **"Quiz bowl,** *see page 6,"* to run at break.

    c. **"Quiz bowl,** *from page 1,"* serves as the jump head for its continuation.

    d. Do not give jumped stories undue prominence on inside pages. Try to run as rectangular modules, not long columns, toward bottom of page.

12. **Keep columns to a readable width.**

    a. Desirable line widths range from 12 to 36 picas or 2 to 6 inches wide in 9- to 12-point type.

    b. Lines narrower than 9 picas (about an inch and a half) are awkward to read.

    c. Lines wider than 42 picas (about 7 inches) create a confusing jump back from the end of one line to the start of the next.

13. **Keep focused on content.**

    a. Experiment with layouts—but remember their purpose is to enhance the news, not submerge it.

    b. Use only original artwork, photos and graphics on your news and feature pages. Remember that copyright laws apply to almost all professional cartoons and photographs.

14. **Use informal rather than formal balance.**

Formal balance
may be tidy
but is
extremely
dull.

15. **Make sure standing elements are assets, not just space fillers.**

    a. Boxed menus or teasers about inside features that stretch across the top or bottom of the front page may take up space better devoted to enhancing a key module. A simple boxed list may serve as well.

    b. On the front page, run only news briefs that deserve such prominence Design news brief modules around the stories instead of scratching for stories to fill a given space.

Example 3-22. (News) "Phone system. . . ," *Explosion,* 11″ × 17″, Glendale H.S., Glendale, CA.

Example 3-23. (News) "Pre-engineering classes. . . ," *TJ Today,* 11″ × 17″, Thomas Jefferson High School for Science & Technology, Alexandria, VA.

Example 3-24. (Features, Entertainment) "On the catwalk," *El Tejano,* 11″ × 16″, W. B. Ray H.S., Manteo, NC.

Example 3-25. (Features, Entertainment) "Before the big time," *Bruin Banner,* 11″ × 17″, Sam Barlow H.S., Gresham, OR.

F E A T U R E S — 7

Hanging on for dear life

■ One person's story reveals challenge of ropes course.

By Evie Daniels
Staff Writer

As I finished harnessing up, I stared up at the 52-foot tall tower upon which I was about to challenge. My excitement and pre-planning route collapsed before my eyes as the feelings of nervousness and fear slowly took over. I glanced back at my fellow classmate who would hold my rope. He was the decider of my fate if anything went wrong.

Inside, I began to have doubts and was going to quit, but I felt that because so much time was spent for preparation of the climb, I had better give it a try.

My partner, Alyson Davenport, and I began the adventure rock-by-rock. With each step above safety, uneasiness took my confidence captive. Every reach became more difficult as the climb not only required more physical strength but mental strength as well.

To reach the half-way goal seemed like a miracle. We had to overcome several obstacles that made our journey much harder. Sitting halfway up, we wrote in a journal of our feelings that we were experiencing at that moment. We could read other entrees by previous climbers, but I thought to myself, "This is no time to sit and read a journal." But Alyson persuaded me that our goal to the top could and would be achieved. So, we put the journal back and began the climb again.

Every step was a risk. We climbed higher and higher as everyone below became smaller. Now, it was all rather funny to me. My confidence and excitement returned at the time when it seemed like it should be at its lowest. With the final stretch we reached the top. Our task was complete and there was such a feeling of relief and satisfaction.

It's hard to explain. Without Alyson, I probably wouldn't have climbed to the top. I had learned so much about teamwork and self confidence in that one climb. As I was lowered down to the ground, I knew I had completed a great feat. A part of me was left at that tower, not only on paper, but in spirit, as well.

Reaching for the top, Evie Daniels and Alyson Davenport work as partners on the ropes course. "It was great!" said Davenport. *(Photo by Ben Quigley)*

Tackling the ropes, senior Jimmy Forrest was among those students in the leadership class that visited the course in December. "It showed me the importance of teamwork," said Forrest. *(Photo by Ben Quigley)*

■ Program helps build confidence and unity.

By T.J. Ward
Copy Editor

Building teamwork, confidence and trust, the ropes course in Kill Devil Hills helps to unify groups and enrich individuals.

Started by the Dare County Sheriff's Department in October of '95, the ropes course was initially built for the Department's Wilderness Program for Dare County youths. Funded by a grant, the program aims to prevent juvenile delinquency and youth related crime, including controlled risk-taking activities like the ropes.

Grant money for the program and the tower was attained by the Wilderness Program coordinator and Kill Devil Hills Town Commissioner Bill Morris. Morris, a Dare County DARE officer, found the land for the project.

Before the construction of the Alpine tower at the Sheriff's Department exported their students in the Wilderness Program on courses owned by other agencies.

"We were sending our youth program out of the county," said Deputy Parker Long, MHS resource officer. "We were having to pay to send our students there."

Since its construction, a number of MHS classes, including Marie Sutherland's peer tutoring and Susan Lee's student leadership classes, have taken field trips to the ropes course to build camaraderie and self confidence.

The program includes team-building warm-ups, such as helping the group walk across a series of logs without touching the ground, scaling a climbing wall and a partner effort to reach the top of the alpine tower.

"The wall was pretty intimidating," said senior Stacy Riggs. "But I knew I'd be upset if I didn't at least try."

Coupled with benefits to students, the course should also produce revenue for the Dare County Sheriff's Department. For a charge, private businesses and programs similar to those in Dare County can use the tower.

Dare County Sheriff's Wilderness Program, as well as the tower serve the community as a new form of education and learning for the county's youth.

"I think it is a very valuable asset to teaching," said Long. "It's just another teaching environment. It is an outdoor environment where students learn different mental skills."

Example 3-26. (Features, Entertainment) "Hanging on. . . ," *Sound to Sea*, 11″ × 17″, Manteo H.S., Manteo, NC.

This student demonstrates a technique students use to shoplift, despite a warning sign in the background. Timesphoto by Katie Piotrowski.

Focus

Shoplifting

For some it is a way to get things they cannot afford. Others do it for the thrill

by Meghan Gordon

First it was a candy bar here, a lipstick there.

Then it got bigger and better until Marie* got caught her freshman year shoplifting after years of stealing.

"I thought I had become invincible, and no one would ever catch me. I thought the people deserved for me to steal from them because they made the prices so high, and I couldn't afford it. Later on, I found out the reason the prices were so high was because of people like me that stole from them," Marie said.

"I went to Drug Mart knowing I was going to steal, and we went in and started grabbing stuff. When we finished with our 'shopping,' we went to leave and an undercover security lady stopped us and said to my friend 'Miss, I would kindly like you to empty whatever is in your pockets out.' My friend tried to deny it, but the lady claimed she saw us," Marie said.

Marie said she was then escorted to a storage room and had to give up everything she and her friend had tried to steal.

"My friend, the one that got caught, only had one thing, but when they searched me, they found $36 worth of stuff ranging from makeup to magazines to books.

"I was escorted home in a police car, the policeman came to my door and talked to my parents, and as I stood there crying, I realized how disappointed I was in myself and the humiliation I felt beyond belief," Marie said.

Jim Lakatos, assistant manager at Drug Mart, said the store's main shoplifting problem is just juveniles and young adults getting what they want and not paying for it.

Lakatos said once someone has been caught stealing in the store, he or she is not allowed back in any Drug Mart store again unless he or she is a minor, and is with a parent or guardian.

If anyone tries to come back in after he or she has been caught and prohibited from the store, it is then

Shoplifter tells of experiences

by Duane Tysiak.

Stealing was all one Lakewood High School sophomore could think about.

"I can't even count the number of times I've shoplifted," the student said.

The student, who has never been caught, says he steals because it's fun and he doesn't have any money to pay for it.

"I've stolen $2000 at least: from malls, grocery stores, drug stores but never anyone's house; that's not cool," the student said.

All you have to do is outsmart the employees, which is not hard, the student said.

"Those electronic sensors are a joke," the student said, "All you have to do is rip off the sensor or demagnetize it," he added.

Stores that have cameras are the biggest deterrent, the student said.

"Avoid them. You will be caught," he said.

It is hard to get caught, the student said, "if you have any brains."

The biggest mistake, he said, is going to the same store in the same day.

"Let's say there's a guy named Fred who steals three pairs of pants. Fred goes back later to steal a shirt. Security is going crazy looking for shoplifters, and Fred gets busted," he said.

The student said the more you steal, the better chances you have of being caught because you get overconfident.

"Most of the stuff I steal, I keep. Some I sell," he said.

The student said he hasn't shoplifted for three months because he

---

Example 3-27. (Features, Entertainment) "Shoplifting"—in-depth double truck, *The Times*, 8-1/2″ × 11″, Lakewood H.S., Lakewood, OH.

Focus

up to the employees to recognize and keep in mind the faces, Lakatos said.

Drug Mart has taken precautions to derail shoplifting, such as increasing security cameras and security personnel, he said.

"We also have sensormatic devices, which are little electronic strips. It's on some products so if you go out the door without being demagnetized, it sets off alarms," Lakatos said.

Rini-Rego's grocery store also has problems with shoplifting but is working on minimizing the problem, one of the assistant managers said.

He said on a scale of 1 to 10, the shoplifting problem at Rego's is a three or four, based partly on how efficient the Lakewood police are when called in.

"It's somewhat of a deterrent that the cop will be here in short period of time after we've called, and we do prosecute," he said.

He said the store is not allowed to so any search procedures, unless the actual consumption of the item is seen.

Rego's hired a security agency that sends in plain clothes people at random hours of the day to give a surveillance check of the store, the assistant manager said.

"We used to have sensors on the doors, but it wasn't cost efficient to have them up," he said.

Even though its not always possible, Lakatos said, Drug Mart tries to stop the shoplifter outside of the store.

"After they get stopped, we just take them in back, the police are called and then (the shoplifter) is realized into the custody of the police," Lakatos said.

Juveniles are caught more than any other age group, Lakatos said.

"At least they are usually the ones that get caught. I don't really know, everyone is probably stealing, but we just seem to catch more kids than anyone else," Lakatos said.

Cosmetics and toys are the top two items stolen the most frequently from Drug Mart, Lakatos said.

"**Cosmetics are really** up there—it may be the price, people just cannot afford it," Lakatos said.

The most stolen item at Rego's, the assistant manager said, is cigarettes. He said they feel this is because the item is a valuable commodity. The store is in the process of relocating the item to make it harder to steal.

Mike Moblay, the assistant man-

'I thought the people deserved for me to steal from them because they made the prices so high, and I couldn't afford it. Later on, I found out the reason the prices were so high was because of people like me who stole from them' -Marie

ager of Revco, said shoplifting is not a immense problem at the store, although it does occur.

Candy and gum are items among the most often stolen at Revco.

"Anything can be stolen, but the smaller the item, the bigger the chance of it being stolen. The impulse items at the front of the store or at any door would be the things that are stolen the most," Moblay said.

A shoplifter may find it easier to steal from stores when it is a certain season, Lakatos said.

"In the wintertime, it is easier because of bulky winter coats, more chance to hide stuff, but as far as the rate goes, I think its pretty much steady all year round. I hate to pin point kids, but the availability of kids being out of school is up in the summer and might have a lot to do with it." Lakatos said.

Like the rise or fall of the amount of shoplifting in the different seasons, the assistant manager of Rego's said he felt the approach of a holi-

day brings on more shoplifters also.

"During a holiday time, shoplifting increases because there is an extra traffic flow in the store, and it's a lot easier to steal things when you have a higher traffic flow. The holidays is also a time when people are in a pinch for money, and then there is an increase of theft," he said.

Drug Mart is trying to make a conscious effort to show it is being aware of who is in the store and what is going on at the store, Lakatos said.

"We just want people to be aware that we are keeping an eye on them. We also train our employees, and they do notify security if they see anything suspicious," Lakatos said.

Revco employees are trained to watch out for anyone who looks suspicious, Moblay said.

"With a watchful eye, we can just try to keep things to a minimum in the store," Moblay said.

Julie*, a sophomore, says she usually shoplifts about three times a month, and when she does she takes large quantities of items.

"I like Dillard's because it is really open, people don't watch and they don't count their items. When I'm stealing clothes, I usually just stuff

Continued on page 15

Revco loses $50,000 yearly to shoplifters

by Duane Tysiak

Stealing a candy bar here and there may not seem expensive, but the cost adds up, Mark O'Brien, Revco manager, said.

"We lose about $40-50,000 a year to shoplifters. To make up for this, we must sell an extra $250,000," O'Brien said.

The store uses product sensors and security cameras on occasion.

"Some customers find the cameras offensive," O'Brien said.

The store has a limit of two students at a time. This is normally enforced after school and when summer vacation starts, O'Brien said.

"Ninety percent of students who come in are nice and well mannered," he said.

Once a student is caught shoplifting, O'Brien says the best thing to do is call the parents and the police. The

student can come in and work off the fine or he or she can do community service.

O'Brien says he wants students to realize what they think is a harmless prank can hurt them in later life. If a person gets a reputation for being dishonest, it is very hard to get rid of that reputation.

Finast has security cameras and plain clothes detectives, Banae Gholston, a store detective, said.

We catch about five students a week, he said.

"They normally don't steal by themselves. They always say they were going to pay," Gholston said.

Half the students get probation or community service. The other half pay a fine, Gholston said.

Only about one percent of the students who walk through the door shoplift, he added.

Example 3-27. *(continued)*

Example 3-28. (Features, Entertainment) "Making the best of Le Bad Cinema," *The Prospector*, 11″ × 17″, Cupertino H.S., Cupertino, CA.

Example 3-29. (Sports) "Mustangs rebound," *Epitaph*, 11″ × 17″, Homestead H.S., Cupertino, CA.

Example 3-30. (Sports) "Sports briefs," *Bear Facts*, 11″ × 17″, Alief Hastings H.S., Houston, Texas.

Example 3-31. (Sports) "The Vance County Civil War," *The Viking*, 11″ × 17″, N. Vance H.S., Henderson, NC.

— EXERCISE 3-32 —
Designing a modular layout

DIRECTIONS:

Work on the five-column grids shown here, created for an 11″ × 17″ tabloid, or use another format assigned by your adviser.

Step 1: Place all standing elements, such as nameplate, teasers and news briefs.

Step 2: Use the elements given below to create your layout. Include the final layout, properly marked to indicate graphics, story, headline and other elements along with your rough versions.

In making the layout, you must make decisions about

- Size of headlines and art
- Use of available photos, pull quotes and/or sidebars
- Whether to run a story full length, cut final paragraphs or jump part to another page
- Whether to vary column widths (measurements given for five-col. base)

Approval of such decisions might normally involve the editor in chief and adviser.

Items on page:

Story 1: SLUG: Senator
            Length: 8″ on five-col. base

Facts in lead: Leaving politics to politicians is dangerous, according to former Senator Carlton Winkleman, who served two terms in the United States Senate. Speaking to an assembly of juniors and seniors on Oct. 28, Winkleman encouraged them to get involved and ask questions.

Quote: 'Nothing's more dangerous than taking your rights for granted.'
                                    Senator Carlton Winkleman

Photo: Winkleman with group of students (should run horizontally)

Possible sidebars: Factoids about 18-year-old voting in the last election, issues of concern to young voters

Story 2: SLUG: Plays
            Length: 7″ on five-col. base

Facts in lead: "On Stage" will present two one-act plays this fall instead of a single drama. Francine Fitzhugh, student director, said this will give more students a chance for roles. Tryouts begin next Monday and are open to any interested student with a C average or better.

The bill will include both a comedy and drama, giving the audience a chance to both laugh and cry, she said.

Photo: Student director and adviser, to run as landscape or portrait

Possible sidebars: Schedule of tryouts; roles being cast

Story 3: SLUG: Smoke
            Length: 6-1/2″ on five-col. base

— EXERCISE 3-32 —
Designing a modular layout (cont'd)

Facts in lead: Great American Smoke-Out Day will get special attention, thanks to Student Council's decision to sponsor a variety of activities, leading up to the day itself. A poster contest with the grand prize a dinner for two at a smoke-free restaurant—gets underway this week. Entries will decorate the halls during the week prior to the annual smoke-out.

Photo: Unidentifiable students in haze of smoke (landscape or portrait)

Quote: Smokers truly bet their lives they won't get cancer.

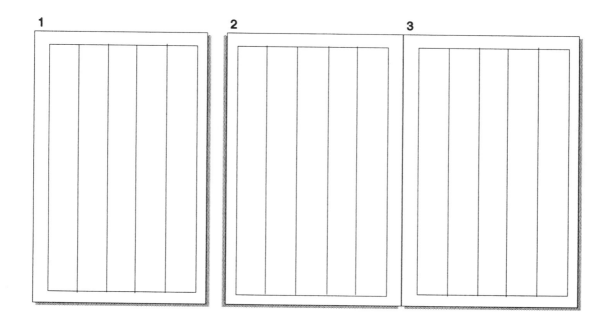

Adding advertising

The pluses of advertising

For some school papers, ads are a necessity. For others, income from ads is a plus that helps purchase desirable extras, such as new and enhanced computer programs.

On the other hand, ads don't even figure in the planning of a number of papers. Yet ads can do more than pay the bills. They can also enhance a newspaper's inside pages and serve as a bridge between school and community. *(For more about advertising sales and management, see "Advertising—boon and bane," Unit 4.)*

To many local business people, running an ad in a student paper is simply a way to support the school. Although they hope to receive a certain amount of good will, they look at the money they spend as a kind of donation, not as a positive step toward gaining more business.

Sometimes they simply hand over their business cards for reproduction in the smallest possible size. It's a way to get rid of their charitable obligations—and the ad staff salesperson—as painlessly as possible. The result is a dull, basically white mass at the bottom of the page, imprisoning 12 to 16 business cards in uniformly ruled cells, each with a few weak lines of type.

Making advertising an asset to layout

Most school and professional papers run no ads on their first and editorial pages, keeping them free of the "taint" of commercialism and purchased influence. On inside or back pages, which usually carry ads, they can provide contrast, movement and even readability (Examples 3-33–3-36). With modular layouts, ads of various sizes combine to make up a rectangular space across the bottom or to the outside of a page as do *a* and *b* on the following ad layouts.

Examples: a   b   c

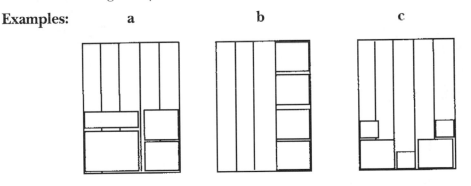

Ads arranged in a modular form should fit a common grid, even though other stories and graphics on the same page are designed with variable columns. Although the upper and lower rules of identically sized ads should align both horizontally and vertically, no two ads should share the same frame or box. Make sure uniform white space and rules separate ads, and make white space an integral part of each advertisement's basic design.

Examples 3-33, 3-34, 3-35. *Sound to Sea*, 11″ × 17″, Manteo H.S., Manteo, NC.

Example 3-36. *B&G* (*The Blue & Gold*), 11″ × 17″, Findlay H.S., Findlay, OH.

Ad placement comes first

One clear advantage of placing ads in a unified block is that it provides a rectangular space for editorial matter—stories, features and graphics. Other methods of laying out ads, as in layout example may result in awkward spaces that make it difficult or impossible to lay out editorial matter in modules.

Space for advertising should be blocked out before laying out editorial matter and not changed simply for convenience. If not enough ads have been sold to fill out a rectangular page module, papers regularly turn to the institutional ad. This type of ad promotes something within the school itself:

1. Self-promotion of the paper
   a. an ad about advertising in the paper
   b. promotion of an upcoming issue

2. Ads for school activities: plays, concerts, dances, other programs

3. Schedules: college representatives, upcoming tests, sports

For other than the paper itself, institutional ads may be sold, perhaps for slightly less than to commercial enterprises, or offered free as a service to the school.

Avoid ads that just say, "Good luck, team," or any message that has no true selling or informational value and is therefore obviously nothing more than a way to fill up space.

Achieving sharp-looking advertising

As with any outlet for advertisers, a school newspaper has only two basic design sources for the ads it runs: the advertisers themselves and its own ad staff.

Along with calling cards, businesses can often supply glossy proofs of ads that they've run in professional papers. Especially with a scanner, these ads are easily fed into the computer and modified to fit. Be sure, however, that all type remains large enough to be legible. Even without a scanner, the advertising artist may cut and paste up an advertiser-supplied proof to create a good-looking ad, or try to reproduce it in the paper's word-processing, draw or desktop publishing programs.

And then there's the business card

Yes, it's a source of money for the paper, and the advertiser may ask for nothing more. Yet a lineup of business cards thinly disguised as ads can only result in lackluster pages and offer little return to the advertiser.

When selling card-size spaces, offer to use the business card as the basis of a custom-designed ad. This compliments the business person, showing the paper is not merely seeking a donation but is sincerely interested in providing effective advertising. When returning the suggested layouts for approval, you may wish to include several more designs in larger sizes as possibilities for future issues.

Here is a typical business card as it might fit into a two-column space:

The Mane Event

'Hair care with a difference!'

LeMan Shopping Center   Rhett Rogers, owner
4182 Wolfe Rd.   (000) 543-2121
Byrnehurst OK 40892   (000) 543-9034

Within a given space and with a limited amount of information, there are limits to what you can do to dress up such an ad. Much depends also upon the type of draw programs at your disposal, as well as time. But even a simple word-processing program and an ounce of creativity can make a difference. This is a spot where clip art might come in handy, too.

On editorial pages, clip art can give a school paper a "canned" look—as if its staff lacks the originality or resources to create its own art. If your paper intends to use some professionally created advertising, however, combining it with hand-drawn illustrations sets up a distracting contrast that makes student art look unfinished and the professional too slick. Judiciously chosen clip art offers a possible solution. Unless the paper can generate professional-looking work from its own graphic programs, it's best not to mix the two kinds of art.

Varying ad shapes and sizes

On a five-column grid, a lineup of ads all the same shape and size makes a page look regimented and dull. Ad salespeople do well to remember that a space measuring two columns wide by two inches deep is sold as a four-inch ad. That ad could just as well measure one column wide by four inches deep—the same size and price but a different shape space that offers variety to the page and a different sort of challenge to the designer (Examples *a* and *b*).

Example a

Sugar 'n' Spice Bakery

We bake "everything nice" in breads,
pastries, and taste-tempting treats . . .
for every day and special occasions

Call ahead or come in
Phone: 541–6362
18 S. Main St.

Hours:
Mon–Fri 8 A.M.–5 P.M.
Sat. 8 A.M.–1 P.M.

Example b

Sugar 'n'
Spice Bakery

We bake
'everything nice'

. cakes . pies
. cookies
. breads . buns
. every sort
of taste-tempting goody

COME IN
Enjoy an after-school
treat . . . take home our
oven-fresh bread...or
a scrumptious dessert.
CALL AHEAD
to order party or
special-occasion fare.
Phone 541-6362
128 S. Main St.

Use this
space

for an ad
that contrasts

with its

neighbors

Make it a rule

When rules surrounding an ad serve both as its outline and a means of separating it from adjoining ads, this kind of double duty forces ad borders to compete with one another. Ads with plainer or narrower borders seem to fade from view, while broader, blacker rules loom threateningly. You can solve this problem by using hairline horizontal and vertical rules between all ads, as well as between ads and editorial matter. Make sure that rules are evenly centered and placed. It is not necessary to place rules at outside margins. Using hairline rules allows the border to become a part of an advertisement's basic design, instead of a barrier separating it from other ads.

In placing ads on a page, consider such factors as their use of overprint on screened grounds, reverse type and other special typographical and design techniques. Ads similar in design and tone tend to cancel one another out if placed side by side. In the same way, ads should be placed so no noticeable pattern—such as checkerboard or an apparent stripe—emerges when the advertising module is viewed as a whole.

Thinking like a copywriter

Ad writers make no claim to be objective. Their purpose is to appeal directly to the reader and to make that person buy or use the product or service offered—or at least think well of it. Copywriters don't pretend to be investigative reporters, yet they are not licensed to distort the truth. In fact, laws protect consumers against deceptive advertising and false claims.

Yet copywriters should attempt to portray a product in its most positive light—through catchy headlines and enthusiastic prose. In designing layouts and writing advertising copy for school papers, there is no set formula to follow except:

1. Keep copy brief.

2. Avoid clichés and overused adjectives.

3. Use white space as a design element—and to guide the reader to and through the key points.

4. Include all needed details: address, phone numbers, contact person, services offered, prices if pertinent.

5. Make sure ads are accurate—or advertisers may demand and deserve a refund, retraction or free repeat.

Exercises 3-37 and 3-38 provide practice in designing ads from business cards or information from an advertiser.

Questioning classifieds

Display ads seek special notice through headline or "display" type and an attractive layout. In contrast, classified advertisements are usually grouped together—each a single paragraph and each printed in the same typeface and size with nothing more than a boldface, all cap lead-in to distinguish it.

In professional papers, classifieds are often separated into "classes" by boldface headings, such as "HELP WANTED," "FURNISHED APARTMENTS" or "PERSONALS."

The cheapest ads of all, classified ads might sell for no more than twenty-five or fifty cents a line in a typical school paper—and they can be much more bother than they are worth. When submitted by students, classifieds can become difficult to police—for they offer temptation for those who wish to discover how much they can get away with. A secret, coded message may cause hurt and heartbreak for someone—with or without the collusion of the student who sold it—and uncertainty about youthful slang may cause the advertising staff or adviser to appear unduly suspicious.

Some papers limit classifieds to personal messages for special occasions such as Christmas, Valentine's Day and graduation. In such schools, they may well be tradition—but not one that all advisers should rush to begin.

— EXERCISE 3-37 —
Designing from business cards

DIRECTIONS:

Below is a sample of a business card submitted as the basis for a four-inch ad in the school paper.

Step one: List additional details that you might secure from the business owner or manager.

Step two: Design two versions of the ad that you would plan to show to the advertiser before creating a finished version to run in the paper.

You may do your layouts on a computer or with pencil and paper. If copy is not clearly readable, supply an extra sheet of paper on which all headlines, subheads and copy blocks are typed or printed.

Family owned and run

Starr Sporting Goods

Active wear . athletic gear . team sportswear

Paul Starr, owner   Open Mon.-Sat.
134 S. Main St.   10 am- 5:30 pm   **541-3441**

Additional information obtained for ad:

_____

_____

_____

_____

_____

_____

_____

_____

_____

_____

_____

_____

_____

Designing from business cards *(cont'd)*

Proposed ad: 2 col. by 2 in. version

Proposed ad: 1 col. by 4 in. version

— EXERCISE 3-38 —
Designing a display ad

PART A. DIRECTIONS:

Using the information below, design an eight-inch display ad to run two columns wide by four inches deep, based on a five-column grid.

Wright Driving School is offering a New Year's Special. Driving lessons for teens, $125, on specially equipped driver's education cars with automatic transmission. Course includes seven separate sessions, each with a 50-minute period of driving and a 50-minute period of observation.

Students must enroll before March 1 to get this low price.

Wright Driving School has been in business for over ten years. Their motto: Get your driver's training the Wright way.

Call: 543-8000
Wright Driving School, 2167 Woodley Rd
(Slogan) *Make safe driving a lifetime habit*

Artwork: As part of your layout, you may wish to incorporate computer-generated geometric design elements, line drawings or photographs. Block off the space and label appropriately if actual samples of this art are not readily available.

Designing a display ad (cont'd)

PART B. DIRECTIONS:

Create another design for the same advertiser to run as a nine-inch display ad three columns wide by three inches deep, based on a five-column grid.

Photography—Picturing the news

The double duty of a good photograph

A good photo does double duty on a newspaper page. First, it serves as an entry point that captures would-be readers' attention and draws them to the text. Of equal importance is a photograph's ability to provide an additional dimension to a story by personifying and giving substance to the people, places and events making the news. Good photos convey a sense of action and exude an emotional appeal that gets readers personally involved in the paper's contents. Although not all photos are worth a thousand words, some can tell a story in themselves with a minimum of accompanying text.

THE PROBLEMS OF PHOTOGRAPHY—Every adviser knows them well—although the problems vary, depending upon the paper's resources and staff.

The picture that didn't turn out or turned out badly, the picture that couldn't be taken . . . it sometimes seems that "resourceful" student photographers have an even handier fund of excuses than student reporters. In addition, while stories can usually be rechecked and rewritten, there is often no second chance for shooting a news or sports photo.

GOOD NEWS PHOTOGRAPHERS—BORN OR MADE? Recruiting and training are part of staffing, and the availability of an in-school film lab and sophisticated computer photo program hinges on the school's size and paper's funding. Whether your paper "has it all" or not, the secret of good photography boils down to the individual photographer's timing, sense of composition and capability in handling his camera, no matter how simple or complex.

Within all the variables, however, a paper can strive to improve its photography through careful planning—from assignment to production. Follow three steps for better photo coverage:

1. the planning stage
2. the photo shoot
3. the process of cropping and refining

Step one to better photography: Planning

1. Before making a photo assignment for a news or feature story, have a clear idea what factor can best be reinforced pictorially. If it's a talk by a visiting dignitary, show her making her presentation or interacting with students, not getting into a car to depart.

2. If the dummy layout is ready, let the photographer know whether it is planned as:

   a. portrait—not necessarily of a person, but oriented vertically

   b. landscape—not necessarily scenery, but oriented horizontally

   Example:

3. Make directions as explicit as possible—but allow room for creativity. Provide an assignment sheet (Figure 3-39) that outlines needed details.

4. Especially with an inexperienced photographer or for group shots, it's often advisable to send a reporter who knows the story well and can also obtain identifications (Figure 3-40).

5. Stress the importance of deadlines—and allow sufficient time for processing.

Step two: The view through the camera

Taking good pictures is one thing; being a news photographer is another. Student newspaper photographers must train themselves to look through the viewfinder with the requirements of a news photo in mind ("Guidelines for better news photos," Figure 3-41). Just as newswriting has a special sound, so do news photos have a special look. Student photographers should make a habit of studying professional newspapers and magazines to get ideas for covering both spot news and features.

Stories that call for posed group shots cause special difficulties for any school paper. Photographers, with the help of the staff's exchange editor, should maintain a clipping file of group photos run in other publications as sources of inspiration.

Sports photography is a field in itself, and much of the dramatic photography done in magazines like *Sports Illustrated* does require sophisticated equipment. Without special lenses, student photographers must rely on their ingenuity to get effective action photos.

Since most school newspaper photographs are printed in black and white, student photographers must understand how many sins of composition and posing are minimized by the distraction of color. News and feature photographers must focus on their subject, not the brilliance of the scene. (Examples 3-42–3-46) Even when photos are printed in color on newspaper, detail is lost and colors look smeary if backgrounds are too busy.

PHOTOS: SERVING AS FEATURES BY THEMSELVES—You can take advantage of the emotional impact, action, and story-telling ability of strong photos by using them individually, as photo features, or as photo pages planned around a theme (Examples 3-47–3-50).

A set of photographs, however, goes to waste as a collage—an assortment of photos that overlap, look randomly placed, and have no center of visual interest to draw viewers' attention and interest.

There are three main kinds of photo pages or features:

*   *Photo event:* usually about a specific activity, such as homecoming or the winter carnival. Although related in time and place, each shows a different phase or aspect. Cutlines and perhaps an introductory paragraph convey the news and identify each picture.

*   *Photo story:* a series of photographs that, taken together, tell a developing story or show how a process unfolds much better than words could. It may be "how to" participate in a sport or construct a science project. May require explanatory cutlines, step by step.

*   *Photo essay:* a situation or problem about which a picture can speak louder than words, such as overcrowding on the stairways or graffiti in the halls. Like a written essay, it too expresses a point of view, but through independent or related photos, not words.

YOUR PAPER'S LOGO

Photo assignment sheet

Story slug _____ Assigned photographer _____

Day, date of shoot _____ Time _____

Location _____

Subject or event _____

Contact person (to arrange photo date or see at site) _____

_____ Contact's phone no. _____

Special instructions: _____

_____

_____

_____

_____

_____

_____

_____

_____

_____

Deadline for proofs or prints: _____

Assignment editor _____

Assigned reporter _____

Note: The reporter _____ will _____ will not accompany you.

YOUR PAPER'S LOGO

Photo identification form

Story slug _____ Assigned photographer _____

Place photographed _____

Total number of people in photograph _____

Sequence of identification (Check one):

_____ Clockwise from _____

_____ Rows, left to right. Number of rows _____

Names, listed in order (Indicate row number, if applicable):

_____

_____

_____

_____

_____

_____

_____

_____

Other data useful for caption or cutline:

_____

_____

_____

_____

_____

_____

_____

_____

Photographer _____

Reporter _____

Guidelines for better news photos

Always keep these basics in mind.

1. Control the technical aspects of your photo.

   - *Focus:* Aim for the main subject—the center of interest needs to be in focus; other areas need not be.

   - *Contrast:* Avoid extremes. Too little contrast adds to grayness of pages; stark black and whites obliterate details.

   - *Lighting:* Be sure of adequate light, but watch out for ruinous glare.

2. Pay attention to timing. Good photos seem to catch their subjects at a defining second that makes the shot say more.

3. Improve a photo's composition by moving yourself and your camera to try varying angles, as well as by rearranging your subject.

4. Concentrate on a center of interest—all good photos have a story to tell, and news photos must reinforce the text they accompany.

5. Remember, what you see in the viewfinder is what you get. Check for unwanted elements that distract from the main subject.

6. Make sure moving objects are moving into, not out of, the picture.

People make news; make their pictures stand out.

1. Posed photos are staples of school papers; strive for ways to keep them from becoming repetitive in pose.

2. Avoid large groups, such as the entire choir or band. Try to determine the newsmakers before going to cover an assignment, and then single them out for a separate shot—perhaps in addition to taking the group.

3. As a rule, heads of subjects should be at least dime sized when reduced for publication if they require identification.

4. Try to help subjects feel relaxed and look natural, not stiffly posed nor staring directly into the camera. Show willingness to take time to make the picture right.

5. Move close for the largest possible image. Notice how professional photos are most effective when they purposely do not show all of a person or thing.

6. Concentrate on five or fewer people in ordinary situations.

7. Beware of snapping partially blocked or rear views of people, especially those who need identification. Friends, family and subjects themselves feel cheated if they see such shots in the paper.

8. Prepare fully, be prompt, know what the assignment calls for, make a point of getting identifications if not accompanied by a reporter.

When photographing news events, timing is paramount.

1. Whether covering a sports event or a play, stay alert, and try to anticipate the defining movement for the type of shot that comes only once.

2. Although a blizzard, a blaze or a building under construction—almost every photo benefits from "people" interest included in the scene.

3. Be aware of force lines. For example, three people moving in the same direction can lead the viewer's eyes right out of the picture. Use force lines to direct attention to your center of interest.

4. Seek photos that contribute to the story and increase its effectiveness by portraying emotion and a sense of action.

5. Know what the layout calls for—a landscape or portrait. If helpful, work with the editor beforehand to plan the shoot.

6. Choose photo scenes that underscore a major point in the story, not a minor one.

Dare to be creative.

1. A paper should always have room for an outstanding photo. Be on the lookout for unassigned news, human interest or story-telling pictures that could stand alone.

2. Strive for a perspective that shows a familiar thing or scene in a new light—yet sends a clear, coherent message to its viewer.

3. Try not to be caught without your camera when a unique photo opportunity comes along.

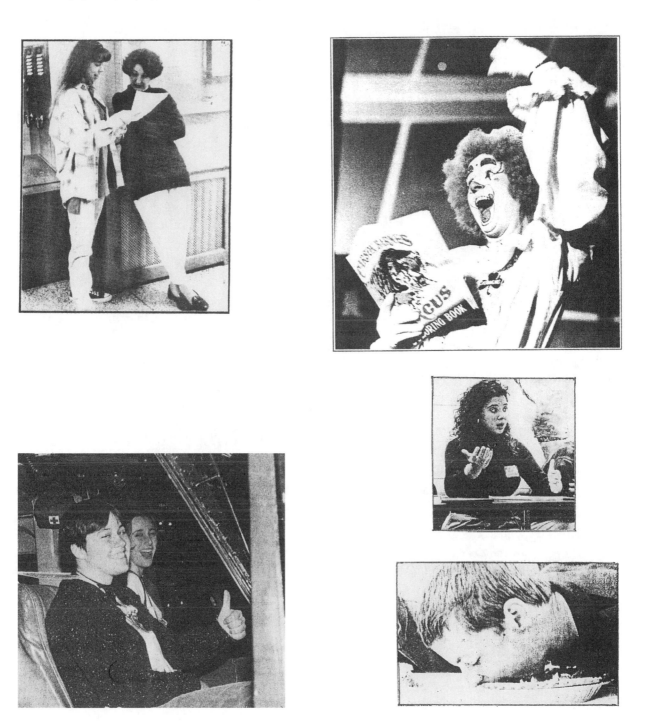

Example 3-42. *Tide Lines*, 11″ × 14″, Pottsville Area H.S., Pottsville, PA. (upper left corner)

Example 3-43. *Hawk's Eye*, 11″ × 17″, Olanthe East H.S., Olanthe, KS. (upper right corner)

Examples 3-44, 3-45. *TJ Today*, 11″ × 17″, Thomas Jefferson High School for Science & Technology, Alexandria, VA. (example 3-44, middle right side of page; example 3-45, lower left corner)

Example 3-46. *B&G (The Blue & Gold)*, 11″ × 17″, Findlay H.S., Findlay, OH. (lower right corner)

Example 3-47. *TJ Today,* 11″ × 17″, Thomas Jefferson High School for Science & Technology, Alexandria, VA.

Example 3-48. *The Times,* 8-1/2″ × 11″, Lakewood H.S., Lakewood, OH.

Example 3-49. *Newshawk,* 8-1/2″ × 11″, Fairborn H.S., Fairborn, OH.

In-line skating wheels into sports world

By Nicholas Moceri

Not many wheeled sports can be adapted to such terrain as streets, stairs, ramps, tennis courts, brick, and subways, as only in-line skating can.

In-line skating, a relatively new phenomenon, was invented by Rollerblade, Inc. in 1987, and has continued to grow in popularity. The sport combines roller-skating, downhill skiing, cross-country skiing, and ice skating. In-line skates are best described as ice-skates with wheels.

In-line skating can be used for performing tricks, aerobic workouts, roller-hockey, and transportation. Much of its popularity has come from word-of-mouth praises instead of the usual publicity hype put on new products.

"I got into it from watching other people and hearing what they said about it," said Kash Wimer ('96). "Not from some magazine advertisement."

Many members of the CWA community are hooked to the concept of the multi-use apparatus.

"There is always something new to do when you skate instead of just going from point A to point B like on a bike," said Wimer.

R.J. Kern ('96) has also found the sport to be both fun and exciting.

"You can skate almost anywhere and tricks add an element of danger and fun," said Kern.

In-line skates have even found themselves in Europe, attached to the feet of English teacher Tom Hajduk. He and a friend toured Europe in 1991 and used in-line skates as a mode of transportation for the three-month duration of their trip. They skated from train stations with their backpacks to their next destination. They even skated on subways. In-line skating was very new in Europe when he visited and has since boomed in popularity there.

"I had never skated before when my friend handed me a pair and said, 'Let's go,'" said Hajduk.

"I had to learn quickly to get around in Europe, but it is an easy sport to learn."

In-line skating offers independent foot movement, which means you can easily control your direction and speed. The motions used to propel the skater forward are similar to roller-skating and ice skating. The sport is easy to learn, taking only minimal balance and coordination to stay on the skates.

"It's just a blast," said Hajduk. "You get into it and are hooked."

"I love the challenge of doing new tricks and being able to skate anywhere," said Kern.

One downside to the sport is its cost to buy equipment. In this sport, price is usually an indication of quality. Brand new skates will cost anywhere from $30 to $300 at most retail stores. On top of the skates, wrist guards are essential to protect from injuries as are knee pads, elbow pads, and a helmet. All of these things together will cost roughly $100.

Some brands of skates recommended by professional stores are Rollerblade and Bauer, companies which specialized for many years in ice hockey skates. Those on a budget can buy skates and equipment cheaply at used sporting-goods stores without compromising quality. Hajduk said that well-made in-line skates should last for at least five years. Some shops that he suggests are REI and Bridgeport Cyclery. Kern also suggests Olympic Sports. According to both, these stores are knowledgeable and can offer tips for beginners.

"Used skates are a great way for beginners to see if they like the sport and to avoid price barriers," said Hajduk.

In-line skating is a sport whose continued popularity has brought it into the level of high-caliber sports.

Example 3-50. *Academy Times,* Charles Wright Academy, Tacoma, WA.

When planning a photo page or picture spread, you may find it easiest to assign the page as a whole and design the layout from actual proofs or prints to make the most effective use of the best shots. In designing the page, remember that fewer good shots are preferable to a crowd of weak ones—and the rule holds that one photo should dominate the page as the center of visual interest (CVI). According to one expert, the chosen CVI should be at least twice the size of anything else on the page. Your choice should be a shot that holds maximum interest and suggests its relative importance.

Make the entire page an effective composition by using a variety of rectangular shapes, both portraits and landscapes—and be sure each person is clearly identifiable. Allow ample white space as part of your page design, with equal spacing between photos and variable space outside, used in a way that draws viewers to the pictures on the page and helps emphasize the theme.

A well-done layout design becomes an intrinsic part of a photo page and can be a tool for telling its story. Do not let one format become your paper's standard, but vary your design to fit each page's photos and their message.

The final step: Creative cropping makes a difference

Whether or not you have the latest scanners and photo equipment, you can get the maximum effect from your photos by careful and thoughtful cropping (Figure 3-51). No, you cannot make a bad picture good. Even computer photo tools can't make a blurry photo clear, but you can make a good photo a far more effective element of your newspaper page.

Manipulating photos by computer

A scanner and computer photo design tools can take a photograph beyond real—and into the realm of the unreal. These tools will allow you to crop, reduce, darken and lighten the original photo, although not to enlarge it or clear up its blurriness. You'll also be able to take off scratches, fingerprints and blemishes, as well as create countless special effects.

Remember, these are tools, not costly toys. Students may need frequent reminders that the professional media—both print and video—rely upon deadlines and face the need to meet them precisely. Don't allow your staff to become so wrapped up in the wonders of photo manipulation and the search for unattainable perfection that they miss deadlines and waste their time and yours.

It's best to assign a limited number of trained students to scan all photos, with deadlines staggered so all work is finished on time. It's important that students know it's unethical to alter a news photograph in any way that affects its verisimilitude. This includes flipping a picture, perhaps to make a person face left instead of right.

There are two basic types of scanner: slide, which is faster and more accurate, and flatbed, which is preferable for art.

Guidelines for creative cropping

1. **The number one rule:** Crop close to the actual subject.

2. **Backgrounds should contribute,** not distract from the center of attention. Trim down to essentials, but don't cut out or break apart a needed element, causing the viewer to ask unanswerable questions.

3. **Crop away waste space.** Do away with parts that do not contribute to the photo's subject; however, be aware of the cropping's potential effect, such as cramping a chubby subject into a too narrow space.

4. **Let the viewer's eye fill in the form.** Concentrate on a person's features in close-up shots and portraits. Cropping off the top of a head or lower portion of the body helps instead of hurts a photo.

5. **Give extra power to the CVI.** Close-cropping the subject of a page's center of visual interest heightens its impact and dominance. Viewers naturally adjust to differing inner proportions within a series of pictures.

6. **The ultimate form of cropping is the cutout**—an outlined figure with essentially all of the background cut away. To keep it from seeming to float in white space, a cutout should be grounded in something—either at bottom, top, or side—to give it substance. Beware of misusing this technique.

7. **Be aware of the *rule of thirds:*** Avoid placing the center of interest in the exact center of a picture.

Centered   Off-center

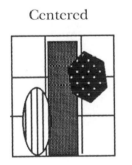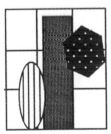

8. **Rules around pictures make them stand out.** Viewers will likely not notice tightly wrapped l-pt. rules, but they keep a photo or piece of artwork from fading away at the edges, and tend to sharpen the focus on the subject.

MANAGING TO FIND TIME, FINDING TIME TO MANAGE

Curing financial woes

For any adviser whose constant worry is selling enough copies of the current issue to cover its cost, it must come as a surprise to discover that more than 36% of the school papers surveyed are distributed free to the entire student body. Yet advisers free of worries about circulation are not home free, for they too are faced by rising production costs, the need for advanced technology and other financial pressure.

To be distributed free, most school papers count on a full or partial subsidy from the local board of education. Other advisers have devised a variety of other techniques to attain this goal. In any case, free distribution to every member of the student body— and in at least one instance, parents—substantiates the value of the school newspaper as an important and necessary element in school life. If sold, circulation can range from under 25% to 50% of enrollment. Although advisers can argue that students buying the paper share it with friends and families, the added readership does not contribute toward the cost of publication nor enhance the paper's status as the voice of the entire student body.

Another advantage of free distribution is that it allows staff and adviser to concentrate on maintaining high journalistic standards, instead of trying to come up with gimmicks to increase per-issue sales or subscriptions. In truth, in the days of fierce competition among professional media, sales figures of the school press may not look too bad.

Believe in the need!

At a time when school newspapers are often discounted as an unnecessary frill compared with academic courses, it is important that you as an adviser believe in the importance of print journalism to the school and in the vital need of society for informed newspaper readers. Students encouraged to develop the habit of reading their school newspaper have already taken a major step toward that goal.

The need for a school paper may also be justified as a vocational course, preparing students for professions in journalism, advertising and other fields of communication. However, the school administration, the board of education and community leaders should recognize that publication of a student newspaper is beneficial not only to members of its staff but also has essential value to the entire school, students and faculty alike, as well as the community and nation.

In "selling" the importance of the school paper, emphasize why today's school newspaper is a vital tool for learning. Figure 4-1 provides members of the school administration, parents, potential advertisers and both critics and supporters with ten reasons for its being a needed school program.

No, THERE'S NEVER ENOUGH MONEY—No matter how it looks from the outside, for a school newspaper and its adviser there is never enough money—just as there's never enough time—to do the kind of job you want to do. It may provide some consolation—though small—to know that almost all advisers face the same situation, even if they're already distributing each edition to every student for free.

Money problems are, and always will be, a major issue, for there's always a need to make a good thing better. If you already have six computers and a scanner, wouldn't it be great to use spot color? Or full color? What about an in-house photo lab? Or...? Dream on, but *do* something to achieve your goals.

There are about as many ingenious ways of adding to a school paper's income as there are advisers. Some require an initial investment of considerable time, organization and effort. Others, once begun, are virtually self-perpetuating. Some work best in a small town setting; others in a larger community. Affluent communities often provide readier sources of support than schools in less fortunate circumstances, but even there, achieving your goals requires asking questions, being prepared, seeking advice from many sources, not letting rebuffs discourage you and being determined to find the formula that works for you.

Sources of support

Have you reached an understanding with your school principal? Does he or she understand why the school newspaper is a vital tool for learning, not just an unessential time waster during the school day? Is the paper already given away free? If so, you may skip the next few paragraphs—and go directly to the main office and remind your principal how wonderful you think he or she is.

If you answered "no" to any of the foregoing questions, you might want to talk with your principal again. Tell him or her you'd like a chance to sit down and talk about your plans for the paper; the need for his or her advice, cooperation and support; the key role that the student press plays in school life; and its importance to the entire student body as a tool for learning. You may want to bring up the many advantages of free distribution when you meet again later.

Have you ever noticed how much people in authority like to give advice? If no money is available at the local school board or administrative level to provide a subsidy of whatever amount, ask your principal's opinion of ways that other advisers have used to broaden circulation to include a majority of students.

1. **Student activity fee.** Paid at the beginning of the year or each semester, it eliminates the need for students to have spare change to pay for each newspaper issue. Activities fees usually include the yearbook, newspaper and admission to a given number of school events.

2. **Newspaper subscription.** Not only offering a discount off the per-issue price, the subscription guarantees that the pocket-change problem won't make a student miss an issue. It also lets the paper know how many copies to print and publish.

Ten reasons today's school newspaper is a vital tool for learning

1. Provides a solid source of information for and by students about school and other events of direct concern to them

2. Develops the habit of looking forward to and reading a newspaper, an important characteristic of a concerned citizen

3. Underscores the importance of the press as an essential element in maintaining a free and democratic nation

4. Serves as a practical example of the school's belief in the value of becoming a habitual reader, inside the classroom and out

5. Promotes a sense of school unity and belonging at a time when many students feel estranged from school as community

6. Demonstrates the level of journalistic writing and ethics that readers should expect and student writers can attain

7. Broadens students' interest in and awareness of the multiple curricular and extracurricular activities their school offers

8. Encourages students to appreciate balanced, objective reporting through reading of issues close to them

9. Offers a forum in which students may express their opinions and learn the responsibilities and rights of the American press

10. Helps prepare students for their future roles and the part newspapers play in helping them become and keep informed

© 1998 by John Wiley & Sons, Inc

One troublesome problem: If subscription sales aren't brisk enough, should the paper allow per-issue purchase, too? A subscription drive takes careful planning and promotion, the design and printing of a subscriber's identification card and an efficient method of distribution to designated students.

3. **Other school-affiliated sources of support.** Ask your principal for advice about other school organizations that might contribute to the newspaper's support, once they are made more aware of its importance. Possibilities include student councils, classes, parent-teacher organizations and clubs.

TURN TO YOUR LOCAL NEWSPAPER—No one should be more interested in developing a new crop of capable newspaper readers than the publisher and editor of your local paper. In fact, nearly 12% of the schools polled stated that their school paper was printed by the local newspaper, with one published and distributed once a month as a pull-out section within the paper itself.

Enlist the help of your community's newspaper, either as a direct source of printing with the possibility of a substantial discount, or as a knowledgeable resource that may offer both direct and indirect aid. It's a place to ask about the availability of financial and informative support from the newspaper itself or from community businesses and foundations. The local press can also give advice about sound journalistic practices, editorial policies and ethics. Cooperation between the professional press and student staffs may extend to tours of the newspaper's offices and visits by reporters to talk with and advise student staff members.

Remember, newspapers in each city and town have their own systems and procedures. What you can expect depends to a great extent upon policies already in place. If you make your local editor or publisher aware of the mutual interests of school and professional papers, however, you may inspire and work with your local paper to develop plans to benefit you both.

ADVERTISING—BOON AND BANE—Several schools with no other sources of income than an official subsidy and advertising reported counting on ads for 45% to 50% of their budgets. With a year's advertising revenue totaling $1,500 to $3,000, this divides out to slightly more than $150 to $300 per issue if ten issues are printed.

No matter what their other means of raising funds, most school papers turn to advertising—either to make up for lack of circulation or to pay for enhancements in technology and printing attributes, such as photography and color. For the adviser—as well as for the staff—advertising can be a boon, as well as a terrible headache. Successful advisers approach the subject of advertising in a number of effective ways, and each school must adopt and adapt the style that works best in its situation.

It's easier for a school paper to sell advertising in an affluent community, or in a small town with strong ties and loyalty to the school from which many townspeople were graduated, than in a large city with a less concentrated citizenry.

Setting your goals

Before planning your advertising campaign, determine how much money you'll need for the coming year's production. You can estimate your budgetary needs in two ways: (1) the basic amount needed to publish a given number of issues and pages, and (2) the amount required to publish a given number of issues plus an allowance for funds to enhance the paper and upgrade its technology.

STEP ONE: PROJECT YOUR YEAR'S BUDGET

A. Expenses

1. How many issues do you plan to publish?
2. What is the cost per issue?
   (a) printing
   (b) supplies
   (c) photography
3. What other expenses must be prorated into the year's total?

B. Income

1. Subsidies
2. Monies from sales, subscriptions or activities fees
3. Income from other sources

C. Determine advertising needs

1. Separately total yearly expenses and projected income other than advertising.
2. Subtract projected income from expenses.
3. Remainder is amount needed yearly in advertising.
4. Divide by number of issues to determine amount of advertising needed each month.

STEP TWO: DETERMINE ADVERTISING SPACE: COLUMN INCHES OR FRACTIONAL PAGE?

A. Figuring ad space by column inches

1. One column inch equals a measured inch in depth—or one—times the number of columns (1×1) regardless of its actual width in inches.
2. Base advertising on a standard grid—for example, five columns for an $11'' \times 17''$ page.
   (a) Allowing for margins, an $11'' \times 17''$ paper measures approx. 15 inches in depth.
   (b) To find the total number of available column inches, multiply 5 (total number of columns) by 15 (depth in inches).
   (c) An $11'' \times 17''$, 5-column page contains 60 inches of advertising space.
   (d) Below is the approximate size of one column inch:

⟵ one col. in. ⟶
$11'' \times 17''$, 5-col. page

3. By the same token, an 8-1/2″ × 11″ page with a 3-column grid contains approximately 28-1/2″ of advertising space.

```
      ◄— one col. in. —►
    8-1/2 ″ × 11″, 3-col. page
```

B. Create a chart showing size options

1. Ads can range from one column inch to a full page, but certain sizes are more popular and effective.

2. For a given number of inches, usage of space is often variable. For example, a four-inch ad could run in either of the following spaces:

```
        This is the approximate size
           of a 4-column-inch ad
            running horizontally
       on a 5-column, 11 ″ × 17″ page
```

```
              This is the
           approximate size
                 of a
           4-column-inch ad
               running
               vertically
             on a 5-column,
            11 ″ × 17″ page
```

C.   Sell ads by the page and its fractions

1.   With a paper that uses variable column widths, you may find it easier to base your advertising space on full-page and fractional page sizes: 1/2 page; 1/4 page; 1/8 page; and so on (Example 4-2).

   Since each fraction sells at a specified price, selling by this method is somewhat less complicated than determining prices by column inches, which requires students to multiply the number of columns by the actual measured inches in depth. (Some students just can't seem to grasp the need to multiply by one, when one column may measure more than two inches wide.)

2.   Selling ads at fractional rates also works well when the paper's design calls for ads grouped together in block form at the bottom or down the outside of pages. This layout provides a rectangular space for editorial copy, clearly separating news from advertising. If there are not enough ads to fit evenly into a rectangular space, it can be squared off effectively by publishing a "house" or institutional ad, run to promote the advantages of advertising in the paper, to publicize a school activity or to call attention to a special feature in this or a coming issue.

3.   On the other hand, selling ads by the column inch offers advertisers a bigger selection of sizes and shapes, although they may be more difficult to square off evenly for modular layouts.

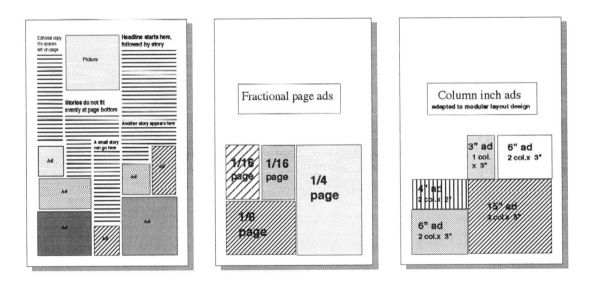

Example 4-2.   Left to right: Page layout with column inch ads; fractional page and column inch ads in modular layouts.

D.   Set ad prices by fractional page rates

1.   Determine your prices based upon a standard number for a full page. You may start from the same figure used in column inch measurements.

   For an 11″ × 17″ paper:

Full page = 60	1/4 page = 15
1/2 page = 30	1/8 page = 7-1/2

2. Choose a base price that meets your budgetary needs and advertising prospects.

3. At a base price of $5, an 1/8 page will cost $37.50 (multiply 7-1/2 by 5). With a base price of $3, it will be $22.50 (7-1/2 multiplied by 3).

4. When you price according to this system, it should be to your advantage to offer proportionally lower prices for larger size ads.

5. For an 8-1/2″ × 11″ paper, it is more convenient to base full-page size on 30 and figure prices in the same manner.

6. The base rate used for calculating prices is noted on sample size and rate charts (examples 4-3 to 4-6) included for duplication. You may insert your own chosen price schedule along with your paper's logo.

STEP THREE: DECIDE YOUR BEST ADVERTISING RATE SCALE

A. Assess your potential and needs

1. Advertising rates depend upon your community and the size of your school as well as your projected budget.

   (a) On a commercial level, advertisers seek to reach the largest number of customers for each advertising dollar they spend. In other words, get "more bang for their buck."

   (b) Advertisers in school papers may seek good will or buy an ad out of loyalty, and you should also take this factor into consideration in setting your price rates.

   (c) Too high a price may scare off would-be advertisers.

   (d) Too low a price may needlessly cut into your potential income.

2. Ad prices reported by school papers range from $2.50 to $10 per col. in.

   (a) At $10 per col. in., a full-page ad in an 11″ × 17″ paper—or 60″ of advertising—could bring as much as $600; at $5, as much as $300.

   (b) If your paper publishes ten issues, selling one page per issue would equal $6000 or $3000 yearly advertising income.

3. If any small neighborhood papers or shopping guides circulate in your community, check their advertising rates before setting yours.

B. Prepare a clear, uncomplicated rate scale

1. Set a single, basic price per column inch or reasonable increments for fractional pages so that student salespeople and potential advertisers can follow it without difficulty.

2. Consider offering discounts as incentives for buying full- or half-page ads.

   (a) *Example:* A full-page ad in an 11″ × 17″ paper, costing $600 at $10 per col. in., might be discounted to $500. A half-page ad, instead of $300, might be $250.

   (b) Other possibilities include a 10% discount for anyone who contracts for a full year's advertising, paid in advance.

(c) Beware of making discounts too complicated, thus creating mistakes and confusion in selling and billing.

C. Consider the need for adding certain extra charges

1. You may want to include extra costs that the paper would have to bear, if not passed along to the advertiser.

2. Make this a one-time charge for ads running in several issues so repeat advertisers are not penalized.

3. Weigh the production costs of these extras against the complications of charging for them before incorporating them into your ad rates.

STEP FOUR: PLAN YOUR ADVERTISING STRATEGY

1. Create a profile of potential advertisers.

2. Decide upon an effective program—who will sell ads, when, and how.

3. Design tools that will convince targeted advertisers of the value and advantages of taking space in your school paper's pages.

Mounting your advertising campaign

A successful advertising campaign must be tailored to your school, the size and makeup of its student body, plus the type of community in which it is located. What works in a small, closely knit community may not succeed in a large urban school, yet cities may offer resources that smaller towns don't have.

Much of the effort involved in conducting a successful advertising campaign must come before anyone attempts to sell the first column inches or quarter page of space. A few hours of planning and preparation beforehand can save the hectic scramble of competition for your attention when everyone on staff needs help at the same time.

LINE UP POTENTIAL ADVERTISERS—Research to develop an adequate list of businesses, groups and professional people who might be interested in reaching the student market. Four main types of advertisers are most readily willing to buy space in school papers.

1. *Business and professional people allied to the school in some way,* either by having businesses in the community or neighborhood, being graduates of the school themselves or having offspring in school. Such people often see advertising in the paper as a worthy donation, a means of securing good will or a way of supporting their school.

2. *Businesses that market to teenagers.* These offer a wide range of possibilities—from fast foods and sporting goods to beauty salons. Although not traditionally thought of as businesses, churches may find school papers a tempting place to advertise, as do colleges and learning centers.

3. *Nonprofit and service organizations with a cause to promote.* Ads warning of the dangers of smoking and drunk driving, information about becoming a foreign exchange student—the list goes on and on. First, consult your local phone book or Chamber of Commerce to discover what organizations are active in your community. Call to discover the person to contact about advertising.

4. *National and local corporations.* The larger the company or organization, the less likely it is that you'll find anyone able to make a quick decision about advertising in a school publication, yet many corporations have yearly budgets that set aside money for institutional advertising or charitable spending for a worthy cause. What could be more worthy than your school paper?

In addition to finding a match, one drawback to nailing down this kind of advertising is that boards approving such expenditures may meet only a few times a year. Resources include the phone book and public library for a list of local foundations. Before seeking support, write or phone the foundation or corporation to discover the contact person and procedure. (Find specific leads for selling ads in Appendix 3.)

CHOOSE YOUR PLAN OF ATTACK—There are as many ways to approach an advertising campaign as there are schools, situations and communities. Here are some possibilities that you might want to adopt or adapt for your paper.

1. *Assign sales goals.* A successful adviser in a suburban school required all members accepted for the incoming staff to sell $250 worth of advertising, due at the beginning of the school year or shortly thereafter. With eighteen members on the staff, their efforts over the summer or at the beginning of the school year ensured $4500 in the coffers right at the start.

Since some might object to what could be viewed as a "pay to play" requirement, your first step in inaugurating a similar system should be discussing it with your principal. Also, be sure to state this requirement on the application for staff membership, along with any other requirements or prerequisites, such as being available to work before or after school, if needed, for a given number of hours each production period.

You will also need a method in place for students who fall short of selling the required amount of ads. To avoid the system's breaking down, make it a known policy that any student not fulfilling the requirement will be assigned a task—a rather tedious but necessary one—as an additional responsibility all year.

2. *Seek major sponsors.* In addition to carrying advertising, another adviser has devised the practice of selling the back page of each issue to an individual patron, such as Student Council, a community awareness campaign or a local corporation. At $500, sponsorship of a page pays the printing cost of one issue of the 12-page, 11″ × 17″ newsprint paper.

The page, carrying the footer "The printing of this issue was paid for by (patron's name)," may be devoted to a staff-written feature story about the sponsor or an advertisement relating to its current campaign or activities.

To mount such a campaign, create a packet that includes examples of the kinds of page layouts and features available to would-be sponsors. Even though targeted groups or businesses decide not to invest in a full page at $500, they may be inspired to sponsor one-half or one-quarter page for proportionally less as a way of doing their share. These can then be grouped together as cosponsors.

Sponsor pages are priced differently from the paper's regular ad rates, which for one-time insertions are $160 for the back page and $140 for inside pages.

3. *Divide responsibilities.* Often students who like to write have no interest in or talent for selling ads and vice versa. Another approach to the problem of advertising is to recruit a special business/advertising staff whose sole responsibilities are selling, producing and billing ads as well as keeping the financial records of the paper. This, of

course, comes closer to the staffing of professional newspapers where business and editorial staffs are fiercely independent (and, where one frazzled person doesn't have to oversee every detail of both).

For advisers who find it impractical to set an early fall deadline to fulfill the year's quota, a separate advertising staff eliminates the need to browbeat editors and reporters about meeting both editorial and advertising deadlines. Also, students who enjoy the full responsibility of advertising and business have the satisfaction of knowing they make a vital contribution, not only to the paper's success but to its very existence.

DUTIES OF AN AD STAFF—Advertising and business require different skills from those needed by writers and editors. In addition to contacting potential advertisers and selling space, business and advertising manager and staff need to design, lay out, compose and place ads on assigned pages before the news staff begins filling the pages with editorial matter.

They also bill advertisers and send tear sheets or copies of ads to each advertiser in each issue; alert advertisers to special occasions; keep records of accounts payable and paid; and maintain the paper's financial books. It is, if not mandatory, at least extremely advisable, to have all members of the business/advertising staff be computer literate.

Handling the business/advertising side of a newspaper requires at least three distinct skills: (1) accounting, (2) art and design, (3) layout and composition by computer. The size of the business staff naturally depends upon the size of the paper, the number of pages produced each issue and the number of candidates for these positions.

Staff positions on the advertising/business side of the paper include business manager, advertising manager and layout artist/ad designer. Each is expected to cooperate in generating the necessary quota of ad sales. The obvious advantage to this kind of staff organization is that it clearly places full responsibility and credit for advertising and business in the hands of students who are chosen expressly to do the job. It does not put the adviser in the awkward position of marking a talented, energetic reporter down on the grading scale at the end of a term because he or she hasn't sold the required number of ads.

In a small school, it may be necessary to divide responsibilities differently.

To recruit students fitted for positions in advertising and business, plan to consult with teachers in the business and art departments for advice and recommendations. Once staff organization is established, staff members also develop the habit of recruiting their friends to take over the positions they are vacating because of graduation. This is a good idea, if they have been doing the job well!

4. *Recruit an outside sales force.* If your school has a special distributive education course, such as DECA (Distributive Education Clubs of America), you may find it possible to solve the problem of selling ads for the paper by turning to them.

Nonprofit organizations such as symphonies and charitable groups sometimes turn over the business of selling ads for their concert programs and newsletters to independent ad salespeople, who receive 10% of their sales in return. (And, most school newspapers certainly qualify as nonprofit groups, especially in the eyes of their advisers.) In school, the 10% of sales would go, not to individual students, but to groups, such as DECA, which need to conduct fund-raising efforts during the year to raise money to send members to state and national conventions.

Before making plans with another teacher or adviser, consult with your school principal to make sure of his or her approval. Also, to the benefit of both organizations and as a learning tool for students, make the agreement between groups on a professional basis, with a contract specifying the amount of advertising needed for each issue, the deadlines for obtaining it and the percentage of sales that go to the newspaper and the club.

As in all areas of newspaper advising, one of the main problems of "hiring out" work such as selling ads is making sure the job is done when needed. For the paper to be successful, everyone must live up to his responsibilities—because every detail depends upon another being done on time and well.

Launching your campaign

PLAN AND PREPARE IN ADVANCE—Being prepared works wonders! It's much easier than trying to control and clean up when a crisis is upon you. If your selling staff is "well armed" and ready to go, they'll be much more enthusiastic when selling.

Plan to conduct a survey of the student body to determine their spending habits and make a summary of its highlights to pass on to potential advertisers. It should surprise them to discover how much money the average student spends each month—and how much this mounts up to over the entire year for the entire student body. These are facts that attract advertising money!

Be sure to sample students from all class rankings and backgrounds to get a true cross section of the student body. The responses can serve both as a valuable marketing tool and as the basis of a feature story sure to interest all the paper's readers.

GET SET TO GO—Divide your list of prospective advertisers among salespeople. If they have leads of their own, remind them to check first with the ad manager to avoid making duplicate calls that waste effort and annoy potential advertisers.

First contacts by phone or introductory letters provide advance notice and avoid annoying prospects with an unexpected sales pitch. Letters are easy to ignore, so plan to make follow-up phone calls, requesting an appointment.

Student salespeople will act and feel more confident—and the paper look more professional—with an advertising promotional packet containing:

1. Introductory letter (if not mailed previously)
2. Sample of ad sizes and space rates
3. Copy of school paper (if suitable example available)
4. Reasons school press is vital tool for learning
5. Results of survey on student spending habits, if available
6. Advertising contract

See the reproducible forms included in this chapter.

KEEP AN UP-TO-DATE CARD FILE—Having names of all advertisers and potential advertisers on $3'' \times 5''$ cards, as well as on the computer, is easier for quick entries and less liable to careless error. Note date of contact, student salesperson, prospects who want "follow-up" calls or say they'll consider buying an ad later. Let appropriate prospects know of special events, for example, flower shops at prom time. Also include notice of such issues as pre-Christmas, Valentine's Day and graduation via inserts included with advertisers' billing and copies of paper.

SET LONG-TERM GOALS—In addition to seeking local advertisers, lay plans for securing major advertisers, such as large local corporations or businesses with national headquarters elsewhere, who may need to be approached far in advance.

Getting started

Following is a list of reproducible forms and letters that you may wish to use or adapt to your needs.

It includes:

1. Rate chart for fractional page ads—8-1/2″ × 11″ papers (Example 4-3)
2. Rate chart for fractional page ads—11″ × 17″ tabloids (Example 4-4)
3. Rate chart for column inch ads—8-1/2″ × 11″ papers (Example 4-5)
4. Rate chart for column inch ads—11″ × 17″ papers (Example 4-6)
5. Letter to potential advertisers (Figure 4-7)
6. Request letter to past advertisers (Figure 4-8)
7. End-of-year thank you for support (Figure 4-9)
8. Advertising contract (Figure 4-10)
9. Invoice (Figure 4-11)

MONEY-RAISING PROJECTS—PRO AND CON: Washing cars, sponsoring bake sales, selling candy, staffing a concession stand at a professional team's stadium—enterprising newspapers staffs and their advertisers have set out to raise money for their paper by these means and many more. The question of course is, is it worth it?

There is no question that publishing a good school newspaper should be the staff and adviser's major occupation. Money-raising events can drain time and attention from that obligation—and turn creating a first-class paper into mere relief at getting it out at all. Nor, should advisers be placed in the position of feeling like indentured servants—forced to devote time, worry and efforts determining how to get the school paper out of financial difficulties.

The "con" side to many money-raising projects is obvious: they waste too much time and effort for too little gain. A bake sale netting under $20 makes too small a dent in an annual budget of thousands of dollars.

There is a "plus" side: If advertising and other financial support aren't enough, look for ways to raise money through one-time activities and events that make a worthwhile profit—and don't take too much time and attention away from your real mission, producing a good paper.

Activities such as "battle of bands" contests after school have appeal for students, or ask your principal if the paper can sponsor a once-a-year, pay-to-attend program during school time. Make this something with both academic and entertainment appeal, such as a version of *Jeopardy* or another game show. School activities of this kind have another advantage. They keep the school paper in the eye of its public—the student body—and make it seem like a group with winning ideas, not a group of losers struggling to exist.

Look for a list of other money-raising ideas devised by advisers across the country in Appendix 3.

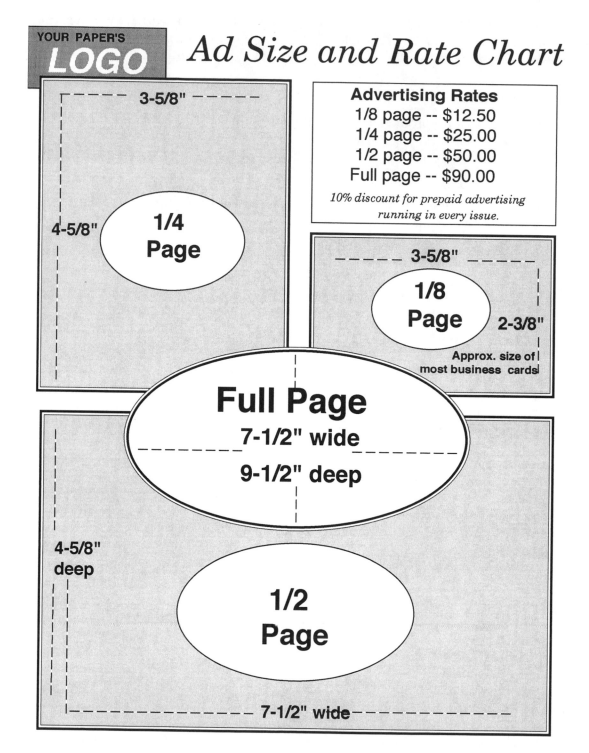

YOUR PAPER'S
LOGO

Ad Size and Rate Chart

3-5/8"

4-5/8"

1/4
Page

Advertising Rates
1/8 page -- $12.50
1/4 page -- $25.00
1/2 page -- $50.00
Full page -- $90.00

*10% discount for prepaid advertising
running in every issue.*

3-5/8"

1/8
Page

2-3/8"

Approx. size of
most business cards

Full Page
7-1/2" wide
9-1/2" deep

4-5/8"
deep

1/2
Page

7-1/2" wide

Example 4-3. Rate chart for fractional page ads (8-1/2″ × 11″).

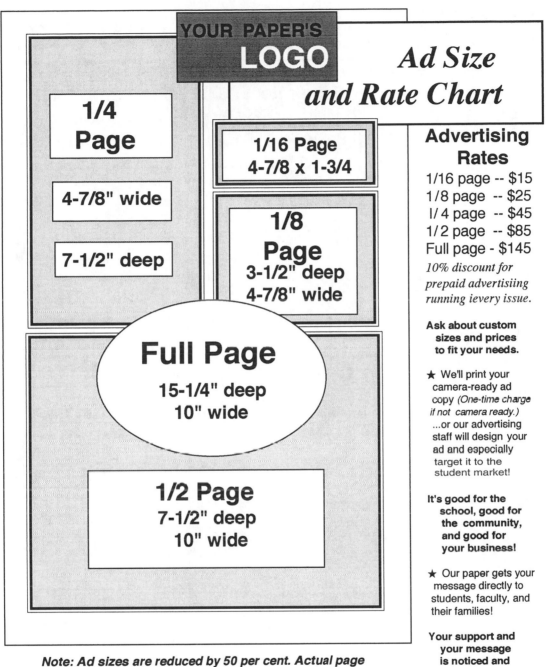

YOUR PAPER'S LOGO

Ad Size and Rate Chart

1/4 Page

4-7/8" wide

7-1/2" deep

1/16 Page
4-7/8 x 1-3/4

1/8 Page
3-1/2" deep
4-7/8" wide

Full Page
15-1/4" deep
10" wide

1/2 Page
7-1/2" deep
10" wide

Advertising Rates

1/16 page -- $15
1/8 page -- $25
I/ 4 page -- $45
1/2 page -- $85
Full page - $145

10% discount for prepaid advertisiing running ievery issue.

Ask about custom sizes and prices to fit your needs.

★ We'll print your camera-ready ad copy *(One-time charge if not camera ready.)* ...or our advertising staff will design your ad and especially target it to the student market!

It's good for the school, good for the community, and good for your business!

★ Our paper gets your message directly to students, faculty, and their families!

Your support and your message is noticed and appreciated!

Note: Ad sizes are reduced by 50 per cent. Actual page size is 11x17-inches, including outer margins.

Example 4-4. Rate chart for fractional page ads (11″ × 17″).

SAMPLE AD RATES AND SIZES

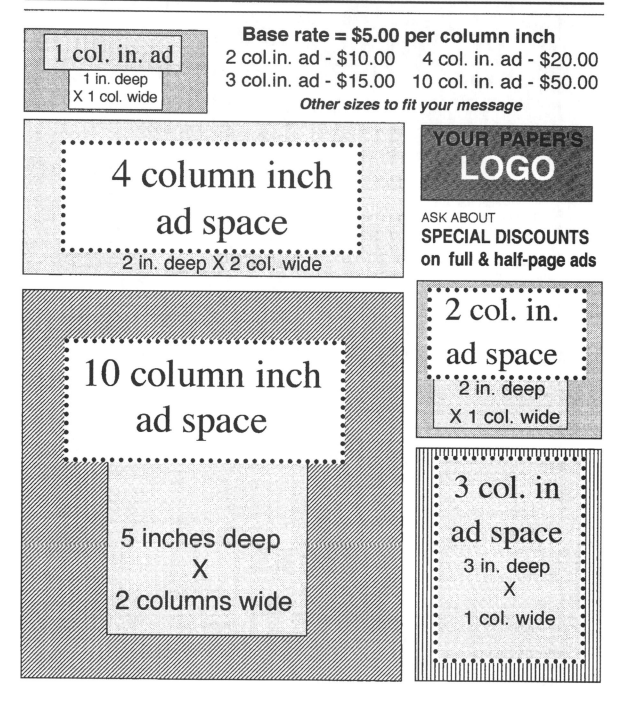

1 col. in. ad
1 in. deep
X 1 col. wide

Base rate = $5.00 per column inch
2 col.in. ad - $10.00   4 col. in. ad - $20.00
3 col.in. ad - $15.00   10 col. in. ad - $50.00
Other sizes to fit your message

4 column inch ad space
2 in. deep X 2 col. wide

YOUR PAPER'S LOGO

ASK ABOUT
SPECIAL DISCOUNTS
on full & half-page ads

10 column inch ad space

5 inches deep
X
2 columns wide

2 col. in. ad space
2 in. deep
X 1 col. wide

3 col. in ad space
3 in. deep
X
1 col. wide

Example 4-5. Rate chart for column inch ads (8-1/2″ × 11″).

Example 4-6. Rate chart for column inch ads (11″ × 17″).

Paula Pen, Editor
Mrs. Adrian Adams, Adviser

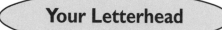

Ken Keen, Business Manager
Andy Arnold, Advertising Manager

BYRNEHURST HIGH SCHOOL • 9119 LYNNWOOD ST., BYRNEHURST, OK 53467 • Phone (003) 821-1065

Date

Business Person, Title
Name of Company
Street Address
City, State, ZIP Code

Dear _____,

As you know, national advertisers like to target teens because they not only have money of their own to spend but also influence other purchases made in their families.

By placing advertising in *The Torch,* the school paper of Byrnehurst High School, you'll be reaching this age group through a medium that is published expressly by and for students.

In addition to getting your message directly to this desirable audience, you'll help to support a worthwhile educational endeavor that not only reports news the student body needs and wants, but also trains staff members in the practices and standards of good journalism.

Because a school paper goes out in the community and is read by students' families, your support of the school through advertising will also create good will toward your business and your company name.

Our rates are extremely reasonable, and we are ready to publish your prepared copy, or our advertising staff will design an ad especially to suit your message. Enclosed is an advertising rate chart, giving you a sample of the sizes and prices we have available.

Please consider the advantages of advertising in our school paper and the valuable contribution you'll make by helping support the student press. One of our salespeople will call on you soon to answer any questions you may have.

We hope we can welcome you as one of our advertisers.

Sincerely,

Advertising Manager

Enclosure: Advertising Rate Chart

Paula Pen, Editor      Ken Keen, Business Manager
Mrs. Adrian Adams, Adviser   Andy Arnold, Advertising Manager

BYRNEHURST HIGH SCHOOL • 9119 LYNNWOOD ST., BYRNEHURST, OK 53467 • Phone (003) 821-1065

Date

Business Person, Title
Name of Company
Street Address
City, State, ZIP Code

Dear _____,

    With another school year just beginning, we want to thank you again for your past support of our Byrnehurst student newspaper, *The Torch.*

    We hope you will choose to advertise again during the coming year and perhaps decide to increase the amount of advertising you choose to place in our pages.

    Enclosed is a copy of our current space rates, along with this year's scheduled publication dates. One of our staff sale representatives will be calling on you soon.

            Sincerely,

            Advertising Manager

Enclosure

Paula Pen, Editor
Mrs. Adrian Adams, Adviser

Your Letterhead

Ken Keen, Business Manager
Andy Arnold, Advertising Manager

BYRNEHURST HIGH SCHOOL • 9119 LYNNWOOD ST., BYRNEHURST, OK 53467 • Phone (003) 821-1065

Date

Business Person, Title
Name of Company
Street Address
City, State, ZIP Code

Dear _____,

    We want to thank you for the support you've given to our student newspaper and Byrnehurst High School by advertising in *The Torch* during the past school year.

    You have helped our newspaper staff to complete a successful year of bringing "the news that students need and want" to our school's student body.

    We hope that you have been well satisfied with our service, and that you'll decide again to place advertising in our pages during the coming year.

                Sincerely,

                Advertising Manager

Paula Pen, Editor
Mrs. Adrian Adams, Adviser

Your Letterhead

Ken Keen, Business Manager
Andy Arnold, Advertising Manager

BYRNEHURST HIGH SCHOOL • 9119 LYNNWOOD ST., BYRNEHURST, OK 53467 • Phone (003) 821-1065

Advertising contract

Date _____

Business or Organization _____

Street Address _____

City _____ State _____ ZIP Code _____

Name of Purchaser _____ Phone _____

ADVERTISING DEADLINES		
Issue	**Deadline**	**Publication Date**
1	Sept. 16	Sept. 30
2	Oct. 14	Oct. 28
3	Nov. 18	Dec. 2
4	Dec. 20	Jan. 17
5	Jan. 30	Feb. 13
6	March 7	March 21
7	April 11	April 25
8	May 21	June 5

Advertising material required on or before deadline date for each issue.

TERMS

- Prepaid ads running every issue receive a 10 percent discount.
- Payment due within 30 days of billing.
- Notification of changes or cancellation should be made at least a month before date scheduled for insertion.
- Advertisements must conform to the standards of ethical journalism.
- Advertisers will receive a copy of the issue containing each insertion of their ad upon publication.

Advertising Agreement:

The above-named advertiser wishes to insert the following ads in the issue(s) indicated:

Size of Ad	Price	No. of Insertions	Date of 1st Insertion	Total Price
		Applicable One-Time Charge:		
		Applicable Discount:		

Price to be billed: _____

Frequency of Insertion: _____ In successive issues _____ Every other issue
_____ Quarterly _____ One issue only

Preparation of Ad: _____ Advertiser furnishes camera-ready copy. _____ Repeat ad each issue per this contract.
_____ Newspaper staff to design, prepare ad.* _____ Phone each issue re possible changes.

Method of Payment: _____ Prepaid; check received before date of publication
_____ Please bill after publication of each insertion

Signed: *Name:* _____ *Title:* _____
for advertiser

Name: _____ *Title:* _____
for newspaper

* Please provide description of ad desired on back of this page or on separate sheet.

371

Paula Pen, Editor
Mrs. Adrian Adams, Adviser

Your Letterhead

Ken Keen, Business Manager
Andy Arnold, Advertising Manager

BYRNEHURST HIGH SCHOOL • 9119 LYNNWOOD ST., BYRNEHURST, OK 53467 • Phone (003) 821-1065

Invoice

Date _____

To: Business or Organization _____

Street Address _____

City _____ State _____ ZIP Code _____

BILLING/PAYMENT RECORD OF ADVERTISING PLACED IN SCHOOL PAPER

Date of Insertion	Description: Ad size or type of charge	Amount Due	Amount of Payment	Date Paid	Balance Due

To our advertiser:

Payment is due within 30 days of receipt of your bill unless prior arrangements have been made with the paper's business manager.

If you wish to purchase additional space or make changes in copy scheduled for future issues, please contact the newspaper advertising manager at least a month before date of publication.

Thank you for your support of our newspaper and our school.

_____
Business Manager

✂ -

STATEMENT:

Date Mailed _____

Mail Payment to:

The Torch
Byrnehurst High School
9119 Lynnwood St.
Byrnehurst, OK 53467

Acount Number _____

Co. Name _____

Address _____

City _____ State _____ ZIP Code _____

Issue # _____ Amount Due _____ Amount Enclosed _____

Please cut statement at dotted line and include with your remittance. Save upper half for your records.

Organizing the school newsroom

Organization in a newsroom—where everything revolves around deadlines and crises—may seem an impossibility. That's doubly true in a school newsroom, where most students have but one or at most a few regularly scheduled hours a day to devote to working for the paper. The rest must be time snatched from other demands and diversions.

Then there's the rule of bells that sends kids scampering away, leaving their work half-finished and their staff room in chaos.

Creating a system within a system

For the school newsroom, success in organization will not come from setting up a model system—no matter how perfect looking on paper—and expecting students to follow it to the letter. A system that attempts to rigidly impose order on a process as fragmented and chaotic as publishing a paper can only produce frustration and potentially rebellion. Instead, the purpose of the system is for everyone to know what should be done, how to do it, where something should go, where to look first and, most important, how to correct a kink in the system when one inevitably occurs.

A SAFETY NET FOR ADVISERS—A notable advantage of a well-organized newsroom is the headaches it saves, both for staffers and adviser. With a system in place, an adviser should have less need to listen to face-saving excuses that often turn into ingenious ways to blame someone—anyone but the student himself.

Instead of indulging in blame and recrimination, students aware of the need for organization can more easily develop the habit of asking themselves, "What is the problem? How can I solve it?" Spending time in advance on organization can save time later, for then the adviser need no longer serve as the sole fixer.

Dealing with space

There is probably no typical school newsroom to hold up as a model. Some school papers share space with the yearbook; others use computers belonging to other departments; some meet in a regular classroom where other subjects are taught throughout the day; and, of course, the nonexistent ideal is a perfectly organized, professional-looking setup with separate areas for editorial work, advertising, business and desktop publishing. Even the adviser blessed with the latter would surely find areas needing improvement.

Although there is obviously no one way to organize a newsroom, there are some basics that every adviser should strive for.

Preparing for action

As much as possible, the school newsroom should look and feel like a place where people transact the business of putting out a paper—not like a regular class in session. This means that stacks of textbooks and similar clutter should go somewhere under cover—at least under desks—at the beginning of each session.

Encourage students to be self-reliant self-starters. Unless there is an announced staff meeting, it's helpful to have an established routine for starting out each day, especially in view of the wide assortment of duties that need doing.

Keeping kids posted

One effective method of staff organization is the bulletin board, kept up as a junior staff member's extra duty assignment. The bulletin board—ideally more than one—can serve a variety of useful purposes. If only one is available, it should be divided into three clearly defined spaces.

1. **For timely messages.** These include two types of communication: brief posted notes to individual students and notices to the entire staff or special teams of staffers. Differentiate these notices by size and perhaps by using colored paper or borders. In order to work, messages must be removed as soon as they're outdated, and staffers must check this part of the board first.

   This is the place for posting assignment sheets and a daily sign-out sheet, unless some other method has been devised.

2. **For press clippings.** Reserve one spot for clippings from professional papers on national and international issues that may inspire features or in-depth reports. You might also include good examples from exchange papers—and even your own last issue. Be sure to keep them fresh, or no one will stop to take notice.

3. **For words to the wise.** Put up posters to serve as reminders of the rules of good journalism, concentrating on points where staff members exhibit weakness. Direct students to the bulletin board—or even post a list of the pages in your journalism text or newswriting workshop files that stress how to correct certain frequently found errors. It's a way to save your time and give notice that reporters need to take responsibility for improving their own work.

Space of their own

Devise a way for each student to have a place to keep such items as hard copy of work in progress, notes from interviews, a diskette holding a copy of current assignments and memos too long to post on the bulletin board, though their presence should be noted here.

The space should be large enough to hold a manila file folder, and it can be as simple as a series of hanging files in inexpensive plastic crates. Be sure the space is large enough so files aren't crammed together. Folders will require a housecleaning after each issue, though reporters should keep their notes longer in case a story's accuracy comes under question.

If your school has a vocational department, you may ask its chairman about building a simple, open-sided cabinet with slots deep enough to hold a letter or legal-size file. Versions in heavy cardboard are also available in office supply stores.

Students having a place of their own, labeled with their names, has many positive benefits—not the least that it proves students really belong. If something comes up missing, the personal file leaves no question of responsibility, and if a student is absent, there is no doubt about where to look first for work in progress.

If students take home diskettes to continue writing or editing a story on a compatible home computer, have them first make a copy and leave a duplicate diskette in the file. Should the student and/or diskette not return the next day, this assures you of having something to work from.

Planning ahead with forms and files

Are you saving too much or saving too little? Of course, it's hardly thinkable that an adviser could save too much time, but there's much else that can pile up around a newspaper office. The result is so many stacks of paper and so much clutter that the essentials—although present—are buried somewhere and just can't be found.

In the age of computers, much once saved as paper can now be stored on diskette—a way to genuinely save time formerly spent shuffling papers.

How many back issues of your paper do you need? Sure, there may be a time 25 years from now when a school alumna wants a copy of "her" paper for a class reunion, but a fellow graduate will likely have treasured one all those years.

Keep a limited number of copies, remembering that, thanks to the computer, there should be no need to cut up an old paper to get a copy of one story or picture. Just slip in the right diskette and reprint the one you need. For current use, plan to keep one copy of each issue, and clamp them together or place in a hard-cover folder. It is much faster and easier to leaf through a newspaper-sized, book-style file of issues than to paw over a stack of papers, look through and put away each one individually. Such a folder is also useful for exchange papers.

At the end of each year, plan to have at least two complete sets of issues bound together as volumes—one for the paper's files and one for the school library. The building principal might appreciate one, too, if space and budget allow.

Contribute to recycling

Most of your old papers and used copy paper do have a place—in recycling bins. Grit your teeth and throw out most of your leftover papers when an allotted time passes after each issue's publication. Have you heard the adage: "Today's news wraps tomorrow's garbage"? The saying is passé, but old paper still has a useful purpose. Have a box exclusively devoted to copy paper destined for recycling. Depending upon your policy about eating and drinking in class, candy and chip wrappers or soda cans are strictly taboo—and might serve as grounds for taking away the privileges if appeals to pride don't work.

File as much as you can by computer

Although you have a hard copy of every form that you use—perhaps in a book like this, it is preferable to obtain the type and number you need by using a copier or printing them off the computer. If scanned or typed into the computer, save them on a diskette reserved exclusively for forms. Be sure to give them clearly assigned file names and keep a separate index, if needed.

Count on the computer—keep it organized

Use the edit menu, and include the date and time under the slug when work begins on every story in your word-processing program. The computer will automatically update this data whenever the story is worked on, and it can serve as a useful record if questions arise.

After each issue comes out, copy all data used in that issue onto diskettes to clear space on your computer.

Depending upon the number and location of computers at your disposal, it is helpful if a box for filing diskettes is kept at each station. Make sure that each record pertaining to a given story is filed with the same slug, which should also appear on story and photo assignment sheets. Since computer file menus list items alphabetically, it may sometimes prove faster and easier to open files from the menu than searching for it and clicking on the screen—as long as the assigned slug is consistently used.

STAMP IT FOR APPROVAL—One quick way to identify the status of copy is to rubber-stamp each edited piece according to a set series of words or symbols. For example, you might buy a happy-face stamp for the okayed final draft or purchase stamps with the words "Final" or "Rewrite" to indicate where the draft stands in the writing/editing process.

Make your space work-oriented

Whether your staff meets in a classroom or newsroom, have it as professional-looking as possible. For editorial board meetings, arrange desks or chairs in an oval or circle if no conference table is available. Let the editor in chief take the head of the oval, while you as the adviser sit to one side.

Students—and you—need to see work actually being done on the paper. To those who say they can't work with distraction, the true answer is that it's a professional skill they need to learn. And, the more people working, the fewer distractions there are.

Shortcuts worth taking

Have laminated printouts available at each computer listing such shortcuts as:

- defined styles for headlines, subheads, text, etc.
- headline schedule showing typefaces and count
- computer commands that save time but are easily forgotten

You might also keep a paper file of good stories. Have it readily available, perhaps in the same place as student's personal files or in a special hanging file, along with skill-sharpening exercises. Put the stories under headings by type: straight news, features, editorials, and so on. This file may include stories from exchange papers and professional papers, as well as your own past issues. When advising a student how to repair a story, direct him or her to the appropriate source to get a better idea of the sound and form of well-written journalism or to get more practice in a specific skill.

Adopt a 'no excuses' policy

The more you can help students develop a sense of responsibility, the more you help them grow as maturing, capable people; the more you free yourself from the irksome duties of cosseting and babying students, who may be feeding you a line; and the more the paper can advance.

When introducing a new system, it is best not to throw too many changes and methods at students at one time—especially if they are already set in the ways of a previous adviser. It is strange how apt students are to forget a new set of rules or the working of a new system—or even assignments. Kids think forgetfulness is natural in young people, while adults always think it an unmistakable sign of old age. Introduce the most needed changes first, then wait until they are accepted and followed before adding others. Good luck!

Organizing for efficient computing

Do computers save time and effort? The answer depends on your viewpoint. One adviser of a highly respected California paper estimates that computers have forced him to double his time commitment. Computers allow you and your students to perform specialized tasks, each of which were formerly left to technically trained experts, and computers can complete most of those tasks with the twitch of a mouse or the touch of a few keys.

Yet, for advisers and students involved with high school journalism, computers should come with a powerful warning: Abandon hope of saving time and effort via desktop publishing. True, a computer system comprising a few pieces of equipment can accomplish electronically—in almost miraculous seconds—tasks that otherwise must be done laboriously by hand. But an ever-present danger for both advisers and students is that exploring the possibilities of desktop publishing can seem to be the end, not the means.

Direct your—and your students'—energies

For a high school newspaper, the purpose of owning and operating an adequate computer system should be to process and package the assembled contents—stories, headlines, photos, infographs, advertising and so on—both attractively and efficiently. Unless your school affords both the facilities and the faculty, the common aim of school newspapers should be to help students acquire the fundamental skills in writing, gathering information, organizing their ideas and thoughts and presenting them effectively. Learning these skills will serve them better, whatever their future plans, than investing much of their time trying to master the absorbing but never-ending, ever-expanding possibilities of the computer.

If you have a love for the computer, succumb to it, but accept the fact that computer technology continually offers its users more power and more capabilities. The computer industry is in the business of making each new development seem indispensable. Is it? Everything depends upon your purse and your needs.

In schools where a number of untrained or barely trained students come aboard the staff each year, advanced equipment and programs can monopolize an adviser's attention and time. While it seems you never have enough computers, programs and equipment, the danger exists of having so much that students lack sufficient time to absorb all the knowledge needed to use them effectively and expend valuable time on unproductive byways.

Assess your true needs

In the field of school journalism today, the need for desktop publishing has become a given. How much remains the question—and its answer depends upon your resources, the size of your school, the number of journalism courses your school offers, the size of your staff and the frequency and number of pages each issue.

STICKING TO THE BASICS—Computers become obsolete so fast that schools, which are famous for having outdated equipment, cannot hope to supply the latest technological advances as soon as they appear. The basics of computer operation remain the same, however. Your aim should be to own computer equipment that allows students to perform all necessary tasks and to learn the professional—not just the game-playing—uses of the computer in a way that enhances their skills and results in an efficiently produced, attractively-composed and inviting-to-read paper. One way to get more techno-logical might for your money is to purchase used computer hardware from a reliable dealer in used equipment.

AMONG YOUR REQUIREMENTS:

- *A sufficiency of memory:* With computers coming with multi megabytes, one with 8 MGs may seem puny, but you'll need less if your plans are to concentrate on fewer areas of the computer's possible uses.

Try to keep your computers compatible so that programs can be linked or shared. You may also find it practicable to buy computers of varying capacities, reserving those with more power for programs requiring more memory.

- *The largest affordable monitor:* Although you can reduce or enlarge the image at will, you can complete a task faster and more efficiently on a screen that lets you see what you're doing as you work.

Available PC monitors range from 13-inch to 21-inch displays, with the size of view-ing image, measured diagonally, running approximately 0.9 to 1.7 inches smaller than the number given. For example, a 14-inch display translates to a 12.4-inch viewable image size. When buying a monitor, the greater the viewing area, the more you pay.

Laptop computers generally feature a 9.5-inch display area, measured diagonally.

- *A printer fit to print:* It's one of the less expensive pieces of equipment if your aim is a workmanlike printer—unable to turn out multiple or large-size copies at a high rate of speed. You can expect such reasonably-priced printers to take only 8-1/2″ × 11″ paper, which will require you to tile and paste if you publish a tabloid-size paper.

While smaller-size printers sell for a few hundred dollars, those handling tabloid-size sheets of paper run into the thousands. For example, one with an 11.69″ × 17″ print-able surface area is priced over $2000.

One inexpensive solution to the problem facing schools that publish tabloid-size papers is to proof and edit the paper with tiled copy. Then take diskettes of the final ver-sion to a professional copy center that is equipped to print tabloid-size sheets from diskettes for a modest price.

And then, there's the printer that also works as a fax, copier and scanner. What next? Dream on.

- *Scanners add can-do to your newsroom.* Priced from just a little over $100 to well over $1000, scanners can bring documents, photos and graphics into your computer for refine-ment and integration into your pages. Scanners for photographs and graphics generally include software for enhancing, sizing and otherwise editing their images. As with other types of electronic hardware, the price depends upon the features they incorporate.

Before buying a scanner or any other equipment, weigh the capabilities you need against the features and prices of those for sale. The biggest and best may be right for professional jobs, but one that's less costly may perform all the functions you require.

For a paper that's short on both funds and equipment, a simple scanner such as the Visioneer PaperPort VX™ may be helpful and practical. This allows you to feed paper documents into your files and includes a program that turns them into editable for-matted text. Using a document scanner makes it possible to readily use printed copy done on a different machine, without reprocessing it

- *Do you need to be on the World Wide Web?* There are pages lying around out there that haven't been touched for many moons. Yes, there's much valuable information on the Internet, valuable if you know what you want and need, but be careful. Surfing the Web can be both alluring and distracting. Schools that provide students access to the Internet find it necessary to require them to sign a contract that attempts to limit their search for restricted sites and provides penalties for abuse of their privileges.

Learning to use the Internet is easy, but developing the intellect and understanding to make good use of the available information should come first. For kids, surfing the Web is dangerously like other compulsive computer games. Unless you have the money and time, and really feel the need, it's probably best for you and your class to research the Web on a computer belonging to another department, the school or the public library. As an adviser, you may find the Internet personally useful for up-to-date information about journalism programs, organizations, computer sources and so on.

• *Software programs—specialists, all:* Every computer store and catalog is loaded with new and newer software—always promising to deliver more and more. Even though these promises are true, it's essential to choose wisely. For school newspaper use, three questions need answering:

1. Will it save time and effort, or will it waste both because of the time spent in learning and the effort expended in using it?

2. Do staff computers have sufficient memory to handle the additional software and if not, can we afford to add more memory?

3. Will the expanded capabilities be worth the expenditure, or is this a nice but unnecessary frill?

Just as you don't want to overload your computer with software that puts a choke hold on its memory, you must be careful about overloading kids with more computer finesse than they can handle. Although it may prove intriguing, deep involvement with advanced programs puts an extra burden on the adviser or advisers. Unless you love it, keep it simple.

As with scanners, computers regularly come with software installed, including a word processing program plus others you may not want or need. For school papers, the most popular of desktop publishing tools is PageMaker™ which has the reputation of being the easiest to learn and use.

Although both word-processing and desktop publishing programs include simple tools for creating graphics, you may also want a more sophisticated graphics program— but remember their capability of eating up time.

Then there are also clip art, additional fonts and expanded memory—the last of which is likely the most practical choice. Be extremely careful when buying clip art to make sure the collection contains what you can use and need. Think chiefly of its use in advertisements, for it's best that the paper's editorial pages present only students' own work. Similarly, overuse of fonts makes the paper look less professional; choose carefully, if desired, for advertisements and occasional features.

Some programs that offer to automatically correct your spelling and grammar serve mainly as crutches, and others may prove to be costly, time-consuming toys.

You'll discover a mind-boggling display of hardware, software and accessories in such computer catalogs as Mac/Multiple Zones, Mac/Micro/Data Comm Warehouse and Mac/PC Mall as well as the periodical catalog, *Computer Shopper,* available at bookstores and newsstands.

Learn by doing

Although teachers generally are expected to know more about a subject than kids do, there are certain advantages to keeping just a step ahead. This helps you to understand the process of learning and, as a result, transmit it more effectively. When you work with computers, it's often a disadvantage to try to learn too much all at once. Since there is always more to learn, an attempt to comprehend unneeded phases of a program's possibilities may make a muddle of the techniques you need. In fact, the computer itself will often reveal its secrets while you work with what you know.

Feel free to randomly combine keys to discover what happens when a pair or trio of keys—such as the option-shift-V—are held and struck together. An expert says that computers are designed to be foolproof. Don't think of yourself as a dummy, as a popular series refers to computer novices, but as an explorer becoming acquainted with the world of computers through hands-on experience.

THINK SAVE! SAVE! SAVE! Two of the most valuable features of a computer are "Save" and "Revert," found under the file menu. The save function can also be performed on the keyboard with the command key + s. Frequently saving your work is not just a form of insurance against power outages and computer crashes. Saving your work allows you to retrieve a version you inadvertently deleted or to do additional experimentation on a page layout or graphic—then return to the last-saved version if it doesn't turn out as well as you hoped.

"Revert," found in the file menu, requires you to "Think SAVE!" regularly. Otherwise, you might lose as much as you gain by reverting to a much earlier version. Remind students to "Think SAVE!" frequently. Help them make it a habit by testing the command key + s, when you pass by to check on student progress, especially at the first of the year. You'll be able to judge their "saving" habits by the number of seconds the process takes. You may also wish to make "Think SAVE!" signs to post at every computer.

Don't forget another keyboard-generated way to correct the last-done step. Under the Edit menu or by using command key + Z, you will find the "Undo Typing" or "Redo Typing" function, depending upon which is available at the time. When this function is inoperable, "Revert" can be a lifesaver. "Think SAVE!"

CREATE YOUR OWN TIME-SAVING SHORTCUTS FOR QUICKER COMPUTING:

1. Add the names of your school, administration, faculty and prominent students to your computer's dictionary. (Keep a list of those you've added so the names of graduating seniors and departing faculty members can be deleted the following year.)

2. Create glossaries of various commands that, once learned, can prove great time savers, both for yourself and staffers. Have copies available at every computer and also in the staff manual so that precious time isn't wasted trying to find instructions for saving time.

There are three main types of keyboard shortcuts you should use:

• *Keyboard shortcuts for most-used computer commands** (Figure 4-12). Although the symbols are listed on each pull-down menu, having them memorized or handily available can save precious time.

• *Glossary of keyboard-generated symbols, icons and dingbats** (Figure 4-13). Limit your glossary to those that are most frequently used and approved. Specify the use of each, for example, • (bullet) for listed items within text and ™ (registered trademark).

---

*Examples given apply to Macintosh™ programs. Check your manual for specific instructions and for other applications.

Glossary of keyboard shortcuts
for computer commands

FILE COMMANDS

To save copy	command key + S
To open a selected icon	command key + O
To close a file window	command key + W
To print the open file	command key + P
To quit the program	command key + Q

EDIT COMMANDS

To undo the most recent edit/change	command key + Z
To cut an item to clipboard*	command key + X
To copy an item to clipboard*	command key + C
To paste an item from clipboard	command key + V
To find/change an item	command key + F

TEXT COMMANDS

Plain text	command key + T
Bold	command key + B
Italic	command key + I
Underline	command key + U
Highlight text	shift + ← , → , ↓ , or ↑
Move insertion point to far left, right of copy block; bottom, or top of file	command key + ← , → , ↓ , or ↑

---

*Saved only until another item is cut or copied.

YOUR PAPER'S
LOGO

Glossary of shortcuts
for keyboard-generated icons

FROM THE STANDARD KEYBOARD

Option + 2 = ™ (registered trademark)

Option + 8 = • (bullet: to introduce listed items within text)

Shift + option + - (dash) = — (em: to set off inserted phrases)

USING TYPEFACE ZAPF DINGBATS

All dingbats created from a family of type also have a choice of sizes. Use dingbats sparingly when called for in staff style manual or needed in advertising design. Find in font menu as ✳❀☐✳ ✳✱■✳❂❀▼▲

Obtained by striking lower-case letter, after selecting type under menu:

3 = ✔ check mark

5 = ✕ mark

u = ◆ square balanced on point

t = ▼ triangle en pointe

y = ▮ medium upright bar

u = ◆ square en pointe

s = ▲ solid black triangle

' = ➜ arrow pointing to right

z = ▮ fat upright bar

x = | thin upright bar

v = ❖ partitioned diamond

n − ■ solid black square

e = ✳ fleurette

Obtained by striking letter, plus shift key:

$ = ✂ scissors

% = ☎ telephone

I = ☆ outlined star

G = ◇ outlined, shapely diamond

Note: Examples given apply to Macintosh™ programs. Check your manual for other applications. In some programs, you may be able to automatically add bullets, numbers or check boxes to paragraphs from the format menu.

© 1998 by John Wiley & Sons, Inc

• *Glossary of keyboard-generated custom styles.* Create a list of most used typefaces, sizes and styles in the "Define Styles" dialogue box in the style menu. When chosen, the assigned type choice for body text, bylines, heads, cutlines, subheads and so on can be made from the style menu or even more quickly from the keyboard, using the command key + number. Some publishing programs are capable of linking type commands and applying them consecutively.

Example: Standard text NY 12 = command key + 1

TRY NOT TO PANIC—At times the computer's pointer will not move, the printer refuses to print or the computer will suddenly send a message about its "peripherals." If there have been no other indications of trouble, it may be a "bad air" day or just the computer wanting to express itself.

Try turning off the computer, leave it off for at least 10 seconds—more may please it better—then turn it on again.

ORGANIZE THE DESKTOP—Make use of folders to keep your desktop organized. Create a folder for each folio heading—news, editorial, sports, entertainment and so forth—or each page in the process of being edited. Another set of folders may hold copy in the process of being roughed. This system works particularly well if files can be shared.

Since it is possible to place folders inside folders, create additional folders, for example, a folder for news briefs inside the Page 1 folder, and place letters to the editor in a folder within the Editorial or Opinion folder.

Although some stories may be roughed on other computers, make sure they are copied to disks and then placed in their appropriate folders as quickly as possible. Slugs of all stories should carry the date and time to show when they were last worked on.

To keep the desktop as clear as possible, copy all outdated material to disks as soon as feasible and discard copy from active computer space. To provide additional memory, it may also be necessary to remove stories, such as investigative reports ready for future issues, and restore from disks when actually needed. Of course, also keep hard copies of stories you intend to run later.

If memory is at an absolute premium, you may on rare occasions need to alter the allocation of memory to a given program. Check your computer reference manual for instructions.

Making a good paper better

Assess your own progress

What qualities combine to create a superior school newspaper? How can you be assured that your hard work and efforts are achieving positive results?

One way to keep you and your staff in focus is by periodically—perhaps at the beginning and end of each year—measuring your paper against a set of standards such as the one that follows (Figure 4-14), inspired by the *Guide to Better Newspapers,* of GLIPA, Great Lakes Interscholastic Press Association.

You may wish simply to check each item "+" (or yes), "o" (or no), or "—" (for needs improvement) in the blank space before each statement. Or, you may prefer to compare your paper against a standard of excellence—or with one or more exchange papers. In this case, judge by the numerical scale from 1 to 5 in order to encourage continued improvement.

This is the same kind of critique that may be used for judging the overall performance of a school paper when entered in journalism competitions.

Self-checking critique:
100 points for judging school papers

DIRECTIONS:

Use the critique in one of two ways:

A. Check each item "+" (or yes), "o" (or no) or "—" (for needs improvement) in the blank space before each statement.

- or -

B. Circle the appropriate number from 1 to 5, based on a scale by which 1 equals weak or missing and 5 equals superior or top-notch.

PART I. Overall layout and design

A. Throughout paper

____ 1. Consistency in design elements, typefaces, use of rules, etc., gives paper an attractive, well-designed character.   1 2 3 4 5

____ 2. Placement of stories and graphics changes from issue to issue to provide variation within continuity.   1 2 3 4 5

____ 3. Page design and headline sizes reinforce relative importance of stories. 1 2 3 4 5

____ 4. Modular design serves as basis for layouts, combining square and rectangular units, varying column widths.   1 2 3 4 5

____ 5. Pages have a center of visual interest and additional entry points to stories.   1 2 3 4 5

____ 6. Layouts have both horizontal and vertical movement with attention paid to bottom half of the page.   1 2 3 4 5

____ 7. White space acts as a unifying design element to focus reader attention and avoid crowding type and graphics.   1 2 3 4 5

____ 8. Internal margins and spacing between elements is kept consistent, with greater space separating one module from another than is used within.   1 2 3 4 5

____ 9. Layout design enhances readability and emphasizes content, rather than calling attention to itself.   1 2 3 4 5

____ 10. Pages have a coherent, positive impact, avoiding such flaws as tombstone headlines, clashing elements and awkward jumps.   1 2 3 4 5

B. Page One

____ 1. Nameplate is effective and uncluttered.   1 2 3 4 5

____ 2. Datelines includes volume/issue number, name and address of school, and issue's publication date.   1 2 3 4 5

____ 3. Standing elements, such as news briefs and teasers, are truly informative, not just page fillers.   1 2 3 4 5

____ 4. Lead story makes a compelling impression through headline, graphics and layout.   1 2 3 4 5

_____ 5. Front page delivers genuine news, a result of solid reporting, instead of a rehash of common knowledge. 1 2 3 4 5

C. Inside pages

_____ 1. Folio lines on each inside page carry the publication name, page number and date of issue. 1 2 3 4 5

_____ 2. Section heads, if used, complement overall design of paper but do not dominate page. 1 2 3 4 5

_____ 3. Whether containing text or advertising, bottom half of pages as well as top half exhibits well-planned design. 1 2 3 4 5

_____ 4. An editorial page, included in each issue, contains the paper's masthead and carries no advertising. 1 2 3 4 5

_____ 5. Facing pages, as well as the double truck, are laid out to complement one another, not compete. 1 2 3 4 5

D. Typography

_____ 1. Body copy is an easy-to-read serif type that is large enough not to "go gray" in longer columns. 1 2 3 4 5

_____ 2. Copy is set in readable column widths, not set too narrow, set too wide nor illegibly contorted by text wraps. 1 2 3 4 5

_____ 3. Typographical devices, such as obvious changes in leading or type size, are not used to make stories fit space. 1 2 3 4 5

_____ 4. Cutlines, bylines, icons, etc., maintain a consistent style throughout the paper. 1 2 3 4 5

_____ 5. One or two headline typefaces in appropriate sizes are used consistently, except for special features. 1 2 3 4 5

E. Headlines

_____ 1. Headlines are proportioned to the page and story, not weak and wordy, nor too large and overpowering. 1 2 3 4 5

_____ 2. Headlines use downstyle with single quotes and a minimum of capitalization and punctuation. 1 2 3 4 5

_____ 3. Headlines clearly direct readers to story modules, serving as umbrellas over their parts. 1 2 3 4 5

_____ 4. Stories avoid label heads, except as kickers, captions above photos or in novelty headlines. 1 2 3 4 5

_____ 5. Novelty headlines (tripods, hammerheads, etc.) are used effectively, but reserved for features and in-depth reports. 1 2 3 4 5

F. Photography, graphics and sidebars

_____ 1. Sidebars and infographs provide additional dimensions to major stories, in-depth reports and features. 1 2 3 4 5

_____ 2. Photo subjects face into the page and, if possible, direct the reader's eye toward accompanying story.   1 2 3 4 5

_____ 3. Layouts use both landscape and portrait-oriented photos, varying in size and content.   1 2 3 4 5

_____ 4. Photographs concentrate on subjects showing action, cropped to highlight center of interest, rather than on stagnant posed shots.   1 2 3 4 5

_____ 5. Cartoons and drawings look clearly, purposefully drawn, not like apparent space fillers or last-minute sketches.   1 2 3 4 5

G. Advertisements

_____ 1. Advertisements show the result of thoughtful design, going beyond mere reproduction of business cards.   1 2 3 4 5

_____ 2. Ads use a variety of techniques, including graphics, logos, screens, photos, typography—to make each distinctive.   1 2 3 4 5

_____ 3. Both layout and copy combine to attract readers and promote the advertiser's message, product and/or service.   1 2 3 4 5

_____ 4. Column rules are used to define and organize advertising space; adjoining ads are indicative of thoughtful placement.   1 2 3 4 5

_____ 5. Page one and editorial pages remain free of advertising.   1 2 3 4 5

PART II. Journalistic content

A. General coverage

_____ 1. The paper concentrates on firsthand coverage that goes beyond known information and superficial facts.   1 2 3 4 5

_____ 2. Coverage directs its appeal to all facets of the student body and shows awareness of faculty, parent and community interest.   1 2 3 4 5

_____ 3. Reporting shows a keen, lively concern for bringing each story home to its readers—whether it's news, opinion, sports or feature.   1 2 3 4 5

_____ 4. Content demonstrates a balance of well-planned, thoroughly researched stories concerning school and wider interests.   1 2 3 4 5

_____ 5. Articles include analysis of some events and issues, stressing the "how" and "why."   1 2 3 4 5

B. News

_____ 1. Reporters have contacted a variety of news sources and use several for major stories.   1 2 3 4 5

_____ 2. News stories concentrate on future events or seek to provide new angles of and insights into past ones.   1 2 3 4 5

_____ 3. School activities, clubs, nonathletic events, curriculum-related news receive adequate coverage.   1 2 3 4 5

____ 4. Student-related, out-of-school events receive coverage when they warrant it. 1 2 3 4 5

____ 5. News value determines length, with a good balance between briefs and longer stories. 1 2 3 4 5

C. Opinion

____ 1. Each issue contains at least one unsigned, well-researched editorial representing the paper's views. 1 2 3 4 5

____ 2. Editorial pages carry the paper's masthead, readers' forum policy and letters, editorial cartoon and/or photographs and editorial columns. 1 2 3 4 5

____ 3. The paper's editorial policy appears in the year's first issue and periodically afterward. 1 2 3 4 5

____ 4. Editorials make their point convincingly and logically without being long-winded. 1 2 3 4 5

____ 5. Opinion pieces and straight news are clearly defined; straight news is free of reporters' opinions. 1 2 3 4 5

D. Features

____ 1. Original, lively features cover their subjects thoroughly and appeal to common human interests. 1 2 3 4 5

____ 2. Each issue offers various types of features, including profiles, behind-the-scenes stories, firsthand experience, etc. 1 2 3 4 5

____ 3. News features take a fresh and unexpected angle on events in order to broaden and increase student interest. 1 2 3 4 5

____ 4. In-depth reports present several articles, resulting from firsthand research when topics merit them. 1 2 3 4 5

____ 5. Entertainment features include coverage of school concerts and plays, as well as brightly written reviews and reports of community resources. 1 2 3 4 5

E. Sports

____ 1. Sports pages afford fair coverage to all sports, both boys and girls—including scholastic sports, intramurals, the physical education department and relatively unfamiliar sports practiced by individual students. 1 2 3 4 5

____ 2. Sports stories concentrate on future events and "inside" information instead of drawn-out coverage of past events. 1 2 3 4 5

____ 3. Graphics, digests of statistics and sports news briefs add impact to pages. 1 2 3 4 5

____ 4. Sports features appeal to general interest, not only fans, via personality profiles, interviews, columns, first-person experience. 1 2 3 4 5

____ 5. Articles concerning pro or college sports have special interest for students, instead of just being fillers. 1 2 3 4 5

PART III. Writing and editing

A. General coverage

____ 1. Writing style is clear, concise, easy to understand.   1 2 3 4 5

____ 2. Reporters rely on the active voice of verbs and use consistent tenses throughout each story.   1 2 3 4 5

____ 3. Stories adhere to standard rules of grammar and spelling; show consistency of journalistic style.   1 2 3 4 5

____ 4. Reporters avoid beginning successive paragraphs—or a number of stories—with identical words.   1 2 3 4 5

____ 5. Stories fully identify each person on first reference, including the person's full name plus profession or other identifying factor.   1 2 3 4 5

____ 6. Stories contain accurate facts, use technical terms correctly and show evidence of effective research.   1 2 3 4 5

____ 7. Well-chosen direct and indirect quotations, properly attributed, add substance, authority and interest.   1 2 3 4 5

____ 8. Reporters avoid clichés and trite phrases, both of their own use and in their choice of quotations.   1 2 3 4 5

____ 9. Stories show the results of effective interview techniques, including the use of follow-up questions.   1 2 3 4 5

____ 10. Writers avoid the use of the school's name, nickname and initials unless required for clarity.   1 2 3 4 5

B. News

____ 1. Stories maintain an objective point of view, not expressing the writer's opinion nor using forms of *I* or *you*, unless in quotations.   1 2 3 4 5

____ 2. Summary leads are brief, lively, grammatically varied and rarely begin with weak words such as *a, an, the* and *there*.   1 2 3 4 5

____ 3. Stories with other than summary leads provide the basic W's and an H in a nutgraph as early in the story as possible.   1 2 3 4 5

____ 4. Stories develop logically from the most important facts to those of lesser importance.   1 2 3 4 5

____ 5. Reporters concentrate on major aspects of the story, emphasize the present and future, not the past, and answer the questions planted in the reader's mind.   1 2 3 4 5

C. Opinion

____ 1. Instead of preaching, editorials emphasize "we," not "you," and avoid directly attacking individuals or belittling their sincerely held views.   1 2 3 4 5

____ 2. Editorials include supporting evidence and examples—and build to a convincing conclusion.   1 2 3 4 5

____ 3. When using humor, editorials and columns refrain from sarcasm and "inside" jokes that may offend or insult some readers.   1 2 3 4 5

____ 4. The paper uses various types of columns—none of which are idle ramblings, written to fill space.   1 2 3 4 5

____ 5. Columns have an original slant, yet make ample use of anecdote, quotation and example.   1 2 3 4 5

D. Features

____ 1. Features exhibit appropriate journalistic style, whether interview, column, personal experience or review.   1 2 3 4 5

____ 2. Stories contain telling quotations to further the writer's theme—not random, inquiring reporter-type responses.   1 2 3 4 5

____ 3. Effective leads get the reader personally involved.   1 2 3 4 5

____ 4. Features show the result of thorough research and interviews that go beyond superficial questioning.   1 2 3 4 5

____ 5. Entertainment reviews and features are fresh, lively and original—with brevity as an asset.   1 2 3 4 5

E. Sports

____ 1. Sports stories downplay the "When" and emphasize the other W's and the H.   1 2 3 4 5

____ 2. Sports writers maintain journalistic objectivity and do not use such phrases as "our team."   1 2 3 4 5

____ 3. Writers avoid lengthy coverage of past games, using scoreboards and graphics to present their results.   1 2 3 4 5

____ 4. Stories refrain from using sports clichés, trite phrases and overly strong writing.   1 2 3 4 5

____ 5. Sports writers show evidence of knowing and using varying techniques appropriate for features, straight news, columns, etc.   1 2 3 4 5

F. Headlines and cutlines

____ 1. Headlines stress the most important facet of each story, concentrating on the lead or nutgraph.   1 2 3 4 5

____ 2. Headlines are tightly written, active statements that include effective verbs or verb forms.   1 2 3 4 5

____ 3. Names, phrases and titles are kept together, not broken between two lines of a headline.   1 2 3 4 5

____ 4. Cutlines contain a brief description of the photo itself and needed identification. They avoid cuteness.   1 2 3 4 5

____ 5. All photographs have cutlines and photo credits.   1 2 3 4 5

More than 50 hints for every phase of publication

Here are ideas from journalism conferences and advisers, articles and books—as well as a few original ones—that you may wish to incorporate into your newspaper pages or journalism program. For that's what journalism is always about: looking for what's new and searching for ways to improve what needs improving and ways to make what's already good better.

Ideas are listed in three categories:

- Sharpen your paper's image

- Strengthen your paper's design

- Smooth your desktop publishing operation

SHARPEN YOUR PAPER'S IMAGE

1. Put your beginning journalism class to work, proofreading for missed errors in the just-published issue. Offer a modest bonus for whoever finds the most. Or, instead of a beginning class, let those not on the editorial board look for errors during the next issue's planning sessions.

   When proofreading a printed page, have students look for

   a. layout errors—missing cutlines, badly aligned text, etc.

   b. typos and other mistakes—spelling, syntax, missing words, incorrect homonyms, faulty punctuation

   c. incorrect capitalization and spelling of proper names

   d. errors in using dates, other numbers

   e. misuse of abbreviations and acronyms

   f. inconsistency of style

2. Post their names on an honor roll or give extra points to the page editor and reporter with the fewest errors—with the goal of being 100% error free.

3. Choose one type of error that seems endemic to your paper—such as the misuse of apostrophes in words like "it's"—and target this error for total elimination in the forthcoming issue.

   Following Ben Franklin's program for self-improvement, target a different problem each issue—until all are eliminated wholly or nearly so.

4. Check paper for legibility after each edition is out. Screened backgrounds add contrast to a page, but make sure they are light enough to preserve legibility of type. Ordinary body copy often looks dim over a screen, and bold copy may seem blurry if densely printed.

5. Be careful that words used creatively don't accidentally (or ingeniously) spell out something questionable when read vertically or diagonally, as in the following:

   FUN
   AND
   GAMES

6. In preparing copy, leave only one space after a period. Check for and correct errors through the Find/Change feature of your word-processing program. First, type "period/space/space" under Find and "period/space" under Change. Then use the Change All command.

7. "Find" features recognize spaces—so this technique works to replace hyphens with em dashes. This -- is incorrect, while this — is right.

8. Letter spacing and kerning are ways to refine the appearance of headlines. Since creators adjust word-processing programs to generally acceptable levels, experimentation by beginners may waste time and have less than satisfactory results.

9. Make a point of having reporters write and editors edit copy to achieve paragraphs of varied lengths. A series of long text blocks look dull and gray; short ones tend to be a choppy-looking series of single sentences. Varied paragraph lengths also avoid the appearance of distracting ribbons of white that sometimes result from equal-length paragraphs.

10. When text runs too short, fill out pages by:
    a. supplying subheads
    b. dropping in an intriguing pull quote
    c. floating more space above—not below—the headline (but don't overdo)
    d. adding a kicker
    e. setting text two or three picas narrower and boxing with a one-point rule

11. If article runs too long for page, options are
    a. to move or cut another story
    b. to change column width and reduce size of photo or graphic
    c. to cut final paragraphs or jump story to another page
    d. to eliminate a second deck of headline

12. Have a policy about touchy matters, such as handling the death of a student or teacher, single parents, suicide. A recommended type of obituary is a regular news story that includes reminiscences of friends.

13. You may consider everyone in your journalism classes to be part of the staff and assign them stories as soon as they can capably handle them.

14. Sidebars attract both scanners and readers. Train reporters and editors to think like page designers, page designers to think like reporters and editors. Encourage both to think of how to use data to make pages content-driven.

15. Evaluate page design by trying the dollar bill test. When you lay it on a page, the bill should touch a visual for your paper to rate an "A."

    Visuals include:
    - pull quotes
    - icons
    - photos
    - mug shots
    - graphics
    - infographs

16. Be consistent in your use of names and identification. You may, however, wish to use different forms for faculty and students.

17. Avoid exaggerating the importance of polls and surveys. Articles and/or infographs about poll results should include answers to the following:
    a. Who did the poll? How was it conducted?
    b. How many were interviewed? Who were interviewed?
    c. How were respondents selected? (Self-selected polls lack validity.)
    d. When was the poll taken? Who sponsored it?

   e. What is the sampling error?

   f. What questions were asked and in what order?

   g. If possible, compare with other polls.

18. Warn students against stretching out stories with unrelated quotes, not pulled together by reporter.

19. Students need you, the adviser, to coach them on the fine points of journalism. They really don't know.

20. "If students are taught that their writing is outstanding when it's not, it does them a great disservice in the long run. If you don't challenge kids, you're underestimating what they can accomplish."—George Curry, *Death by Cheeseburger,* p. 46.

STRENGTHEN YOUR PAPER'S DESIGN

1. Use reverse type wisely and sparingly. Use white type only against dark grounds. The lighter the background, the more legibility suffers when reversing small type or multiple words. Reversing type to white on black runs the risks of spotty printing and hard-to-read type if too small.

2. Use lead-ins to bridge headline and text with long or important stories. Occasionally set introductory paragraphs in a size larger type, spanning several columns. Pull quotes can also make effective lead-ins.

3. The purpose of rules is to separate things; and unneeded rules are both redundant and distracting.

   Not needed: A rule after a headline wrongly separates two parts of a story that clearly belong together.

   Column rules are redundant for justified stories with straight edges that serve as natural boundaries themselves.

   Worth using: Rules do serve to separate stories with ragged right edges.

4. When experimenting with special effects, add one element at a time and carefully weigh the results. Keep pages clean, not cluttered.

5. Run an outstanding photo as a front page feature—or perhaps as an attention-getting teaser for an inside story.

6. Set pull quotes in plus column, alongside story, if using a multicolumn grid.

7. In news brief sections, maintain a uniform headline style—including type font, size, style and number of lines.

8. Page one menus touting inside stories are no longer new. If used, make sure they offer newsworthy tidbits and aren't just filling space.

9. Use white space to draw readers from outside into the page, not away from the copy and photos.

10. Vertical type is generally hard to read.

H
E
A
D
L
I
N
E

11. Words lose their effect if arty headlines don't emphasize their point.

What's the poin**t**?

Are you l**OO**king for trouble**?**

12. When using text wrap, allow about one pica to separate text and item inside.

13. As a rule of thumb for determining point size for secondary headlines, divide the size of primary head by two, then choose the nearest standard size.

14. Too much color dilutes its effect. Use it sparingly.

15. Beware of gutters that run the full length of the page, dividing it into long, identical columns, which lead the reader's eye away from the rest of the paper's content.

16. Proportion headlines to your page size and to each other; make them neither too big nor too small, yet not all the same.

17. Keep ads of competitors away from one another—not on the same or facing pages.

18. Have staff photographers take pictures of students for use as exclusive illustrations for local advertisers. It may require an extra charge.

SMOOTH YOUR DESKTOP PUBLISHING OPERATION

1. To insure uniform spacing, set automatic formatting under Paragraph in Format menu. For example, a first line indention of 0.167 will indent paragraphs 1/6 inch, or approximately two to three letters of body copy type.

2. Some papers set the first paragraphs of a story minus indentions—on the theory that indents signal a new, not a first, paragraph.

3. Others omit all indentions but allow extra space between paragraphs. This breaks up grayness of long stretches of text and makes paragraphs seem more self-contained.

4. To provide extra space between paragraphs, refer to automatic spacing command under Paragraph in Format menu. Relying on two carriage returns creates an overly long gap that distracts from story continuity.

5. Although the standard default serves for body copy, you may wish to change the proportion and use tighter leading for larger headline type. Check your desktop publishing manual for directions.

6. Save time by creating custom style sheets in your computer for predetermined formatting of characteristics of type style, size, leading and alignment.

7. When creating infographs using pie charts, limit number of pieces to ten or fewer.

8. Screen extra-large type, and consider its effectiveness.

9. Some advisers report finding the use of color fraught with problems—requiring all equipment to match.

10. For spot color, use screens to give effect of medium shade of color.

11. With one color, you have the option of creating 256 grays; with two colors you can go to 1000, and do quad tone with blacks.

12. Most professional presses are set up for two colors—one of which is black. It does not cost much more to add the second color. Four-color printing is another story.

13. Save frequently, frequently, frequently! Use "Revert" to get back to last-saved version when you get in a mess. Don't blunder ahead, making things worse . . . and wasting time.

14. Save materials under consistent file names for ease of opening via File menu. Make sure time/date is current.

15. Back up materials to disks during each session, and protect disks from damage. Keep them away from magnetic fields, and other danger zones.

16. Before file is open, any command selected becomes a program setting. Commands can also be changed in an individual file.

Appendix 1

GLOSSARIES FOR DESKTOP PUBLISHING AND JOURNALISM

Included are specialized terms concerning the two areas most involved in publishing a school newspaper. For convenience, they are divided into two sections: desktop publishing and journalism. Since some apply to both, check the second if not found in the first.

Desktop publishing terms

bullet list—related information, such as types of scholarships available, presented as a list and introduced with a bullet or other dingbat. A bullet list may run within a story or separately as a sidebar

centered—copy set with even margins from right to left

classified ad—a list of offerings, often classified by type, run together in a special section. All are generally paragraph form in the same typeface with all-cap or boldface lead-ins

clip art—stock illustrations purchased from a software supply catalog, including permission to use without breaking a copyright. Clip art tends to look canned, and finding appropriate designs is often difficult

clipboard—a temporary storage area in computer memory for most recent selection cut or copied

column inch—unit of space one inch deep and one column wide—useful for measuring ad sizes

cut—term for a newspaper photo or art, taken from engraving terminology

cutout—a photo published with most of the background eliminated and the central figure or object outlined

default—the proportion of line spacing used by a desktop publishing program. Standard default leading in most computer programs is 20% greater than the type size used, which sets the leading of 10 point type at 12 point

dingbat—asterisk (star), bullet (small black circle), check mark, square box or other decorative symbols—used to draw attention to beginning of paragraphs or items in a list

display ad—an ad that attempts to attract the reader through headlines, artwork and design techniques in contrast to classified ads

display type—sized larger than body type, used for headlines and advertising

double truck—the two facing pages in the center of a paper; often laid out as a single unit, running across the fold

dummy—model layout of a newspaper page, showing position of every intended element, that serves as a guide for computer placement

entry point—a visual element, such as an initial cap, icon, photo, subhead or dingbat, which serves to attract readers to a story

family—all of the sizes, weights, widths and variations of a particular type design

font—a complete set of a single size of type in all its variations

flush left—copy aligned to the left of a column or columns of type and having ragged right margin

flush right—copy aligned to the right of a column or columns of type and having a ragged left margin

format—the basic physical characteristics of a paper as to size, kinds of headlines and other variables on which individual issues are based

golden mean—a ratio of .62 to 1, which some prefer as the most pleasing proportion for cropping a photo or designing a layout module

graph—short for a paragraph (sometimes spelled *graf*)

gutter—the space between columns on the printed page of a newspaper

initial letter—a single letter at the beginning of a paragraph, printed in a larger size and often embellished to serve as an entry point to a story

jump—to continue a story in a different place or on a different page

jump head—a key word or words in headline type to signal the continuation of a story from another page

jumpline—information at the end of a story, signaling its continuation to a certain page

justified—copy spaced for even alignment at right and left margins

kerning—adjusting type on a computer to control spaces between individual letters

landscape—any cut, not necessarily of scenery, that runs horizontally

lead (**led**)—space between lines of type *(see also, under Journalism)*

letter spacing—stretching a word across a space

logo—the distinctive typographical design created to identify the name of a product, manufacturer, newspaper, etc.

lower case—small letters of a typeface

master page—a page holding the text, graphics and guides repeated on every page in a publication

menu—in computer terminology, the list of choices available in a certain category, such as Edit or Style *(see also, under Journalism)*

modular design—layout style by which all elements in a story—text, headlines and graphics—are designed as a whole in rectangular or square units

mug shot—portrait picture showing subject's head and shoulders

nameplate—the designed space displaying the name of the paper and any accompanying information; sometimes also called the paper's logo or flag

overprint—printing of one color over another, such as type over a screened background

pica—a type measurement equaling 12 points or 1/6 of an inch

point—standard measurement for type—there are 72 points to an inch

portrait—a picture emphasizing a person's head and shoulders; sometimes called a mug shot; also, any cut run vertically instead of horizontally as a landscape

proofreader—someone who reads printed material for errors

reverse—printing type in white against a dark background

rule—a line used on a page—for example between columns or ad modules—to serve as a separation and/or enhance the design

sans serif—a typeface with letters that have straight ends

scanner—a type of computer hardware that reads information from a photograph or graphic, converting it for computer processing

screen—a technique creating a shaded type or background tone instead of full-strength black or color. Ranges of shades are classified by the percentage of black or full-strength color they contain

serif—a small stroke finishing each end of a letter in a typeface

sidebar—a secondary item providing additional information, sidelights or graphics related to a major story

spot color—one color used in addition to black to create special design effects

standing head—a headline used over a regular column in every issue

subhead—a headline dividing a column of type, printed in a boldface version of the body copy or a different typeface and/or larger type size

template—a computer-created dummy that serves as a model for another similar publication and/or page

tile—for computer-created pages too large for the printer used to handle—the portion printed on a single sheet. To assemble a complete page, tiles are pasted together

tombstone—headlines of the same typeface and size running side by side which may appear to run together; sometimes called "bumping heads"

tracking—automatically governs space between characters

type style—**bold** (type that is blacker and heavier than the basic type of its font), *italic* (letters that slant toward the reader's right), ***bold italic***, Small Caps, shadow, outline, underline, extended, condensed

widow—a stray, partial line of type that is cut off from the rest of its paragraph and stands alone at the head of a column

Note: For terms not included, check under Journalism, and also see glossaries in your computer program manuals.

Journalism terms

ad—abbreviation for advertisement

advance (advance story)—news of an event to occur in the future

all caps—a word or word written in all capital letters

AP—abbreviation for Associated Press, a news-gathering service

banner—type of headline stretching full width, usually at the top of a page; also called a streamer

beat—news source that a reporter is assigned to cover regularly

box—material enclosed, either completely or partially, by a printed rule

byline—the name and identification of a story's author

caption—the heading placed above a photograph; sometimes used to refer to the descriptive copy below a photo

center of visual interest (CVI)—the dominate item on a page—usually a photo, graphic or headline

classified advertising—ads run in small type in a separate section, which is often classed into different categories, such as "Help wanted" or "Lost and found"

column (1)—a type of feature that is regularly run in a paper, featuring a single writer

column (2)—the vertical sections of type, which may have varying widths to story on a page

column width—the actual measurement in picas or inches; also measured in character count as a way to determine the character count of the entire story

copy—a story or article written for a newspaper; also used to describe a page or block of text

copyreading—checking copy for errors before it is entered into computer or receives its final rewrite

crop—to eliminate unwanted portions of a photo to emphasize its center of interest

cut—term for a newspaper photo or art, taken from engraving parlance

cutoff test—reporter's check that final-paragraphs are not essential to story

cutline—the descriptive copy below a photo

dateline—line at beginning of news story giving point of origin, if not local, and date, if significant

deadline—time at which job must be handed in or completed to make issue date of publication

deck—each part of a headline in a single font, whether one or more lines (once used to define a single line of a headline)

direct quote—the reproduction of a speaker's exact words, set within quotation marks and correctly attributed

downstyle—the use of a minimum number of capital letters in headlines and body copy, where good usage permits an option

editorial—an article that represents the paper's opinion

editorial column—an article representing the opinion of an individual writer

editorializing—inserting the writer's opinion into a news story, which should be written objectively

euphemism—a milder word used instead of another word, possibly offensive—not an acceptable way to soften a quote from a news source

feature story—an article of special interest with a quality other than its timeliness as main attraction

5 W's and an H—the Who, What, When, Where, Why and How—the key questions answered by a summary lead

folio line—the heading of inside pages, indicating section, school name, issue date and page number

follow-up—a news story written after an event has occurred

graph—short for a paragraph (sometimes spelled *graf*)

hammerhead—a large headline of only one or two words, followed by a longer and smaller head underneath—the reverse of a kicker

headline—lines of display type printed above a newspaper story, calling attention to relative importance and attracting readers to the story's content

headline schedule—list of styles and sizes, often with counts, for use in a newspaper

in-depth report—a story that goes beyond the surface to discover the news behind the news; also called an investigative report

indirect quote—using a version of a speaker's words without quotation marks. Example: *He said that he expected to reject the plan.*

infograph—a chart, diagram or graph presenting statistical information, such as survey results and enrollment figures, in easy-to-grasp form

inverted pyramid—a method of writing a story using a summary lead and facts in diminishing order of importance

kicker—short, lead-in phrase above main head

label head—a headline without a verb; to be avoided

lead (leed)—the first paragraph of a story *(see also, under Desktop publishing)*

libel—untrue statement or material that damages a person's reputation

masthead—list of the paper's vital statistics, including school name and address, staff members and other pertinent data, such as editorial policy; usually found on editorial pages

menu—in newspaper terminology, a front-page box or boxes announcing a paper's inside contents, sometimes called a teaser *(see also, under Desktop publishing)*

nutgraph—paragraph giving the key details of a news story—the 5 W's and an H—when a variation on the summary lead is used

objectivity—an attempt to write a story without showing bias or injecting the writer's opinion

photo release—a permission form used by photographers for persons in photos not taken at news events, granting the right to print the photo

plagiarism—unauthorized copying of another's work. Reproducing copyrighted material without permission—whether words or art—is a crime

profile—feature story about a person; personality piece

pull quote—quote from a story or news source that is "pulled out" and set as a graph in a distinctive format and type to attract readers to a story and add visual interest

retraction—a printed correction of an earlier error in the paper

slug—one or two words that specifically identify a story, typed in the upper left-hand corner of work to be edited or processed; also includes reporter's last name, plus date/time from edit menu

stet—a term meaning "let it stand"—or disregard a change that was previously marked or indicated

style—rules regarding punctuation, capitalization, abbreviation, etc.

style book, style manual—compilation of style rules for a newspaper

summary lead—a first paragraph that contains the essential 5 W's and an H of a news story

teaser—a front-page box or boxes announcing a paper's inside contents, sometimes called a menu

trademark—the legal, registered name of a product or business. Be sure to use capital letters when using such trademarked names as Kleenex and Coke, which are sometimes used generically

STYLE MANUAL

Note to advisers:

Style rules may vary from school to school, but it is important that each paper consistently follow a set style of capitalization, punctuation and word choice. Some schools use the *Associated Press Stylebook;* however, this book may prove too extensive for school journalists to use conveniently. Depending upon an individual school's journalism program, it may be preferable to choose a more manageable list to introduce students to the concept of becoming stylistically uniform. A manual written specifically for school use, such as this, can concentrate on those topics of most concern in the student press and provide guidelines for such matters as different forms of address for students and faculty.

To all staff members:

This style manual will direct you making the right choices where there is a question of usage or when common errors need special attention.

The manual is divided into categories:

Capitalization
Proper use of names
Numbers
Abbreviations
Punctuation
Special points about usage

Capitalization

For all capitalization, the acceptable choice is *down style,* which means the minimum use of capital letters.

DO's:

1. Do capitalize the initial letter of a sentence, headline or caption in addition to all proper nouns.
   Example: Anyone can belong to Booster Club.

2. Do capitalize proper names of groups and clubs.
   Example: Student Council, Council president, French Club

3. Do capitalize proper names of events.
   Example: Homecoming, Junior-Senior Prom

4. Capitalize a person's title, including coach or assistant principal, used before a person's name.
   Example: Ms. Helen Swift, Dr. Daniel Dove, Principal Kevin Claypoole

   Note: a. Capitalize *only* proper nouns when used after the name as identification.
   Example: Mr. Kevin Claypoole, Byrnehurst principal

   b. Do not capitalize such identification as teacher or faculty member, even when used preceding a person's name.

5. Do capitalize principal words of literary, theatrical, art or musical titles, as well as prepositions of four or more letters and all initial letters, including *The, A* and *An.*
    > *Example:* "A Tale of Two Cities," "You Can't Take It With You," "Where the Wild Wind Blows"

    Note: Use quotes around all but the Bible and catalogs of reference materials in body copy; use only single quotes in headlines.

6. Do use capital letters with proper names and titles, whether of a place, group or organization, but do not use them otherwise.
    > *Example:* French Club—Chess Club
    > Student Council—Council committee
    > Byrnehurst Board of Education—the board

7. Do capitalize the days of the week. Do not abbreviate unless in tabulated forms, then use without periods at end.

8. Always capitalize trademarked names of products such as Nintendo, Nike and so on. Use generic name instead of trademark, if possible.

DO NOT's:

1. Do not capitalize classes—senior, junior, sophomore, freshman—except when part of a proper noun.
    > *Example:* Senior Week
    > The senior class elected officers.

2. School subjects such as math, biology, history do not take capital letters; however, those words referring to national identities do.
    > *Example:* English, French, American history

3. Do capitalize proper names of specialized subjects.
    > *Example:* Contemporary Living

4. Do not capitalize club offices: president, vice-president, etc., when used after a name.

5. Do not capitalize a word just because it sometimes is part of a proper word to which it relates.
    > *Example:* Byrnehurst High School—when the high school opened
    > Fenwick Auditorium—the new auditorium
    > principal's office—German language teacher
    > English department

6. Use capital letters without periods for common abbreviations, even though not capitalized when written out.
    > *Examples:* DECA—Distributive Education Clubs of America
    > JV—junior varsity

7. Capitalize *room* when used with its number.
    > *Example:* Some think Room 333 is the school's busiest.

8. Do not capitalize *a.m., p.m.* Write in lower case with periods.

9. Do not capitalize the descriptive names of athletic teams.
    > *Example:* The junior varsity basketball team overcame a . . .

Proper use of names

1. Include first and last names, with identification, on first reference to an adult.
    > *Example:* Mrs. Lillian Howard, Latin teacher

2. On following references, use title and last name.
    > *Example:* Mrs. Howard, Mr. Claypoole, Coach Kraft

3. For students, use first and last names, with significant identification, on first reference.
    > *Example:* Ron Freeman, Chess Club president
    > Tressa Jordan, sophomore

4. On following references, use a student's first name.
    > *Example:* Ron, Tressa

    Note: Avoid using unorthodox nicknames by which a student is known familiarly by friends.

5. When listing names, adopt a definite pattern and stick to it.

    a. With no other determining factor, use alphabetical order.

    b. If grouped by class, list seniors first, then juniors, sophomores, freshmen.

    c. When listing officers, give names first, followed by office.

       Example: Juan Lopez, president; Shannon Smucker, vice-president; Marv Crawford, secretary; Audrey Wilkins, treasurer.

    d. When listing winners of honors or awards, begin with highest places.

Numbers

1. Write out words for numbers one through ten, except in scores, dates and street numbers.

    Example: No more than ten will be chosen.

             Byrnehurst defeated Central 27–3.

             The play debuts March 10.

2. Use numerals for numbers 11 and higher.

    Example: Byrnehurst's senior class has 450 members.

3. Spell out a number at the beginning of a sentence. Rephrase the sentence if number is large. A year can be in numerals, however.

    Example: Twenty students received superior ratings.

             A record $1,596 in pledges . . .

             2001, not 2000, marks the century's beginning.

EXCEPTIONS:

4. When numbers are mixed, use the same form for both.

    Example: Students in grades 9 through 12 are eligible.

5. Do not use *rd, th, st* or *nd* after dates or other numbers.

    Wrong: The meeting will be Feb. 10th.

    Right: The meeting will be Feb. 10.

6. When writing dates of a current event, do not include the year.

7. Spell out words for numbers and write out *cents* instead of using cent sign for amounts less than $1. Use dollar sign ($) with decimal system for larger amounts. Do not use zeros after decimal point with even numbers.

    Example: Your two cents, worth counts for little.

             This book costs $19.95. That one is $17.

8. Use of ordinal numbers, such as tenth or 112th, is the same as for cardinal.

    Example: Their new address is 10 Tenth St.

Abbreviations

1. Write out the names of clubs, organizations, tests and other words on first reference, even though commonly known by their acronyms.

    Example: Distributive Education Clubs of America, not DECA

             Scholastic Aptitude Test, not SAT

    Note: a. It is at times permissible to use the acronym in a headline or lead, but the full name should be written out in full as early as possible.

        b. On further reference, a shortened form of the name may be used in addition to the acronym.

        Example: In distributive education, students . . .

2. Abbreviate E. for East with numbers; don't without.

    Example: 5 E. Milbury Lane

             East Milbury Lane is just one block long.

3. With street addresses, capitalize and abbreviate the words *avenue, street* and *boulevard* when the number is included; however, spell out these words if numbers aren't given.

    Example: 538 Bacon Blvd.

             She lives on Bacon Boulevard.

Note: Always spell out words for other types of thoroughfares, such as *drive, alley, circle* or *lane,* and capitalize as above.
> *Example:* 7614 Radcliffe Circle

4. Without dates, names of months are written out.
> *Example:* September no longer means the first day of school is at hand.

5. Months of more than five letters are abbreviated when written with dates.
> *Example:* Jan. 15, Feb. 15, March 15

6. Do not abbreviate *assistant, associate, association.*

7. Never abbreviate *Christmas* nor use the un-X-ceptable *X.*

8. Do not abbreviate the names of academic degrees, unless used in a listing.
> *Example:* He holds a doctorate in history.

9. Use the abbreviated form of the word *versus,* which should never be used as a verb as in "The Blazers are versing the Saints.
> *Example: Byrnehurst* vs. *Longchamps*

Punctuation

1. Write correctly punctuated sentences. Use periods and commas carefully to avoid run-ons and fragments.

2. Remember the importance of paired commas when setting off dates, nouns in apposition and phrases. This usage requires commas before *and* after.
> *Example:* A deadline of Monday, May 4, has been set for applications.
> Mr. Kevin Claypoole, Byrnehurst principal, led the discussion.
> *Blazer Follies,* the annual student musical, will open May 17.

3. When using quotations, use end punctuation inside quotation marks.
> *Example:* "Surprised?" said Mrs. Perkins. "I was overwhelmed."
> She added, "It was a moment I'll never forget."

4. Do not use quotation marks with indirect quotations.
> *Example:* Mrs. Perkins said she was not just surprised, she was overwhelmed.
> According to Mrs. Perkins, it was a moment she'll always remember.

5. Do not use commas before the last "and" in a series, unless needed to avoid confusion.
> *Example:* Sophomores, juniors and seniors are eligible.

6. When listing a series of names and identifications, follow names with commas and groupings with semicolons.
> *Example:* Superior ratings went to Tom Anderson, Bill Jennings and Cybil Hubbard, violin solos; Loria Davis and Dave Beck, flute solos; and Lynn Reyna, drum solo.

7. Avoid excessive use of contractions.
> *Poor:* Mr. Claypoole doesn't expect the ruling until next week.
> *Preferred:* Mr. Claypoole does not expect the ruling until next week.

8. Make use of hyphens (-) and em dashes (—) in the following ways.

   a. Use a hyphen at the end of a line to divide a word that will not fit. Generally created by auto hyphenation.

   b. Use a hyphen to join modifying words that precede a noun.
   > *Example:* The senior guard played a near-perfect game.

   c. Use a hyphen to show the relationship of numbers in scores, ratios, some fractions and vote tabulations.
   > *Example:* The recipe calls for 2-1/2 cups of flour.
   > The last-minute touchdown put Byrnehurst ahead, 14–13.

   d. Do not use the hyphen to link adverbs ending in *ly* or the adverb *very* to a compound modifier.
   > *Example:* It was a clearly open-and-shut case.

   e. Do not use a hyphen when writing editor in chief.

9. Use an em dash instead of a pair of hyphens to denote a break in sentence continuity. Include a space both preceding and following each em dash used.

> *Example:* The ugly duckling—or so the story goes—often turns out to be a swan.

> *Note:* a. Do not overuse this kind of punctuation.
>
> b. Create the em dash on a computer by using the shift-option-hyphen keys.

10. Use the bullet (•) to call attention to items in an unnumbered list.

> *Example:*This year's Student Council goals include:
> - More student participation in Council planning
> - Greater recognition of all sports at pep rallies
> - Further study of . . .

> *Note:* a. Although not strictly punctuation, the bullet or a similar type of dingbat helps differentiate items and also has graphic appeal. Do not overuse.
>
> b. Create the bullet by using the option-8 keys on a computer.*

Special points about usage

1. Do not use the word *on* before a day or date unless its absence creates confusion.
> *Example:* Play tryouts begin Monday.

2. Avoid using times such as *today, tomorrow* or *yesterday* in newspaper stories, since their meaning depends upon when a paper is read.

3. When stating time, specify a.m. or p.m.—do not use the vague *o'clock*.

4. Do not write 12 midnight or noon; the 12 is redundant.

5. Omit zeros for even hours or prices.
> *Example:* Doors open at 5 P.M.
> Student tickets are $5.

6. The words *boy* and *girl* apply until someone's eighteenth birthday. After, *man* and *woman, young woman* and *young man* are appropriate.

7. According to the *AP Stylebook,* prefer *his* as the choice with singular indefinite pronouns (or rewrite to avoid the decision).
> *Example:* Everyone has his own opinion of that.

8. Use obscenity only if necessary to prove a point. Do not use euphemism in place of taboo words.

9. When using quotations, do not alter wording nor use abnormal spelling to indicate speaker's dialect or mispronunciation.

10. Strive for correct use of plurals. A dictionary provides most of the answers. If no form is shown after a noun, the word forms its plural regularly by adding an s.
> *Exceptions:* words as words—*ifs, ands, buts*
> proper names—add *s* if they don't end in s, and add *es* if they do end in s
> figures—add *s—1950s*
> multiple letters—*ABCs*
> individual letters—*A's*

11. Avoid squinting modifiers—adverbs able to modify more than one word.
> *Example:* Someone who tells a joke often gets a groan, not a laugh.

12. In referring to those in their teens, use *teen-ager* as the noun form and *teen-age,* not *teen-aged,* as the adjective.
> *Example:* A teen-ager is often stereotyped.
> The teen-age chess champion defeated his adult challenger.

13. The phrase *a total of* is often redundant but sometimes useful when beginning a sentence with a large number.

14. Use a comma with numbers of four or more digits, except in the case of years.
> *Example:* In 1957 an anonymous donor gave $5,000 to create a scholarship fund, which has since grown to . . .

---

* Procedure given for Macintosh™ programs.

IDEAS FOR STORIES, ADS, MONEY RAISERS

Ideas for in-depth reports

1. *Where parents are coming from: why parents feel as they do*
   Research the times of their teens. • Learn about their fashions. • Interview parents. • Talk with counselors about parent/teen conflicts. • Note similarities as well as differences. • Ideas for conflict resolution.

2. *Is winning everything?*
   How have attitudes in professional sports filtered into schools? • Do an objective comparison. • Interview local grads who played pro or semi-pro sports. • Is school athletic code realistic? • Interview coaches and players.

3. *Are teen-agers victims of society?*
   How media, advertisers, manufacturers target kids. • Do research nationally, locally. • Also focus on problems, cures. • Interview nonconformist students for their reaction. • When and how do kids get blame although cause may lie elsewhere?

4. *Education: Getting somewhere or going nowhere*
   Research three or four chief critics of education. • Compare their criticisms to results of local findings. • Assess your school's standings in test results, college entrance, curriculum. • Draw conclusions about strengths, future needs.

5. *Sex: Media glamour vs. daily reality*
   Channel-surf situation comedies and soaps; excerpt love scenes. • Research psychologists' and local authorities' opinions. • Compare media portrayal to approach in sex education classes, student reality.

Additional ideas:

6. *Siblings: blessing or pain?* • Poll to see average size family in your school; take it from there.

7. *Genes or lack of will power?* • Who's in charge; what qualities lead to success in school—or the real world?

8. *Addiction: Is any one free?* • Drugs, smoking, gambling, the Internet—why someone is addicted and how to break away.

9. *Stresses on kids* • Pressure—is it real or imaginary? How can students take control and not defy society or parents?

10. *Teachers—from the other side* • Then and now photos, teachers' pranks, changes they've seen, their views of students today.

11. *Keeping fit: the right and wrong ways to try* • Is fitness or looks more important? How to start a fitness program.

12. *Dating dilemmas* • What experts say, pressures on boys and girls to date, standards of today vs. those of the past.

Story and feature ideas

1. Rivalries—spirited or silly
2. Pressure of school athletics
3. Being a twin
4. Shoplifting—petty crimes
5. Class projects
6. Ever wonder why . . .
7. Employability
8. Beating the system
9. Gambling
10. School food
11. Is there life after dark (in your town)?
12. Teen drivers—the good and bad of it
13. Hanging out
14. Graffiti
15. Visit to an abortion clinic
16. Stereotyping
17. Teachers' "other" lives
18. Junk food
19. Overcoming obstacles—students with disabilities
20. A popular new game or fad
21. Crime on campus
22. Where have all the heroes gone?
23. Interesting cars in lot
24. A local hero
25. A special pet
26. Horror stories on the job
27. Assignment: go to traffic court
28. Making the weight as athletes
29. Out-of-way sites, such as air raid shelter, in school
30. How town and school got their names
31. How mascot was chosen, yearbook named, etc.
32. Test anxiety
33. School nurse—anecdotes, stats, quotes
34. Story behind incoming press releases
35. Community plays/student participation
36. Lost and found bin
37. Vegetarianism
38. Trials of a cigarette smoker
39. Personal experience
40. Students' rights—do kids have more now
41. Volunteering
42. In locus parentus—the school as parent
43. Dress codes
44. Juvenile court system
45. Student knowledge
46. Dropping out—what happens next
47. Is bigger (or smaller) better—visit another school
48. Do kids really believe they're invincible?
49. An out-of-the-ordinary sport
50. A behind-the-scenes look at anything intriguing

Column ideas

1. Class distinctions
2. Freshman vs. senior
3. Typecasting—a look around your school
4. Unexpected side of someone or something
5. Sexism
6. Computers
7. Classrooms—those that beckon, those that don't
8. If I were . . .
9. Prom: stresses and dresses
10. Reciting in class—differences in attitudes
11. Advice: give and take
12. Hall talk
13. Have a makeover
14. Try weight lifting—or something else new
15. Unconscious fashion statements
16. Soap operas vs. my life
17. Desktop decor
18. Slang
19. If I had a big star's salary
20. News
21. Those warning labels
22. Book review
23. Playing favorites
24. Daring to be different
25. Any story in the list of features ideas

Advertising leads

Ads from all these of businesses appeared in school papers surveyed.

Local advertisers

Animal hospital	Earring shop	Pregnancy counseling
Athletic store	Florist	Pretzel shop
Attorney	Food and pet supplies	Print shop
Bank	Frame shop	Putt-putt golf
Beauty salon	Gas station	Realtor
Bike world	Grocery, carryout	Refinery
Bookstore	Health foods	Resale merchandise
Bowling lanes	Home repair	Restaurant
Bus charter service	Ice skating rink	Résumé writing service
Car care	Insulation company	Rollerblades
Card shop	Insurance agency	Sandwich shop
Chiropractor	Jewelry store	School events
Church teen program	Lawn maintenance	Screen printing
Cleaners	Learning center	Shoe store
Coffee house	Local manufacturer	Smoke-free organization
Community college	Local newspaper	Sports cards and awards
Dance studio	Mail and office service	Tanning center
DECA school store	Merchandise mall	Tuxedo rental
Decorator	Modeling school	Vision center
Dentist	Motorcar company	Women's health center
Driving school	Photography shop	Yearbook
Drugstore	Poolroom	

National advertisers, franchises

Subway fast food	Merle Norman cosmetics	Coke
TCBY yogurt	Josten's class rings	Pepsi
Wendy's	McDonald's	Taco Bell
Penney's	Crabtree & Evelyn	Marine Reserves

Reader's Digest Foundation—substance awareness committee

Note: Contact the local outlet first, although national advertisers and chains may require you to contact their headquarters. It may be necessary to seek this type of ad far in advance.

Money-raising projects

1. Battle of bands
2. Senior photographer contributes cut for publications
3. Candy sales
4. Printing athletic programs with ads
5. Biannual bake sales
6. Skating party
7. Work concession stands at pro games
8. T-shirt sales
9. Carnation sales on holidays
10. Sponsoring a dance
11. Selling holiday messages at Christmas and Valentine's Day
12. Sales of candy, gift wrap
13. Pizza
14. Community supper
15. Selling personals
16. Selling ads to be put on paper placemats, distributed to local restaurants
17. Heart to Heart—dating match-up
18. Selling full back page to patrons
19. Sock hop
20. Concession sales at school musicals
21. Selling candy and soda at yearbook distribution party
22. Selling buddy pictures taken by professional photographer

RESOURCES FOR ADDITIONAL INFORMATION AND SUPPORT

Two outstanding sources for a wide range of journalism texts and materials:

1. JEA Bookstore
   Kansas State University
   103 Kedzie Hall
   Manhattan, KS 66506-1505
   Phone: (913) 532-5532
   Web: http://www.jea.org/

2. Journalism/The Writing Company
   10200 Jefferson Boulevard, Room JL3
   P.O. Box 802
   Culver City, CA 90232-0902
   Phone: (800) 421-4246
   Web: http://writingco.com/writing

Specific titles

1. *Looking Good in Print,* Roger C. Parker. Ventana Press, Chapel Hill, NC, 1993.

2. *Desktop Publishing with Style,* Daniel Will-Harris. And Books, South Bend, IN, 1987.

3. *Death by Cheeseburger,* a publication of the Freedom Forum. Arlington, VA, 1994.

4. *High School Journalism,* Homer L. Hall. Rosen Publishing Group, New York, NY, 1993.

5. *From News to Newsprint,* Robert Bohle. Prentice Hall, Englewood Cliffs, NJ, 1992, 1984.

6. *Scholastic Journalism,* Earl English, Clarence Hach, Tom Rolnicki. Iowa State University Press, Ames, IA, 1990.

7. *Journalism Today,* Donald L. Ferguson, Jim Patten. National Textbook Company, Lincolnwood, IL, 1995.

8. *The Academy Times Staff Manual,* Steve Matson, editor. Available JEA Bookstore,1995.

9. *Hi-Times Staff Handbook and Style Manual,* Vince Aleccia. Available JEA Bookstore,1995.

10. *OSU School of Journalism Handbook,* OSU School of Journalism. Columbus, OH, 1994.

11. *The Associated Press Stylebook and Libel Manual,* Norm Goldstein, editor. Addison-Wesley, New York, NY, 1996.

12. *Associated Press Guide to News Writing,* René J. Cappon. Prentice Hall, New York, NY, 1991.

National Associations, Resources

1. Association for Education in Journalism and Mass Communication
   (Also contact for Scholastic Journalism Division, AEJMC)
   1621 College St.
   University of South Carolina
   Columbia, SC 29308-0251
   Phone: (803) 777-2005
   Web: http://www.aejmc.sc.edu/online/home.html

2. Columbia Scholastic Press Association
   Columbia University
   Box 11, Central Mail Room
   New York, NY 10027
   Phone: (212) 854-9400
   Web: http://www.columbia.edu/cu/cspa/about.html

3. The Freedom Forum
   1101 Wilson Blvd.
   Arlington, VA 22209
   Phone: (703) 528-0800
   (800) 830-3733 for ordering material or information
   Web: http://www.freedomforum.org

4. Journalism Education Association (see first entry)

5. National Scholastic Press Association
   University of Minnesota
   620 Rarig Center
   330 21st Avenue South
   Minneapolis, MN 55455
   Phone: (612) 625-8335
   Web: http://studentpress.journ.umn.edu

6. Quill and Scroll Society
   School of Journalism and Mass Communication
   University of Iowa
   Iowa City, IA 52242-1528
   Phone: (319) 335-5795
   Web: http://www/uiowa/edu/~quill-sc

7. Student Press Law Center
   Suite 1910
   1101 Wilson Blvd.
   Arlington, VA 22209
   Phone: (703) 807-1904
   Web: http://www.splc.org

Note: Approximately 80 regional and state school journalism associations exist throughout the country. Check one of the major organizations, listed here, for the address of the one serving your locality.